JAINA STUDIES

PAPERS OF THE 12TH WORLD SANSKRIT CONFERENCE
Vol. 9

Jaina Studies

Edited by
COLETTE CAILLAT
NALINI BALBIR

MOTILAL BANARSIDASS PUBLISHERS
PRIVATE LIMITED • DELHI

PAPERS OF THE 12TH WORLD SANSKRIT CONFERENCE HELD IN HELSINKI, FINLAND, 13-18 JULY 2003
VOL. 9

General editors:
PETTERI KOSKIKALLIO & ASKO PARPOLA

First Edition : Delhi, 2008

ISBN: 978-81-208-3247-3

MOTILAL BANARSIDASS
41 U.A. Bungalow Road, Jawahar Nagar, Delhi 110 007
8 Mahalaxmi Chamber, 22 Bhulabhai Desai Road, Mumbai 400 026
203 Royapettah High Road, Mylapore, Chennai 600 004
236, 9th Main III Block, Jayanagar, Bangalore 560 011
Sanas Plaza, 1302 Baji Rao Road, Pune 411 002
8 Camac Street, Kolkata 700 017
Ashok Rajpath, Patna 800 004
Chowk, Varanasi 221 001

PRINTED IN INDIA
BY JAINENDRA PRAKASH JAIN AT SHRI JAINENDRA PRESS,
A-45 NARAINA, PHASE-I, NEW DELHI 110 028
AND PUBLISHED BY NARENDRA PRAKASH JAIN FOR
MOTILAL BANARSIDASS PUBLISHERS PRIVATE LIMITED,
BUNGALOW ROAD, DELHI 110 007

PREFACE

For the first time since the foundation of the International Association of Sanskrit Studies, the 12th World Sanskrit Conference held in Helsinki included a whole session on Jain Studies.[1] Though some prominent scholars of Jainism unfortunately could not attend the meeting, others were able to participate and most of them were keen to deliver the revised text of their paper in time to meet the requirements of the Helsinki organizers and general editors of the Conference, and of the publishers Motilal Banarsidass. As for the colleagues who were not able to do so, a summary of their contribution, based on the preliminary abstract and/or text they had submitted to the organizers is included in this preface.[2]

It had been agreed that, among other subjects, our attention might focus particularly on Jain literature(s), an important aspect in the life

---

[1] It should nevertheless be mentioned that papers on Jainsm had been read in panels on "Middle Indo-Aryan and Jaina Studies" at the VIIth and VIIIth World Sanskrit Conferences in Leiden (1987) and Vienna (1990). Furthermore, information concerning recent Jain conferences has been given by Colette Caillat in the *Bulletin d'Études Indiennes* 21.1 (2003), p. 265-277. Would it be immodest to note that the first Jaina conference in Europe was the International Symposium on Jaina Canonical and Narrative Literature (Strasbourg, 16th-19th June 1981): proceedings (edited by Nalini Balbir and Colette Caillat) in *Indologica Taurinensia* 11 (1983), pp. 7-340?

[2] In the present conspectus, which is meant to reflect the Helsinki meeting, reference will be made both (i) to the articles that are reproduced in the present volume, and (ii) to those of which the summary or a preliminary version, as the case may be, has reached the editors. The latter are inserted between square brackets. They are by: Suchitra (Ray) Acharyya, J. E. Cort, H. P. Devaki, S. C. Goswami, and O. Qvarnström

of this comparatively small but dynamic community. For their elite has always been eager to teach and advise their members, while, on the other hand, it has been keen to be well-informed about both their own doctrine and their opponents' positions: thus it would be easy to detect the latter's weak points and defeat them definitely. Whether oral or written, literature plays an important part in the Jain strategy. It is never ideologically neuter, but always didactic (a common feature in Indian literature, it is true). At all levels, at all times, education – whether elementary or sophisticated, theoretical or practical, serious or humorous – plays a significant role in the life of all Jain followers. This is reflected in the present volume, in which all epochs (from antiquity to the present day) are taken into account and all strata of the society play their role. Due to the variety of the literary genres, the hearer or reader is acquainted with philosophers, with *ācārya*s and community leaders, or with various rulers, as well as with humble faithful lay followers and with mankind in general, whose fate it is to die.

The participants in the Jain section did not aim at a theoretical approach to Jain literature as a whole, an attempt which would seem premature. Even a general synthesis of Jain narrative literature, despite several excellent monographs, would appear too ambitious for the present (cf. Paul Dundas's remarks in the introduction to his contribution). Our wish was simply to consider aspects of the Jains' literary activity through the ages – the variety of their audience, methods and skill – which always has edification in view. Further, the papers in the present volume focus mostly on the contents and the aims of the texts that are being examined, only occasionally on their structure and formal stylistic characteristics.

* * *

In several canonical treatises or developments, everyday life and realia come to the front. [Dr. Suchitra Ray Acharyya, for example, summarizes observations and recommendations concerning staple commodities and the good but sober diet prescribed in the *Uvāsaga-dasão* for a well-to-do lay follower of Northern Bihar who wishes to embrace an ascetic way of life.[3]] Various information on the condition of and the role played by women in a Jain household and the Jain community are collected from several passages of the *Aṅga*s and *Purāṇa*s (J. R. Bhattacharya[4]). Thus ever since the beginning ethical considerations have constituted a not negligible item in Jain literary activity.

Several papers bear on philosophical issues. Two of them examine discrepancies that can be detected in the positions defended in some parallel treatises.

Fujinaga Sin considers the possible evolution of meaning of *dharma* and *adharma* denoting the medium of motion and rest in Jain ontology. Referring to the *Dravyālaṃkāra* (by Rāmacandra and Guṇacandra, 13th century, recently published by Ācārya Muni Jambūvijayajī), he suggests that probably, according to some schools of thought, *dharma* had been considered to exist only in *loka*, not in *aloka*.

Kristi Wiley, continuing her comparative, systematic, and critical analysis of Śvetāmbara and Digambara *Karma* literature, shows how some apparent discrepancies between, e.g., the Śvetāmbara canonical *Prajñāpanāsūtra* and the Digambara *Ṣaṭkhaṇḍāgama* are best explained not by the anteriority of one or the other of the treatises, but by differences of interest or emphasis that prevailed among the redactors of the two sects. In fact, the similarities are undeniable and fundamental.

---

[3] "Data on ancient Indian agronomy in the *Uvāsagadasão*".

[4] "Woman in ancient Jain literature", pp. 33-41 in this volume.

[Olle Qvarnström draws attention to a Jaina-Mīmāṃsā debate, and suggests that "the medieval debate between Jaina philosophers and Hindu theologians concerning the source of knowledge and the valid means of knowing *dharma* is parallel in many respects to Western debates on faith versus reason".[5]]

As for N. L. Jain, he reviews "the traditional basic postulates of *Anekāntavāda*", claims that "they can be expressed in current relativistic and statistical language", and draws practical advice from the *Syādvāda-Anekānta* theory. Referring to modern authors, in particular to Ācārya Śrī Mahāprajña, he shows the importance of *Anekānta* for "conflict resolution", admits its limitations but finally recommends "methods of developing anekāntic vision".

That antique beliefs and practices can be and have been successfully handed down and constantly recast is shown by the *Maraṇa-vibhatti-/Maraṇasamādhi-paiṇṇaya*, by far the longest of the Śvetāmbara pamphlets in the (more or less canonical) Prakīrṇaka section: many of its *gāthā*s recur elsewhere in these "Miscellanea", as well as in a Digambara treatise, the *Mūlācāra*. A kind of "pot pourri", this *Prakīrṇaka* (known by eight different names!) can be seen as a good example of "intertextuality", a feature that has been shown to characterize various developments of the *Dharmaśāstra*s (cf. Patrick Olivelle's paper, on "Manu and the Arthaśāstra. A study in Śāstric intertextuality", in Section 13 of the present Conference on *Law & Society*[6]).

Even if canonical and paracanonical teachings never ceased to be referred to, various readjustments have always taken place and Jain literary traditions naturally testify to change as well as to continuity.

---

[5] "The Jaina-Mīmāṃsā debate on omniscience." Published in: Peter Flügel (ed.), *Studies in Jaina History and Culture. Disputes and Dialogues*, pp. 89-106. London: Routledge, 2006.

[6] See also M.-C. Porcher, "Remarks on some new approaches to Sanskrit literature" (pp. 335-337 on intertextuality) in *Indologica Taurinensia* 11 (1983), pp. 331-337.

[A conspicuous example is presented by John E. Cort, who examines the works of the mystic Tāraṇ Taraṇ Svāmī (1448-1515): an aniconic Digambara author, who "is credited with authoring fourteen texts in an ungrammatical amalgam of Sanskrit, Prakrit, Apabhramsha and Bundelkhandi" and can be shown to exhibit continuities with the Digambara philosophical and mystical traditions and to expose "his own distinctive vision of Jain teaching and practice".][7]

Not all original attempts are as satisfactorily documented as Tāraṇ Taraṇ Svāmī's. Peter Flügel concentrates on the scarce and uncertain literature concerning the aniconic Loṅkāgaccha, founded also in the 15th century by the Gujarati layman Loṅkā. He draws attention to ancient texts in Sanskrit and Old Gujarati and to materials that have appeared in scattered form in 20th century Jain publications in Hindi and Gujarati, that can be supplemented by recent fieldwork (of December 2002, January 2003).

Such attempts as those of Tāraṇ Taraṇ Svāmī and Loṅkā certainly need more investigation. Another original project is Nalini Balbir's preliminary study of "autobiographies of Jain monks and nuns" written in the 20th century by the Jain mendicants, whether monks or nuns, in Hindi or Gujarati. Until now a neglected literary genre, such *ātmakathā*s are to be viewed in relation to models in Sanskrit or Prakrit literature and with the hagiographies more recently published by the mendicants' disciples on auspicious occasions.

The remaining papers can be regarded as variously focussing on the "belles-lettres" as conceived by Jain authors, who never lose sight of the didactic aim. More than once it can be seen how the Brahmanical tradition is both well-known, echoed, and has been adapted, rewritten so to say, in order to praise Jain values and "Great Men".

This is particularly conspicuous in the analysis of various hymns and of important epic compositions. [In the *Bhaktāmarastotra*

---

[7] "The literature and language of the Digambara polyglot mystic Tāraṇ Taraṇ Svāmī (1448-1515)." Published in: Peter Flügel (ed.), *Studies in Jaina History and Culture. Disputes and Dialogues*, pp. 236-311. London: Routledge, 2006.

(48 verses revered by all Jains, composed prior to the 9th century CE.), S. C. Goswami detects a "monistic undercurrent" which he compares with "the Upaniṣadic theme of the identity of the Knower of Brahman and Brahman itself".[8]] On the other hand, Jean-Pierre Osier, studying the "Jain Tradition and the *Sahasranāmastotra*" and comparing those written by Jinasena (9th century) and Āśādhara (13th century), identifies four main characteristics of Āśādhara's hymns and commentary: (i) "acquaintance with Jain mythology (ii) assimilation, i.e., transformation of Hindu names into Jain conceptions, (iii) openness and relevancy of the Jinas' names, and (iv) originality of the Jain *bhakti*".

All people who live in the Indian cultural sphere being familiar with the great epics, and in particular with the *Rāmāyaṇa*, it is to be expected that the Jains would draw on the Rāma epos for their followers' edification. As a matter of fact it has been shown that there are two distinct versions of the Rāma story. Eva de Clercq here considers three poems of the "older version": by Vimalasūri (1st century, in Prakrit), Raviṣeṇa (7th century, in Sanskrit), and Svayambhūdeva (9th-10th century, in Apabhramsha). She circumscribes the "doctrinal passages", which, she observes, are remarkably few, but convey all the basic elements of the doctrine, ethics being the main topic discussed. She concludes that "their real function appears to be that of an intermezzo, a moment of reflection within the lengthy Rāma epic" – certainly an essential one.

[H. P. Devaki draws attention to a remarkable literary masterpiece, Somadeva's "religious romance written in Sanskrit prose and verse", *Yaśastilaka*, composed in 969 CE. Both a *kāvya* and an *upadeśa*, it deals with a well-defined subject, central in Jainism, *ahiṃsā*. Whether physical or intentional *ahiṃsā* is always to be condemned

[8] "The monistic undercurrent of the Bhaktāmara". On "the Ātman theory and Brahman theory" in Jainism and the Upaniṣads, see A. N. Upadhye, *Śrī Yogīndudeva's Paramātmaprakāśa (Paramappapayāsu)*. (Śrīmad Rājacandra Jaina Śāstramālā, 3) Agas 1973, p. 39.

and it always backfires. The topic is shown to be connected with the doctrines of *karma* and rebirth (both also prominent in Jain philosophy and recurrent in Jain narratives). It is shown how the reader will be overwhelmed and perturbed by the picturesque and pathetic scenes that are depicted. Somadeva evidently aimed at making such a strong intellectual and emotional impact on his audience that it would determine their general conversion.][9]

Paul Dundas claims that even if, at first sight, a narrative is trivial or if the aim is not clear, it will prove rewarding to try to determine what its use is or has been intended to be. For it is not a secret that Jain authors played an important pedagogical role and often lived in a world of debates and conflicts in which they more than once took a prominent part. Thus Dundas shows how, if read with the historical background in mind, a narrative that is generally considered to be dull, e.g., Jineśvarasūri's *Kathākoṣaprakaraṇa* (written in Maharashtri Prakrit in 1051 CE), becomes an exciting document, especially if one remembers that "Jineśvara is famous in Śvetāmbara Mūrtipūjak Jain tradition as the conqueror in the court of King Durlabha and the inspiration if not the founder, of the lineage known as Kharatara Gaccha".

The papers submitted in respect of the Jain Studies Session remind us of the extreme depth and diversity of Jain literature, as well as of its special informative value. At the same time it should not be overlooked that various formal and rhetorical patterns are used, which are quite similar to those that are analysed by critics interested in the theory of literature.

We are all thankful to the organizers of the 12th World Sanskrit Conference for all the work they did, and so nicely, before, during and after the Conference. Petteri Koskikallio, in particular, was always available for questions and queries. Thanks are also due to the

[9] "The doctrine of Ahiṃsā in Jainism with special reference to Somadeva's *Yaśastilakacampū*".

Finnish Cultural Foundation for having supported the Conference, and to Paul Dundas, K. R. Norman and Peter Skilling who read some of the papers collected in this volume and corrected their language.

COLETTE CAILLAT
NALINI BALBIR

CONTENTS

CONTRIBUTORS

NALINI BALBIR
UFR Orient-Monde arabe
Université Paris-3
13, rue de Santeuil
F-75231 Paris Cedex 05
FRANCE
e-mail: nalini.balbir@wanadoo.fr

JAGAT RAM BHATTACHARYYA
Department of Prakrit and Jain Agama
Jain Vishva Bharati Institute
Ladnun, Rajasthan, 341 306
INDIA
e-mail: jrb@vbi.org

COLETTE CAILLAT
Académie des Inscriptions et Belles-Lettres
23, quai Conti
F-75006 Paris
FRANCE

EVA DE CLERCQ
Department of Indology, University of Gent
Blandijnberg 2-146
B-9000 Gent
BELGIUM
e-mail: evadeclercq@hotmail.com

PAUL DUNDAS
Department of Sanskrit, The University of Edinburgh
7 Buccleuch Place
Edinburgh EH8 9LW, Scotland
U.K.
e-mail: p.dundas@ed.ac.uk

PETER FLÜGEL
Centre for Jaina Studies, SOAS, University of London
Thornaugh Street, Russell Square
London WC1H 0XG
U.K.
e-mail: pf@cix.co.uk

SIN FUJINAGA
Miyakonojo Kosen, Kimazaki Ken
Miyakonojo si
JAPAN
e-mail: fujinaga@miyakonojo-nct.ac.jp

NAND LAL JAIN
Jain Centre, 12/644 Bajrang Nagar
Rewa, Madhya Pradesh, 486 001
INDIA
e-mail: amitdas_rewa@rediffmail.com

JEAN-PIERRE OSIER
4, avenue Marcel Doret
F-75016 Paris
FRANCE
e-mail: jean-pierre.osier@wanadoo.fr

KRISTI L. WILEY
Department of South and Southeast Asian Studies
University of California, 7303 Dwinelle Hall
Berkeley, CA 94720
U.S.A.
e-mail: Kristi.Wiley@gmail.com

On the Composition of the Śvetāmbara Tract *Maraṇavibhatti-/Maraṇasamāhi-Paiṇṇayaṃ*

COLETTE CAILLAT

In the section *Law and Society* of this 12th World Sanskrit Conference, Prof. Olivelle has presented "A study on śāstric intertextuality".[1] Though the term is not frequently in use, scholars who have analysed the Jain Scriptures, especially the Śvetāmbara Canon, have more than once shown how the texts are often interrelated, and how developments have been borrowed from, and grafted onto one another.[2] This of course is particularly conspicuous in cases where the texts bear on identical or connected subjects, or aim at being a sort of compendium of comparable teachings. Thus in his Dissertation *Über die vom Sterbefasten handelnden älteren Paiṇṇa des Jaina-Kanons*, Kurt von Kamptz could trace the numerous interconnections between the oldest of these pamphlets, viz. those bearing on disciplinary matters.[3] He concentrated his analysis on the oldest of these, especially the *Ā(urapaccakkhāṇa)*, *Bh(attapariṇṇā)*, *C(ausaraṇa)*, *M(ahāpaccakkhāṇa)*, *S(aṃthāraga)*, all in

[1] Cf. Olivelle 2004. Further, e.g., Bailey 1999 (*ubi alia*); also Fezas 2005, comparing *Yājñavalkyasmṛti* 1.327-333, *Arthaṣāstra* 1.19 and *Daśakumāracarita* 8. Concerning P, see JAS 17.2, A. M. Bhojak's Introduction, p. 27ff.

[2] Compare similar features in the Buddhist tradition, cf. the precious *Pāli Tipiṭaka Concordance*. Cf. also the numerous "floating stanzas" and *subhāṣita*s in the Indian literatures.

[3] Kamptz 1929: 8ff. For a comparison of C, Bh and S, see p. 10ff., for the "Mosaikarbeit" in M, p. 14. On the *Paiṇṇaya*s [henceforward: P] in general, Doctrine § 50.

Jain Māhārāṣṭrī Prākrit, and noted how identical or similar *pāda*s or stanzas (generally *āryā*s), recur in these pamphlets: this is not to be wondered at, since all five deal with death, and teach how to conduct one or the other of the main phases of the voluntary death recommended for the Wise, the *paṇḍiya-/paṇḍita-maraṇa*. Whereas the *Causaraṇa* exalts the "Recourse to the Four" (i.e. the Arhats, Siddhas, Sādhus and the Dharma), the other four texts mostly (though not exclusively) concentrate on the praxis. Ā (70 *gāthā*s) deals in particular with the "Renunciation of the Sick", Bh (172 *gāthā*s) with the ritual for the "Renunciation of Food", M (141 *gāthā*s) with the "Greater Renunciation", S (123 *gāthā*s) with the "Death Bed". Kamptz also points to agreements with some other *Paiṇṇaya*s, e.g. the *Cand(āvejjhaya)*, "Hitting the mark" (171 *gāthā*s),[4] but does not take into account the longest of these treatises (apparently composed later)[5] which, "given the ultimate goal of a religious", proposes to present "a full account of the rules concerning death".[6] Though, in a manuscript, the text is given eight

[4] The last development of Cand (gā. 117-173) deals precisely with the "*maraṇa-guṇa*". Towards the end of this section, the JAS edition quotes 75 additional *gāthā*s [*infra*: Cand 000 (Add 00)] which were known to Muni Caturavijaya, but have not been traced in the extant manuscripts. Remarkably they are appended after Cand 167-169 where it is emphatically recalled that there is no external support at the hour of death. The 75th of these additional *gāthā*s – a sort of colophon – is in the form of an exhortation addressed to the listeners of this tract. It reads: *āurapaccakkhāṇaṃ eyaṃ soūṇa* ... (cf. Caillat 1992: 35-44). – Compare, in JAS 17.1, the three different pamphlets entitled *Āura-paccakkhāṇa*! Also see footnote 7, *infra*. Evidently *āurapaccakkhāṇa* is considered a topic of utmost importance.– Compare the "Méthode(s) pour bien mourir", *Ars moriendi*, composed in the 15th-16th century in Western countries; further the *Préparations à la mort*, quoted in Jean Delumeau 1989: 319ff., 324ff., *ubi alia* [I thank Prof. Delumeau who drew my attention to these tracts]. Further, Montaigne: "Que philosopher c'est apprendre à mourir" (*Essais*, Book I, chapter 20): "Cicero dit que Philosopher ce n'est autre chose que s'aprester à la mort ... Il est incertain où la mort nous attende, attendons-la partout ... Le savoir mourir nous afranchit de toute subjection et contrainte".

[5] Cf. Alsdorf 1966: 11/163): "a late but important text the composition of which deserves a special study".

[6] Mar 1 c-d: *samaṇassa uttim'atthe maraṇavihī-saṃgahaṃ vocchaṃ*.

different names, it is generally known as *Maraṇavibhatti-* or *Maraṇasamāhi-pakaraṇa* (Henceforward: Mar).[7] According to the JAS edition, it encompasses 661 *gāthā*s,[8] explaining the "Distinction between the (auspicious and the inauspicious) death" / the "Concentration on death".

Given the importance which, in India, is attached to the last moments of a person at the point of death, it is but natural that the "Seniors of the Canon" had already drawn attention to this critical period. The example had been set by Mahāvīra, as recalled in the first *suyakkhandha* of the *Āyāraṅga-sutta*. Further, the fifth lecture of the *Uttarajjhāyā* is known as *akāmamaraṇijjaṃ*, and thus bears on "death against one's will", the death of the fool. The subject therefore is a crucial one at all periods of Jainism and in all circles. Hence it is not surprising that, more than once, even the wording of the prescriptions assembled, e.g. in the Ā, have an exact counterpart also in the second chapter of an old Digambara treatise in Jain Śaurasenī, the *Mūlācāra*. Further, the fact that death and preparing for death have been a major concern among the Jains, whatever their sectarian affiliation, is also proved by archaeological and epigraphical evidence.[9] Hence it can be surmised that the Jain authors or digests shared a common heritage of floating stanzas and *pada*s, which, in turn, could give rise to a number of new developments, the texts remaining open. A certain degree of fluidity can therefore

---

[7] Cf. JAS ed., p. 99 and p. 159, n. 2: *eyaṃ Maraṇavibhattiṃ 1, Maraṇavisohiṃ ca nāma guṇarayaṇaṃ 2* | *Maraṇasamāhī taiyaṃ 3 Saṃlehaṇasuyaṃ cautthaṃ ca* || 1 || *pañcama Bhattapariṇṇā 5 chaṭṭhaṃ Āurapa[c]cakkhāṇaṃ ca 6* | *sattama Mahapaccakkhāṇaṃ* [sic] *7* | *aṭṭhama Ārāhaṇapaiṇṇo 8* || 2 || ... *Maraṇavibhattī raiyaṃ biya nāma Maraṇasamāhiṃ ca* || 3 || Cf. Doctrine § 50.

[8] The number varies, cf. Doctrine § 50 (660, 663...).

[9] Cf. Rice 1873; Narasimhacharya 1973; Settar 1986; 1990. – Voluntary termination of life has also been reported in Śatrunjaya, Shah 1968: 162-164 (quoted in Caillat, 1977: 43-66). In a short article, published in the journal *Études*, two French scholars, Louis and Marie-Simone Renou (1951) summarize the voluntary death of a Terāpanthī *sādhvī*, which they witnessed in 1949, at Rajaldesar (Rajasthan): "une religieuse d'une trentaine d'années était étendue sur un drap à même le sol: elle en était au quinzième jour de jeûne ... Des sœurs lui tenaient compagnie, en psalmodiant des versets sanskrits pour adoucir sa fin ..."

be expected in the composition of the above tracts, even though they bear specific names. Moreover the same, or nearly identical, titles have been given to different pamphlets,[10] in particular (naturally) when they did not belong to the same sect. Thus the name *Ārāhaṇa-paiṇṇa* (one of the names of the *Maraṇavibhatti*) is not without counterparts. In particular the "Accomplishment" which the Śvetāmbaras teach is also prescribed and detailed by the Digambara (or perhaps Yāpanīya) author Śivārya.[11] As for the title of the present *Maraṇa-samāhi/-vibhatti*, the editors retained the latter, following the *Nandisūtra-cūrṇi* (and Haribhadrasūri's gloss),[12] which points to the "Distinction between the (auspicious and inauspicious) death".

* * *

The structure of this P(aiṇṇaya) is not totally clear. According to Puṇyavijaya (quoting the colophon), "it should have five chapters (Uddeśas)", but this assertion proves to be a problem, which is left unsolved:[13] in fact the development often seems entangled, as (apparently) similar topics are taken up and abandoned more than once. Nevertheless, the general line can be tentatively traced. The introductory *maṅgala* and the disciple's questions (*gāthās* 1-9) precede two main parts, a shorter and a longer one (gā. 10-99, 100-640), the limits of which are not absolutely clear-cut. But it can be

---

[10] Cf. *Paiṇṇayasuttāiṃ* II (JAS 17.2) in which two *Ārāhaṇā-paḍāyā/-patākās*, one *Ārāhaṇā-sāra*, one *Ārāhaṇā-paṇaga* are edited.

[11] Cf. Oetjens 1976. On Śivārya and the Yāpanīya sect, P. S. Jaini 1979: 79. Several other works are mentioned in Settar 1990.

[12] Cf. JAS Introduction, p. 99, n. 1; Text, p. 159, n. 2. Compare Mar 1d, *maraṇa-vihī-saṃgaha*.

[13] Muni Puṇyavijayaji writes (Introduction, p. 100): "This tract should have five chapters (Uddeśas). My old age does not allow me to dive deep into the problem of its five chapters. So I request scholars and revered *munis* to throw light on this problem". But apparently Pt. Amritlal Mohanlal Bhojak has not been more successful than the Muni. Nevertheless the JAS edition is provided with a very helpful analytical table of contents.

maintained that the approaching end of each of these two sections is signalled, in both of them, by the quotation of a series of *bhāvaṇās* (*bhāvanās*), each of these series being different, and independent, from the other one (gā. 60-67 and 570-640).[14]

(A) The first part of Mar is comparatively short (gā. 10-99).

1. It consists of a general exposition of the subject (gā. 10-77), followed by a sort of conclusion/transition which includes notes on the well-prepared heroic death, the *abbhujjaya- (abhyudyata-) maraṇa*[15] that is reached after the soul's purification. The latter is obtained thanks to a full confession addressed to a well qualified ācārya (78-99).

(B) The second part (gā. 100-640/659), which is much more developed, can be broadly divided into four chapters, or four groups of detailed observations and recommendations, preceding two concluding stanzas (660-661):

2. gā. 100-209, which bear on well-known necessary (in fact *life-long*) exercises, teach how to train for *ārāhaṇā* (*ārādhanā*)[16], so as to manifest "loyalty", thus to ensure the successful "accomplish-

---

[14] Also see *infra*, gā. 380ff. Compare, in the *Uttarajjhāyā*, the last stanzas of the last chapter (six of which are nearly identical with those of Mar 59-65). – Cf. *infra*, and Alsdorf 1966: 163ff., including a definition of the three different types of *bhāvanās*. On *bhāvanā/anuprekṣā*, the twelve "mental reflections" (Jaini 1979: 248ff.), *infra*, section B-5 (ii).

[15] "That death which one voluntarily submits to after having known the remaining life-span by supernatural knowledge", P I, Introduction, p. 101, n. 1. – Bh 9 distinguishes three varieties: *vanniyaṃ tivihaṃ | bhatta-parinnā 1, iṅgiṇi 2, pāovagamaṃ 3 ca dhīrehiṃ*. Cf. Kamptz 1929: 18. – For the 3 sorts of death mentioned in Ā 36, see *infra*, ad Mar 240ff.

[16] An important technical term, in evidence in the title of several *Paiṇṇayas* (cf. JAS 17.2). As an equivalent, Schubring suggests "Treue", "loyalty", Doctrine § 185, etc., cf. Deleu's translation of the corresponding *ārādhaka*, Viy I 3.3 etc., "loyal", III 1.2d, etc., "perseverant in the hour of death", III 4.6. According to Mar 318-321 (M 137-139), it has 4 constituents and 3 varieties: *daṃsaṇa (1) – nāṇa (2) – caritte (3) tave (4) ya ārāhaṇā cau-kkhandhā | sā c'eva hoi tivihā ukkosā (1) majjhima (2) – jahaṇṇā.*

ment", the "realization" of the Doctrine in the hour of death. This passage insists on confession (*āloyaṇā, ālocanā*) and on the various sorts of *tapas*, the qualities of knowledge, conduct and faith, on self-purification and the two aspects (external and internal) of the "voluntary submission to death" (*saṃlehaṇā, saṃlekhanā*).

3. This leads to the "renunciation of the sick", further reinforced by the strict observance of the five great vows:

gā. 210-412, starting with the *āurapaccakkhāṇa* (or "Renunciation of the Sick"), trace the way to the Goal, concentrate more specifically on *ārāhaṇā*, show how to succeed, and to ultimately lift the banner of *ārāhaṇā*.[17] The development quotes *gāthā*s also known, *inter alia*, from two other P, the *M(ahāpaccakkhāṇaP)* (142 *gāthā*s, cf. Mar 210-324), further the *S(aṃthāragaP)* (Mar 335f.: S 103f.; Mar 353: S 89: Bh 46; Mar 403-405: S 93-97, the latter, towards the end of this pamphlet, proposing a short list of *bhāvanā*s!).

4. gā. 409-412 recall Saṇaṃkumāra's fortitude, and thus introduce gā. 413-485, in which the Jain ideal is illustrated by referring to the examples set by religious heroes, or religious leaders (413-485 + 486-503) who resisted *uvasagga*s (*upasarga*s) or *parīsaha*s (*parīṣaha*s).[18] Examples set by animals are finally adduced (507-524);

5. gā. 525-569 show how the whole teaching culminates (i) in the final going forth, the "*pāovagamaṇa (prāyopagamana)*" rites,[19]

---

[17] Mar 311d = 315d = M 129d = 134d: *harāhi ārāhaṇa-paḍāgaṃ*; Mar 313d = Cand 169 (Add 40): *harāmi ārāhaṇa-p.*; Mar 319a-b = 320a-b = 321a-b = M 138a-b = 139a-b: *ārāheūṇa ... -ārāhaṇaṃ*.

[18] Compare "die Beispiele aus der Legende" in S and Bh, commented upon by Kamptz 1929: 24-38. On the use of examples in Jain (and Indian) demonstrations, H. Jacobi, *Ausgewählte Erzählungen*, Ernst Leumann, *Die Āvaśyaka-Erzählungen*, etc. quoted in Balbir 1993: Bibliographie and pp. 105ff., *ubi alia*; Caillat 1975: 28ff.

[19] Skr. *prāyôpagamana*. Leumann 1883, Glossar, s.v., "entering into trespass", cf. Alsdorf 1965: 45f. (the traditional commentaries generally render *pādapa-*).

coupled with (ii) the observance of the twelve topics for meditation, the *bhāvaṇās* (*bhāvanās*) or *aṇupekkhās* (*anuprekṣās*) (570-640).

To conclude, the final *gāthās* (641-661), reverting to the *paṇḍiya-maraṇa*, exhort immersion in both the right mental concentration and the pure one (*dhamma-*, *sukka-jjhāṇa*; *dharma-*, *śukla-dhyāna*).[20]

Puṇyavijaya's Preface and the subtitles of the edition help to follow the meanders of this tract, in which the same, or similar, reflexions are seen to occur more than once. Further, some *gāthās*, and *padas*, of "part A" recur in "B", as if two tracts had been pieced together, or, rather, as if it had been deemed necessary (thanks to a sort of preliminary summary, or *Textus simplicior*) to prepare for subsequent, more detailed, teachings.[21] As for the above mentioned series of 5 inauspicious +1 auspicious *bhāvaṇās* (gā. 60-65 + 66-67), they could be seen as one possible approach to the subject, contrasting with the list of the 12 positive "reflections", the *bhāvaṇās* recommended in gā. 570-640, as "taught in the Jina's Doctrine".[22] For, as shown by Alsdorf, the first set refers "not so much to the mental disposition itself but a certain behaviour, in word and action, resulting from it and creating (*bhāvana*) a certain karmic effect, viz. the corresponding *deva-durgati*",[23] but not *siddhi*. On the contrary the second series (of gā. 570-640) refers to the twelve topics recommended for meditation (on impermanence, etc., *infra*).

Thus it could be that, to account for various, technical, more or less discontinuous, statements aimed at answering a disciple's ques-

---

[20] Mar 660c-d: *dhammammi tao jhāṇe sukke ya maiṃ niveseha.*

[21] E.g.: 8 cf. 308abd; 22 cf. 101, 224; 54cd cf. 135cd; 57cd cf. 165cd ... Cf. *infra* and footnote 101.

[22] Mar 570: *bhāvehi bhāvaṇāo bārasa Jiṇa-vayaṇa-diṭṭhāo*, cf. *infra*. Cf. also Ārādh (1), gā. 713-722 + 729-745 ("*ku-bhāvaṇā-*" + "*bārasa-suha-bhāvaṇā-āṇusaṭṭhi-*").

[23] Cf. Alsdorf 1966: 164-165, referring to the *Uvavāiya-sutta*.

tion on *maraṇa-samāhi/abbhujjaya-maraṇa* (7f., 10f.), redactors have "composed" a comprehensive treatise in which specific old material is encompassed in more general, perhaps more recent and somewhat differently oriented reflexions. For it appears that in some passages of "part A" and towards the end of "part B", several stanzas have counterparts in the *Ārāhaṇā* treatises of the *Paiṇṇaya* group, whereas numerous *gāthā*s of the central portion are identical with the ancient statements of the specialized pamphlets analysed by Kamptz. Therefore, in contradistinction to these comparatively older, shorter, tracts which appear to concentrate on praxis, the Mar could be seen as a sort of compendium in which both specialized, traditional, and on the other hand, more recent and more general teachings have been voluntarily merged. Further this long development has been interspersed with several mnemonic lists of catchwords.

* * *

Let us read more in detail.

(A) 1. Naturally, the perfect death is possible only for those who have gone forth, who have thoroughly confessed themselves and have remained free from thorn-like faults for a long period of time (12): only those who are thus well prepared can strive to attain the full accomplishment, *ārāhaṇā*,[24] i.e., in the words of Puṇyavijaya, "Devoted adherence to the ascetic ideals", which is said to be threefold, as it pertains to Faith, Knowledge and Conduct,

> *sammattammi ya paḍhamā, nāṇa-carittehiṃ 2-3 do aṇṇe* (15),

three aspects which will be glorified later (53-58). Those who have no right faith will experience *bāla-maraṇa* a number of times (21), in opposition to the *paṇḍiya-maraṇa*, the conditions of which are

---

[24] Compare, in Pali, CPD II, s.v. *1. ārabhati*, 2. [*viriyaṃ ā.*, *vipassanaṃ ā.*]. Compare Mar 59-65: Āradh (1) 713-722.

summarized (*samāsao*, 22-44). In particular it is essential to extract all the thorns (*sall'uddharaṇa*, 45-50) that prick and alter the *jīva*, so that, thus freed from all unconfessed faults, it recovers its innate state of purity. This is achieved thanks to confession (*āloyaṇā*, *ālocanā*), a necessary prerequisite if one is to perform the *paṇḍiya-maraṇa*. The above considerations lead to a reminder, on the one hand, of the disadvantages or advantages resulting from the presence or absence of such thorns and, on the other hand, of the important value of right knowledge, conduct and faith (51-52 + 53-58).

At this point it is to be observed that Mar 51 is identical with gā. 330 of the second *Ārāhaṇā-paḍāyā*, whereas Mar 54 announces Mar 135,[25] the latter being identical with *Mahāpaccakkhāṇa* 101 and *Saṃthāraga* 114, further with one of the additional *gāthā*s inserted in the last section of *Candāvejjhaya* (ad 169 Add 38). As for Mar 57, it is practically the same as Mar 165.[26]

Finally, gā. 58 invites one to remain totally stainless, thus serving as a transition to the enumeration first of the five impure *bhāvaṇā*s (*bhāvanā*s, which are to be avoided, 59-65), later of the pure ones (to be practised, 66-67). Here is undoubtedly an important topic. It is linked with considerations bearing on self-purification, renunciation and meditation – and death: the fool's death (70-77),[27] and, on the contrary, the well prepared, "loyal" death: the latter implies the total extraction of all that alters the *jīva*'s essential purity, thus a sincere full confession, addressed to a perfectly qualified ācārya (78-83 + 84-99).[28] The teachings concerning the "topics" (*ṭhāṇa*, *sthāna*) beneficial to a soul at the time of death

---

[25] Mar 135: *jaṃ annāṇī kammaṃ khavei bahuyāhī vāsa-koḍīhiṃ* | *taṃ nāṇī tihī gutto khavei ūsāsa-metteṇaṃ*. "He who knows, who abides by the three restraints (of mind, body and speech) eliminates in a breath the *karman* which he who does not know eliminates in numerous crores of years." Cf. Mar 59-67: Ārāh (1) 713-722.

[26] Mar 57 in the singular, 165 in the plural. Cf. Cand 119.

[27] Mar 77d: *maranti te bāla-maraṇāiṃ*.

[28] Mar 78: ... *mohaṃ mottūṇa guru-sagāsammi* | *āloiya nissallā mariuṃ ārāhagā te vi*.

(14 + 6), and those concerning the virtues of an ācārya (18 + 8 + 10) are imparted by means of enumerations.

To conclude, attention is again drawn to confession (the pre-requisite of the *paṇḍiya-maraṇa*), and to the importance of a firm attachment to the Teaching. It is recalled that the spiritual shafts (*bhāva-salla*, *-śalya*) are of three kinds, as they are liable to affect faith, knowledge and conduct. It is further emphasized that "he who has totally extirpated this triple spiritual shaft and passes away, he, being in exact conformity with the going forth, adheres devotedly to the ascetic's ideals at the hour of death",

> *tivihaṃ pi bhāva-sallaṃ samuddharittā u jo kuṇai kālaṃ*
> *pavvajjāī sammaṃ sa hoi ārāhao maraṇe* (99).

(B) Now starts the second, more detailed development of the *Maraṇavibhatti* and its ritual.

2. It begins with a sort of preamble, a preliminary rehearsal of Jain fundamental tenets and obligations (ca. one hundred *gāthā*s, 100-209). Among them several either announce later Mar statements or prescriptions, or are partly identical with, partly very similar to, stanzas of other old *Paiṇṇaya*s. These *gāthā*s mostly deal with major themes and obligations constant in Jain soteriology: **(i)** the initial normal confession (cf. *supra*), **(ii)** the fundamental triad (right faith, knowledge, conduct), **(iii)** austerities, all leading to, and culminating in, **(iv)** *saṃlehaṇā*. Taken together this ritual amounts to a preliminary confession to the guru, followed by the appropriate atonements.[29]

(i) The first of these teachings (100-120 + 121f.),[30] that bears on the regular confession (*āloyaṇā*), insists on the relief that ensues[31] and

---

[29] Cf. Bh 18ff., Kamptz 1929: 18f.

[30] To these *gāthā*s are appended set lists (of the 10 defects of confession 123; of the 6 external + 6 internal *tapas*); further, the ācārya's recommendation to abide diligently by the right faith, knowledge, conduct, austerities (123-128).

on the constant obligation to confess exactly, totally (*sammaṃ āloyae savvaṃ*, 100d): "just like a child who while murmuring tells what he has done and has not done in a straightforward way, thus should one confess it, totally, without deceit",

> *jaha bālo jampanto kajjam akajjaṃ ca ujjuyaṃ bhaṇai*
> *taṃ taha āloejjā māyā-maya-vippamukko ya* [v.l. *u*].[32]

This recommendation is essential, for only sincere confession can restore Truth.[33] The above simile is met with more than once in the old Jain scriptures. It recurs (with small variations) in Mar 224,[34] as well as in several other *Paiṇṇaya*s;[35] it had been insisted upon in Śvetāmbara disciplinary texts.[36] Further, the Digambara tradition also (e.g. in the *Bhagavatī Ārādhanā* 549) similarly recommends:

---

[31] Mar 102 = 230 = M 30: Ārādh (2) 332: *kaya-pāvo vi maṇūso āloiya nindiuṃ guru-samāse* | *hoi airega-lahuo ohariya-bharo vva bhāravaho.*

[32] Mar 101. Compare Bh 22 (*āryā vipulā*!): *aha so āloyaṇa-dosa-vajjiyaṃ ujjuyaṃ jahâyariyaṃ* | *bālu vva bāla-kālā u dei āloyaṇaṃ sammaṃ*. Bh appears to have the disciplinary rules exactly in mind: it invites one to respect them strictly (including the chronology of the facts) and to be exhaustive (cf. *Vavahāra-sutta* 1, especially 1.17). The statements in Mar etc. are more general (cf. concordances, *infra*). But Mar does add later: *jaṃ puvvaṃ taṃ puvvaṃ; jahâṇupuvviṃ jaha-kkamaṃ savvaṃ* | *āloijja su-vihio kama-kāla-vihiṃ a-bhindanto* (105).

[33] The essential role of confession in Jainism is recalled in Caillat 2003, § 5 (referring to Calvert Watkins, "On Confession in Slavic and Indo-European" in Watkins 1994, II: 602-621, quoting Sylvain Lévi, *La doctrine du sacrifice dans les Brâhmaṇas*, Paris 1898: "L'aveu rétablit les faits; il ne répare pas moralement la faute, il la fait disparaître, en effet, puisque l'acte et la parole sont dès lors conformes").

[34] Mar 224c-d: *taṃ taha āloyavvaṃ māyaṃ mottūṇa nissesaṃ*. – In the present perspective, minor spelling variants and v.l. need (hence will) not be taken into account.

[35] The same saying occurs in older as well as in more recent P: in Ā 33 (*māyā-mosaṃ pamottūṇa*), M 22 (*-vipamukko u*); Ārādh (2) 332 (*āloyavvaṃ māyā-maya-vippamukkeṇa*).

[36] See *Vavahāra-sutta* 1; *Vyavahāra-ṭīkā*, ad *Vav-bhāsa* 1.133 = *Nisīha-bhāsa* 6392 = *Ohanijjutti* 801... Cf. *Mahānisīha* 1.199 *bhūṇe muddhaḍage bāle jaha palave ujju-paddharaṃ* | *aviuppannaṃ tahā savvaṃ āloyavvaṃ jaha-ṭṭhiyaṃ*. "Straightly and unrestrainedly as a baby [or] a lad [or] a boy would babble thus,

jaha bālo jaṃpaṃto kajjam akajjaṃ va ujjuaṃ bhaṇadi
taha ālocedavvaṃ māyā-mosaṃ ca mottūṇa.[37]

On the other hand, Mar 120 (the last stanza of this passage) recurs later (in Mar 222), as well as in other P, whether early or late (viz. M 20 = Ārādh (1) 207), and is very similar to Ā (2) 31 and Cand 132. Several further agreements are conspicuous in this set of 21 *gāthā*s. In particular, affinities between Mar and M are remarkably numerous: Mar 102 = 230 (M 30); Mar 110 = 227 (M 27) = Ārādh (5) 5; Mar 111 = 228 = M 28 = Ārādh (1) 216 = (2) 296 = (5) 6; Mar 112 = 229 = M 29 = Ārādh (1) 217. Many such agreements will be met with in the following developments.

The present passage insists on the benefits to be derived from a full and sincere confession if made by one who is genuinely intent on avoiding the defects liable to vitiate this difficult exercise – intent in particular on avoiding all possible fraud, etc., that would increase the risk of future bad rebirths (119 a-b = 124 a-b; 119c-d: 124 c-d). It further behoves the ācārya to prescribe the adequate atonement and to recommend indefatigable zeal:

daṃsaṇa-nāṇa-caritte tave ya kuṇa a-ppamāyaṃ (126).

As a sort of conclusion and transition, two lists are quoted: gā. 123f. list the ten faults to be avoided by one who confesses, while gā. 127f. enumerate the six sorts of external and six sorts of internal *tava*s (*tapas*): among the latter, *pāyaccchitta*s here rank third;[38]

---

in an inerudite way, everything must be accurately confessed" (ed. & transl. J. Deleu).

[37] Ed. Shastry. The *gāthā* is quoted by A. N. Upadhye, *Bṛhatkathākośa*, p. 74 (referring to gā. "547"). Remarkably, the next *gāthā* concludes: "After this total perfect confession concerning faith, knowledge, conduct, being free from thorns, having completed the purifying penances (prescribed by the guru), step by step perform saṃlekhanā." (*daṃsaṇa-ṇāṇa-caritte kādūṇâlocaṇaṃ suparisuddhaṃ* | *ṇisallo kada-suddhī kameṇa sallehaṇaṃ kuṇāsu.*)

[38] Mar 128: *viṇae 1, veyāvacce 2, pāyacchitte 3, vivega 4, sajjhāe 5,* | *abbhiṃtaraṃ tava-vihiṃ, chaṭṭhaṃ jhāṇaṃ 6 viyāṇāhi.* Elsewhere *pāyacchitta* is mentioned first, before *viṇaya* and *veyāvacca* (Uvav § 30, etc.). As for "confession", *āloyaṇā* (*ālocanā*), it is the first of the *pāyacchitta*s.

the fifth is study (*sajjhāya*, *svādhyāya*) – which has no equal among the austerities, and will never have:

na vi atthi na vi ya hohī sajjhāya-samaṃ tavo-kammaṃ (129 c-d).

(ii) This asseveration, which is also proclaimed in Cand 89 c-d[39] as well as in Ārādh (1) 589 c-d and Ārādh (2) 85 c-d, here introduces an important passage (Mar 129-149), on the merits and supreme value of the association knowledge-conduct, *nāṇa-carittāṇaṃ guṇā māhappaṃ ca*,[40] a sound knowledge of the Doctrine being the necessary condition (*sine qua non*)[41] for a true religious life: *n'atthi carittaṃ viṇā nāṇaṃ*, for it is due to knowledge that a monk can distinguish between what is to be done, and what to be avoided.[42] At the same time, as indicated by the title of the passage (*nāṇa-carittāṇaṃ guṇā māhappaṃ ca*), knowledge has to be firmly propped up by right belief and by the observance of righteous conduct, as stressed by the title given to gā. 150-153 (*sammatta-juttāṇaṃ caraṇa-karaṇāṇaṃ guṇā*). In fact, from a soteriological point of view, knowledge and conduct cannot be dissociated: they are equally important, and equally necessary, for "the *karman* which the ignorant needs an enormous number of years to annihilate, the knowledgeable one who controls his mind, speech and body annihilates in one and the same breath".[43]

---

[39] It occurs in the fifth section of Cand (*nāṇa-guṇe tti pañcamaṃ dāraṃ*, gā. 68-99), which, as in Mar, precedes sections on the *caraṇa-* and *maraṇa-guṇas* (100-116 and 117-173). Note the slight difference in the titles of the parallel sections of Cand and Mar: in Cand, *nāṇa* is mentioned independently, in Mar, it is associated with *caritta*.

[40] Mar 129-149, a chapter in several respects comparable to Cand 68-99 (and the Add[itions] to Cand registered in JAS), cf. *infra*.

[41] Comparable to the "irradiance" of the moon, such is the right Doctrine taught by the learned, according to Mar 145a-b = Cand 82a-b.: *candāu nīi joṇhā, bahussuya-muyāo nīi Jiṇa-vayaṇaṃ*. In various passages knowledge is proclaimed to be superior to fasting, Mar 131 = Cand 95 (Add 11).

[42] Mar 138d, 137d.

[43] Mar 135 (see footnote 25) = M 101 = S 114 = Cand 169 (Add 38). In this connection, Mar appears to insist on discipline more than the parallel P do. Com-

(iii) On the other hand, the monk should never depart from discipline, but, on the contrary, must strictly adhere to the recommendations of the master(s) who have the responsibility to "guide" him in his ascetic efforts in order to achieve "purity" (154-175: *nijjavagā āyariyā atta-sohī ya*)[44]: several *gāthās* of these passages (129-175) are common with the teachings imparted in the central part of Cand (*nāṇa-guṇe*, gā. 68-99a-b + *caraṇa-guṇe*, 99cd-126):[45] in both P the monk is invited to train in view of his last moments, to do it as soon as possible, while the material, intellectual and spiritual circumstances are favourable, while good masters are available, and he himself is in full vigour.[46]

(iv) Ultimately, the ācārya will assist the ascetic so that he will become strong enough to successfully perform the last death-preparatory rites. They are of two sorts (176: *duvihā saṃlehaṇā)*, physical (177-188: *sarīras.*), and spiritual (189-209: *ajjhappas.*), and are alluded to in ca. 30 *gāthās*, the teachings of which also recur in the Ārādh treatises. They will be dealt with in the next section.

3. When thus prepared and fortified, the ascetic will finally be deemed fit to let life progressively abandon his body, to face the

---

pare Mar 54, where, in a similar context, only self-control is mentioned: *jaṃ nijjarei kammaṃ asaṃvuḍo subahuṇā vi kāleṇaṃ* | *taṃ saṃvuḍo tigutto khavei ūsāsa-mitteṇaṃ*. Also see (in a comparable context) the titles of Cand 68-99 *nāṇa-guṇe tti*, and the title of the parallel reflexions, Mar 129-149.

[44] On the *nijjavagas*, cf. also *infra*, Mar 325-334.

[45] Cf. Mar 129acd = Cand 89acd = Ārādh (1) 589 = (2) 1017; Mar 131: Cand 95 (Add 11); Mar 135 = Cand 169 (Add 38); Mar 139abd = Cand 76 (Add 1abd); Mar 140 = Cand 79 Add 2 (corr.); Mar 141a(corr.)cd = Cand 68acd; Mar 144f. = Cand 81f.; Mar 147a-b: Cand 73a-b; Mar 150 = Cand 85; Mar 151 = Cand 114; Mar 152acd = Cand 113acd; Mar 153acd (corr.) = Cand 115acd.

Further: Mar 165a-c (corr.) = 276a-c; Mar 166 = 283 = Cand 125 = M 93; Mar 167acd = 275acd = Cand 122ac; Mar 169 = Cand 124; Mar 170 = Cand 170.

[46] Mar 177ff.: *jāva u suī na nāsai, jāva ya jogā na te parāhīṇā* ... ‖ *jāva ya khema-subhikkhaṃ, āyariyā jāva atthi nijjavagā* | *iḍḍhī-gārava-rahiyā nāṇa-caraṇa-daṃsaṇammi rayā* [!] ‖ *tāva* ...

voluntary and heroic death, the *abbhujjaya-maraṇa*,[47] and thus reach *ārāhaṇā* (210-324). The whole process is explained in almost the same terms in the 142 *gāthā*s of the *Mahāpaccakkhāṇa*.[48]

(i) The first step consists in the so-called "Renunciation of the Sick", *āura-paccakkhāṇa* (*ātura-pratyākhyāna*), i.e. an exhaustive confession implying the complete, total, definitive, renunciation of all that is not the Self (210-269). To judge from the name of this exercise, it is to be resorted to, in principle, by staunch believers with badly failing health. According to the JAS *Paiṇṇayasuttāiṃ* edition, several independent pamphlets are given this title, among them the old *Āurapaccakkhāṇa-paiṇṇaya.*[49] Several *gāthā*s or *pada*s of the latter also occur in the first section of Mar, as well as in M, in Cand (and Cand Add). Further the exact Digambara counterparts of several stanzas are met with in the second chapter of the *Mūlācāra*, named *Bṛhatpratyākhyāna-saṃstara-stavâdhi-*

---

[47] Mar 308 (abd = 8abd) – 309. Mar mentions the three varieties quoted Bh 9: ... *vanniyaṃ tivihaṃ* | *bhattaparinnā 1, iṅgiṇi 2 pāovagamaṃ 3 ca dhīrehiṃ* || But it does not elaborate. This last *pāovagama(ṇa)* will have been preceded by many other *paṇḍiya-maraṇa*s (cf. 240-246). Cf. Doctrine § 165; Kamptz 1929: 17.

[48] Hence the concordances need not be given in detail in the following summary.

Mar 210 = M 1: *esa karemi pamāṇaṃ* ...; Mar 323 = M 142 (the last *gāthā*): *eyaṃ paccakkhāṇaṃ aṇupāleūṇa suvihio sammaṃ* | *vemāṇio va devo havijja ahavā vi sijjhejjā*.

As shown by Kamptz (1929: 14f.), M is dependent on Ā, in which three layers can be distinguished. The (old) ritual is analysed in Ā "43ff.: M 41ff.", the latter being almost identical with Mar 240. Kamptz further refers (among others) to the old canonical texts, especially Viy II 2 (JAS ed. 4.1, p. 84f.) where two kinds of wise death (*paṇḍiya-maraṇa*) are defined, viz. "[voluntary] death by [1] complete immobility (*pāôvagamaṇa*) or [2] the renunciation of food (*bhatta-paccakkhāṇa*)", cf. Deleu 1970: 89f.

[49] JAS 17.1, no. 16, pp. 329-336 (71 *gāthā*s). Further, two so-called *Āura-paccakkhāṇa*: [1] no. 6, pp. 160-163 (30 *gāthā*s); [2], no. 13, pp. 305-308 (34 *gāthā*s). On the other hand, an additional set of 75 *gāthā*s inserted in Cand (after gā. 169) has also been given this name (*supra*). – Compare Mar 211: Ā 19: M 3; Mar: *jaṃ kiṃci vi duccariyaṃ tam ahaṃ nindāmi savva-bhāveṇaṃ* | *sāmāiyaṃ ca tivihaṃ tiviheṇa karem'* <*a*>*ṇāgāraṃ* (Ā (b): *taṃ savvaṃ vosirāmi tiviheṇaṃ*; (d): *karemi savvaṃ nirāgāraṃ*; M (d): *karemi savvaṃ nirāgāraṃ*.

kāra. Given the number of precise agreements or nearly identical statements concerning the *āurapaccakkhāṇa*, there can be little doubt about the fundamental importance and high antiquity of this rite, which involves the total adherence of those who resort to it.[50]

It essentially consists in the detailed confession of all possible categories of faults. Apart from a preliminary homage to the Tīrthaṃkaras, etc., and the sincere condemnation of all past bad deeds,[51] it is a reminder of the main Jaina principles and beliefs, and the solemn proclamation that the Self, rooted in renunciation, restraint, austerity, exercises and meditation, is firmly attached to the Jina's word and rule.[52] Further, having again taken the great vows (233), the dying man proclaims his determination to die the "death of the Sage" (*paṇḍiya-maraṇaṃ marīhāmi*, 240f.),[53] or even, more drastically, the *pāovagama(ṇa)* death of those who vow to remain totally immobile during their agony (246). The aim of the

[50] In spite of small (mostly grammatical) differences, the following *gāthās* are almost identical: Mar 213: Ā 35; Mar 216 c-d: Ā 25 (a-b): Māc 2.46; Mar 217: Ā 29: Cand 169 (Add 9) = Māc 2.50 (c: *te savve nindāmī*, Mar: *tam ahaṃ savvaṃ ninde* Ā = Māc); Mar 220: Ā 31: Cand 169 (Add 26 a-c); Mar 222 = 120 (c: *te haṃ āloemī*): Cand 132 (*te savve āloe*): Ārādh (1) 207 (*te haṃ āloeuṃ*); Mar 222: Ā (2) 31: Cand 132 acd; Mar 227 = 110: Ārādh (1) 215 = (5) 5; Mar 228 = Ārādh (1) 216 = (5) 6: (2) 296; Mar 233: Ā 13, 21: Cand 169 (Add 11): Māc 2.41 = 3.109; Mar 240, cf. Ā 47; Mar 241 (a: *jammaṇa-*: Ā 48 (*jāi-*) = Cand 169 (Add 24) = Māc 2. 76 (*jādi-*) = 3.119; Mar 244: Ā 48; Mar 247: Ā 50: Māc 2.79 (ab: Mar *cakkavāle savve vi ya* ...: Ā Māc *cakkavālammi mae savve vi*); Mar 248: Ā 52: Cand 169 (Add 18): Māc 2.82; Mar 249: Ā 51: Cand 169 (Add 20): Māc 2.80; Mar 250: Ā 51: Cand 169 (Add 19); Mar 255: Cand 169 (Add 29); Mar 256: Ā 57: Cand 169 (Add 33): Māc 2.90 – It will have been observed that, in several places, the wording of Ā (a comparatively old Śvetāmbara P) and Māc (Digambara) is remarkably close. On such connections, see Okuda 1975, *passim*.

[51] Mar 210ff., cf. M 1ff., Ā 19.

[52] Mar 216: *āyā paccakkhāṇe āyā me saṃjame tave joge*: M 11: Ā 25: Cand 169 (Add 8): Māc 2.46.

[53] Mar 240d = 241d = 244d = Cand 169 (Add 24d) = (Add 25d): Ā 47d (*aṇumarissaṃ*): 48d (*marasu iṇhiṃ*). – Ā 36 defines three sorts of deaths, the third one being precisely the *paṇḍiya-maraṇa*, which is that of the *kevalins*: *tivihaṃ bhaṇanti maraṇaṃ: bālāṇaṃ 1 bāla-paṇḍiyāṇaṃ 2 ca* | *taiyaṃ paṇḍiya-maraṇaṃ jaṃ kevaliṇo aṇumaranti.*

āurapaccakkhāṇa is to help the aspirant to be well prepared and to remain calm in the expectation of death (cf. 255-257): he should be immune from all worldly temptations, and be ready for death at any time, an aim that the five great vows should help to attain:

paṃca ya mahavvayāiṃ ... āruheūṇaṃ .... sajjo maraṇaṃ paḍicchejjā (257).

At this point, Mar, as well as M, emphatically extols the help and benefits to be derived from the *mahāvrata*s (258-269).

(ii) This somewhat rhetorical praise of the mendicants' great vows also serves as a sort of solemn transition to the next, the important, teachings, that focus on *ārāhaṇā* (270-324 + 335-385).

After preliminary considerations aimed at bracing the aspirant (270-272), the text points to the various conditions that are normally to be respected in order to attain *ārāhaṇā*: the presence of monks (*sāhu-majjhe*, 273c), a hard, ritually pure, couch (*silā-tala*, 274c, cf. 286), and, more important still, a long previous preparatory training (*puvviṃ kāriya-joga*, 277f.), both physical and spiritual (fasts, immobility, meditation), which, normally, is prescribed and supervised by the ācārya,[54] and will have fortified the dying man. Failing this preparation, his efforts would be of no avail, as the *jīva* would be overwhelmed by insuperable obstacles.[55] Now, confession to the guru is once more to be performed, *āloyaṇā seyā*,[56] this exercise being obligatory before the aspirant finally mounts the ritual death bed. The latter should be evidently free from all living beings.[57] In fact, the true bed is the pure *jīva* of the dying man:

appā khalu saṃthāro hoi visuddho marantassa.[58]

---

[54] Cf. 281f.: *kiṃ taṃ paṃḍiya-maraṇaṃ? ...* || *aṇasaṇa pāovagamaṃ, ... jhāṇa-bhāvaṇāo a* ||

[55] Cf. Mar 276, 283 = 166, Cand 125.

[56] Mar 259d, cf. Bh 47-49, S 91f.

[57] Mar 286: Cand 169 (Add 62). This prescription underlines the difference between the Jain and the Brahmanical customs, the latter implying the use of water, fire ..., as recalled ibid. a-b.

[58] Mar 287c-d = S 53 = Cand 169 (Add 63).

His mind, plunged into meditation and engrossed in other spiritual exercises, totally adheres to the Jina's teachings (288): Mar once more insists on the soteriological qualities of knowledge,[59] which is comparable with fire and burns all *karman* (290-292).[60] Hence, not only is it necessary to be well versed in the Doctrine, it is moreover advisable to remember precisely those teachings – the *pada*, sentence, verse, or even single word – which have determined one's conversion.[61]

At this point, one is to declare a total, complete adherence to the Law taught by the Jina (*dhammaṃ ... saddahāmi ...*) and to the Way leading to *nirvāṇa*, that is beneficial to all beings;[62] further the aspirant proclaims his being a *samaṇa* and a perfect ascetic,

> *samaṇo 'haṃ ti ya paḍhamaṃ, bīyaṃ savvattha saṃjao mi tti,*
> *savvaṃ ca vosirāmī Jiṇehī jaṃ jaṃ paḍikkuṭṭhaṃ,*[63]

he rejects all possible wrong doing,[64] attains *samādhi* (301), further, relying whole-heartedly on the Siddhas, Arhants, Sādhūs,[65] and thanks to the above memorized Dharma taught by the *kevalin*s, he attains the Goal.[66] Continuing his meditation in spite of the pains and difficulties he endures (304-307), he progressively procedes to the so-called well prepared heroic death, *uvei abbhujjayaṃ maraṇaṃ* (309d). Finally, when he has overcome all obstacles, he is invited to lift the banner of success, *harāhi ārāhaṇa-paḍāgaṃ* (311d ff.). Then, having ascended the death-bed, he proclaims that he has indeed crossed over; hence: *harāmi ārāhaṇa-paḍāgaṃ* (313). He is

---

[59] Cf. *supra*, section 2. (i).

[60] Mar 290a-cd = Cand 169 (Add 36acd), Mar 290b: Cand ibid. (b); Mar 291 = Cand 169 (Add 37).

[61] Mar 293-296: Cand 96, 94, 95.

[62] Mar 297: Ā 58: Cand 169 (Add 45): Māc 2.91.

[63] Mar 298 = Cand 169 (Add 12): Ā 63: Māc 2. 98.

[64] Mar 299.

[65] Cf. C 11: *Arihanta 1 Siddha 2 Sāhū 3 Kevali-kahio suhâvaho Dhammo 4 | ee cauro ... saraṇaṃ lahai dhanno.*

[66] Mar 303.

further advised to remain vigilantly faithful to the Jina's doctrine (316f.).

To conclude, seven scholastic *gāthā*s recall the four branches and three degrees of *ārāhaṇā*,[67] and draw attention to the benefits derived from this controlled renunciation of life, viz. rebirth among the Vaimānikas or even *siddhi*:

> *vemāṇio va devo havijja ahavā vi sijjhejjā* (323).

This stanza, on the other hand, serves as the conclusion of the 142 *gāthā*s which compose the *Mahāpaccakkhāṇa*.

(iii) As for Mar, it adds some more remarks concerning the ritual, several of which are also met with in the *Bhattaparinnā-* and *Saṃthāra-Paiṇṇaya*s, and in the *Ārāhaṇā*s.[68]

(a) First a group of ten *gāthā*s (325-334) deals with the help that the now pure *sāhu* will request from the learned, wise and firm masters (*dhīrā*, 333) who will have to guide him (*nijjavae maggejjā*, 325).[69] Their qualities are innumerable (334). Their knowledge, character and religious conduct should be perfect, they should be conversant with the various monastic procedures and the various forms of heroic deaths (327), be perfectly well versed in discipline as well as in the canonical texts (333). To attend on the dying man in his ultimate, heroic enterprise, eight guides are mentioned, whose qualities are so numerous that they cannot be enumerated:[70]

---

[67] Mar 318 (-324): *daṃsaṇa 1 nāṇa 2 caritte 3 tave 4 ... | ... ukkosā 1 majjhima 2 jahaṇṇā 3 ||*

[68] The controlled, gradual, serene, passing away of the heroic Jaina ascetic or lay-follower is also described or alluded to in several other canonical passages, cf. Khandaga's career, as detailed already in Viy II 1 (JAS 4.1, p. 76ff.; cf. Deleu 1970: 89f., *ubi alia*); compare *Antagaḍadasāo*, *Aṇuttarovavāiya-dasāo*, *Uvavāiya* ...

[69] Cf. the formal request addressed to the guru, Bh 17f.: ... *guru-pāmūle 'bhigamma viṇaeṇaṃ | ... vandiuṃ bhaṇai: ||* "*āruhium ahaṃ, supurisa, bhattapainnā-pasatthabohitthaṃ | nijjāmaeṇa guruṇā icchāmi bhav'annavaṃ tariuṃ*". On the necessity of *nijjavaga*s, cf. already gā. 155. Good masters precisely help one to cross over: *saṃsāra-mah'aṇṇava-tāraya*, Cand 31c.

two ācāryas, with two attendants for the service, two others in order to take care of the ascetic's life, two learned ones, who help him in all his movements and never leave him alone.[71] "Such are the superior teachers under whose guidance the *samaṇa* will pursue his perfect death",

paḍivajjijja mahattham samaṇo abbhujjayaṃ maraṇaṃ (335).

(b) The topic is detailed in 30 *gāthās*,[72] which deal with the "thinning of passions and extraction of darts" or unconfessed offences, (*kasāyâi-khāmaṇā sall'uddharaṇâi-nirūvaṇaṃ*, 335-365). The ascetic first asks for pardon from all the superiors and colleagues, and, conversely, he himself pardons them.[73] He blames himself, repents, becomes one with the Āgama (339), practises such extreme *tapas* that he is like a corpse (340); he endures all possible hardships, is totally detached, shakes off the blemish due to thirst for the objects of the senses. He reduces his diet, renounces all care for his physical condition; further, in the presence and with the help of the above superiors, he proceeds with the last, the supreme, purification (*parikamma*).[74] He prepares his death-bed, on a carefully arranged layer of bark, or grass or leaves, or on a board or a slab of stone, oriented so that the head is in the North or in the East.[75] In the presence of the highest gurus, he will mount this death-bed arranged according to the rule (*vihi-vihia saṃthāra*), observing the

---

[70] Mar 334: *ee te nijjavayā parikahiyā aṭṭha uttim'aṭṭhammi* | *jesiṃ guṇa-saṃkhāṇaṃ na samatthā pāyayā vottuṃ*. Cf. the *aṇega-guṇa-sayasahassa* of the ācārya, Cand 22-36.

[71] Mar 330f.: *doṇhaṃ āyariyāṇaṃ do veyāvacca-karaṇa-nijjuttā* | *pāṇaga-veyāvacce tavassiṇo vi do pattā* || *uvvattaṇa-parivattaṇa-uccār'ussāva-karaṇa-jogesuṃ* | *do vāyaga tti ṇijjā asunna-karaṇe jahanneṇaṃ* ||

[72] From now on, more concrete details are added. Compare Bh, S, and Kamptz's description.

[73] Mar 336f.: S 103f.: Ārādh (1) 488f.: (3) 118f.: (6) 48.

[74] Mar 345f.

[75] Mar 347f.: ... *ajjhusira-vāga-taṇa-patta-kaḍae ya* | *kaṭṭha-silā-phalagammi*.

three restraints (of mind, body and speech), being well-possessed of the Teaching, adhering to the Discipline. And he fasts. First, while he reduces the usual fourfold meal, he nevertheless takes some liquid so that he can attain *samādhi*. But, in due time, he also, progressively, excludes liquids;[76] he remains on this couch, with absolutely no desire (*a-niyāṇa*), listening to his guides' sermons: the masters aim at guiding the dying man so that he partakes of a good destiny, being free from *saṃsāra*'s dangers and fears (354-365).[77]

To encourage detachment from wordly preoccupations, the guides' words recall basic Jaina instructions (many of which are also developed elsewhere):[78] more than once, they are reinforced by similes. Gā. 366-385 insist on the miseries of *saṃsāra*, and further on the fundamental difference between the body and the Self, an opposition which should prevent any attachment to the body,

annaṃ imaṃ sarīraṃ, anno haṃ ... | ... dehe ko tattha paḍibandho?[79]

The "solitude, uniqueness" of every *jīva* is emphasized (*vaccai egāṇio imo jīvo*),[80] hence Mar pathetically invites one to practise *dhyāna* and be conscious of the incommensurable chain of *saṃsāra*.[81]

(iv) The above considerations are prolonged by the enumeration of the well-known miseries experienced by the embryo, or at the time of birth, etc. (386-401). To conclude, gā. 402-405 are a pressing

[76] Mar 352f.: ... *savvo cauvvihâhāro | tava-saṃjamu tti kiccā vosiriyavvo ti-guttenaṃ || ahavā samāhi-heuṃ kāyavvo pāṇagassa āhāro | to pāṇagaṃ pi pacchā vosiriyavvaṃ jahā-kāle* || Cf. S 89: Bh 46: Ārādh (2) 432.

[77] Cf. Bh 52d: *aṇusaṭṭhiṃ dei gaṇi-vasabho.*

[78] Cf. also the twelve *bhāvanās*, *infra*.

[79] A very common remark, Mar 369 = 590: 403: S 99, etc.

[80] Mar 378b.

[81] Mar 381-385: S 93-95. Compare S 88-122 (in JAS entitled *paḍivanna-saṃthāragassa khāmaṇā bhāvaṇā ya*).

exhortation to suppress all sense of ownership, all interest in the body, etc., whereas 406-408 warn against the various obstacles and disagreements facing the *sādhu*, and hence recommend the avoidance of all passions,

> *rāgo vā doso vā īsi maṇeṇaṃ na kāyavvo* (408 c-d).

* * *

4. Having thus recalled fundamental Jain tenets, developed the relevant theoretical arguments and detailed the steps to be taken by those who aim at the perfect *paṇḍiyamaraṇa*, Mar corroborates the teachings by referring to illustrious examples of saints or great men who were not deterred from their faith and observances in spite of their diseases or the pains they endured, or the terrible obstacles they had to face (409-503). Similarly, in order to support their recommendations, Bh and S adduced examples of courageous deaths. But, whereas these "Legenden von Märtyren" are interspersed in the texts of Bh,[82] Mar reserves a specific chapter to this topic (gā. 409-503), and deals in some detail with several heroic deeds. A number of these legends are common to the three *Paiṇṇaya*s.[83]

After four *gāthā*s in praise of the courage of Saṇaṃkumāra *cakkavatti* (409-412), two groups of 22 heroes each are distinguished. Undoubtedly life is always difficult for staunch believers, but some men traditionally serve as examples of faith and fearlessness: gā. 413-485 concern those who have had to endure one of the 22 *uvasagga*s (*upasarga*, "calamity"), gā. 486-503 deal more rapidly with those who had to cope with one of the 22 *parīsaha*s (*parīṣaha*, "affliction").[84] At the same time the latter is expressly linked

---

[82] References in Kamptz 1929: 25-38.

[83] Cilāiputta: Mar 428-31, Bh 88, S 86; Avantisukumāla: Mar 436-40, Bh 160, S 65f.; Daṇḍaaṇagāra: Mar 466, S 61; Sukosalamuṇi: Mar 67f., Bh 161, S 63f.; Cāṇakka: Mar 79, S 73-75.

with the second lesson of the *Uttarajjhayaṇa*.[85] To these illustrious examples Mar further adds that of nine animals who also heroically practised religion (507-524).[86] According to Kamptz, by inserting examples of heroic deaths, Bh and S also call attention to the preparatory concrete aspects of the *paṇḍiya-maraṇa*[87] which they embrace. So does Mar. At the same time, these texts follow the teaching scheme traced by the Jains (and the Indians in general) who insist on the importance of the "example" (*udāharaṇa*).[88]

5. In Mar, it is further recalled that all the nuisances that have been alluded to have, in fact, been created by the *deva*s in order to frighten animals and men, to dissuade them from lingering in the pleasures of the senses (525): only the *sādhu* who is physically and morally strong as well as thoroughly versed in the Jain fundamental teachings (the *Puvva*s, *Pūrva*s, etc.) can victoriously undertake one or other of the two kinds of death by fasting (the twin *iṅgiṇi-pāovagamaṇa* deaths, 526).

---

84 On the *parīsaha*s, Utt, chapter 2 (*parīsah'ajjhayaṇaṃ*); on the *uvasagga*s, Sūy, chapter 1.3 (*uvasagga-parinnā*). Most of the heroes mentioned in Mar are referred to in Nemicandra's *ṭīkā* on Utt., cf. JAS, Introduction, p. 102. See also Mehta & Chandra 1970-72.

85 Mar 485: *samuiṇṇesu ya ... ghoresu parīsahesu sahaṇeṇaṃ* I *so attho saraṇijjo jo bīe Uttarajjhayaṇe*. Mar follows the Utt sequence. Some minor differences in the name of the afflictions can be observed. In Mar they are: 1 *bhikkhāvaṇa* (Utt *digiṃcchā-p.*), 2 *taṇhā* (Utt *pivāsā-p.*), 3 *sīya* (*sīya-p.*), 4 *usiṇa* (*usiṇa-*), 5 *masaya* (*daṃsa-masaya-*), 6 *acelayatta* (*acela-*), 7 *araiya* (*arai-*), 8 *itthiga* (*itthī-*), 9 *cariyâi* (*cariyā-*), 10 *nisīhiyā* (*nisīhiyā*), 11 *sijjā* (*sejjā*), 12 *akkosa* (*akkosa-*),13 *vaha* (*vaha-*), 14 *jāyaṇā* (*jāyaṇā*), 15 *alābhaga* (*alābha-*), 16 *roga* (*roga-*), 17 *taṇa-phāsa* (*taṇa-phāsa-*), 18 *jalla* (*jalla-*), 19 *sakkāra* (*sakkāra-purakkāra*), 20 *pannâi* (*pannā-*), 22 *daṃsaṇa* (*daṃsaṇa/sammatta*). Exceptionally, the 21st is *nāṇa* in Mar (503), *annāṇa* in Utt; but the implications are evidently identical.

86 Cf. *Nāyādhammakahāo*. Further see Jaini 2000: 261f.

87 Kamptz 1929: 24.

88 Cf. Balbir 1993: 105: "Les niryukti considèrent l'exemple [Pk *diṭṭhānta* (Skt *dṛṣṭānta*) et *udāharaṇa*] comme une composante essentielle des méthodes d'enseignement, au même titre que les moyens de preuve". More generally, see Katsura & Steinkellner 2004.

(i) As far as the latter is concerned, two varieties, *sa-/a-nihāri*,[89] are mentioned, a statement later followed by a glorification of this remarkable austerity that has ensured all the Tīrthaṃkaras' *siddhi*:

savve vi ya Titthayarā pāovagayā u siddhi-gayā (540c-d).

Three *gāthā*s emphasize that *pāovagamaṇa* is exceptionally meritorious as it is based on the total abstention from all aliment, *āhāra*, which, according to this passage, is the supreme, essential treasure to which all living beings are inevitably always attached.[90] Thus, well prepared, lying on a slab of stone (*silāyala-gaya*), the dying man is ready to face death, unflinching though in solitude and wilderness (547), comforted by his faith and doctrinal knowledge, in particular convinced of the heterogeneity of the body and the soul, the *jīva*,

iya me anno jīvo anno deho tti mannejjā (532).

Hence, when the body has perished, the "soul" goes free, the soul which has been proclaimed to be imperishable:

... *dehaṃ mottūṇa vaccae jīvo | so jīvo aviṇāsī bhaṇio* ... (567 b-c).

(ii) This truth as well as a set of other fundamental tenets must have been thoroughly mastered, especially those tenets that have determined a man's "conversion"; for they will, normally, have forged his character and personality, and will thus remain present in his mind at any time.[91] As a matter of fact, Mar now devotes a

---

[89] Mar 527: *eyaṃ pāovagamaṃ sanihārī 1 vā anīhāriṃ 2*, cf. Utt 30.13. On *(a)nīhāri*, Deleu, Viy II 1.2 (*ubi alia*) [Viy, chapter II, JAS 4.1], referring to Abhayadeva's commentary: "taking place under circumstances (e.g. in a house or in a wood resp.) that make the subsequent removal of the dead body necessary or not"; Kamptz 1929: 16f., Leumann 1883, Glossar s.v.

[90] Mar 543 c-d: *āhārāo rayaṇaṃ na vijjae uttamaṃ loe*; 544c-d: *savve savvâvatthaṃ āhāre honti āuttā*; 545: *taṃ tārisaṃ rayaṇaṃ sāraṃ jaṃ savva-loya-rayaṇāṇaṃ | savvaṃ pariccaittā pāovagayā paviharanti.*

[91] Cf. Mar 293-295 (+296) = Cand 96-94-95 = 102-105-103.

set of 71 *gāthās* to reflections and meditation, as expressed in the "twelve *bhāvaṇās*", an important topic (often termed *aṇupekkhā/ anuprekṣā*, "deep reflection"),[92] that has been developed at all epochs of Jain literature. These should be meditated upon by the dying man, when lying well composed on his death bed. They are enumerated in gā. 573-574, several of them are further detailed in gā. 575-640.[93] Most of them can be regarded as summarizing some of the fundamental teachings of the Doctrine. If well assimilated and present at the ultimate moment, they will pervade the believer's thoughts, so that he thoroughly controls his mind, and hence imperturbably keeps it set on fundamental, auspicious, objects of meditation, even when he is passing away.

Though various (comparatively minor) discrepancies have been noted in the order as well as in the names of some of these items, the list is well established. As for the Mar scheme, it recurs in Maladhāri Hemacandra's *Bhavabhāvanā*, composed in AD 1131.[94] In Mar 573f. (= Ārādh (1) 731f.) it runs thus:

> *paḍhamaṃ aṇiccabhāvaṃ1 asaraṇayaṃ2 egayaṃ3 ca annattaṃ4 saṃsāra5m asubhayā6 vi ya viviham loga-ssahāvaṃ7 ca* (*asuhayaṃ6 ciya* Ārādh) *kammassa āsavaṃ8 saṃvaraṃ9 ca nijjaraṇā10m uttame ya guṇe11 jiṇasāsaṇammi bohiṃ ca dullahaṃ12 cintae maimaṃ*,
>
> impermanence, helplessness, loneliness, separateness of the Self and non-Self, cycle of transmigration, impurity of body, universe, influx of *karman*, stoppage of karmic influx, shedding of *karman*, Law expounded by Jina, rarity of religious Enlightenment.[95]

---

[92] So rendered by Sukhlalji [& Dixit] 1974, ad TS IX 7. On *bhāvaṇā*, *supra* footnote 15, referring to Alsdorf. On *aṇupekkhā*, *aṇuprekṣā*, cf. Upadhye 1960, Introduction (especially pp. 6-42). Also TS IX 7 and Sukhlalji's (1974) and N. Tatia's (1994) commentaries *ad loc.* Further, Williams 1963: 244, "The Anuprekṣās", 245f. "The Bhāvanās"; Bruhn 2003: 35f.

[93] Mar 570: *evaṃ bhāviya-citto saṃthārammi, suvihiya, sayā vi | bhāvehi bhāvaṇāo bārasa Jiṇavayaṇa-diṭṭhāo*. These *bhāvaṇās* are 12, i.e. the same number as the traditional number of the Aṅgas: *vaṇṇei bhāvaṇāo bāras' imā bāras' Aṅga-viū*, cf. Ārādh I 729-745. A different list had been mentioned *supra*, Mar 59-67 (cf. footnote 14). Further, Bruhn 2003: 34, § 5.14 "Technical Matters".

[94] On the *Bhavabhāvanā* (531 *gāthās*), Upadhye 1960: 28ff.

"Impermanence" (*aṇicca*, *anitya-*),[96] invariably seems to be mentioned as the starting point of the reflections. On the other hand, to judge from the length of the related developments, the triad *āsava-saṃvara-nijjaraṇa*, which is dealt with in (20+5+5 =) 30 *gāthā*s, appears to be deemed particularly important,[97] inserting as it does some of the most popular teachings of the "śramaṇic" poetry.[98] Further the *āsava* passage in particular is remarkable not only for the number of the *gāthā*s it includes, but, also, for the rhetoric and pathetic tone of several of them, for the numerous comparisons and interrogations it uses, as well as for the inclusion of more than one *vipulā āryā*, a comparatively old rhythmic scheme (602, 613, 618).

> Thus, in brief, have all the twelve reflections been thoroughly dealt with: reflecting upon them the *jīva* accedes to freedom from desires. Do reflect upon the reflections, do keep the vows – they are jewel-like: all evil will be thoroughly destroyed, before long you will reach *siddhi*, precisely,
>
> *bārasa vi bhāvaṇāo evaṃ saṃkhevao samattāo* I
> *bhāvemāṇo jīvo jāo samuvei veraggaṃ* II 639 II
> *bhāvijja bhāvaṇāo, pālijja vayāī rayaṇa-sarisāiṃ* I
> *paḍipuṇṇa-pāvakhamaṇe airā siddhiṃ pi pāvihisi* II 640 II

The remaining 20 *gāthā*s do not add any new material, but pathetically recall one *locus communis* or an other (e.g. the helplessness and loneliness of every life, 645ff.) that has been more elaborately dealt with previously. A comparison reminds one how difficult it is to obtain a human birth, how rare to gain *bodhi* and enlightenment

---

[95] Upadhye 1960: 44. In other treatises, e.g. in the *Tattvārtha-Sūtra* (IX 7) among others, the sequence of the *anuprekṣā*s differs slightly: *anityâśaraṇa-saṃsāraikatvânyatvâśucitvâśrava-saṃvara-nirjarā-loka-bodhidurlabha-dharma-svākhyātatvânucintanam anuprekṣāḥ* (cf. Mar 1-2-5+(3-4)+6-7+(8-9-10)+12-11).

[96] Mar, TS, etc.: *adhruva*, Śivārya, Vaṭṭakera, Kundakunda (cf. Upadhye 1960).

[97] Compare the number of *gāthā*s reserved for the other topics: for nos. 1+2+3+4: (4+5+6+1 =) 16 *gāthā*s; for nos. 5+6+7 (3+4+3 =) 10 *gāthā*s; for nos. 11+12 (2+6 =) 8 *gāthā*s.

[98] E.g. Mar 625: *jo samaṃ bhūyāiṃ pāsai bhūe ya appa-bhūe ya* I *kamma-maleṇa na lippai so saṃvariyâsava-duvāro*. Cf. BhG 6.28.32, Dhp 10.1, etc.

(646ff.). Finally one is warned against "the torments suffered by the miserable heretics deluded by the poisonous sprouts of false systems" which they mistake for "the sublime savoury flavour of the Jina's teaching, this *kalpataru*. Hence, blissfully addicted to the sweet taste of this blissful great tree, one should abandon the world and die the death of the sage."[99]

It will have been observed that the emotion which arises from the Mar *gāthā*s is fundamentally (though not exclusively) based on arguments of a rational character: the Paiṇṇa aims at convincing the listener and providing him with a number of main guidelines in order finally to conclude: "Mould your mind with the Jina's doctrine, purge it from the impurity of mundane traditions, and keep it immersed in the *dharma-* and *śukla-dhyāna.* Listen how, with a heart fashioned by the Jina's word, the *samaṇa* is to remain absorbed in mental concentration, on which concentration, on which subjects, he should concentrate".[100] Well taught, well trained, perfectly disciplined, the *samaṇa* will master his life unto the last.

As recalled by Muni Shri Puṇyavijayaji, the Mar has traditionally been described as being composed of five *uddeśa*s, the limits of which are sometimes more or less blurred. Nevertheless it appears that the topics successively dealt with are the following:

1 (gā. 10-99) a general preamble/overview (including several mnemonic *gāthā*s and a comparatively long passage dealing with confession): in many respects this "*śataka*" could be viewed as a *Textus simplicior*, introducing a detailed description of the topic;[101]

---

[99] Mar 658f.: *taha para-titthiya-kīḍā visaya-visaṅkura-vimūḍha-diṭṭhīyā* । *Jiṇa-sāsaṇa-kappataruvara-pārokkha-rasā kilissanti;* ॥ *tamhā sokkha-mahātaru-sāsaya-sivaphalaya-sokkha-satteṇa* । *mottūṇa loga-saṇṇaṃ paṇḍiyamaraṇeṇa mariyavvaṃ* ॥

[100] Mar 660f.: *Jiṇamaya-bhāviya-citto loga-suī-mala-vireyaṇaṃ kāuṃ* । *dhammammi tao jhāṇe sukke ya maiṃ niveseha* ॥ *suṇa jaha Jiṇa-vayaṇa-maya-bhāviya-hiyaeṇa jhāṇa-vāvāro* । *karaṇijjo samaṇeṇaṃ jaṃ jhāṇaṃ jesu jhāya-vvaṃ* ॥

2-5 (gā. 100-640) the main development dealing successively with:
– the necessary lifelong preparation in view of a successful death;
– the ultimate preparation and rites in view of the impending *paṇḍiya-* or the *pāovagamaṇa-maraṇa*, and *ārāhaṇā*;
– examples of heroic deaths;
– topics to be meditated upon when lying on the pure death-bed.

On a cursory reading, the reason why some subjects (e.g. confession, *āloyaṇā*, *ālocanā*) recur in several places of the Mar is not immediately obvious. In fact it appears that the Mar invites one to take into account not only the final, ultimate rites and passing away, but also, more or less implicitly, the whole religious life of the Jain *samaṇa*. This also explains the fact that so many of the Mar *gāthā*s are apparently borrowed from, or in any case common with, those of other *Paiṇṇaya*s: *ārāhaṇā* has to be viewed as the conclusion, the accomplishment, of a life-long process.

REFERENCES

Primary Sources

Ā = *Āurapaccakkhāṇa-Paiṇṇaya*. Ed. Puṇyavijaya & A. M. Bhojak (JAS 17.1.) 1984.

Ārādh = *Ārādhaṇā-Paiṇṇaya*. Ed. Puṇyavijaya & A. M. Bhojak. (JAS 17.2.) 1987.

Aup = *Aupapātika-Sūtra*. See Leumann 1883.

Āyār = *Āyāraṅga-Suttaṃ*. Ed. Jambuvijaya. (JAS 2.1.) 1976.

Bh = *Bhattaparinnā-Paiṇṇaya*. Ed. Puṇyavijaya & A. M. Bhojak (JAS 17.1.) 1984.

Bhagavatī Ārādhanā. By Śivārya. Ed. Kailaschandra Shastri. (Jivaraja Jaina Granthamala, 36-37.) Sholapur 1978.

C = *Causaraṇa-Paiṇṇaya*. Ed. Puṇyavijaya & A. M. Bhojak (JAS 17.1.) 1984.

---

[101] Cf. Bruhn 1993: 20: "In the Śvetāmbara canon we notice a few cases where a single work can be split into two parts ... distinctions ... take mostly the form of dichotomy ...".

Cand = *Candāvejjhaya-Paiṇṇaya*. Ed. Puṇyavijaya & A. M. Bhojak (JAS 17.1.) 1984.

Dhp = *Dhammapada*. Ed. Pali Text Society, 1995.

JAS = *Jaina Āgama Series*. Bombay: Shri Mahāvīra Jaina Vidyālaya, 1968-.

M = *Mahāpaccakkhāṇa-Paiṇṇaya*. Ed. Puṇyavijaya & A. M. Bhojak. (JAS 17.1.) 1984.

Māc = *Mūlācāra*. Ed. Pt. Kailash Chandra Shastri. Delhi: Bhāratīya Jñānapīṭha, 1984, 1986.

Mar = *Maraṇasamāhi*. Ed. Puṇyavijaya & A. M. Bhojak. (JAS 17.1) 1984.

P = *Paiṇṇayasuttāiṃ*. Ed. Puṇyavijaya & A. M. Bhojak. (JAS 17.1-2.) 1984, 1987.

S = *Saṃthāraga-Paiṇṇaya*. Ed. Puṇyavijaya & A. M. Bhojak. (JAS 17.1.) 1984.

Sūy = *Sūyagaḍa*. Ed. Muni Jambuvijaya. (JAS 2.2.) 1978.

TS = *Tattvārtha-Sūtra*. See Sukhlalji 1974; Tatia 1994.

Utt = *Uttarajjhayaṇāiṃ*. Ed. Puṇyavijaya & A. M. Bhojak (JAS 15.) 1977.

Uvav = *Uvavāiya-Sutta*. See Leumann 1883.

Vav = *Vavahāra-Sutta*. Ed. W. Schubring. Leipzig 1918. Ed. by K. P. Modi with Malayagiri's commentary. Ahmedabad 1925-28.

Viy = *Viyāhapaṇṇatti-Suttaṃ*. Ed. Bechardas J. Doshi. (JAS 4.1.) 1974. See Deleu 1970.

Secondary Sources

ALSDORF, Ludwig 1965. *Les études jaina. État présent et tâches futures*. Paris: Collège de France.

—— 1966. *The Āryā Stanzas of the Uttarajjhāyā. Contributions to the History and Interpretation of a Canonical Jaina Text.* (Abhandlungen der Geistes- und Sozialwissenschaftliche Klasse 1966, Nr. 2.) Mainz: Akademie der Wissenschaften und der Literatur, 1966.

BAILEY, Greg 1999. Intertextuality in the Purāṇas: a neglected element in the study of Sanskrit literature. In: M. Brockington & P. Schreiner (eds.), *Composing a Tradition: Concepts, Techniques and Relationships:* 179-198. Zagreb: Croatian Academy of Arts and Sciences.

BALBIR, Nalini 1993. *Āvaśyaka-Studien*, I: *Introduction générale et traductions.* (Alt- und Neu-Indische Studien, 45.1.) Stuttgart: Franz Steiner Verlag.

BRUHN, Klaus 1993. Sectional studies in Jainology II. *Berliner Indologische Studien* 7: 9-58.

BRUHN, Klaus 2003. The Mahāvratas in early Jainism. *Berliner Indologische Studien* 15-17: 3-98.

CAILLAT, Colette 1975. *Atonements in the Ancient Ritual of the Jaina Monks*. (L.D. Series, 49.) Ahmedabad: L.D. Institute of Indology.

—— 1977. Fasting unto death according to the Jaina tradition. *Acta Orientalia* 38: 43-66.

—— 1992. Interpolations in a Jain pamphlet or the emergence of one more *Āturapratyākhyāna*. *Wiener Zeitschrift für die Kunde Südasiens* 36: 35-44.

—— 2003. Gleanings from a comparative reading of early canonical Buddhist and Jain texts. *Journal of the International Association of Buddhist Studies* 26.1: 25-50.

CPD = *A Critical Pāli Dictionary*. Ed. by V: Trenckner et al. Copenhagen: Royal Danish Academy of Sciences and Letters, 1924-48.

DELEU, Jozef 1970. *Viyāhapannatti (Bhagavaī)*. (Werken uitgegeven door de Facultett van de Letteren en Wijsbegeerte, 151.) Brugge: "De Tempel", Rijksuniversiteit te Gent.

DELUMEAU, Jean 1989. *Rassurer et protéger. Le sentiment de sécurité dans l'occident d'autrefois*. Paris: Fayard.

FEZAS, Jean 2005. The daily routine of the king: From commentary to literary creation. Paper read at the *International conference "Forms and Uses of the Commentary in the Indian World"*, Pondicherry, February 22-25, 2005.

JAINI, Padmanabh S. 1979. *The Jaina Path of Purification*. Berkeley: University of California, Center for South and Southeast Asia Studies.

—— 2000. Indian perspectives on the spirituality of animals, (Revised version) in: P. S. Jaini (ed.), *Collected Papers on Jaina Studies*: 253-266. Delhi: Motilal Banarsidass, 2000. [Originally published in D. Kalupahana & W. G. Weeraratne (eds), *Buddhist Philosophy and Culture: Essays in Honour of N. A. Jayawickrema*, Colombo 1987.]

KAMPTZ, Kurt von 1929. *Ueber die vom Sterbefasten handelnden älteren Paiṇṇa des Jaina-Kanons*. Dissertation, Universität Hamburg.

KATSURA, Shoryu & Ernst STEINKELLNER (eds.) 2004. *The Role of the Example (dṛṣṭānta) in Classical Indian Logic*. (Wiener Studien zur Tibetologie und Buddhismuskunde, 58.) Wien: Arbeitskreis für tibetische und buddhistische Studien.

LEUMANN, Ernst 1883 *Das Aupapâtika Sûtra, erstes Upânga der Jaina*, I: *Einleitung, Text und Glossar*. (Abhandlungen für die Kunde Morgenlandes, 8.2). Leipzig: F.A. Brockhaus (Reprint: Nendeln: Kraus Reprint, 1966.)

MEHTA, M. L & K. R. CHANDRA 1970-72. *Prakrit Proper Names*. (L.D. Series 28, 37.) Ahmedabad: L.D. Institute of Indology.

NARASIMHACHARYA, R. 1972. *Sravanabelgola*. (Epigraphia Carnatica, 2.) Mysore: Kannaḍa Adhyayana Saṃsthe.

OETJENS, Karl 1976. *Śivāryas Mūlārādhanā. Ein Beitrag zur Kenntnis der Sterbefasten-Literatur der Jainas*. Dissertation zur Erlangung der Würde des Doktors der Philosophie der Universität Hamburg.

OKUDA, Kiyoaki 1975. *Eine Digambara-Dogmatik. Das fünfte Kapitel von Vaṭṭakeras Mūlācāra herausgegeben, übersetzt und kommentiert*. Wiesbaden: Franz Steiner Verlag.

OLIVELLE, Patrick 2004. Manu and the *Arthaśāstra*: A study in śāstric intertextuality. *Journal of Indian Philosophy* 32: 281-291.

RENOU, Louis & Marie-Simone RENOU 1951. Une secte religieuse dans l'Inde contemporaine. *Études* 268, 341-343. [Reproduced in Louis Renou, *Choix d'études indiennes*. Réunies par Nalini Balbir et Georges-Jean Pinault. Paris 1997. (Réimpression de l'École Française d'Extrême-Orient 9, p. 927.)]

RICE, L. B. 1873. Jain inscriptions at Śravaṇa Beḷgoḷa. *Indian Antiquary* 2: 265-266 & 322-324.

SCHUBRING, Walther 1935. *Die Lehre der Jainas. Nach der alten Quellen dargestellt*. (Grundriss der Indo-Arischen Philologie und Altertumskunde, 3.7.) Berlin: Walter De Gruyter & Co.

SETTAR, S. 1986. *Inviting Death. Historical Experiments on Sepulchral Hill*. Dharwad: Institute of Indian Art and History. Karnatak University.

—— 1990. *Pursuing Death. Philosophy and Practice of Voluntary Termination of Life*. Dharwad: Institute of Indian Art and History. Karnatak University.

SHAH, Ambalal Premchand 1968. Some inscriptions and images on Mount Śatruñjaya. In: *Shri Mahavir Jaina Vidyalaya Golden Jubilee Volume*, I: 162-169. Bombay: Shri Mahavira Jaina Vidyalaya.

SUKHLALJI 1974. *Pt. Sukhlalji's Commentary on Tattvārtha Sūtra of Vācaka Umāsvāti*. Translated by K. K. Dixit. (L.D. Series, 44.) Ahmedabad: L.D. Institute of Indology.

TATIA, Nathmal 1994. *Tattvārtha Sūtra. That Which is*. Translated with an Introduction by ... San Francisco, London, Pymble (Institute of Jainology).

UPADHYE, A. N. 1960. *Svāmikumāraviracitā Kārttikeyānuprekṣā (Kattigeyāṇuppekkhā): prāmāṇikarītyā Śubhacandra-viracitayā saṃskṛtaṭīkayā sametā*. (Śrīmad Rājachandra Jaina Śāstramālā.) Agas: Śrīmad Rājachandra Āśrama.

WATKINS, Calvert 1994. *Selected Writings*, I-II. Ed. by Lisi Oliver. (Innsbrucker Beiträge zur Sprachwissenschaft, 80.) Innsbruck: Institut für Sprachwissenschaft der Universität Innsbruck.

WILLIAMS, R. 1963. *Jaina Yoga. A Survey of the Mediaeval Śrāvakācāras.* (London Oriental Series, 14.) London: Oxford University Press.

Woman in Ancient Jain Literature

J. R. BHATTACHARYYA

In India, the time of Jain canonical literature was an important phase for rearrangement of cultural values. Be it the canons of the Śvetāmbaras or the *Anuyoga*s of the Digambaras, and the Śvetāmbara *Carita sāhitya* or Digambara Purāṇas, a meagre amount of the sociological aspect peeping inside the position of women had not been overlooked. Naturally the ethical codes of asceticism and household righteousness have been taken into great consideration in the Jain canons and the commentary literatures.

This article does not attempt to focus on the exhaustive study keeping in view of each and every aspect of woman life but it encompasses the two broad aspects: domesticity and asceticism.

On the aspect of spiritual liberation of a woman, Digambaras and Śvetāmbaras express different opinions. Digambaras vehemently discard the attainment of *mokṣa* of women while Śvetāmbaras strongly admits *strīmukti*, emancipation of a soul (as it has no gender) from the cycles of birth and death. Digambaras, in a straight way refuse to accept any possibility of attaining salvation of any person wearing clothes. Professor Padmanabh S. Jaini in his book *Gender and Salvation* (1992) has referred to some of the Jain treatises where spiritual liberation of women has been mentioned and critically analysed, viz. *Suttapāhuḍa* of Ācārya Kundakunda (c. 150 AD), *Strīnirvāṇaprakaraṇa* with the *svopajñavṛtti* of the Yāpanīya Ācārya Śākaṭāyana (c. 814-867), *Nyāyakumudacandra* of the Digambara Ācārya Prabhācandra (c. 980-1065), *Tātparyavṛtti* of the Digambara Ācārya Jayasena (c. 1180), a commentary of the *Pravacanasāra* of Kundakunda, *Tarkarahasyadīpikāvṛtti* of the Śvetāmbara Ācārya Guṇaratna (c. 1343-1418), a commentary on the *Ṣaḍdarśanasamuccaya* of Haribhadra, and the *Yuktiprabodha* with the *svopajñavṛtti* of the Śvetāmbara Upādhyāya Meghavijaya (c. 1653-1704).

It will not be improper to keep in mind the social position and dignity of women as depicted in the contemporary Hindu and Buddhist literatures. In partial view, Manu seems to be a strong accuser of woman as he considers that in childhood a female must be subject to her father, in youth to her husband, when her lord is dead to her sons; a woman must never be independent.[1] *Manusmṛti* does not allow women to study or chant Vedic mantras in performing sacraments, except marriage. And this ceremony was considered to be the sacred initiation of women. As for their property or *strī-dhana*, it is strictly defined.[2] The Veda allows sharing of parental properties:

> A daughter, always living with her parents, like a woman aging at home, begs money to her parents. Let the parents think over the matter. Calculate and give her share to her for her maintenance and for her serving the guests. (RV 2.17.7.)

Jain Ācāryas vividly advocate for the protection of women. Thus their father, husband and son should protect women in different phases of life.

> *janako bhartā putrāḥ strīṇām etāvad eva rakṣā-nimittam*
> (*Padmapurāṇa* 78.91)

The same is repeated in the Jain Commentary literature as

> *jāyā piti-vvasā nāri, data nārī pati-vvasā* |
> *vihavā putta-vasā nārī natthi nārī svayaṃ-vasā* ||
> (*Vyavahārabhāṣya* 3.233)

---

[1] Manu 5.148.

[2] Manu 3.56.

The Hindu Dharmaśāstras also have advocated the protection of women in the society:

> *pitā rakṣati kaumāre bhartā raksati yauvaṇe* |
> *rakṣanti sthavire putrā na strī svātantryam arhati* ||
> (Manu 9.3; Gautama 8.1; Vaṣiṣṭha 5.13)

In the *Manusmṛti*, on one hand, women were prohibited from participating in state politics. The reason behind it was that, being light-hearted, whimsical and eccentric in their nature, they were held to be inefficient as rulers, governors and even councilors. On the other hand, in ancient India women were considered to be fit for domestic work. But in broader view the reverse image comes into existence for Manu even advocates the appointment of females in the royal service. It is also cited in the *Manusmṛti* that

> where women are honoured, there the Gods are pleased, but where they are not honoured, no sacred rite yields rewards (Manu 3.56).

At first Buddhism believes that the inherited intellectual inferiority of women does not allow them to be fit for practical life. Buddha says:

> Womenfolk are uncontrolled, Ānanda. Womenfolk are weak in wisdom, Ānanda. That is the reason, that is the cause why womenfolk do not sit in a court of justice, do not embark on business, do not reach the essence of the deed. (*Aṅguttara-nikāya*, II, p. 93.)

So he prohibited women to be admitted into his order. But later on women from all corners of the society were admitted into the Buddhist order. And once they were admitted, they were given a good deal of latitude and they were trained properly to be useful in charitable work and other popular benevolent service to the society.

While discussing the position of women in Jainism, let us first take reference of the status of a daughter. Like in Hinduism son-birth always remains a first choice, though in some cases the birth of a female child seems to be an occasion of earning as well as flourishing the fame of the clan.[3] Daughters from childhood up to the age of marriage used to enjoy all happiness. In childhood days playing ball with other children and youthful pranks with girls of equal age at rather mature stage are depicted in the Jain scriptures in a well-liked manner. In inner houses daughters were free to be unveiled. They were, in most cases, allowed to move freely and attend public functions and gatherings. All this is mentioned sporadically in *Jñātādharmakathā*, *Antakṛddaśā*, *Uttarādhyāyana*, *Bhagavatīsūtra* and so on.

The Jain Purāṇas categorize the status of women into seven classes, viz., daughter, wife, mother, widow, heroic woman, nurse and prostitute. The social position of women, in the period of Jain Purāṇas seems on the whole to be sympathetic. Though women were depicted as the source of vices, it is meant particularly in the case of spiritual upliftment. From the religious point of view women were considered inferior since earlier than the Puranic age. The holy custom like sacred-thread ceremony of women had already been obsolete during the early stage of the Purāṇas. Since then womanhood and Śūdras are tabulated in the same status.[4]

The contribution of Jain Puranic literature to the upliftment of the status of women was exceedingly great. The Jain Purāṇas are ambiguous. It is true that they were more liberal in support of the sacred thread ceremony for women. In the Jaina Tantra literature woman is depicted as the source of divine power.[5]

On the other hand, Jain Purāṇas also have mentioned the social status of womenfolk: women in general were strictly prohibited in rituals and religious doings. Only women observing penance and austerity were considered to be virtuous and were allowed to join sacrificial ceremonies.[6] Social evils like abduction of another

---

[3] *Uttarādhyayana*, chapter 18.

[4] Altekar 1959: 429.

[5] Sharma 1972: 71.

[6] *Mahāpurāṇa* 72.92.

man's wife also took place in Jain Purāṇas and Guṇabhadra, as mentioned there protested harshly and condemned such act as a deadly sin.[7] *Harivaṃśapurāṇa* (43.180) in such case prescribes cutting off of limbs of the accused. In the *Padmapurāṇa* women are stated to be under control of men in all activities. Even the *Mahāpurāṇa* denies salvation for women. The Jain Purāṇas seem to be influenced by Hindu Dharmaśāstras in many ways. Only some necessary alterations have been made in the Jain point of view. Jain Purāṇas depict the woman character as faint-hearted and draw the inference that this is why women are dominated by men in society. Jain Ācāryas on this matter have given solutions from time to time how to rescue women from social evils.

Jain literature considers both systems of life, dwelling in a house and renunciation of worldly affections.

A daughter and a sister could draw much care and affection from their father and brother. For instance, the elder sister of a brother was so respected that she was always considered as being the representative of the mother. A story says that a merchant and his son threw their lives into danger in order to rescue the lost girl from death; that having failed to rescue his daughter the king left worldly pleasure and opted for asceticism.[8]

Considering the physical, mental and emotional characteristics, the females, from their early childhood to adolescence, were sent to attend the art school. It was quite natural that the Jaina fathers prescribed the art education for the girls instead of the Vedic education. The course of studies prescribed for females were exclusively practical and physiologically sound, having a special attention to the mental aptitude of the students and their prospects in the future as members of the state, of the monastery, of the school or of the family. Music was also part of the curriculum. As it is today, specialization was also very much in vogue. Some chose dancing as their field of specialization, some painting, some singing and so

---

[7] *Mahāpurāṇa* 68.490.

[8] *Nāyādhammakahāo* 1.16.7.

on. On these there are a number of interesting episodes to be found in Jain literature.[9] Dancing, games and physical education were of immense value in satisfying the physical needs of the young girls and early adolescents. As in Brahmanic households, the princesses utilized their skill in physical exercises, games and dancing in the proper use of their amusement and physical exercise.[10] Like the Brahmins in the same way, the Kṣatriya and Vaiśya females enjoyed the blessings of higher learning and culture.

As for female education, it was mainly based on moral values. Women had to learn such aspects and acquire knowledge, which would be related with and caused to the upliftment of womanhood and ultimately in dealing a life of an ideal daughter, wife and mother. In such cases, the education was given mostly by the mother and in some occasions by the housemaids. Scriptural education was given mainly to the nuns but women in general were free to learn scriptures from the qualified nuns.

In the Indian tradition, the second vital phase of woman life may be drawn to be within the periphery of espoused state. There is no mention in the Jain texts of the suitable age of marriage. Only it is said that the boy and the girl should be of an equal age. This means simply that late marriages were prohibited in ancient India. The *Piṇḍaniryukti* (verse 509) advocates that if after the attainment of puberty of a maiden, her guardians fail to arrange her marriage, they fall into hell. Manu (9.88) is also in support of the same.

The household life begins with marriage and when the identity of a daughter converts into that of a wife. Unlike the Hindus who teach eight types of marriage the Jains usually restrict the number to three, viz., marriage arranged by the parents of both parties, *svayaṃvara* and *gāndharva*.

But some Jain Purāṇas have numbered the marriage systems as four and in some places as five, while the Hindus prescribe from

---

[9] *Triṣaṣṭiśalākāpuruṣacarita*, II, p. 60.

[10] Haribhadrasūri, *Samarāiccakahā*, p. 23.

six to eight. According to P. Thomas the Jain system of marriage is of four kinds, such as, arranged by parents, *svayaṃvara*, *gāndharva* and *āsura*, while the Jain Purāṇas admit that marriage is of five kinds which are *svayaṃvara*, *gāndharva*, arranged by parents, *prājāpatya* and *rākṣasa*. Generally, marriage within one's own caste was prevalent. It is found commonly that the parents brought a wife for their son from a family of the same status. For instance, Meghakumāra was married to eight princesses of equal age, beauty and virtue, belonging to the same royal rank.[11] But exceptions with regard to caste and rank are not unknown. For instance, we hear of minister Teyaliputta who married a goldsmith's daughter.[12] Gayasukumāla, a Kṣatriya by caste, was betrothed to a Brāhmaṇa girl.[13] King Jiyasattu married a painter's daughter. Prince Brahmadatta married girls from Brāhmaṇa and merchant families.[18] In fact, as propounded in the *Manusmṛti*, the system of inter caste marriages was in vogue in a flexible manner in ancient India.

One interesting point to be noted is that the dowry system was prevalent at that period and on the other hand the system of marriage by purchase was also customary.

In most cases the dowry system existed in the form of money, goods or estate which a girl brought to her husband's house in marriage. A popular story is that a king of Vārāṇasi gave one thousand villages, one hundred elephants, plenty of treasure, one lac of foot soldiers and ten thousand horses to his son-in-law in marriage. But the system of marriage by purchase shows that a wife was obtained for money paid to her father's family by the boy or his father. The story of Teyaliputta is the example here. Other such stories are available in Jain literature.

Women could be free to take decision in their own marriage. Although parents usually played a vital role in the selection of an

---

[11] *Nāyādhammakahāo* 1.

[12] *Nāyādhammakahāo* 14.

[13] *Antagaḍadasāo* 3.

ideal bridegroom, *svayaṃvara* marriage was also very popular at that period, especially in royal families. *Mahāpurāṇa* approves equal right of men and women in parental properties.

Woman deserves a very important place in motherhood as well. This is no doubt a vital phase regarding the relation of a woman with her child and her husband as well. The Jain Purāṇas and the Hindu Dharmaśāstras have praised extensively the qualities of a mother. The filial relation of a mother is considered the highest on many occasions in Jain literature. Conjugal relation cannot reach to the same intensity of affection. There are plenty of examples where a mother's attribution is depicted as higher than that of a father.

The most pathetic condition of a woman is widowhood. The death of a husband brings a tremendous solitariness to the life of a widow. In such situations, the Jain Purāṇas show leniency to some extent whereas the Smṛtis seem to be most merciless towards them. The life of a woman in widowhood is not found so restricted so clearly in Jainism as it is in Hinduism, especially in the context of *Manusmṛti*.

REFERENCES

ALTEKAR, A. S. 1959. *The Position of Women in Hindu Civilization*. 2nd edition. New Delhi: Motilal Banarasidass.

Aṃtagaḍadasāo. Ed. by Ācārya Mahāprajña. Ladunun: Jain Vishva Bharati, 1992.

Aṅguttaranikāya. Vol. II. General editor Bhikkhu Jagadish Kashyap. Nalanda: Pali Publication Board, 1960.

JAINI, P. S. 1992. *Gender and Salvation*. Delhi: Munshiram Manoharlal Publishers.

Manu = *The Laws of Manu*. Transl. by Georg Bühler. (Sacred Books of the East, 25.) Oxford: Clarendon Press, 1886. (Reprint: New Delhi: Atlantic Publishers and Distributors, 1990.)

Mahāpurāṇa of Puṣpadanta. Ed. by P. L. Vaidya. Hindi translation by Devendra Kumar Jain. Varanasi: Bhāratīya Jñanapīṭha, 1983.

Samarāiccakahā of Haribhadrasūri. Ed. by M. C. Modi. Ahmedabad: Shambhulala Jagadish Shah – Gujar Grantha Ratna Kāryālaya, 1936.

SHARMA, Brijendra Nath 1972. *Social and Cultural History of Northern India (c. 1000-1200 A.D).* New Delhi: Abhinava Publishers.

Triṣaṣṭiśalākāpuruṣacarita of Hemacandrasūri. Transl. by Helen M. Johnson. Baroda: Oriental Institute, 1962.

Uttarādhyayana-ṭīkā. Ed. by Muni Puṇyavijaya. Ahmedabad: Prakrit Text Society, 1973.

Uttarajjhayaṇāṇi. Ed. by Yuvācārya Mahāprajña. Ladnun: Jain Vishva Bharati, 1992.

Early Śvetāmbara and Digambara Karma Literature: A Comparison

KRISTI L. WILEY

In their introduction to the *Prajñāpanā-sūtra*, the fourth Upāṅga of the Śvetāmbara canon, the editors of the Jaina Āgama Series, Muni Puṇyavijaya, Paṇḍit Dalsukh Mālvaṇiyā, and Paṇḍit Amṛtlāl Mohanlāl Bhojak, have noted some important differences in the treatment of *karma* theory in this text and in the *Ṣaṭkhaṇḍāgama*, the earliest extant Digambara text. They have observed that in the *Prajñāpanā-sūtra*, there is no mention of *yoga* as a cause of karmic bondage. The reason that *yoga* is not mentioned, they have concluded, is that only three types of karmic bondage (*bandha*) are discussed, namely, *prakṛti-bandha* (type bondage), *anubhāva-bandha* (feelings produced by the realization of *karma*), and *sthiti-bandha* (duration bondage).[1]

> The crystallised and subtle stage as well as the terminology of the *karma* speculation which we come across in the later works written by Śvetāmbara and Digambara theoreticians are not present in the *Prajñāpanā* version of *karma* speculation. ... This account does not contain the discussion about *karmapradeśa* (quantity bondage). Hence, it is but natural that it could not mention *yoga*, which is the cause of *pradeśa-bandha*. This proves beyond doubt that the *Prajñāpanā* account represents the old stage of *karma* speculation.[2]

---

[1] *Anubhāva-bandha* or *anubhāga-bandha*, which in classical *karma* theory deals with intensity bondage, or how forcefully *karma* yields its effects when coming to fruition, is understood here as *vedanā*, or the effects produced by the rise of *karma*.

In contrast, in the *Ṣaṭkhaṇḍāgama*, the description of the influx of *karma* and its bondage with the soul agrees with passages in the *Tattvārtha-sūtra* and with later Śvetāmbara *karma* texts. Influx (*āsrava*) of karmic matter to the soul (*jīva*) is caused by vibrations (*parispanda*) of its space points (*ātma-pradeśa*s). These vibrations occur when *vīrya-antarāya karma* obstructs the infinite and perfect energy (*ananta-vīrya*) of the soul and when there is activity (*yoga*) expressed through the body (*kāya*), speech (*vacas*), or mind (*manas*).[3] This subtle matter is bound (*bandha*) with the soul whenever an action is motivated by desires or passions (*kaṣāya*s), which are characterized by feelings of aversion or hatred (*dveṣa*) in the form of anger (*krodha*) and pride (*māna*) as well as attachment (*rāga*) in the form of deceitful manipulation (*māyā*) and greed (*lobha*).[4] In addition to *yoga* and *kaṣāya*, there are three additional causes for the binding of *karma*: false views of reality (*mithyātva*), a lack of self-discipline (*avirati*), and carelessness (*pramāda*).[5]

According to tradition, the *Prajñāpanā-sūtra* and the *Ṣaṭkhaṇḍāgama* were both composed on the basis of material contained in the *Pūrva*s and the *Dṛṣṭivāda*, the twelfth Aṅga, into which portions of the *Pūrva*s were thought to have been incorporated.[6] It is impossible to know what, if any, information about *karma* theory was contained in the *Pūrva*s and the *Dṛṣṭivāda* and what, if any, of this material was incorporated into either the

---

[2] Puṇyavijaya 1971: 384.

[3] TS VI.1-VI.2. As mentioned in *Sarvārthasiddhi* (SS 610), in the absence of *vīrya-antarāya karma*, vibration of the soul is still present in an omniscient being with activity (*sayoga kevalin*) in the thirteenth *guṇasthāna*.

[4] TS VIII.2-VIII.3. These four passions, which are caused by sub-varieties of *cāritra-mohanīya karma*, are realized in four degrees of intensity (SS 751).

[5] TS VIII.1. The four aspects of karmic bondage, variety or type bondage (*prakṛti-bandha*), duration bondage (*sthiti-bandha*), intensity bondage (*anubhāva/anubhāga-bandha*) and quantity bondage (*pradeśa-bandha*), are listed at TS VIII.4 (= SS VIII.3). *Prakṛti-* and *pradeśa-bandha* have as their efficient cause activity (*yoga*) and *sthiti-* and *anubhāga-bandha* have as their efficient cause passions (*kaṣāyas*) (SS 735).

[6] Puṇyavijaya 1971: 223.

Prajñāpanā-sūtra or the *Ṣaṭkhaṇḍāgama*. As Paul Dundas has noted,

> there can be no doubt that any accurate knowledge of what its (the *Dṛṣṭivāda*'s) contents might have been had disappeared by about the sixth century CE,

and

> it came to be regarded as a convenient repository where elements of developed Jain literary culture which could not be provided with an impeccable scriptural pedigree, such as the complete version of the Universal History, could be fictitiously stated to have had their origin.[7]

Scholars who are members of the Jain community usually accept the statements of authors and commentators that the *Pūrva*s and the *Dṛṣṭivāda* are the sources of knowledge contained in these two texts. For example, Hiralāl Jain and A. N. Upadhye, the editors of the printed edition of the *Ṣaṭkhaṇḍāgama*, state that its publication was "throwing light for the first time upon the only surviving pieces of the lost *Dṛṣṭivāda*".[8] The editors of the Jaina Āgama Series believe that the subject-matter in the *Prajñāpanā-sūtra* may be associated with three of the fourteen *Pūrva*s: *Jñānapravāda*, *Ātmapravāda*, and *Karmapravāda*.[9]

Some scholars, however, have questioned the validity of the lists of the contents of the *Dṛṣṭivāda* that are found in the *Samavāyāṅga-sūtra* and in the *Nandī-sūtra* and the association of the *Dṛṣṭivāda* with later texts. For example, Ludwig Alsdorf has concluded that the statement that these texts contain "everything" indicates that the contents had been lost at an early time, "conveniently permitting to derive from the *Dṛṣṭivāda* or the *Pūrva*s any text or

---

[7] Dundas 2002: 69. According to the *Bhagavatī-sūtra* (BhSū), as foreseen by Mahāvīra, knowledge of the *Pūrva*s died out one thousand years after the death of Mahāvīra (Dundas 2002: 68, citing BhSū 20.8).

[8] As quoted in Alsdorf 1973: 2.

[9] Puṇyavijaya 1971: 213.

subject which it was desired to invest with dignity".[10] However, as Paul Dundas has noted:

> The resilience of the literary tradition about the *Pūrvas* is such that no Jain scholar has seen fit to seriously challenge its validity. Indeed, despite both the absence of specific proof of the existence of these scriptures in the form of manuscripts and the occurrence of obviously fanciful statements calculating the amount of ink required to write the *Pūrvas* as equivalent to the volume of a number of elephants, Śvetāmbara and Digambara texts alike record broadly similar names and descriptions for the *Pūrvas* and their contents which point to a common origin of the tradition. The fact that it is not unknown in classical Indian literature for later, better-formulated works to render otiose earlier writings suggests that the possibility of some sort of lost precursor of the currently existing scriptures, the memory of which predates sectarian division, should not be completely discounted.[11]

There are many similarities in *karma* theory in *Prajñāpanā-sūtra* and the *Ṣaṭkhaṇḍāgama* that may be indicative of some common origin. For example, the maximum duration of bondage (*sthiti*) for each of the individual varieties of *karma* is identical in these two texts. And with respect to type bondage (*prakṛti-bandha*), the eight main varieties (*mūla-prakṛti*s) are the same. Most of the subvarieties (*uttara-prakṛti*s) of *karma*s are also identical, although the effects produced by some of the varieties are understood differently.[12]

Given the number of similarities in these two texts, one should examine the validity of the assumption that activity (*yoga*) is not a cause of karmic bondage in the *Prajñāpanā-sūtra*. And one should speculate on reasons for the absence of a discussion of *pradeśa-bandha* in *Prajñāpanā-sūtra*. Was this aspect of karmic bondage unknown at the time that the *Prajñāpanā* was composed?

---

[10] Alsdorf 1973: 4-5.

[11] Dundas 2002: 68.

[12] For example, *gotra-karma*. See Wiley 1999.

ACTIVITY (*YOGA*) AND KARMIC BONDAGE IN THE *PRAJÑĀPANĀ-SŪTRA*

One should examine the absence of *yoga* as a cause of karmic bondage in the *Prajñāpanā-sūtra* because the statement by the editors of the Jaina Āgama Series that "the *Prajñāpanā* considers *rāga* (attachment) and *dveṣa* (aversion) alone to be the cause of karmic bondage"[13] contradicts a theory advanced by William Johnson in a book entitled *Harmless Souls: Karmic Bondage and Religious Change in Early Jainism with Special Reference to Umāsvāti and Kundakunda* (1995). Here, Johnson has discussed how the question of what is perceived to be the immediate cause of bondage of the soul has changed over time. After comparing passages in the earliest portions of the Śvetāmbara canonical texts with those found in the *Tattvārtha-sūtra*, he has concluded that prior to Umāsvāti,

> in these earliest Jaina texts the influx of karmic particles and their bondage to the soul is seen as being the inevitable result of activity (*yoga*) ... and that for early Jainism volition is not a relevant factor in bondage. ... The instrumentality of passion (*kaṣāya*) is a relatively late addition to Jain belief.[14]

The absence of *yoga* as a cause of karmic bondage in the *Prajñāpanā-sūtra*, as postulated by the editors of the Jaina Āgama Series, is based on a passage at the beginning of the twenty-third chapter entitled *Karmaprakṛtipada*.[15] In answer to the question, "How are the eight *karmaprakṛtis* bound with the soul?" the process is described as follows: "With the rise (*udaya*) of *jñānāvaraṇīya karma*, there is the *niyacchati* of *darśanāvaraṇīya karma*." The editors of

---

[13] Puṇyavijaya 1971: 384.

[14] Johnson 1995: 15, 18.

[15] The numbering of the *sūtras* in the Jaina Āgama Series edition of the *Prajñāpanā-sūtra* differs from that in the Āgamodaya-Samiti edition, which contains Malayagiri's commentary. This edition has been reprinted in 1988 by the Śrī Ādināth Jain Temple Trust (Bangalore). For reference, I have included the *sūtra* numbers from the Jaina Āgama Series edition (PrSūJā) and from Āgamodaya-Samiti edition (PrSūĀs) and the page numbers from 1988 reprint edition.

the Jaina Āgama Series interpret the verb *niyacchati* as *āgamana*, or influx, in agreement with the definition "to bring near".[16] Thus, in accordance with their understanding of this verb, the passage reads,

> With the rise of *jñānāvaraṇīya karma*, there is the *niyacchati* (influx) of *darśanāvaraṇīya karma*. With the rise of *darśanāvaraṇīya karma*, there is the *niyacchati* (influx) of *darśanamohanīya karma*. With the rise (*udaya*) of *darśanamohanīya karma*, there is the *niyacchati* (influx) of *mithyātva*. With the premature realization (*udīraṇā*) of *mithyātva*, eight varieties of *karma* are bound with the soul.

Thus, according to their reading, "*yoga* does not cause the influx of *karma*, *karma* causes the influx of *karma*," with *jñānāvaraṇīya karma* causing the influx of *darśanāvaraṇīya karma*, and so forth.

There is, however, another way to understand this passage. In his commentary, Malayagiri interprets the verb *niyacchati* as *nirgacchati*.[17] Regarding the mechanism of how *karma* is bound with the soul, Malayagiri explains that

> with the rise (*udaya*) of *jñānāvaraṇīya karma*, *darśanāvaraṇīya nirgacchati*, *niścayena gacchati*, in other words, it departs or goes away, it absolutely must go. A *viśiṣta udaya* is obtained, which means that the rise of *jñānāvaraṇīya* is *utkarṣa prāpta*, forcefully obtained. With the rise of *darśanāvaraṇīya karma*, they experience wrong views. This is the internal cause of *kujñānavāsis*, those who have wrong views of reality, or see things the opposite of what they are. And with the rise of *darśanāvaraṇīya karma*, *darśanamohanīya karma nirgacchati*, which means that by this rise, it has attained a

---

[16] PrSūJā 166; PrSūĀs 289 (p. 302). "While explaining as to how a living being binds each of these eight types of *karmas*, we are told that at the time of the rise (*udaya*) of *jñānāvaraṇīya karma*, the influx (*āgamana*) of *darśanāvaraṇīya karma* takes place. For this the term '*niyacchati*' is employed" (Puṇyavijaya 1971: 389).

[17] Malayagiri's commentary on PrSūJā 1667; PrSūĀs 289 (p. 303). *Nirgacchati* is found in two manuscripts used to prepare the Jaina Āgama Edition: a palm-leaf manuscript of the Jaina Jñāna Bhaṇḍāra, Jesalmer (catalogue no. 27), dated V.S. 1389; and a manuscript in Muni Puṇyavijayajī's collection at the L.D. Institute of Indology, Ahmedabad (catalogue no. 6709), undated, probably from V.S. 17th century. "*daṃsaṇamohaṇijjassa kammassa udaeṇaṃ micchattaṃ ṇiggacchati.*"

> state of maturity (*vipākāvasthā-udaya*). And with the rise of *darśanamohanīya karma*, *mithyātva nirgacchati*, which means that one regards the unreals (*atattvas*) as real (*tattvas*) and the reals (*tattvas*) as unreals (*atattvas*). With the rise of *mithyātva*, the *jīva* binds eight varieties of *karma*. Thus, the ultimate internal cause for binding the eight *karma-prakṛtis* is *mithyātva*.[18]

The problems with this formulation, of only those with a false view of reality (*mithyātva*) binding eight varieties of *karma*, must not have escaped Malayagiri's attention. He states that this should be understood as a general explanation, since some with a proper view of reality (*samyagdṛṣṭis*) bind eight varieties of *karma* while others, those who are *sūkṣma-sāmparāya*, and so forth, do not.[19] He justifies the explanation of the rise of *karma* ultimately causing the binding of *karma* with the statement

> from the power of the *pariṇāma* (modification or ripening) of previous *karma*, there is the coming into existence of new *karma*, like a seed, which produces a shoot, which produces a leaf.[20]

Regardless of Malayagiri's attempt to bring this passage in line with classical *karma* theory, the explanation here for how karmic matter is bound with the soul is different from that found in the *Ṣaṭkhaṇḍāgama* and in later Śvetāmbara and Digambara texts on *karma*.

There are several reasons to assume that activity (*yoga*) may have been implicitly understood to be one of the causes of karmic

---

[18] Malayagiri's commentary on PrSūJā 1667; PrSūĀs 289 (p. 303).

[19] Those who have attained the fourth through the seventh stages of spiritual purity (*guṇasthānas*) also can bind eight varieties of *karma*, including *āyuskarma*. It is only those *samyagdṛṣṭis* in the eighth *guṇasthāna* and above who do not bind eight varieties of *karma*. *Sūkṣma-sāmparāya* is the tenth *guṇasthāna*, a stage of purity attained for a short period of time (*antarmuhūrta*) while the soul is ascending either the ladder of the suppression of *karma* (*upaśama-śreṇi*) or ladder of the destruction of *karma* (*kṣapaṇa-śreṇi*) during the meditative practice of the first two types of *śukladhyāna* (pure trances). A soul in the tenth *guṇasthāna* does not bind *āyus* or *mohanīya karma*. For details on the binding and realization of *karma* in the various *guṇasthānas*, see Glasenapp 1942: 75-92.

[20] Malayagiri's commentary on PrSūJā 1667; PrSūĀs 289 (p. 303).

bondage in the *Prajñāpanā-sūtra*. At the beginning of his commentary on chapter twenty-three, Malayagiri states that in the previous chapter entitled *Kriyāpada*, there was a discussion of the topic "by what kinds of activities (*kriyās*) is there the binding of *jñānāvaraṇīya karma*, and so forth". Activities, such as injury to living beings, are the external cause of the binding of *jñānāvaraṇīya karma*, and so forth. The effect (*kārya*) is the binding of *karma*. But here [in chapter twenty-three] only the internal cause of binding *karma* is explained.[21] Also, in chapter thirty of the *Prajñāpanā-sūtra* entitled *Samudghāta*, there is a discussion of the *kevalin* bringing to an end all suffering (*duḥkha*) by stopping the gross and subtle activity of the mind, speech, and body. Once *yoga* has been stopped, there is the destruction of an uncountable number (*asaṅkhyāta)* of molecules (*skandhas*) of the four remaining *aghātiyākarmas*, namely, *vedanīya*, *āyus*, *nāma* and *gotra karmas*. After this, the soul abandons the body of the *kevalin* and instantly ascends to the *siddha-loka*. If *yoga* had not been understood as a cause of the influx of *karma* in the *Prajñāpanā-sūtra*, then it would not have been necessary for the *kevalin* to bring to an end the activity of the mind, speech, and body. This was acknowledged by the editors of the Jaina Āgama Series, who have observed,

> as soon as he becomes free from all sorts of activities he becomes a *siddha*. It is so because he does not acquire new *karmas* (as the cause of the acquisition of new *karmas* is activity) and at the same time he dissociates gradually the accumulated ones.[22]

Also, according to the *Prajñāpanā-sūtra*, in the case of the omniscient *kevalin*, *yoga* is the only cause that remains for the binding of *vedanīya karma*, which continues until all activity is brought to an end. In chapter twenty-four entitled *Karmabandhapada*, the question is raised regarding how many varieties of *karma* can be bound when *vedanīya-karma* is bound. The answer is seven if *āyus*

[21] Malayagiri's commentary on PrSūJā 166 /; PrSūĀs 289 (p. 302).

[22] Puṇyavijaya 1971: 423.

karma is not bound, eight if *āyus karma* is bound, six if *mohanīya karma* is not bound, or only one variety of *karma*, namely *sātā-vedanīya karma*, may be bound.[23] In the absence of passions (*kaṣāyas*), when *mohanīya karmas* have been suppressed in the eleventh *guṇasthāna*, or eliminated in the twelfth and thirteenth *guṇasthānas*, only one variety of *karma* is bound, namely *sātā-vedanīya karma*. In this case, the only cause remaining for the binding of this *karma* is activity (*yoga*). Thus, although it is not specifically mentioned in chapter twenty-three, *yoga* must have been understood as one of the causes of karmic bondage in the *Prajñāpanā-sūtra*.

QUANTITY BONDAGE (*PRADEŚA-BANDHA*) AND PROCESSES OF ENERGY (*KARAṆAS*) IN EARLY KARMA TEXTS

One should also ask why there is no discussion of *pradeśa-bandha*, the aspect of bondage dealing with the quantity of karmic matter bound with the soul, in the *Prajñāpanā-sūtra*. This is relevant because the possibility that in earlier times *karma* was thought of as a non-material force rather than a type of subtle matter (*pudgala*) has been discussed by Suzuko Ohira.

> The Jaina doctrine of *karma* took a most dilatory course of development in the canonical period, for it could never have been advanced until the scheme of *pudgala* began to be developed, which took place after the adoption of the atomic theory.[24]

---

[23] Unlike the other seven main varieties (*mūla-prakṛtis*) of *karma*, *āyus karma* is bound just once in each life and must come to fruition in the next life. Thus, a soul in the first through the seventh *guṇasthānas* can bind either seven or eight *mūla-prakṛtis* of *karma*. In the tenth *guṇasthāna*, six *mūla-prakṛtis* are bound: *jñānāvaraṇīya*, *darśanāvaraṇīya*, *vedanīya*, *nāma*, *gotra*, and *antarāya* (*mohanīya* and *āyus* are not bound). In the eleventh, twelfth, and thirteenth *guṇasthānas*, only *sātā-vedanīya karma* is bound. With the absence of *yoga* in the fourteenth *guṇasthāna*, no *karma* is bound. For details on the binding and realization of *karma* in the various *guṇasthānas*, see Glasenapp 1942: 75-92.

[24] Ohira 1980: 45.

She concludes that *karma* was first understood as a material substance in the late first canonical stage (first stage = 6/5th-4th centuries CE).[25] A similar view is held by the editors of the Jaina Āgama Series. They state that

> there were believers in the *kriyā*, who did not accept material veil of the *karma* over and above acts (*kriyā*). Their knowledge is described by the derogatory term, viz. *vibhaṅgajñāna*. This suggests that the tenet of the material veil of the *karma*, recognised in the *karma* doctrine propounded in the Āgamas, was not originally present in the Kriyāvāda at its early stages. If *kriyā* or *karma* (act) were regarded as giving its fruit and that too after a gap of so many years or lives, then *kriyā* (act) being destroyed as soon as it is performed, the theoreticians could not help postulating *karma* as a veil or impression or disposition (*āvaraṇa*, *vāsanā*, *saṃskāra*) resulting from the *kriyā* (act); and gradually it was concluded and determined that this *karma* which is viewed as a veil or impression should be material. Thus, the two terms *kriyā* and *karma* which at one time conveyed the identical sense came to mean different things.[26]

However, this could not be the reason for the absence of *pradeśa-bandha* here, because in the *Prajñāpanā-sūtra*, the variety of *karma* that causes the formation of the karmic body (*kārmaṇa-śarīra-nāma karma*) is listed, and the karmic body must be formed from karmic matter.[27] The karmic body is mentioned in chapter twelve (entitled *Śarīrapada*) in which the various types of bodies of living beings are discussed.[28] There is also mention of the karmic body and *karma-skandha*s in chapter thirty (entitled *Samudghāta*) in the context of the *kevalin* bringing the activities of the body to an end.[29] Following the description of *kevali-samudghāta*, which is performed by some *kevalin*s just prior to death in order to equalize the duration (*sthiti*) of *vedanīya*, *nāma*, and *gotra karma*s with *āyus*

---

[25] Ohira 1994: 7-8 (#24).

[26] Puṇyavijaya 1971: 376.

[27] PrSūJā 1694.6; PrSūĀs 293 (p. 311) states that there are five varieties of *śarīra-nāma karma*, beginning with *audārika-śarīra-nāma karma* and ending with *kārmaṇa-śarīra-nāma karma*).

[28] PrSūJā 901; PrSūĀs 176 (p. 179).

[29] PrSūJā 2175; PrSūĀs 349 (p. 405).

karma, Indrabhūti Gautama asks whether the *kevalin* who performs *samudghāta* has activity (*yoga*) of the mind, speech, and body. Mahāvīra replies that there is no activity of mind and speech, but there is activity of the gross physical body (*audārika-śarīra*) and the karmic body (*kārmaṇa-śarīra*). Thus, even though *karma* is considered to be a subtle type of matter here, details regarding *pradeśa-bandha* are not discussed in this text.

In contrast to the *Prajñāpanā-sūtra*, various aspects of *pradeśa-bandha* are discussed in great detail in the *Ṣaṭkhaṇḍāgama*. For example, there are descriptions of how the individual particles of karmic matter are arranged into groups or bundles at the time that they are bound, and the order in which these bundles will come into fruition. There are discussions about the force or energy contained in various particles of karmic matter as measured in units called *avibhāgapraticcheda*. There are also descriptions of the various processes of energy (*karaṇas*), which are relevant in the context of *pradeśa-bandha*. These include explanations of various types of *saṃkramaṇa*, or transformation of karmic matter from one sub-variety into another, for example, the transformation of previously bound *asātā-vedanīya karma* into *sātā-vedanīya karma*.

In looking at these two texts, one might conclude that the mechanical processes associated with karmic bondage were not well understood by Śvetāmbaras. If one assumes that the *Pūrvas* were the source of knowledge of *karma* theory that is expounded in both of these texts, then one explanation for this difference could be that only a handful of mendicants had memorized those portions of the *Pūrvas* that described these intricate physical processes. Indeed, in comparison with other aspects of *karma* theory, the technical details associated with physical processes that operate during the binding and realization of karmic matter are so detailed and complex that this material would have been difficult to master, even for those mendicants whose specialty was the study of *karma* theory.[30]

---

[30] For an idea of the intricacies of this aspect of *karma* theory, see *Gommaṭasāra Karma-kāṇḍa* (GKK) verses 409-450 as translated by J. L. Jaini (pp. 11-35).

Thus, one could speculate that Dharasena, the teacher of Puṣpadanta and Bhūtabali, who composed the *Ṣaṭkhaṇḍāgama*, was in contact with mendicants who had learned this aspect of *karma* theory while Śyāmācārya, the author of the *Prajñāpanā-sūtra*, was not.

If one discounts the *Pūrva*s as a possible common source for these two texts, then one could postulate that the details of *karma* theory associated with the physical processes of bondage and realization had not been worked out when the *Prajñāpanā-sūtra* was composed, and therefore that it is earlier than the *Ṣaṭkhaṇḍāgama*. But this is unlikely to be the reason for the absence of the *karaṇa*s in *Prajñāpanā-sūtra* because some of the processes of energy are mentioned in the *Vyākhyāprajñapti* (*Bhagavatī*)-*sūtra*, the fifth Aṅga of the Śvetāmbara canon, which predates the *Prajñāpanā-sūtra*. In *Bhagavatī-sūtra*, *Śataka* 1, *uddeśaka* 1, in the section entitled *calana* (movement), the names of the following processes of energy are mentioned: premature realization (*udīraṇā*) of *karma*, the maturation and falling away of karmic matter from the soul (*nirjarā*), increased realization (*udvartanā*) of *karma*, decreased realization (*apavartanā*), the transformation of one sub-variety of *karma* into another sub-variety (*saṃkramaṇa*), and the binding of *karma* in such a way that, under normal circumstances, it cannot be changed through some of the processes of energy (*nidhatti* and *nikācita*).[31]

---

[31] BhSū 1.1, verse 6.1.6. *Nidhatti* prevents the premature operation of *karma* that has been brought under subsidence (*upaśama*) and it prevents the transformation of one sub-variety of karma into another sub-variety (*saṃkramaṇa*). *Nikācita* prevents the premature operation of *karma* that has been brought under subsidence (*upaśama*), the transformation of one sub-variety of karma into another sub-variety (*saṃkramaṇa*), increased realization (*udvartanā*), and decreased realization (*apavartanā*).These two processes of energy are overcome (i.e., they become inoperable) when the soul is in the eighth, ninth, and tenth *guṇasthāna*s. The *karaṇa*s do not operate in the absence of passions (eleventh *guṇasthāna* and above). See GKK 440 and 450. Although it is not discussed in the *sūtras*, *saṃkramaṇa* was also known to Umāsvāti, for he describes it in his commentary on TS VIII.22.

It is not possible to determine how much was known about the operation of these processes of energy because no details regarding them are given in the *Bhagavatī-sūtra*. However, to conclude that Śvetāmbara mendicants were unaware of this aspect of *karma* theory at the time of the final redaction of their Āgamas is problematic in light of another Śvetāmbara text entitled *Karmaprakṛti*, a Prakrit work of some 475 *gāthā*s composed by Śivaśarmasūri.[32] Śivaśarmasūri states that his source for this work was the *Agrāyaṇīyapūrva* of the *Dṛṣṭivāda* called *Karmaprakṛti*.[33] *Karmaprakṛti* contains detailed descriptions of all of the mechanical processes of karmic bondage found in the *Ṣaṭkhaṇḍāgama*, including those processes of energy (*karaṇa*s) mentioned by name in the *Bhagavatī-sūtra*.

There are some minor differences in the material in the *Ṣaṭkhaṇḍāgama* and *Karmaprakṛti*. For example, there are some variations in the listings of the categories (*vargaṇā*s) of matter. However, there are enough similarities in these two texts that there might have been some common source of knowledge on which they are based. Although one could argue that *pradeśa-bandha* and the processes of energy (*karaṇa*s) were not included in the *Prajñāpanā* because the details were not known to its author, one could also argue that they may not have been included because of their

---

[32] Mehta & Kapadia 1968: 114-115. It is thought that Śivaśarmasūri lived in the fifth century of the Vikrama era and was a predecessor of Devarddhigaṇi Kṣamāśramaṇa, who presided over the last Council of Valabhī where the final redaction of the Śvetāmbara Āgamas took place.

[33] Glasenapp 1942: xiv. According to Mehta and Kapadia (1968: 115), some have claimed that Śivaśarmasūri might have been a knower of ten *Pūrva*s (*daśapūrvadhara*). However, this does not correspond with the listings in Hemacandra's *Pariśiṣṭaparvan* (also known as the *Sthavirāvalīcaritra*). In addition, Śivaśarmasūri wrote the *Śataka*, a work on *karma bandha* that is sometimes included as the fifth of the *Prācīna Karmagrantha*s. Some believe he was the author of the *Saptatikā*, the sixth of the *Prācīna Karmagrantha*s, although most attribute this work to Candrarṣi-mahattara, who was also the author of the *Pañcasaṃgraha*. Assuming this work was written by Candrarṣi-mahattara, the date is uncertain. He may have lived during the 9th or 10th century (Mehta & Kapadia 1968: 125).

complexity. The author might have intentionally omitted the technical details of the binding and realization of karmic matter that would have been of interest to only a small group of mendicant-scholars, since the main focus of the *Prajñāpanā* is on the soul, while the main focus of the *Ṣaṭkhaṇḍāgama* and the *Karmaprakṛti* is on *karma* theory.

There is at least one example of such an omission in the later *karma* literature. Devendrasūri, the author of the *Karmagrantha*s, which probably are the most widely read of the Śvetāmbara texts on *karma* theory, was acquainted with the *Karmaprakṛti*, because he states: *Devendrasūriṇā likhitaṃ karmaprakṛti-pañcasaṃgraha-bṛhacchatakādi-śāstrebhyaḥ.*[34] Devendrasūri discusses *pradeśa-bandha* and he lists the various categories (*vargaṇā*s) of matter. He also mentions the process of energy (*karaṇa*) of premature realization (*udīraṇā*). However, he does not discuss three other processes of energy that are described in detail in the *Karmaprakṛti*, namely, increased realization (*apavartanā*), decreased realization (*udvartanā*), and the transformation of one sub-variety of *karma* into another (*saṃkramaṇa*). A lack of knowledge of the author regarding the technical details of karmic bondage does not explain their absence in the *Karmagrantha*s. Therefore, it would be erroneous to conclude that everything that was known about *karma* at any given time was necessarily included in each and every text that discussed *karma* theory.

CONCLUSIONS

One should be cautious in attempting to reconstruct a pre-classical form of *karma* theory based on what is present in, and what is absent from, the discussions of *karma* in these early texts. In their efforts to determine the chronological order of the early *karma* texts, the editors of the Jaina Āgama Series have recognized the limitations of this approach. They have concluded that

---

[34] Glasenapp 1942: xiv, quoting Kg. II 144a.

> we would be making a great blunder in fixing up the chronological order of the *Prajñāpanā* and the *Ṣaṭkhaṇḍāgama* if we were guided only by the fact that the treatment of the subject-matter in the *Ṣaṭkhaṇḍāgama* is more detailed and subtle than that found in the *Prajñāpanā-sūtra*. ... According to both these works, literature of both these types is rooted in the *Dṛṣṭivāda*. This means that innumerable Ācāryas have variously presented the subject-matter of the *Dṛṣṭivāda* itself to achieve different objectives.[35]

K. K. Dixit has also pointed out the problem of reconstructions of early *karma* theory based on these early texts.

> One applying this method must have an adequate acquaintance with the content of the standard form of the doctrine whose historical evolution one is out to delineate, then one must be in a position to convincingly argue out why a particular version of the doctrine ought to be earlier (or later) than another. ... The difficulty remains essentially the same also in the case of the non-Āgamic texts particularly the earlier ones, for here too the relevant chronology is a matter of dispute.[36]

---

[35] Puṇyavijaya 1971: 230.

[36] Dixit 1971: 4. Indeed, the dating of the *Prajñāpanā-sūtra* and *Ṣaṭkhaṇḍāgama* remains a matter of sectarian dispute. The editors of the Jaina Āgama Series identify the author of the *Prajñāpanā-sūtra* with a person named Kālaka, who flourished between 335-376 Vīra Nirvāṇa (192/90-151/49 BCE – first date = traditional dating of the *nirvāṇa* of Mahāvīra, 527 BCE, the beginning of the Vīra Nirvāṇa era (V.N.); second date = 425 BCE, recent scholarly assumptions on Mahāvīra's *nirvāṇa* based on the revised dating of Gautama the Buddha). As discussed below, they date this work prior to the *Ṣaṭkhaṇḍāgama* (Puṇyavijaya 1971: 235). In response, Hiralāl Jain and A. N. Upadhye, the general editors of the *Ṣaṭkhaṇḍāgama*, state that nothing definitive is known about the author of this work, and date it much later, around 993 V.N. (466/568 CE) (*Ṣaṭkhaṇḍāgama*, I, p. 10 of the editorial section dated 1972). They conclude, "the *Prajñāpanā*, though it contains a good deal of old material not properly preserved, in its present form cannot be dated earlier than the Valabhī Council when it was put under the category of Upāṅga and interpolatory verses became a source for the name of its so-called author" (*Ṣaṭkhaṇḍāgama*, I, p. 10 of the editorial section dated 1972). Regarding the dating of the *Ṣaṭkhaṇḍāgama*, in his introduction to volume one of the *Ṣaṭkhaṇḍāgama*, based on *paṭṭāvali* lists, Paṇḍit Phūlcandra Siddhānta Śāstrī gives two possible dates, 614 V.N. (87 BCE / 189 CE) and 683 V.N. (156 CE / 258 CE) for the composition of this work. The date most commonly cited for the completion of the *Ṣaṭkhaṇḍāgama* is 156 CE. Hiralāl Jain and A. N. Upadhye state that "the age of the *Ṣaṭkhaṇḍāgama* is 683 years after the *nirvāṇa* of Mahāvīra ... and it is accepted by all", with "all" referring to

At first glance, the *Prajñāpanā-sūtra* and the *Ṣaṭkhaṇḍāgama* look quite different in their presentations of *karma* theory. However, it is not out of the realm of possibility, as the editors of the Jaina Āgama Series have suggested, that the authors of these early *karma* texts, and the author of the *Karmaprakṛti* as well, were all drawing from some common source of knowledge.

REFERENCES

ALSDORF, Ludwig 1973. What were the contents of the *Dṛṣṭivāda*. In: *German Scholars on India: Contributions to Indian Studies*: 1-5. Varanasi: Chowkhamba Sanskrit Series Office.

BhSū = [*Bhagavatī-sūtra*] *Viyāhapaṇṇattisuttaṃ*. Ed. by Pt. Bechardas Doshi. (Jaina Āgama Series, 4.1.) Bombay: Shri Mahāvīra Jaina Vidyālaya, 1974.

DIXIT, K. K. 1971. *Jain Ontology* (L.D. Series, 31.) Ahmedabad: L.D. Institute of Indology.

DUNDAS, Paul 2002. *The Jains*. 2nd edition. London: Routledge. [1st edition: 1992.]

GLASENAPP, Helmuth von 1942. *The Doctrine of Karma in Jain Philosophy*. Transl. of 1915 text by G. Barry Gifford, revised by the author, and ed. by Hiralal Kapadia. Bombay: Bai Vijibhai Jivanlal Panalal Charity Fund.

GKK = [*Gommaṭsāra Karma-kāṇḍa*] *Gommaṭsāra Karma-Kāṇḍa* of Nemicandra, II. Transl. by Brahmachari Sital Prasad (The Sacred Books of the Jains, 10.) Lucknow: The Central Jain Publishing House, 1937. [Reprint: New Delhi: Today and Tomorrow's Printers & Publishers, 1990.]

JOHNSON, W. J. 1995. *Harmless Souls: Karmic Bondage and Religious Change in Early Jainism with Special Reference to Umāsvāti and Kundakunda* (Lala Sundarlal Jain Research Series, 9.) Delhi: Motilal Banarsidass.

---

the editors of the Jaina Āgama Series (*Ṣaṭkhaṇḍāgama*, I, p. 9 of the editorial section dated 1972). What the editors of the Jaina Āgama Series actually state is as follows: "*Ṣaṭkhaṇḍāgama*, in its present form is a work of two Ācāryas, Bhadanta Puṣpadanta and Bhūtabali, who are posterior to Dharasena who, in turn, flourished sometime after 683 V.N. From this we can safely conclude that the *Prajñāpanā* (which, as mentioned above, they have dated to 335-376 V.N.) is prior to *Ṣaṭkhaṇḍāgama*" (Puṇyavijaya 1971: 235).

MEHTA, Mohanlal & Hiralal KAPADIA 1968. *Jain Sāhitya kā Bṛhad Itihāsa, IV: Karma-Sāhitya va Āgamika Prakaraṇa*. Ed. by Dalsukh Malvania & Mohanlal Mehta. Varanasi: Pārśvanātha Vidyāśrama Śodha Saṃsthāna.

OHIRA, Suzuko 1980. Problems of the Pūrva. *Jain Journal* 15 (July): 41-55.

—— 1994. *A Study of the Bhagavatīsūtra: A Chronological Analysis*. (Prakrit Text Series, 28.) Ahmedabad: Prakrit Text Society.

PrSūĀs = [*Prajñāpanā-sūtra*, Āgamodaya-Samiti Series] *Śrī Prajñāpanopāṅgam* of Pūrvadhara Śrī Śyāmārya with the commentary of Ācārya Malayagirisūri. (Āgamodaya-Samiti Series, 19-20.) Bombay: Śrī Āgamodaya Samiti, 1918-19. [Reprint: Bangalore: Śrī Ādināth Jain Temple Trust, 1988.]

PrSūJā = [*Prajñāpanā-sūtra*, Jaina Āgama Series] *Paṇṇavaṇāsuttaṃ*. (Jaina Āgama Series, 9.) Ed. by Muni Puṇyavijaya, Pt. Dalsukh Mālvaṇiā, & Pt. Amritlāl Mohanlāl Bhojak. Bombay: Shri Mahāvīra Jaina Vidyālaya, 1969 [part 1 (text)]; 1971 [part 2 (introduction & index)].

PUNYAVIJAYA, Muni 1971. See PrSūJā (part 2).

SS = [*Sarvārthasiddhi*] *Sarvārthasiddhi* of Pūjyapāda. Ed. by Phoolchandra Shastri. 8th edition. Delhi: Bharatiya Jnanapith, 1998.

Ṣaṭkhaṇḍāgama of Puṣpadanta and Bhūtabali, vol. 1, book 1. Ed. by Phoolchandra Siddhanta Shastri. Revised 3rd edition. Solapur: Jaina Samskriti Samrakshaka Sangha, 1992.

TS = [*Tattvārtha-sūtra*]. *That Which Is*. Transl. by Nathmal Tatia. London: Harper Collins, 1994.

WILEY, Kristi L. 1999. Gotra karma: A contrast in views. In: N. K. Wagle & Olle Qvarnström (eds.), *Approaches to Jaina Studies: Philosophy, Logic, Rituals, and Symbols* (South Asian Studies Papers, 11): 113-130. Toronto: University of Toronto, Centre for South Asian Studies.

——, forthcoming. Karmic bondage and kaṣāyas: A re-examination of "Umāsvāti's Jainism". In: *Proceedings of the International Symposium on Umāsvāti and His Works*. Delhi: Motilal Banarsidass.

Dharma and *Adharma* in Jain Ontology

SIN FUJINAGA

The word *dharma* has various meanings in Indian philosophy. Mainly this word and its counterpart *adharma* are used to denote a moral idea, that is a good deed and an evil one respectively. Unique to Jain ontology is the use of these two terms to denote the media of motion and rest.[1] The two principles of *dharma* and *adharma* play a very important part in Jain ontological thought as they make up two of the five *astikāya*s or the fundamental categories along with *jīva*, *pudgala*, and *ākāśa*.

Adequate research, however, has not been done on these two applications of *dharma* and *adharma*.[2] The main questions to be examined regarding the ontological use of these terms are: when did the Jains begin to use these ideas, and why do they have to be part of Jaina ontology?

Dharma functions, as is well known, to support the movement of *jīva*, the principle of life, and *pudgala*, matter, while *adharma* works as the medium of bringing them to rest. In other words, *jīva* and *pudgala* can move and stop by their own nature, but only with the help of *dharma* and *adharma*.[3] Though they concern all move-

---

[1] This does not mean that the Jains use the two words only in that sense. They also use the words to denote merit and demerit.

[2] For the monographs on *dharma* and *adharma*, see References.

[3] TS V.17: *gatisthityupagrahau dharmādharmayor upakāraḥ*. All Digambara recensions read *upagrahau*, and Akalaṅka argues in support of the dual number (See note on V.17, p. 111), but the reading *upagraho* is also known (see the

ments and rest of *jīva* and *pudgala*, their main function seems to help a liberated *jīva* move up to the top of the universe and stay there. Some Śvetāmbara canonical texts illustrate this with a number of examples.[4] Then a question arises: why is *adharma* needed as a separate ontological category? In a traditional and common understanding, both *dharma* and *adharma* exist only in this universe and there is nothing outside the universe, that is in *aloka*. But I would argue that even without the help of *adharma* a liberated soul can stay at the top of the universe because beyond that point there is no *dharma* or medium of movement.[5] This suggests a new and different understanding of *dharma* and *adharma*.

On the chronology of the development of the concept of *dharma* and *adharma* scholars express different opinions. W. Schubring[6] regards *dharma* and *adharma* as a mark of an archaic form of Jaina philosophy while Dr. Ohira,[7] following E. Frauwallner, maintains that the twin ideas are comparatively new in the history of Jaina philosophy and have been introduced from Vaiśeṣikas. Even for the ancient Jain philosophers the concepts of *dharma* and *adharma* seem to have been difficult to understand when these words were used in ontological contexts.[8]

Taking the above remarks into account, it is possible to suppose two stages in the development of the ideas of *dharma* and *adharma*. In the earlier conception, *dharma* was regarded as the medium of vertical motion and was thought to exist in the central portion of the universe which was called *lokanāḍī* while *adharma* was considered to help *jīva* and *pudgala* move horizontally, and to

---

Bhāṣya and Sukhlalji's translation, where the reading *-au* is also indicated and preferred).

[4] Umāsvāti shows four of them in TS X.7 which reads: *āviddhakulālacakravad vyapagatalepālābuvad eraṇḍabījavad agniśikhāvac ca*.

[5] TS X.8 clearly mentions that the liberated soul remains to stay at the top of the world because there is no *dharma* beyond that point.

[6] Schubring 1935: 12 (§ 6).

[7] Ohira 1994: 251.

[8] Such confusion can be found in *Bhagavatī* XX.2.2.

be located in the peripheral part of the universe where only *nigoda* can exist.[9] The *nigoda* in this part of the universe is said to be able to move only horizontally.[10] In the course of time, however, these concepts must have changed so that *dharma* as well as *adharma* are regarded as existing and functioning as we understand them now, that is both of them pervade the whole universe and *dharma* works as a medium of vertical and horizontal motion while *adharma* is the medium of rest for *jīva* as well as *pudgala*. The reason for this change remains unclear and no Jain text supports this hypothesis. Theoretically speaking, however, the more recent understanding is not logical. Further studies on *nigoda* and the structure of the universe in Jainism may show that the earlier understanding is supported by Jain philosophical literature.[11]

Now let us consider this in a Jain ontological text. Generally speaking, the Jain philosophers explain only how *dharma* and *adharma* work and seldom explain why the two are required in Jain ontology. Rāmacandra and Guṇacandra, authors of the *Dravyālaṃkāra*,[12] are exceptions. Their 13th century book on Jain ontology has recently been published for the first time.[13] In it they discuss the reason why *dharma* and *adharma* must be independent categories among the five elemental ones (*pañcāstikāya*) along with *jīva*, *pudgala*, and *ākāśa*.

The *Dravyālaṃkāra* consists of three chapters. The first chapter discusses *jīva*, the second *pudgala*, the third deals with *dharma*, *adharma* and *ākāśa*. The feature which distinguishes the last three from the first two is non-movability (*akampa*).[14] This means that

---

[9] The concepts of *lokanāḍī* and *nigoda* are difficult to understand. So far, no monograph on these topics seems to have appeared.

[10] See Schubring 1935: 133 (§ 104).

[11] Among the texts on *lokanāḍī* and *nigoda*, *Lokanālidvātriṃśikā* and *Nigodaṣaṭtriṃśikā* are worth detailed studies.

[12] For their life and works, see Jambūvijaya 2001.

[13] The title of DA had been known because Malliṣeṇa mentions it in his *Syādvādamañjarī*. See DA, p. 2, fn. 4.

though *dharma* and *adharma* help the motion and rest of *jīva* and *pudgala*, they themselves do not move. The authors cite their omnipresence as the reason why they do not move. *Dharma-adharma* pervade the universe. On the other hand, *jīva* and *pudgala* exist only in certain portions of this universe and that is why they can or must move. In this connection the authors clearly mention the horizontal movement of *jīva* which is not clearly mentioned in other works such as the *Tattvārthasūtra* and commentaries on it.[15]

Then a question arises: why do *dharma* and *adharma* function as media of motion and rest? We observe motion and rest as ordinary events. But what is the cause of them? According to the Jains, *jīva* and *pudgala* (more accurately *pudgala* combined with *jīva*) move and stop by their own nature.[16] But they cannot do so without the help of *dharma* and *adharma*. The authors support this opinion by a process of elimination. We must admit the fact that a thing, say a liberated *jīva*, the sun, or a bird, moves and stops and we cannot explain the fact with any principle except *dharma* and *adharma*.

Rāmacandra and Guṇacandra, the authors of the *Dravyālaṃkāra*, show that neither the earth, water, sky nor air are appropriate for the logical explanation of motion and rest of a thing. Take the earth for example. At a place where the earth does not exist, say in the sky, a bird can move, so the earth cannot be the universal or omnipresent medium of moving.[17]

The most important point to be discussed in this context is the difference between *dharma-adharma* and *ākāśa*. Some may say: *ākāśa* works as the omnipresent medium of motion and rest be-

---

[14] The third chapter of DA begins with the phrase *athākampāni*, and in DA 133,9-10 the meaning of *akampāni* is explained as follows: *kampanaṃ kampo deśād deśāntaraprāptihetuḥ paryāyaviśeṣaḥ, sa yeṣāṃ nāsti tāny akampāni*.

[15] DA 135,17-18: *na caivam adhas tiryag api vā gamanaprasaṅgaḥ, gater anekaprakāratvāt, anyaiva hi muktātmanāṃ gatir anyā ca saṃsāriṇām*.

[16] DA 137,9-10: *jīvapudgalānāṃ svata eva vidyamānāyā gater ....*

[17] DA 137,23-25: *yadi hi gati-sthityoḥ kṣityudakatejāṃsy apekṣākāraṇāni bhaveyus tadā te gaganacāriṇāṃ na bhavetām eva. Na hi gagane kṣityādayaḥ sambhavantīti dharmādharmāv evāpekṣākaraṇe, na kṣityādayaḥ*.

cause it exists all over the cosmos, thus *dharma* and *adharma* are not necessarily the unique agents of the movement of *jīva* and *pudgala*. To this the authors answer: if it is so, we could not differentiate *loka* from *aloka.*[18] Only in the *loka* or this universe can we act, that is move and stop. Outside this *loka*, the *aloka* spreads without limit. There nothing exists, therefore neither motion nor rest can occur. *Dharma* and *adharma*, according to the Jains, pervade only the loka while *ākāśa* permeates *aloka* as well as *loka*. In other words, in *loka* all three exist while *aloka* is occupied by the *ākāśa* only. If *ākāśa* works in the place of *dharma-adharma*, then, the authors argue, it would be impossible to distinguish the *loka* from the *aloka*. As we have seen above, *jīva* and *pudgala* can move and stop only in the *loka*, not in the *aloka* where the *dharma-adharma* do not exist. If *ākāśa* were the medium of motion, *jīva* and *pudgala* would go beyond the *loka* and move in the *aloka* too. We would then be unable to differentiate the *loka* from the *aloka*. This would make the universe limitless and unsteady. Our universe or the *loka* has a boundary surrounded by the *aloka*, which in turn has no limit. For the Jains the *loka* should be limited and steady (*saṃsthāna*).[19] Though the reason for this is not clearly mentioned in the Jain literature, I suggest it has to do with the position where a liberated soul stays.

In this manner the authors try to show that nothing except *dharma* and *adharma* are the universal media of motion and rest for *jīva* and *pudgala*. Here it should be noted that the authors explain the function of the pair *dharma-adharma* in the terms of *loka* and *aloka* (*lokālokavyavasthāhetu*).[20] This point is repeatedly emphasized in the *Dravyālaṃkāra*. But why do both *dharma* and *adharma* work as determinants of the boundary between *loka* and

---

[18] DA 139,12-14: *mā bhūt kṣityādau vāyau vāpekṣā gati-sthitimattvāt, ākāśe punar astu, tasyānyonyāpekṣagati-sthitirahitatvād iti. Atrāha: nāpy ākāśe, lokālokavibhāgasyābhāvaprasaṅgāt...*

[19] Cf. DA 140,20-24.

[20] DA 139,14: *lokālokavibhāvasyābhāvaprasaṅgāt.*

aloka? Their fundamental functions are, as we have seen, concerned with motion and rest. Moreover without *adharma*, *dharma* can determine this boundary if we suppose that *dharma* exists only in the *loka* and not in *aloka*. And is it impossible to suppose that *dharma* and *adharma* pervade different parts of the universe, that is *dharma* in the *trasanāḍī* and *adharma* in the rest? Clearly not, when we take into consideration the existence of *nigoda*, especially the *nigoda* which exists in the portion outside *lokanāḍī* and is not developed and does not move vertically.

At the end of their discussion on *dharma-adharma* the authors quote passages from the *Bhavagatī* (13,IV,24-25),[21] to show that even Jain scripture supports the existence of *dharma-adharma* and their function as media of motion and rest of *jīva* and *pudgala*. This might suggest that the authors lack confidence in their analysis of *dharma-adharma* based on logic alone. It might also suggest they have some underlying doubts about the traditional concept of *dharma-adharma*.

Fundamentally *dharma* and *adharma* are congruent with Jain ontology, but when we study their relationship with *karma*, especially with the unique existence of *nigoda*, their nature will be clearer. It is also hoped that more evidence will be found that brings their historical development into clearer focus.

REFERENCES

Primary Sources

Bhagavatī. Ed. by M. O. Shah. (Āgamodayasamiti Series, 12-14.) Mehesana: Āgamodaya Samiti, 1918.

DA = *Dravyālaṃkāra* of Rāmacandra and Guṇacandra with Auto-commentary. Ed. by Jambūvijaya. (L.D. Series, 126.) Ahmedabad: L.D. Institute of Indology, 2001. [References to page and line numbers.]

Lokanālidvātriṃśikā. Ed. by Caturvijaya. (Jaina Ātmānanda Grantha Ratnamālā, 3.) Bhavnagar: Jaina Ātmānanda Sabhā, 1911.

[21] DA 144,14-20.

Nigodaṣaṭtriṃśikā. Ed. by Caturvijaya. (Jaina Ātmānanda Grantha Ratnamālā, 12.) Bhavnagar: Jaina Ātmānanda Sabhā, 1913.

SS = *Sarvārthasiddhi*. Ed. by C. S. Mallinathan. Jaipur: Shree Digambar Jain Atishaya Kshetra Mahaveerji, 1951.

TS = *Tattvārthasūtra*. See *Sarvārthasiddhi*.

Secondary Sources

KOHL, Josef Friedrich 1956. *Das Physikalische und Biologische Weltbild der Indischen Jaina-Sekte*. (The Jaina Academy Publications, 3.) Aliganj: The World Jain Mission.

JAIN, Jagdish Chandra 1933. The metaphysical significance of dharma and adharma in Jaina methaphysics. *The Indian Historical Quarterly* 9: 792-794.

JAMBŪVIJAYA 2001. See DA.

OHIRA, Suzuko 1994. *A Study of the Bhagavatī sūtra. A Chronological Analysis*. (Prakrit Text Series, 28.) Ahmedabad: Prakrit Text Society.

SCHUBRING, Walther 1935. *Die Lehre der Jainas. Nach der alten Quellen dargestellt*. (Grundriss der Indo-Arischen Philologie und Altertumskunde, 3.7.) Berlin: Walter De Gruyter & Co. [References to pages and paragraphs.]

Anekāntavāda and Conflict Resolution

N. L. JAIN

Jain Philosophy is stated to be an aggregate of all the philosophies. It could be characterized by the coordinated practice of triad of non-violence (N2), non-absolutism (N3) or Anekānta and non-attachmental possession (N_3) – *ahiṃsā*, *anekānta* and *aparigraha* to regulate the activities of mind, speech and body for a peaceful and spiritual life of the individual, society, nation and globe. If one observes this triad, one experiences multiplying rather than additive effect:

$$N2 + N3 + N_3 \equiv N2\ N3\ N_3 \qquad \textbf{(1)}$$

The factor of non-absolutism represents a factor of vocal speech which is a connecting link between non-violence and action. The link is always a focal point for the quality of action.

Most of the traditional authors have described it qualitatively and in figurative and over-extolled language suggesting the theory as the

1. highest reach of intuitive human mind,
2. dynamic dialectics for deeper comprehension and
3. guide and inspiration for studies in science and mathematics – though it may be more statistical and relativistic.

They have supported it on philosophical, logical, ethical, spiritual, religious and non-violence ground. They have called it a (1) lamp,

(2) coin, (3) key, (4) chain, (5) collyrium, (6) spectacle, (7) eye, (8) guide, (9) teacher and (10) kind, with their specifics given in Table 1. They have illustrated it with the parable of the elephant and the blind men and pictures drawn from different angles.

TABLE 1:
Illustrations for *Anekānta*

	Illustration	Quality
1.	Lamp	Enlightenment
2.	Coin	Common acceptance
3.	Key	Resolution of locked problems
4.	Chain	Coordinates the various aspects
5.	Collyrium	Clarifies/improves the vision
6.	Spectacle	Improves/widens the vision
7.	Third eye	Holistic sight
8.	Guide	Gives proper directions for action
9.	Teacher	Motivation
10.	Royal kind	Administers body, mind and spirit properly
11.	Razor	Mind-cleaning

In contrast, many modern authors like Kothari[1], and even Lenin, have supported it on physical, statistical and intellectual grounds and many are now trying to support it on the basis of its applications in fields like social, political, economic and even in managerial science etc. That is why, it is said to be a vision or idea rather than a theory of ultimate truth.

TRADITIONAL BASIC POSTULATES OF *ANEKĀNTAVĀDA*

1. Every knowable object or entity is endowed with more than one (up to infinite) attributes – quite a number of times, seeming to be contradictory. It is a conglomerate of attri-

[1] Kothari 1975: 368.

butes. The term *aneka* is, thus, not a negative but a positive quantity.

2. The seemingly contradictory attributes are nothing but complementary parts of the whole in the multi-aspectal approach.
3. The entity could not be described as a whole until it is integrally studied with respect to all its aspects. Thus, *anekāntavāda* is an integrated form of different partial truths about an entity. The relative partial truths are called standpoints or *naya*s (see equation 2 below).
4. Our descriptions about entities do not reflect the ideal truth, but the truth with respect to some realistic aspectal prominence. Every description may represent a partial or relative truth.
5. Different observers under different conditions may have different truth about the same phenomena.
6. Our language is not capable of describing multi-aspectal truth. Our statements are, therefore, prefixed with the word *syāt* ('in some respect'). The word 'may be' is not an accurate expression for *syāt*.
7. The language of *anekānta* is the seven-fold predication (*sapta-bhaṅgī*) system with the word *syāt* attached to each statement.

The above postulates can be expressed in current relativistic and statistical language in the form of the following formulae:[2]

1. The holistic nature (character, T, truth) of an entity can be expressed by summation of all its attributed aspects with respect to all standpoints (S), or

$$T \equiv \Sigma \text{ Nayas or Standpoint} = \Sigma S \qquad \textbf{(2)}$$

This indicates the relativity of our knowledge and limitation of the omniscient for communicating it through out language.

---

[2] Jain 1997: 33-34.

2. Kothari has stated that the seven-fold predication theory could be explained through the complementarily principle of atomic physics through the example of a particle in a closed box. This illustration indicates its superb intellectualism. However, the fourth predicate of indescribability (T ≡) moves this theory beyond the principles of uncertainty which could be expressed as

$$\int_{-\infty}^{+\infty} P.dp \equiv T \equiv 0 \quad \text{(Where P = aspects, T = Truth)} \qquad \textbf{(3)}$$

It means that the holistic truth may be one only but it cannot be expressed by the common man.

3. The seven-fold predicative nature of the entity could also be expressed through integration which again supports indescribability:

$$\int_{1}^{7} P.dp \equiv T \equiv 24 \quad \text{(virtually non-soluble parameters)} \qquad \textbf{(3)}$$

4. Mahalanobis and Haldane have analysed the theory on statistical grounds and suggested the correctness of its seven-fold predications in the form of

$$^3C_1 + {}^3C_2 + {}^3C_3 = 7 \qquad \textbf{(3)}$$

Thus, *Anekāntavāda* finds support on the basis of traditional and current knowledge.

IMPLICATIONS OF *ANEKĀNTAVĀDA*

The above traditional and scientific support for this theory implies that

1. As our knowledge is relative, it does not describe absolute truth, but only relative truth. This means one should cultivate

the multi-dynamic vision in thoughts and phenomena. They could be universal or particular or they may have opposing or non-opposing character.

2. The theory encourages the concept of "unity of oppositions". This kind of vision leads to develop equanimity, an attitude of respecting all opinions as partial truth and regarding non-absolutism as the key-stone for various kinds of harmonies and avoidance of conflicts. The truth is manifold, but, in general, it could be described three-foldly in terms of origination destruction and permanence. The truth means tolerance and truth minus tolerance is untruth.

   Truth – Tolerance = Untruth

3. It does imply that one should cultivate an attitude of reasoning, rationality towards different areas of this diverse world. In simple words, it cultivates independent, moderate and liberal sympathetic and coordinating mental attitudes which are basic for a peaceful world. However, it is not only mental attitude, but it is also expressible vocally through aspect-based statements. These are more important forms.
4. It develops the concept of thinking (and acting) not only from one's standpoint but also from others' standpoint. It avoids the confusion created by absolutism. The Jains have always been multi-aspectal thinkers and that is why they adopted middle-way theories on many philosophical issues and have won many debates in the past. This involved tolerance of others' views and agreement as far as possible.
5. This theory also encourages non-violent practices (like Bharata and Bāhubali to avoid wars and conflicts).
6. This theory has a capacity to transform one's (or national) life from hatred to love, compassion and peace like the emperor Aśoka. It cultivates moral values so desired today.

7. The scientific, technological and economic growth has presented many kinds of scandalous problems well-known to us. This theory suggests to move towards inside to cultivate ethical and moral values for better stress free and peaceful life.
8. *Anekānta* theory is democratic and dynamic in orientation to develop better understanding for solution of problems.
9. It is a prejudice-free, non-insistent and guiding concept for life.
10. *Anekānta* induces wisdom which involves seven pillars: (i) revelation, (ii) elevations, (iii) reduction (iv) elucidation (v) variation, (vi) enumeration and (vii) rejuvenation or transformation. These are the basics of intellectual and physical progress. It makes one progressive and liberal in his cherished direction avoiding religious conflicts etc.[3]
11. It is stated to be the third eye (internal) like the god Śiva looking over all the aspects of living and non-living entities to coordinate their smooth relationship. It induces a flexibility in attitude and behaviour like the thermodynamic theory of elastic body preserving the common qualities of momentum and energy. This flexibility represents interpersonal relationships and mutual understanding.[4]
12. Its concept of aspect-based consideration leads us to a synthetic attitude to solve an issue. It is an adjunction rather than rejection.
13. It lays more importance on ethical orientation through non-violence.

With these implications, the principle could take many forms under different conditions like non-violence and peace, dialogue and mediation, religious tolerance, inter-religious exposure, removal of prejudices, respect and equality for life, development of self-respect, self-content and sharing, healing and reconsideration, re-

---

[3] Jain 2002: 31.

[4] Drago 2000.

moval of negative emotions, developing multi-dynamic vision and integral personality.

CONFLICTS AND THEIR CAUSE

The word "Jain" is derived from the root √*ji*- which means the winning over internal and external enemies. It should, therefore, not be surprizing that this system describes various kinds of enemies like delusion, violence, internal and external conflicts and methods to subjugate them for better physical and spiritual life of individual, society and now nation and globe. The above enemies have negative and distortional character and the religion redirects them towards positively through scientific and psychological methodology. Antonino Drago has mentioned that conflicts are also there in the scientific world on account of different views on nature. Capitany suggested these conflicts could be unified by conversion of philosophical mind into an ethical attitude. This looks like non-violent theory of conflict resolution in the world of science. Why can we not adopt it in the human world of conflicts? Is it so difficult?

The psychologists have stated that the living beings have about sixteen natural instincts which include acquisition and pugnacity.[5] This leads to the emotions of (a) desires (b) my-ness (c) passions like anger, pride, deceit and greed and (d) scarcity and increase. Differences in thinking, ego, ambitions and dreams also form the part of these conflicts. Puranik[6] states that men living with ideals always live in conflicts usurping the peace of mind. When we elaborate the instincts, we can find that the current conflicts of various kinds the world over could be included under them. In fact, the materialistic view of life is the basic cause of conflicts.

---

[5] Jain 1998: 107.

[6] Puranik 2002: 46.

CLASSIFICATION OF CONFLICTS

In general, all the conflicts are a form of eighteen kinds of violence – behavioural pattern based on emotions related with the deluding karma. They may be two-foldly classified.

1. **Minor or interpersonal** like stressful life, family troubles, personal egos, landlord-labour problems etc. which may include soft violence including internal harm (imbalance in proper secretions) and external harm like vocal or physical fights, which may later grow into major war-like conflicts. Many major conflicts start from another issue.
2. **Major or intergroup** like murders, wars, terrorism, genocides, communal riots, religious, political, social, economic, psychological, civilizational and other conflicts which involve hard or physical violence involving killings and curbs. Localism, regionalism, fundamentalism, nationalism, dictatorship, foreign influence, inter- and intra-statism, power politics and the concept of self-interest over morality and the like have also played a part in these types of conflicts. Women, wealth, loyalty, expansion of territory, religious conversions and conservatism, racial or other kind of superiority complex, immunity or insensitivity of political/powerful leaders, overpopulation, illiteracy, pollution, arms race etc. have also been responsible in this area. Conflicts of goals and means have also been stated. All these conflicts may also be classified in the form of short and long term ones. In fact, conflicts of any type are the worst enemies of progress. Kofi Annan has stated that poor countries have more conflicts due to horizontal inequalities. In contrast, democracies have low frequency of conflicts in comparison to non-democracies. They can fight the external conflicts better.

The above instincts cannot be eliminated altogether, but looking to their undesirable effects on individual, society and globe, the religious teachers and thinkers have stressed the need of minimizing or lessening the degree of conflicts through short and long term reduction of the intensity of factors causing them. In fact, complete resolution of conflicts is a mirage and impossible.

The minor level conflicts are minimized through some methods like

1. observing diet and mental purification-based vows to control balanced secretions in the body system leading to reduce the excess production of harmful ones and making up the under production of the useful ones.
2. undertaking meditational practices and postures for about half-an-hour a day leading to the above effects as well as cultivation, and transformation of mental and emotional disturbances. In fact, they reduce the emotional coefficients.
3. developing the Anekāntic attitudes of tolerance, interactions, dialogue, reconciliation, harmony, coexistence and desireless actions etc. For example, counseling services are proving attractive for family conflicts.[7] Many examples can be quoted for the effect of these methods in the transformation of many individuals to better life-styles.
4. In olden times[8] four to seven methods were employed to resolve the conflicts of any type: (i) Negotiation, (ii) Bribery, (iii) Punishment or war, (iv) Espionage or dissensions, (v) Deceit, (vi) Neglect and (vii) Conjuring. It is clear that the first preference was for non-violent or Anekāntic ways to try reconciliation involving mutual understanding of the view of each other and agreeing to avoid the conflict. The soft and hard violent methods were given the secondary positions. When all the soft option proved void, war or vio-

[7] See ICPNA 4: 152.

[8] See for instance *Manusmṛti* 7.109 or Somadeva Sūri, *Nītivākyāmṛta*, Varanasi, 1976, Mahavira Granthamala: 244-245.

lent method of resolving conflict was applied. These methods are applied even today.

The major conflicts affecting the society, nations and now the globe are of major concern for us today. They can never be eliminated. They may, however, be managed and the crisis avoided. Waldemar Kaempffert – the Kalinga prize winner – has stated that during the last 2500 years (in 1945), 902 wars and 1615 internal disturbances have taken place. Moreover, the concept that more effective means of killing should lead to end of wars has been belied.[9] In a more recent data, during 1990-95, 93 wars have taken place in seventy states, killing 55 lakhs of peoples.[10] Thus, the 20th century has been called a war century. We find today different kinds of short and long-span major conflicts throughout the world as shown in Table 2, illustrating their diverse fields.

TABLE 2:
Different Types of Major Conflicts

	Nature of Conflict	**Countries**
1.	Tribal ethnic	Somalia, Rwanda-Burundi, Kosovo, Chechnya, Bosnia, Sri Lanka etc.
2.	Muslim-Christian	Sudan
3.	Jews-Muslim	Israel-Palestine
4.	Gulf war	Arab countries, US
5.	Civil war (political)	Afghanistan, Liberia
6.	Border conflict	China, India, Pakistan
7.	Islamic – western leadership war	Iran, Iraq, US
8.	Terrorist proxy wars	In different parts of the world
9.	Hindu-Muslim	India-Pakistan-Bangladesh
10.	Muslim-Muslim	Iran-Iraq, many Countries

---

[9] Kaempffert 1947: 3.

[10] *Anuvibha Reporter* (Jaipur), Sept-Dec 2000 (no. 5), p. 28.

Most of these conflicts have arisen due to 20th-century technological development from arms to nuclear weapons. They have resulted in arms race, depletions of natural resources, scarcity of water, pollution of natural and moral atmosphere and probability of warming up of global temperature and destruction of even human race along with killing of millions of people. These effects seem devastating for the overall welfare of human kind. That is why moralist thinkers have given deep thoughts and action plans to stop these conflicts: they have many examples of non-violent successes like disintegration of Soviet Union, democracy in South Africa, Philippines and other areas, army of frontier people of India and concept of army-less states. They, therefore, are hopeful for non-violent methods of conflict resolution.

RESOLUTION OF CONFLICTS

The psychologists indicate that conflicts are not purely destructive. They lead to search for ways resulting in constructive outcomes, stimulation for better approaches and results and exercitation for better creativity. They are like ferments or catalysts for producing general welfare. Despite this, they have always been condemned by all. Various ways and means have been suggested to minimize them. As they result from the multiplicity of diverse factors, detailed earlier, seemingly too complex to be resolved for general sustainability, not only ethicists, saints, psychologists and religious leaders have indicated many ways to check them, but all conscious people have realized their ill effects. They have given an idea of degree of conflict in terms of

$$C = \text{Sum of negative factors} / \text{Sum of positive factors}$$

The higher this ratio, the larger will be the conflict. In conflict resolution, therefore, all positive and negative factors are to be considered which give a gradient of approach or avoidance, leading to four kinds of results in terms of win-win, win-lose, lose-win and lose-lose situations. These may be taken as newer forms of the four-fold Indian system of conflict resolution. Thus, the degree of conflict resolution is 1-C.[11]

Another term named

Emotional Quotient: EQ = Negative emotions / Positive emotions

has also been devised where increase in positivity will result in lowering the degree of conflict.[12]

A third term named

MmE (Major – minor – Equivalency)

has also been devised by Pratfort[13] where two models have been combined. The 'Major-minor' model leads to violence while the equivalency model is the basis of freedom from violence or conflicts. Though this method is more theoretical, it could be tried for its objective with a little higher level of the society.

There are two ways of dealing with conflicts: (1) Prevention i.e. preparing suitable condition so that they may not occur and (2) Redressal, reduction of intensity of their ill effects, restraint and redirection where they occur. Both ways are similar to the two-fold objects of medical science (physical) and religious science (psychical).

It is said that conflicts can be resolved in two ways: (1) violent way and (2) non-violent way. The first way has been the traditional way. It has been taken as the most satisfying way. However, the people have realized that violence generates violence and there can be no end of conflicts and wars and establishment of normalcy. Moreover, the ambitious mentality increases not linearly but exponentially, leading to more and more complex conflicts. There is an absolutist vision in this type of conflict. It is set without taking the other side into consideration.

---

[11] Hall & Gardner 1980: 541.

[12] Ghoshal 2002: 17.

[13] Pratfort 2003: 24.

Meredith and Mental have stated that conflicts can be resolved in an effective way or ineffective way. The effective way involves all the methods stated earlier while ineffective resolution consists of forcing or penalization and even dismissal of the conflict through violent means.

There are many methods to avoid major conflicts of any nature, most of which involve reconciliation and agreement with the opponent. Many thinkers and peace-promoting agencies including Malachi O. Orondo[14] have given thoughts over this problem. All of them have suggested the following methods:

1. Change of attitude towards ethical nature by the concerned groups or leaders.
2. Promotion of spiritual revival through evangelization for peace and reconciliation.
3. Mutual talks among the conflicting party to resolve the conflicts. This requires conflict resolution workshops, one of which was organized by Orondo. This suggestion involves dialogues, integration, mutual understanding, agreement and multi-dimensional vision: all direct forms of *Anekāntavāda*.
4. Promotion of democratic values and democracies to minimize the conflicts.
5. Training of crisis management to produce crisis managers for resolving conflicts.
6. Visits of various peace-aware groups to conflict-prone areas.
7. Continuous promotion of conflict resolution concepts through different kinds of media.
8. Introduction of courses on social ethics in educational institutes.
9. Each country should have a ministry of peace-making and conflicts prevention along with UNO taking the lead of this direction.

---

[14] *Anuvibha Reporter* (Jaipur), Sept-Dec 2000 (no. 5), p. 147.

10. Promotion of peace in distant conflict areas through dialogues. Establishment of peace model centers, organization of conflict workshops and regular review conferences to assess the progress.
11. Undertaking balanced development benefitting all groups throughout the nation and world involving removal of poverty.
12. Promotion of change in food habits like vegetarianism.
13. Conflict fractionation or creation of smaller issues out of a complex issue.

On analysing these suggestions and practices, we find that they involve some short term methods and many long term methods. The first ones apply when conflicts are there and the second ones are meant for their prevention and creating an atmosphere for conflict free world.

Almost all thinkers and religions have propounded observance of moral and ethical values for peaceful world. These values require control over the instincts of acquisition, pugnacity, ego and ambitions. The saints have stated that it is only the human being who has also the instincts of surrender and peace to control the above negative instincts. Thus, he can create a peaceful world also. The materialist view of life has to be remodeled or reconceptualized in the spiritual or ethical direction. This means feelings of equality of livingness in all, respect for life, compassion for all and the like. This has a motto: "To initiate a conflict is as sinful as to tolerate or not to oppose it." Thus, pragmatically, the redirectional attitude has a capacity to develop one's latent potential non-violent power for resolution. The concept of redirection arises through the application of the theory of multi-dynamic vision.

With change in direction, grows the seven-pillared wisdom and liberalism which enables one to subside one's negative instincts of self-interested desires and ambitions leading one to meet even the opponent for dialogues etc. for conflict resolution. In fact, all these processes do evolve from multi-dynamic vision principle.

The multi-dynamic vision makes one a keen observer of the processes and effects which lead one to decide the course of action in proper direction. This is the process of internal and external democratization where conflicts of any nature are attempted to be resolved by the above processes. It improves 1-C, and MmE, and reduces EQ.

The long-term suggestions for conflicts prevention and cure are also the resultant of multi-dynamic vision. They are dependent on various global, national or non-governmental agencies which have an Anekāntavādic vision.

We thus see that almost all the pragmatic ideas for conflict prevention and cure are the direct offshoots from multi-dynamic vision. This visionary concept is specific to Jainism and very few have proper conceptualistic ideas about it. We should make efforts to promote this principle far and wide so that the world may be as conflict-free as possible.

LIMITATIONS OF *ANEKĀNTAVĀDA*

Despite the multi-faceted utilitarian aspect of this principle, many limitations to it are observed now-a-days. For example, it is not applicable in case of many Jain fundamental or absolute truths like (1) existence of the soul, (2) the liberated beings, (3) five or six fundamental realities, (4) persons not fit for liberation, (5) eternal *nigoda* lives and (6) extreme conditions of absolutism etc. Ācārya Mahāprajña[15] also states that it is not desirable to apply this principle everywhere, for instance in the case of mathematics and some other abstract sciences. However, *Anekānta* does not commit the policy of 'tit for tat' or violent conflict, but under extreme conditions like taking hostages, sudden terrorist attacks, World Trade Centre-like attack, plane abductions or proxy wars like that in

[15] Ācārya Mahāprajña 2001: 17.

Kashmir which may have to be resolved beyond non-violent policy. Of course, one should try the earlier stated methods before applying different kinds of violent penalization.

Anekānta has, thus, a buildup mechanism for preventing and avoiding conflicts except under extreme and absolute conditions. It could be an ideal for the issue to be approached as far as possible, though reality and ideals are said to be poles apart as per Krishnamurti. However, it will always remain as one of the conductive avenues for conflict resolution.

METHODS OF DEVELOPING ANEKĀNTIC VISION

Despite some limitations, people have gone far to state that Anekāntic vision could act as a panacea for minimizing or ending different types of conflict. It is, therefore, necessary to develop this vision. There are many tools and methods through which this could be achieved. The Anuvibha conventions have been trying to develop an all-encompassing and pooled up training program in nonviolence. The Jain Vishva Bharati (Ladnun) has also established a department for this program with manifold objective.

The aim of the program is mainly three-fold. It involves (1) change of heart, (2) change of attitude and mind and (3) change of life style. Others have also suggested the concept of this type which is comparatively given in Table 3.

The program may cover individual, family, group and society. The development of Anekāntic vision should start through early educational courses on social ethics up to the intellectual development stages – virtually throughout life. The studies of scriptures and biographies of the saints, short and long company with genuine saints or listening to their lectures, incantation, repetition, meditation and genuine dietary habits are some of the tools which awaken our consciousness towards Anekāntic vision and reduce the degree of conflict and Emotional Quotient. The study of subjects like sociology, economics, ethics and spirituality etc. with a wider intellec-

TABLE 3:
Training program in Anekāntic Vision and Non-violence

	Training[16]	JVB Program
1.	Physical training	Breath controls, physical postures, meditation for better inner and outer health.
2.	Mental training	Psychology of violence and non-violence, change of heart, mind and attitude for better emotional health, reduction in emotional coefficient and degree of conflict.
3.	Intellectual training	Structural changes in the life styles and traditional thought processes, cultivation of holistic values through lectures, classes, discussions and self study for developing the Anekāntic vision, study of science of life, optimistic attitude, studies of sociology, economics, health science and psychology, studies on transactional analysis and group dynamics of individual and society.

tual perspective builds up the positivities of emotional intelligence and health which is one of the key elements for *Anekāntic* vision. Lesser the number and intensity of conflicts, more the reduction in our earning of evil karmas and increase in earning of auspicious karmas and, thus, better the world. It must be added that there is only a very small minority (approx. 3%) which causes major or minor conflicts. It is the duty of the majority to impress upon them the good effects of a conflictless state of affairs.

REFERENCES

ĀCĀRYA MAHĀPRAJÑA 2001. *Anekanta: Reflections and Clarifications.* Ladnun: Jain Vishva Bharati.

DRAGO, A. 2000. Non-violence as a science of conflict resolution. *Anuvibha Reporter* (Jaipur), Sept-Dec 2000 (no. 5): 111-116.

GHOSHAL, S. 2002. Article in *Times of India*, 29 October 2002.

---

[16] See *Anuvibha Reporter* (Jaipur), Sept-Dec 2000 (no. 5), p. 147.

HALL, C. S. & L. GARDNER 1980. *Theories of Personality. Primary Sources and Research*. New Delhi: Wiley Eastern. [First edition: New York, 1965.]

ICPNA 4 = *Ahimsa, Peacemaking, Conflict Prevention and Management: Fourth International Conference on Peace and Nonviolent Action, New Delhi, Nov. 10-14, 1999; Proceedings and Presentations*. New Delhi: Anuvrat Global Organization, 2000.

JAIN, N. L. 1997. *Sarvodayi Jain Tantra*. Tikamgarh: Potadar Nyas.

—— 1998. *Jaina Karmology*. (Parshvanath Vidyapeeth Series, 109.) Varanasi: Parshvanath Vidyapeeth – Ahmedabad: Navadarshan Society for Self-Development.

—— 2002. Article in *New Scientist*, London, 17 September 2002.

KAEMPFFERT, W. 1947. *Science Today and Tomorrow*. London: Dennis Dobson Ltd.

KOTHARI, D. S. 1975. Reality and physics: Some aspects. In: *K.C.S. Felicitation Volume*. Rewa.

Nītivākyāmṛta = Somadeva Sūri, *Nītivākyāmṛta-dīpikākhyayā bhāṣāṭīkayā sametam*. Ed. by Sundarlāla Śāstrī & N. K. Devarāja. (Mahāvīra Granthamālā.) Varanasi: 1976.

PRATFORT, F. R. 2003. Building non-violence. *Anuvibha Reporter* (Jaipur), April-June 2003.

PURANIK, T. S. 2002. Article in *Tirthankar Vani*, Ahmedabad, September 2002.

Doctrinal Passages of the Jain *Rāmāyaṇa*s

EVA DE CLERCQ

Literary renderings of Jain versions of the popular story of Rāma are plenty, as is clear from the surveys of different Jain *Rāmāyaṇa*s given by V. M. Kulkarni.[1] In this paper I examine and compare the passages concerning the Jain doctrine of three selected Jain Rāma stories, in order to clarify the position and function of these passages.[2] The works under scrutiny are (1) Vimalasūri's *Paumacariyaṃ* (PCV) in Māhārāṣṭrī Prakrit (1st century?),[3] (2) Raviṣeṇa's *Padmacarita* (PCR), also called *Padmapurāṇa*, in Sanskrit (7th century), and (3) Svayambhūdeva's *Paumacariu* (PCS) in Apabhraṃśa (9th-10th century).

These three poems are very similar in story line. In fact, the *Padmapurāṇa* of Raviṣeṇa, has repeatedly been referred to as a mere extended translation of Vimalasūri's work.[4] The third poet,

---

[1] Kulkarni 1959; 1960; 1990.

[2] The classification of the doctrinal elements I have used, is based on Glasenapp's survey of Jainism (Glasenapp 1925).

[3] The colophon of Jacobi's edition of the PCV contains a statement that the author completed his poem 530 years after Mahāvīra's *nirvāṇa*, which would situate him in the 1st century of our era. Many scholars refute this statement as being corrupt and assign a later date to the work. The editor believes Vimala must have lived in the 3rd or 4th century, while K. R. Chandra argues he lived in the 5th century. For discussions on the date of Vimalasūri, see Kulkarni's introduction to the revised edition of the PCV (PCV, Introduction, pp. 8-15) and K. R. Chandra's analysis (Chandra 1964; 1970: 4-17).

[4] Kulkarni 1959: 189; 1990: 91-103; Chandra 1970: 283; Bulcke 1950: 63.

Svayambhū, explicitly mentions Raviṣeṇa as his predecessor.[5] In table 1 a schematic outline is given of the passages referring directly to the doctrine in these texts.

All three poets commence their story with a description of the *samavasaraṇa* of Mahāvīra, attended by king Śreṇika of Magadha. Vimalasūri and Raviṣeṇa here include a summary of Mahāvīra's teachings (1). They primarily refer to the Jina's instruction on metaphysics: the *dravya*s, *jīva* and *ajīva*, and the mechanics of *karman* that binds the soul to *saṃsāra*. Svayambhūdeva excludes this passage. On the request of Śreṇika, Indrabhūti Gautama starts to narrate the "true" story of Rāma. Firstly, he creates a setting for the narrative with a description of the three worlds, Jambūdvīpa, *bhoga-bhūmi* with its *kalpadruma*s, the different eras, and similar aspects of traditional cosmology and history (2). Raviṣeṇa and Vimalasūri also insert a few verses on the essence of *dāna* (3). The three poets then devote several chapters to the biography of the first Jina, Ṛṣabha, followed by the account of the origin of the *Vidyādhara-vaṃśa*, of which the Rākṣasas and Vānaras later form different offshoots. The *samavasaraṇa* of Ṛṣabha presents an occasion to list briefly some essential elements of the Jain faith (4). These elements are not explained, they are merely enumerated. The poets continue with the story of Bharata and Bāhubali and the biography of the second Jina, Ajita, including the account of the origin of the *Rākṣasa-vaṃśa*. On the occasion of Ajita's *samavasaraṇa*, all three authors specify the past and future Jinas and other *mahāpuruṣa*s (5). The following chapters are dedicated to the lineage of the Rākṣasa and Vānara dynasties. A visit by the Rākṣasa king Taḍitkeśa to a monk is exploited by all three poets to elaborate on the Jain faith, albeit in different ways: Vimalasūri and Raviṣeṇa let the monk preach about the vows specifically, while Svayambhū has him glorify the fruits of the Jain *dharma* (6).

---

[5] PCS 1.2.9.

When, generations later, Rāvaṇa visits the monk Anantavīrya, he takes a vow to never enjoy any woman against her will. Vimalasūri and Raviṣeṇa use this opportunity to elaborate on the Jain *dharma* (7). Their emphasis is mostly on the Jain vows and Jainism as the solution to worldly suffering. Before proceeding to the actual Rāma story, Vimalasūri and Raviṣeṇa enumerate the birthplace, parentage, age, height, etc. of the *śalākāpuruṣa*s (8a). In addition to this, they also illustrate in a few verses the fruits of *puṇya* and *pāpa* (8b). They continue with the biography of the twentieth Jina, Muni Suvrata, in whose *tīrtha* the events of the Rāma story take place and describe the lineage of the *Ikṣvāku-* and *Hari-vaṃśa*, in which Daśaratha and Janaka are born. At the renunciation of Ikṣvāku king Vajrabāhu, Vimalasūri has a monk delivering a sermon on the forms of *karman* and the different methods of hindering and eliminating it (9). In the story of Saudāsa, another Ikṣvāku king, who takes a fancy to meat, Vimalasūri elaborates on the Jain ideas about eating animal food (10). The poets then go on to the actual Rāma story. Daśaratha wants to leave the material world and because of Kaikeyī's boon the younger son Bharata is chosen to ascend the throne, instead of the oldest son, Rāma. Bharata refuses as he also wishes to renounce the world. Vimalasūri and Raviṣeṇa here insert a long sermon by a monk addressed to Bharata on the benefits of *gṛhasthāśrama*, the life of the lay householder as opposed to harsh asceticism (11). Svayambhūdeva has Daśaratha himself explaining why Bharata should spend some years as a layman before becoming an ascetic. During their travels Rāma, Sītā and Lakṣmaṇa encounter a Brahmin, Kapila, who is converted to Jainism after a visit to a Jain monk. Svayambhūdeva uses this visit to elaborate on the fruits of *dharma* and *pāpa* (12). Raviṣeṇa and Vimalasūri merely refer to the monk's preaching. Some time later Rāma, Lakṣmaṇa and Sītā meet the monks Kulabhūṣaṇa and Deśabhūṣaṇa.[6] When these monks attain *kevala-jñāna*, in the PCS Indra comes to honour

[6] The PCS refers to this person as Deśavibhūṣaṇa.

TABLE 1:
Outline of the Doctrinal Passages

	PCV	PCR	PCS
1. Mahāvīra's teachings	2.60-96	2.153-198	–
2. cosmology and history	3.17-41	3.30-63	1.11.1-8
3. *dāna*	3.42-47	3.64-72	–
4. summing up of the elements of the Jain faith	4.22-30	4.34-51	3.11.1-10
5. summing up of the Jinas and heroes	5.145-157	5.189-226	5.9.5-9
6. sermon to Taḍitkeśa	6.116-130 (vows)	6.273-312 (vows)	6.14.2-9 (*dharma*)
7. Anantavīrya's sermon	14.8-150	14.15-352	–
8. a) *śalākāpuruṣas* b) fruits of *pāpa* and *puṇya*	20 20.161-168	20 20.195-204	–
9. sermon to Vajrabāhu	21.49-64	–	–
10.sermon on eating meat	22.79-89	–	–
11.sermon on the *gṛhasthāśrama*	32.56-94 (monk)	32.142-183 (monk)	24.4.1-11 (Daśaratha)
12.fruits of *dharma* and *pāpa*	–	–	28.9.1-11
13.Jainism: the solution to all problems	–	–	32.14.1-9
14.sermon on the ephemeral nature of things	39.53-60	39.112-126	33.5.1-6.9
15.sermon on the different vows	–	–	34.1.1-8.9
16.praise of the gift of food	–	–	35.1.4-9
17.discussion on Buddhism, *nyāya* and *anekānta*	–	–	35.5.1-7.2
18.description of the hells	–	–	35.12.9-15.9
19.the working of *pāpa*	–	41.98-101	–
20.instructions to Jaṭāyu	41.65-69	41.140-153	–
21.consolation of Rāma	–	–	39.3.5-10.8
22.Mandodarī's discourse on the vows	–	–	41.6.1-9

23.Hanumān's sermon on the *anuprekṣās*	–	–	54.5.4-16.9
24.the evil of desiring another man's wife	69.30-38	72.49-62	73.12.1-13.8
25.Aprameyabala's sermon	75.44-58 (*karman*, vows, etc.)	78.prose: 19-35 (*karman*, vows, etc.)	78.2.1-4.9 (*kāla*)
26.sermon on the two forms of Jain *dharma*	82.11-16	85.17-25	–
27.Sakalabhūṣaṇa's sermon to Rāma	102.63-197	105.106-266	83.20.7-10 (enumerated)
28.sermon on eating after dark	103.23-35	106.30-34	84.6.6-7.10
29.Indra's sermon	109.5-26	114.7-56	87.2.1-5.10

them and extols the Jain faith as the only solution to all worldly problems (13). On Rāma's request the monks narrate the story of their previous life. In this story a monk instructs a heathen king on the ephemeral nature of possessions, on pleasures and on the uselessness of the body (14). Thereupon the king converts to Jainism. Next, Svayambhūdeva has the monks giving a very elaborate discourse on the different vows for ascetics and laymen (15). Neither Vimalasūri, nor Raviṣeṇa give such a passage here. After their encounter with those two monks Rāma, Sītā and Lakṣmaṇa continue their journey and reach the Daṇḍaka forest. Again two monks arrive, and Rāma and Sītā honour them and offer them a meal. Svayambhūdeva describes how the gods in the heavens praise the gift of food as superior to all other alms (16). At that time, Jaṭāyu[7], the vulture, spots the monks and as he remembers the evil deeds he committed during a former life, he faints at their feet. One of the monks explains the bird's previous existence. Jaṭāyu once was a king, called Daṇḍaka. One day he saw a Jain ascetic performing dreadful austerities in the royal park and became frightened. He tried to get the ascetic to leave by throwing a dead snake

[7] This Jaṭāyu is often referred to as Jaṭāyin.

around his neck in order to disturb his yogic practices, but the man remained unaffected. Thoroughly impressed with the ascetic's perseverance, the king immediately became a protector of Jain ascetics. Svayambhū describes king Daṇḍaka as a Buddhist. He inserts a discussion between him and the ascetic on *asti* and *nāsti*. The ascetic refutes the doctrines of the Buddhists and of the *nyāya* philosophy and then explains in short the Jain theory of *anekānta-vāda* and *nayavāda* (17). Through the intrigues of his relatives, king Daṇḍaka later becomes resentful towards the ascetics and has them killed. As a result of this, he and his relatives spend numerous existences in different hells which are elaborately described by Svayambhūdeva (18). After this, he is reborn as a vulture. Concluding the story of Jaṭāyu's previous life, Raviṣeṇa adds a few verses on the workings of *pāpa* (19). Before they leave, the monks instruct Jaṭāyu on how to live his life in order to attain a better existence. These instructions basically describe the vows of Jainism (20).

The story continues. After Sītā's kidnapping, Svayambhūdeva describes how two *cāraṇa* ascetics attempt to console Rāma with a discourse on the evils of attachment to women and to bodily pleasures (21). Rāma and Lakṣmaṇa start their search for Sītā and meet up with Sugrīva and Hanumān. Meanwhile Rāvaṇa asks his wife Mandodarī to go and try to convince Sītā into accepting him. Svayambhūdeva describes how pious Mandodarī is reluctant and gives a short speech on the Jain vows (22). Next, in the PCS Hanumān, on the occasion of his capture after his visit to Sītā, tries to change Rāvaṇa's mind and bring about a peaceful release of Sītā by instructing him in the twelve *anuprekṣā*s (23). The story proceeds and the battle begins. One day, as the fighting ceases for a festival, Rāvaṇa visits Sītā and tries to convince her into accepting him as her husband. Sītā faints and, in shock, Rāvaṇa realizes that he should give her back to Rāma. However, since giving Sītā back in full battle would make it appear as if he were afraid, Rāvaṇa decides he shall give her back after winning the war. On this occasion all three poets elaborate on the evils of desiring another man's wife (24). After Rāvaṇa is killed and the funeral rites have been performed, a group of ascetics arrives in a park near Laṅkā. In the PCS the head of the monks, Aprameyabala, gives a sermon on the unavoidable, destructive *kāla*, here as "time", upon which Rāvaṇa's sons renounce the world (25). In the PCV and the PCR, he preaches about *karman*, the vows, *saṃsāra*, and the different hells. Rāma, Lakṣmaṇa and Sītā stay in Laṅkā for six more years. When they hear of the sorrows of Rāma's mother, they decide to return to Ayodhyā. On their return, Bharata renounces the world. One day a mad elephant on the loose sees Bharata bathing. He remembers his previous existence in which Bharata was his best friend. From that moment on, the elephant abstains from food and water. The two monks, Kulabhūṣaṇa and Deśabhūṣaṇa, arrive in Ayodhyā and explain why this elephant refuses to consume anything. In this explanation Vimalasūri and Raviṣeṇa have them preaching on the two varieties of the Jain *dharma*: one for ascetics and one for laymen (26).

The story continues. Sītā is banished and gives birth to two sons, Lavaṇa and Aṅkuśa. Years later, she is brought back to Ayodhyā where she passes a fire ordeal to prove her chastity. Rāma begs her to accept him back as her husband, but she refuses and takes ordination from the monk Sakalabhūṣaṇa. Vimalasūri and Raviṣeṇa then have this monk giving an extensive sermon to Rāma on the Jain beliefs of cosmology, epistemology, metaphysics and ethics, more specifically asceticism and vows (27). Svayambhūdeva enumerates the aspects of the *dharma*, but does not give the actual sermon itself. The monk then narrates the previous births of Rāma, Lakṣmaṇa, Sītā, Rāvaṇa, Vibhīṣaṇa, Sugrīva, Vālin, Lavaṇa and Aṅkuśa. In one of his previous existences Rāma accepted the *aṇuvratas* after hearing a sermon on the Jain vows, more specifically on the vow prohibiting the eating after sunset (28). In the following chapters, all poets describe how one day, Indra instructs the other gods on *saṃsāra*, the solutions to worldly suffering offered by

Jainism and the merits of a human birth in which *mokṣa* can be attained (29). The story continues. Lakṣmaṇa and Bhāmaṇḍala, Sītā's brother, die. Hanumān, Lavaṇa and Aṅkuśa, Vibhīṣaṇa, Sugrīva and several others become ascetics. Finally Rāma attains *kevala-jñāna* and dies.

Even from just glancing at table 1, it is clear that the three poets only share a relatively modest number of doctrinal passages. Only nine of the twenty-nine passages referred to are shared among all three of them (2, 4, 5, 11, 14, 24, 27, 28 and 29). The PCV and the PCR share eight additional doctrinal passages (1, 3, 6, 7, 8, 20, 25 and 26). They differ from each other on three occasions (9, 10 and 19). The third poet, Svayambhūdeva, is different in over half of all the doctrinal passages. This digression of Raviṣeṇa and especially Svayambhūdeva from the example of their foregoer contrasts significantly with the close similarity of the three poems in the story line.

In table 2, the numbers referring to the doctrinal passages from table 1 are arranged according to subject matter. As far as the topics are concerned, ethics gets most attention by far. Twelve of the passages referred to in table 1 concern only ethics, generally one or several vows. But also most of the passages on metaphysics in the three Rāma stories are linked to ethics (1 and 9). They centre around *karman* and its impact on living beings, and are offered explicitly as incentives to follow the ethics of the Jains in order to destroy and inhibit this *karman*. In passage 25 of the PCS *kāla* ("time") rather than being described as a neutral *dravya*, is portrayed as the "all destroying time", one of the key elements in *saṃsāra* and in the suffering of living beings. The poet explicitly refers to the Jain *dharma* as the only escape. Some of the passages on cosmology, particularly those describing the horrors of hell (18 and 25 in the PCV and the PCR) promote the Jain *dharma* in a similar fashion. The doctrinal portions categorized below under the heading "general" draw attention to the sorrows of this world and – implicitly (14, 19, 21 and 24), sometimes even explicitly (6 in the

PCS, 8b, 12 and 29) – on the benefits of the Jain *dharma* as the supreme remedy. Predominantly instructive doctrinal passages, i.e. those which do not seem to be fundamentally aimed at the promotion of Jainism and especially the Jain ethics, are scarce. In passage 17 the philosophical viewpoints of the Buddhists and the adherents of the *nyāya* school are refuted in favour of Jainism, thus again emphasizing the superiority of Jainism to other doctrines. Only some passages describing elements of traditional cosmology and history are more or less void of any element of promotion (2, 5 and 8a). This can also be said of passage 4, where the elements of the *dharma* are merely enumerated, and of passage 27 where in the PCV and the PCR a concise, neutral survey of the entire doctrine is given, while the PCS here merely enumerates the subjects discussed. Despite the prevalence of the topic of ethics and an ever-present undertone glorifying the Jain *dharma*, all the basic elements of the faith are represented in the texts, albeit disproportionately.

TABLE 2:
Arrangement According to Subject Matter

General a) this world b) J = solution	 14, 19 (PCR), 21 (PCS), 24 } 6 (PCS), 8 (PCV, PCR), 13 (PCS), } 12 (PCS), 29
Epistemology	17 (PCS)
Metaphysics (~ ethics)	1 (PCV, PCR), 9 (PCV), 25 (PCS / PCV, PCR)
Ethics	3 (PCV, PCR), 6 (PCV, PCR), 10 (PCV), 11, 15 (PCS), 16 (PCS), 20 (PCV, PCR), 22 (PCS), 23 (PCS), 25 (PCV, PCR), 26 (PCV, PCR), 28
Cosmology / history	2, 5, 8a (PCV, PCR), 18 (PCS; ~ethics), 25 (PCV, PCR; ~ethics)
The whole *dharma*:	4, 7 (PCV, PCR; esp. ethics), 27

In total less than 500 verses of the 8,651 *gāthā*s (approx. 5.6 %) of the PCV concern the Jain doctrine directly. Raviṣeṇa's doctrinal passages are spread over about 800 verses (mainly *śloka*s) of 16,942 in total (approx. 4.7%). For the PCS the percentage is still lower: little more than 400 of a total of 12,684 (approx. 3.1%) concern these doctrinal passages.

Beside these passages, the three Rāma stories naturally also contain other, less direct references to the Jain faith. One type of such references is for instance found in the many lamentations of loved ones at the death of a character. All these words of mourning are very similar. They do not deal with a specific subject of the Jain doctrine, but speak in general of the shortness of life, the pain caused by their attachment to the deceased, etc. Similar references are for instance found in the words of characters who are about to renounce the world. They also speak in general of the ephemeral nature of life and the pain caused by desires. A second indirect type of reference is found in the stories of previous births. These stories explain the current birth and actions of characters based on what happened to them in previous lives. All these narrations are essentially examples of the mechanics of *karman*. The same applies to the stories of future births, such as those narrated by Rāma after his attainment of *kevala-jñāna* in the final chapters. Thirdly, certain actions or words of characters give concrete descriptions of specific aspects of the faith, for instance *stotra*s, *pūjā*s, the giving of alms, rituals performed at festivals, etc. Besides this, most chapters in Vimalasūri's and Raviṣeṇa's poems end with Indrabhūti reciting a religious proverb to Śreṇika. A final, even less direct, type of reference is found in the metaphorical use of technical, doctrinal terms, for instance something consisting of eight units is compared to the eight forms of *karman*, or something consisting of four units is compared to the four *gati*s or the four *kaṣāya*s. Since the Jain Rāma story is believed to have been told by the Jinas, the poems themselves can in effect be considered as representing part of the doctrine.

The first two of these forms of indirect reference to the doctrine again centre on the glorification of Jainism, especially Jain ethics, as the solution to worldly problems.

When weighing the importance of the direct doctrinal passages in their respective contexts, they do not appear to have any definite influence on the narrative itself. For an understanding of the story or of the psychology of the characters none of these passages seem truly indispensable. In the majority of the passages the doctrinal words are put in the mouth of a Jain monk (6, 7, 9, 11 in the PCV and PCR, 12, 14, 15, 17, 18, 20, 21, 25, 26, 27 and 28). In many cases, the result of these sermons is a renunciation or at least some form of acquiescence of one or more characters. As has been noted before, the three poets often do not share these doctrinal passages (7, 9, 12, 15, 17, 18, 20, 21 and 26), without any significant effect on the plot or the actions of the characters. As far as the renunciation of characters following a sermon by a monk is concerned, the mere mention of the monk giving a sermon is sufficient to explain this action. Equivalent to Svayambhūdeva's insertion of a sermon on *dharma* and *pāpa* in passage 12 for instance, the PCV[8] and PCR[9] simply mention that the monk instructs the Brahmin in the doctrine and consequently the Brahmin converts to Jainism. The subject of these particular sermons is largely ethics or related to it; however, the exact elements described vary among the poets (6, 25 and 27). In passage 11 the PCS puts a sermon on *gṛhasthāśrama-dharma* in the mouth of Daśaratha, whereas Vimalasūri and Raviṣeṇa have a monk preach this. In the PCS Bharata, to whom the words are directed, refutes his fathers sermon, yet in the PCR and the PCV, he accepts living as a householder for the moment, following the words of the monk, however still intent on a life as an ascetic as soon as his brother returns from his banishment. In this case, the doctrinal passage in the PCV and the PCR merely results in a differing detail of Bharata's feelings as opposed to Svayam-

[8] PCV 35.40.

[9] PCR 35.85.

bhūdeva's Bharata, but not in any substantial action of the character with effect on the story line. The same can be said about passage 21, where Rāma is consoled by two monks directly after Sītā's abduction in the PCS. This episode is absent from the PCV and the PCR. Following the words of the monks Rāma is consoled for just a few moments, upon which he again starts to bewail his loss, just as he does in the PCV and the PCR.

Most of the remaining doctrinal passages are told by the narrator, Indrabhūti Gautama, to king Śreṇika as part of the narrative frame (2, 4, 5, 8, 10, 19 and 24), with no effect on the plot. Furthermore, three passages consist of the words of Indra or other gods (13, 16 and 29). Besides Daśaratha's words in passage 11 in the PCS, only two other passages are put in the mouths of one of the main characters, both only in the PCS: Mandodarī's words in passage 22 and Hanumān's teachings in 23. The influence of these words on Rāvaṇa's thoughts is minimal and momentary. The fact that the poets, particularly Vimala and Raviṣeṇa, evidently eschew having the main characters preach on the doctrine is noteworthy.

Given their relatively modest amount and size compared to the volume of the three poems and their insignificant influence on the plot, the doctrinal passages of these three Rāma stories can be considered as more or less superfluous to the story. The fact that the three poems do not share all these doctrinal passages, supports this. These passages mainly centre on the topic of ethics; nevertheless, all the basic elements of the doctrine are represented in these works. Their only real function appears to be that of an intermezzo, a moment of reflection within the lengthy Rāma epic, promoting and glorifying the ideals of Jainism before the audience.

REFERENCES

Primary Sources

PCR = [Padmacarita/Padmapurāṇa] *Padmapurāṇa of Raviṣeṇācārya – with Hindi translation*, I-III. Ed. by P. Jain. (Jñānapītha Mūrtidevī Jaina Granthamālā – Samskrita Grantha, 20, 24, 26.) Kāshī: Bhāratīya Jñānapītha, 1958-59.

PCS = [Paumacariu] *Paumacariu of Kavirāja Svayambhūdeva*, I-III. Ed. by H. C. Bhayani. (Singhi Jain Series, 34-36.) Bombay: Singhi Jain Shastra Shikshapith – Bharatiya Vidya Bhavan, 1953-60.

PCV = [Paumacariyaṃ] *Ācārya Vimalasūri's Paumacariyaṃ with Hindi translation*, I-II. Ed. by H. Jacobi & M. S. Punyavijayaji. (Prakrit Text Society Series, 6, 12.) Varanasi – Ahmedabad: Prakrit Text Society, 1962-68.

Secondary literature

BULCKE, K. 1950. *Rām-kathā – utpatti aur vikās*. Prayāg: Hindū Pariṣad Viśvavidyālay.

CHANDRA, K. R. 1964. New light on the date of Paumacariyaṃ. *Journal of the Oriental Institute* 13.4: 378-386.

—— 1970. *A Critical Study of Paumacariyaṃ*. Vaishali: Research Institute of Prakrit, Jainology and Ahimsa.

GLASENAPP, H. von. 1925. *Der Jainismus – Eine Indische Erlösungsreligion*. (Kultur und Weltanschauung, 1.) Berlin: A. Hager.

KULKARNI, V. M. 1959. The origin and development of the Rāma story in Jaina literature. *Journal of the Oriental Institute* 9.2: 189-204.

—— 1960. The origin and development of the Rāma story in Jaina literature. *Journal of the Oriental Institute* Vol. 9.3: 284-304.

—— 1990. *The story of Rāma in Jain literature*. Ahmedabad: Saraswati Pustak Bhandar.

The Uses of Narrative: Jineśvara Sūri's *Kathākoṣaprakaraṇa* as Polemical Text

PAUL DUNDAS

Ernst Leumann's work on canonical and post-canonical stories, published in the 19th century, may justifiably be regarded as inaugurating the serious study of Jain narrative (Leumann 1998: 125-206 and 228-238) and this area of scholarly activity has remained significant within the Indological subdiscipline of Jainology up to the current day.

Jain narrative studies have tended to take several forms. The following examples are representative, although by no means exhaustive:

1. Parallels traced between various versions of a narrative, as in the case of Bloomfield's work on the Mūladeva cycle (Bloomfield 1913). Sometimes parallels are examined across sectarian boundaries, with the cycle of stories dealing with King Brahmadatta studied by Oberlies being a recent notable example (Oberlies 1996).
2. Micro-studies centring on a particular topic or institution. Balbir's study of a small narrative collection dealing with *dāna* is representative of this approach (Balbir 1982).
3. Sanskrit and Prakrit stories as part of the background to wider issues involved in editing narrative versions composed in Apabhraṃśa and early vernaculars such as Gujarati. Hiralal Jain's work on the *Sugandhadaśamīkathā* (Jain 1966) and

Bender's on the *Śālibhadracarita* (Bender 1992) are noteworthy examples.

4. Overall assessments of Jain story literature as a genre. A paper on the forms and terminology of early Jain narrative by Balbir is seminal in this respect (Balbir 1994).

Other approaches to Jain story literature are of course possible. So Pfeiffer has called for a massively ambitious consideration of the Indian narrative tradition as a whole and the identification of what he calls "sets of phenomena", located at all times, languages and areas of South Asia, oral and written, emphasising his belief that a Proppian approach which reveals underlying and interrelated patterns in this vast material will be essential, if the cultural expression of different communities is not otherwise to be regarded as self-contained (Pfeiffer 1994). Such a project would require a complete knowledge of Jain narrative and a willingness to integrate it into a total revisioning of South Asian story literature.

Nobody could underrate the vital importance of the investigations and programmes thus described and the philological skill of those who have conducted them during the last hundred years or so. Yet many of us working in Jain studies (and I include myself here) have often tended to lose sight of the practical cultural function of narrative, namely the instilling within an audience, both lay and ascetic, of everyday knowledge about Jainism and the concurrent legitimising of the ethical propositions of the religion. Unfortunately, perhaps in excessive concern for purely philological or historical issues, we have been inclined to ignore the strong interconnection between Jain narrative and Jain community, that is to say, the manner in which people who identify themselves as Jains are enabled to have confidence that things are truly the way they are in a Jain-centred universe because that is precisely how celebrated stories declare them to be (cf. Narayan 1989: 243-244).

Most Jainologists will be familiar with the landmark volume on Jain narrative edited by N. Balbir and C. Caillat which contains compelling examples of the various philological methodologies which can be brought to bear on the subject (Proceedings 1983). One paper from this volume by B. K. Jain has been largely ignored, no doubt because it is anecdotal and not couched in formal "academic" style, simply taking the form of charmingly described reminiscences. The title of this paper conveys its content: "Ethics and narrative literature in the daily life of a traditional Jain family of Agra during the nineteen thirties" (Jain 1983). Therein we find reference to a range of stories about heroic figures told by the author's mother which makes clear how for the young members of his family, to adapt a statement by Ranjini Obeyesekere about the manner in which she and other youngsters in Sri Lanka were socialised into Buddhism, listening to stories was how they became Jains (Obeyesekere 1992: x).

Anybody who has spent time among Jain laypeople or heard Jain ascetics preach will be aware of the role of narrative allusion in forming and perpetuating a sense of self-awareness and understanding among members of the Jain community. However, the indisputable significance of stories within the experience of Jainism has not yet been seriously investigated by the small band of fieldworkers on the Jain community, and doctrine has consistently been privileged as the dominant mode of discourse, with narrative marginalised as supposedly providing little more than an inferior, irrational version of this (cf. Tatelman 2000: 31-33). While stories in other Indian religious traditions have come to be perceived by informed scholarship as possible areas where latent tensions or difficulties can be exposed, I am hitherto unaware of any academic work which seriously focuses on Jain narrative as a vehicle for philosophising in the manner, say, of Patton's treatment of Vedic narrative (Patton 1996), or of any analysis of a Jain story which has been made to yield the same sort of rich results as recent interpretations of Buddhist tales, such as those of Vessantara (Collins 1998) or Paṭācarā (Hallisey & Hanson 1996). Even if narrative can never reveal the full actualities of the religious experience of earlier times, it may none the less be accepted that it can still give invaluable access to many dimensions of meaning which might otherwise have remained in obscurity.

Those who have actually carried out serious investigation into Jain narrative might well proffer a ready made reply to criticism of this neglect. Bruhn (quoted by Balbir 1982: 109, n. 2) describes the "unchangeable" nature of Jain stories inserted in scriptural commentaries, a judgement which might be viewed by some as excessively euphemistic, for without doubt the continual repetition of stock characters in Jain narrative combined with a certain flatness of style has come to be regarded as a consistently recurring component of its idiom, the literary counterpart, as it were, of the innate austerity of the narrators, which may have had the unfortunate result of the genre being underrated or ignored. Yet we know that from the time of the Ardhamāgadhī Āgama Jain writers were as capable as any of purveying a luxurious and complex style. The sixth *aṅga* of the Śvetāmbara canon, the *Nāyādhammakahāo*, is an obvious example, as are later Prakrit works such as the *Kuvalayamālākathā*. Furthermore, Bruhn's criticism of a near unchanging Jain narrative content might well imply an equally unchanging Jain social context over fifteen centuries. But this is surely implausible. Does every retelling of the story of Śālibhadra encode exactly the same meaning on every occasion and does the notional audience which hears and responds to it in some putative ahistorical manner always evince the same reaction? Rather, it seems obvious that Jain narrative should best be regarded as a changing historical phenomenon deployed in highly variable contexts. As Kirin Narayan has pointed out in her instructive study of modern Hindu narrative,

> Each time a story is told [orally] it can be stretched and moulded to accommodate changing historical circumstances (Narayan 1989: 245).

These reflections have been prompted by one particular Jain narrative text and my aspiration eventually to translate it. Jineśvara Sūri's *Kathākoṣaprakaraṇa* (henceforth KKP) was written in Māhārāṣṭrī Prakrit in 1051 CE (Jineśvara seems to have been born around 990 CE and died some time between 1054 and 1064 CE) and consists of a *mūla* text of thirty verses, with thirty-six illustrative stories. Jineśvara Sūri (henceforth Jineśvara) is of course famous in Śvetāmbara Mūrtipūjaka Jain tradition as the conqueror in debate of the "temple-dwelling" (*caityavāsin*) monks in the court of King Durlabha and the inspiration, if not the founder, of the lineage known as the Kharatara Gaccha. He lived in complex times in which economic change played a significant role, near the beginning, in fact, of the massive expansion of trade in western India which was to cushion the Jain community throughout the period of Muslim dominance and partly compensate for the erosion of any exercise of political power. Jinapati Sūri in his commentary on the *Pañcaliṅgīprakaraṇa* (p. 1) explains why Jineśvara had written his works, namely because he had seen the physical and mental decline of his contemporaries owing to the influence of the Kali Yuga and wished to favour those individuals whose true religious natures had been attenuated by corrupt circumstances. The 11th century involved radical attempts to refocus the integrity of Jain practice, as was also the case at the same time within the Christian community in Europe, and it is surely by no means fanciful to interpret the content of Jineśvara's writings as being connected with this period of reinvigoration and attempted reform in the Śvetāmbara community.[1] At this juncture of consideration of the KKP, then, I advocate consideration of a point to which Jainologists have been slow to

---

[1] Haribhadra's *Aṣṭakaprakaraṇa* (ca. 8th century CE), which prompted a commentary by Jineśvara, seems to have represented a kind of blueprint for the Kharatara monk to respond to the current situation. His introduction (p. 2) describes the dissemination of false doctrine and bad teaching which prevailed in Haribhadra's time, an account which can without too much difficulty be transposed to what is known of Śvetāmbara Jain circumstances in the 11th century. On p. 33, for example, Jineśvara rails against monks who take money from temples, a practice associated with the *caityavāsin*s, while his commentary displays a generally polemical attitude to false coreligionists.

Jineśvara's authorship of a *Caityavandanabhāṣya*, now lost, may well have been an important symbolic act for the leadership of a new sectarian lineage. One might compare the production of a similar work by Devendra Sūri not long after the emergence of the Tapā Gaccha as self-consciously reforming group.

respond, namely the possibility that at least one example of Jain story literature was not located in some sort of timeless realm of pure narrativity but rather was prompted by specific historical and social circumstance.

The KKP is Jineśvara Sūri's last work and it is not unreasonable to assume that his choice of stories for the anthology played some part in what Kharatara Gaccha writers portray as a struggle against the forces of corruption within the Jain community.[2] The Kharatara chronicler Jinapāla describes in his *Yugapradhānācārya-paṭṭāvalī* (p. 5) how the very writing of the KKP was a product of controversy and the uneasy relations which existed between revivalist mendicant ascetics such as Jineśvara and the sedentary temple-dwelling monks:

> At the village of Ḍiṃḍiyā (in Marwār) Jineśvara composed (*kṛtaḥ*) an anthology of stories (*kathānakakośaḥ*) for (public) explication. Initially he asked for a book from the *caityavāsin* teacher who was in that place so that he could use it for explication. But he did not oblige him. So Jineśvara started to compose the anthology in the final two watches of each night and explicated it in the morning. So he composed the whole anthology in the four month rain retreat period.

In the light of this description of the refusal of the *caityavāsin* leader to help Jineśvara, it might well be wondered whether the anthology in question was merely a run-of-the-mill story collection reiterating well-known narrative exempla. This is very much the view of A. K. Warder, the only recent scholar to give any conside-

[2] The themes of the stories of the KKP can be described as follows: nos. 1-7 deal with the results of worshipping the Jina; no. 8 deals with the results of praising the Lord, no. 9 deals with the results of resorting to monks; nos. 10-25 deal with the results of *dāna*; nos. 26-28 deal with the results of spreading the fame of Jainism (*prabhāvanā*); nos. 29-30 deal with the bad results of pointing to the faults of monks; no. 31 deals with the good results arising from preventing contempt of monks; no. 32 deals with the bad results of not having faith in the Jinas; no. 33 deals with the good results arising from giving encouragement in the *dharma;* no. 34 deals with the bad results arising from contradicting one's teacher; and no. 35 deals with results of giving encouragement in the *dharma*.

ration to any of Jineśvara's writings (Warder 1992: 261-281). After a long summary of Jineśvara's lost Prakrit romance, the *Nirvāṇalīlāvaīkahā* (which has been preserved in Jinaratna's Sanskrit version of 1283), Warder turns briefly to the KKP which is, he claims, by contrast with the other production "hardly a literary work, its stories bare of narrative development and description, details of situation and turns of expression" and he suggests a comparison between KKP story no. 8 which includes the narrative of Tosalī and Sundarī and the similar story of Padmaratha in the romance which is not to the former's advantage. Warder's conclusion is that the purpose of the KKP "must simply have been to serve as a handbook of examples for preachers, who might themselves elaborate as seemed desirable on particular occasions" (Warder 1992: 280).[3]

Warder's treatment is clearly not based on any systematic analysis of the Prakrit text. For him, and, I might hazard, other students of Jain literature, the KKP is merely one Jain storybook among many, useful only in the quest for narrative motifs and clearly inferior to those works such as the *Nirvāṇalīlāvatī* which can bear some passing resemblance to the western novel or romance. What I want to suggest once more in this short contribution (a point that will really only be borne out by a full translation and study of the text) is that the KKP emerged at a historically particular moment and that Jineśvara's choice of stories for the anthology (manifestly selective, unlike the huge *omnium gatherum* of Bhadreśvara's *Kahāvalī* written a century later which tries to include virtually every significant Jain narrative; cf. Malvania 1983) reflects the socio-religious pressures experienced by the nascent Kharatara Gaccha in a pluralist western Indian world in the first half of the 11th century. Jineśvara's selection of narratives was surely not random but prompted by a specific situation, namely the need to present his brand of reforming Jainism in a morally and

---

[3] In his introduction to the *Līlāvatīsāra*, Bhayani (1983: 53, n. 15) suggests that the KKP story is an abridgement of Jineśvara's original version which had been part of his lost *Nirvāṇalīlāvaīkahā*.

intellectually superior relationship to other interpretations of Jainism and a culturally dominant Hinduism.

Structurally the KKP can be regarded as an original production in that Jineśvara provides narrative commentaries on his own root text, a practice which does not seem to have been prevalent prior to him. At the same time the KKP can also be judged to be traditional in its use of narrative. Jineśvara's employment of stories from the Āvaśyaka tradition has been referred to by Balbir (1993: 121, 141, 148, 150, 183 and 189), while Caudharī points out that the stories of the KKP have been taken from old Jain works but have been put by their author into a new style and form (Caudharī 1973: 237). Indeed, Jineśvara signals awareness of this himself when in passing he states that some stories in the KKP are old and others new:

1. At the end of the first story of the collection, almost unique in the KKP because it deals with the rebirth of animals (but cf. KKP no. 17), Jineśvara takes care to point out (KKP, p. 11) that his account of the lives of two parrots (who unwittingly offer flowers to a Jina image and experience positive rebirths) is not the same as the version found in Municandra's commentary on Haribhadra's *Upadeśapada*.
2. KKP no. 9 is put in the context of Bharata's attentive care towards monks (*vaiyāvṛttya*) in a previous existence which led to his success in subsequent births (and contains a version of the famous narrative of King Śreyāṃsa's gift to Ṛṣabha). Jineśvara describes how precise details of these matters are to be gained from the Āvaśyaka commentary (*vivaraṇa*).
3. Jineśvara gives a Sanskrit pendant at the end of KKP no. 11, a version of the story of Kṛtapuṇya, in which he states:

> I am giving a version of this story different from that which is maintained by various traditions (*saṃpradāya*) but one which has been communicated (*bhāṇitaḥ*) by Mahāvīra. It would certainly involve serious disrespect (*āśātanā*) resulting in endless rebirth to suggest that he does not speak the truth. In my opinion there is no fault in providing a likely (or, appropriate) (*saṃ-*

bhavita) meaning. People at large accept an alteration of words in respect to a change of meaning. Nothing here has been spoken contrary to Āgama. If it is not appropriate, let the good tolerate it and pardon me.[4]

4. Jineśvara gives a pendant to his version of the story of Śālibhadra in which he makes clear that it can only make sense in the context of other stories about giving (*dāna*).

It might also be noted that at a much later time, in the 17th century, the Tapā Gaccha teacher Vijayasena Sūri refers in the *Senapraśna* (p. 60b) to the KKP as the only source for a particular narrative dimension of the story of Tamāli. The KKP thus manifestly evinces traditional and original features in respect to structure and content.

As for the intended audience of the KKP, there is no evidence that it was directed towards the laity only, as is often thought to be the case in respect to religious narrative. While the anthology unquestionably raises issues pertinent to the Jain laity, it also attacks lax monastic practice and those who would attempt to destabilise Jain behaviour by casting into doubt the validity of Jain practices through an appeal to an ideal situation based on an unrealistic privileging of scriptural injunction, controversial matters which were of real significance to the ascetic community. In addition, the KKP stakes a firm case for the integrity of Jain identity in the face of various forms of Hindu and (occasionally) Buddhist opposition. In effect, this story collection can be regarded as a kind of didactic or polemical cycle dealing with issues of public ritual (image worship, the role of temples and *dāna*), the evils of calumniating monks and praising brahmans and the nature of sectarian identity directed towards the whole Śvetāmbara Jain community which is envisaged as being a component of the larger Indian social world,

[4] KKP, p. 69, lines 17-20: *iha ca nānāsaṃpradāyavaśād anyathābhūto 'py artho bhagavanmukhena bhāṇitaḥ. tatra ca kila bhagavato 'nṛtābhidhāyitā saṃśitā bhavati. āśātanā caiṣā anantaphalabhaveti na cintanīyam. saṃbhavitam artham abhisaṃdhāya vadato na doṣaṃ manye. tattvārthānyathābhidhāne hi tadvacanānyathātvaṃ saṃbhāvayanti janāḥ. iha ca kiñ cid āgamaviruddham abhihitam. yadi ca na yuktaṃ marṣaṇīyaṃ, mithyā duḥkṛtam.*

yet at the same time transcending it because of the rigour, when properly practised, of its brand of knowledge-derived practice.

Often in the longer later stories of the KKP there is barely any narrative dynamic at all (to that extent, Warder was correct; see above) but merely dialogue between various characters concerning ritual and doctrinal issues. The discussions enacted in these stories do not simply conclude in the triumphant validation of Jainism for an audience which already understands the true situation; rather they frequently initiate debate about major issues of practice which only gradually leads to a final confirmation of the orthodox (from Jineśvara's point of view) position, often by reference to the description of the unhappy rebirth of a protagonist who has refused to accept the force of his opponent's argument. One of the most obvious signs confirming Jineśvara's espousal of this mode of "narration as vehicle for discursive analysis" is his designation in the work's title of his collection of stories (*kathākoṣa*) as a *prakaraṇa*, that is to say a treatise which relates to one topic within a broader intellectual discourse.[5] This sense of *prakaraṇa* as designating a type of learned work can be seen in the titles of two other works by Jineśvara, the *Pañcaliṅgīprakaraṇa* and the *Ṣaṭsthānakaprakaraṇa*, as well as in that of Haribhadra's *Aṣṭakaprakaraṇa* on which he commented. Many philosophical texts were designated *prakaraṇa* in the first millennium CE, but it seems to have been only after Jineśvara's KKP that the Jains repeatedly applied this designation to narrative texts, as e.g. Pradyumna Sūri's *Mūlaśuddhiprakaraṇa* with Devacandra Sūri's commentary, Hemacandra Maladhārin's *Bhavabhāvanāprakaraṇa*, Vardhamānasūri's *Dharmopadeśamālāprakaraṇa* and Yaśodeva's *Dharmopadeśaprakaraṇa*.

---

[5] In the Sanskrit *maṅgala* verse to the KKP (there is also a Prakrit equivalent), Jineśvara states: *Kathākośasya vivṛtiṃ vakṣye sūtrānusārataḥ*. In the Sanskrit commentary he explains: *atas tadutsāhajanakaṃ kathakoṣākhyaṃ prakaraṇaṃ cikīrṣur ācāryaḥ*....

Kulkarni (1994b: 131) quotes the following verse which gives the sense of the term *prakaraṇa*: *śāstraikadeśasaṃvaddhaṃ śāstrakāryāntare sthitam* | *āhuḥ prakaraṇaṃ nāma granthabhedaṃ vipaścitaḥ*.

There do, of course, occur "learned" stories at earlier periods of Jain literature, such as that of Śailaka in chapter five of the *Nāyādhammakahāo*, which contains a discussion of how the Sāṃkhya brahman Śuka is converted to Jainism in the course of a debate over the nature of purity.[6] Yet there is nothing comparable to what is frequently found in the KKP, namely scenarios in which after a little scene setting there occur virtual set piece debates between members of the Jain community, lay and monastic, exposing the difficulties or ambiguities involved in basic Jain practices. To that extent, the KKP can indeed be regarded as a "treatise", one intended to instruct the community not just in morals but in the rationale underlying correct institutional practice.

I have elsewhere drawn on KKP no. 16 to show how Jineśvara creates a narrative context for an elaborate discussion of the potential difficulties and inconsistencies involved in *dāna* (Dundas 2002) and on KKP no. 32 which critiques the motivation behind temple building and image worship (Dundas 1987-88). Another good example of the manner in which Jineśvara deals with learned and controversial matters in narrative guise is KKP no. 34. This story centres on an arrogant monk called Municandra, who is described as "relying on the word of the scriptures alone without having actualised their meaning" (*suttamettaggāhī abhāviyattho*), as a consequence of which he undermines the tolerant teachings of another senior monk by persuading the lay community that it should take literally the scriptural statement which warns against honouring the gods and holy places of non-Jains. Furthermore, he sneeringly denies the capacity of laymen to become renunciants on the grounds of their mercantile background with its inevitable attendant flaws.

---

[6] Kulkarni 1994a: 96-104 gives an English version. The later portion of the story describes how King Śailaka, who had taken renunciation, could not adjust to life as a monk and continued to maintain his sense of royal dignity so that, contrary to monastic rule, he was given medical treatment by his son King Maṇḍūka. The overall theme of this story is the inappropriateness of Jain monks staying in the same place for too long, one which would have struck a chord of recognition in Jineśvara's time.

Thoroughly demoralised by Municandra's doctrinaire teaching that renunciation should only come after fully mastering the twelve *pratimās*, the lay people lose their faith. However, another monk, Sāgaracandra, who is the narrative representative of the correct Jainism advocated by Jineśvara, appears to restore the integrity of the teaching by means of a lengthy appeal to the practicalities of life and the diversity of human attainment and aptitude. By Municandra's strict scripturalist standards, he asserts, nobody at all would have qualities sufficient to justify receiving the doctrine and a whole range of characters from Jain legend and narrative would have had to be debarred from the path because of their birth as merchants. Sāgaracandra accuses Municandra of disrespect towards the word of the Jinas by his literalist interpretation of it and so totally discomfits him. The story ends with a lengthy account of Municandra's terrible rebirths amongst barbarian tribes and prophesies endless wandering through *saṃsāra* for him because of preaching what is untrue.

It is difficult to avoid reading the story of Municandra, a narrative analogue for which does not seem to appear elsewhere, as anything other than a product of its time intended to make pointed comment on a particular style of monastic teaching. While Municandra may not appear to be the exact equivalent of the *caityavāsin* monks who were Jineśvara's and the nascent Kharatara Gaccha's main opponents, he does seem to embody an early version of a trend, alluded to elsewhere in the KKP, which was to manifest itself most markedly in Śvetāmbara Jainism in the 15th century. At that time both Kaḍuā Śāh and Loṇkā Śāh appealed to a literalist reading of scripture to reject, in the former's case, the possibility of true renunciation and, in the latter's, the validity of image worship. Such views were obviously subversive of orthodox Śvetāmbara Jainism and in their rejection of a millennium of authoritative scriptural commentary were also totally in opposition to the central legitimitating institution of the religion, the ancient teacher lineage stretching back to Mahāvīra's disciple Sudharman. The KKP both bears witness to and shows a willingness to discuss the implications of a range of similar "deviant" perspectives deriving from a literalist reading of the scriptures clearly in existence in the first half of the 11th century which reforming ascetics such as Jineśvara must have been required to confront along with the laxity of the domesticated temple-dwelling monks.

Had space allowed, I could have drawn on several stories in the KKP to show how Jineśvara demonstrates the superiority of Jainism to Śaiva and Vaiṣṇava Hinduism and of the Śvetāmbara monk to the brahman. However, in concluding this paper, I simply wish to repeat that Jineśvara's *Kathākoṣaprakaraṇa* might profitably be regarded as more than a collection of moralising narratives. This text seems to have played a polemical role in an ideological battle within the Jain community over the nature of orthodox Śvetāmbara Jainism and its place within the socio-religious context of the western India of its time. It is hoped that a translation of the KKP and a fuller study of Jineśvara's Sūri's other works and those of his contemporaries will eventually lead to a more developed demonstration of this.

REFERENCES

Primary Sources

Haribhadra, *Aṣṭakaparakaraṇa*. With the commentary of Jineśvara Sūri. Ed. by Vijayajinendra Sūri. Śāntipurī: Śrī Harṣapuṣpāmṛta Jain Granthamālā, 1991.

Jinapāla, *Yugapradhānācāryapaṭṭāvalī*. Ed. by Jinavijaya. Reedited and corrected in Vinayasāgar (ed.), *Kharataragaccha-Gurvāvali*. Jaypur: Prākṛt Bhāratī Akādamī, 2000.

Jineśvara Sūri, *Kathākoṣaprakaraṇa*. Ed. by Muni Jinavijaya. Bambaī: Siṃghī Jaina Granthamālā, 1949. [= KKP]

Jineśvara Sūri, *Pañcaliṅgīprakaraṇa*. With Jinapati Sūri's commentary. Bombay: Shri Jinduttsuri Prachin Pustakoddhar Fund, 1919.

Senapraśna. Compiled by Śubhavijaya Gaṇin. Muṃbaī: Devcand Lalbhāī Jain Pustakoddhār Granthamālā, 1919.

Secondary sources

BALBIR, Nalini 1982. *Dānāṣṭakakathā. Recueil jaina de huit histoires sur le don*. (Publications de l'Institut de civilisation indienne, 48.) Paris: Institut de civilisation indienne

—— 1993. *Āvaśyaka-Studien*, I: *Introduction générale et traductions*. (Alt- und Neu-Indische Studien, 45.1.) Stuttgart: Franz Steiner Verlag.

—— 1994: Forme et terminologie du narratif jaina ancien. In: Nalini Balbir (ed.), *Genres littéraires en Inde*: 223-226. Paris: Presses de la Sorbonne nouvelle.

BENDER, Ernest 1992. *The Śālibhadra-Dhanna-Carita*. (American Oriental Series, 73.) New Haven: American Oriental Society.

BHAYANI, H. C. 1983. *Jinaratna's Līlāvatī-sāra. A Sanskrit Abridgement of Jineśvara Sūri's Prakrit Līlāvaī-Kahā*. (L.D. Series, 96.) Ahmedabad: L. D. Institute of Indology.

BLOOMFIELD, Maurice 1913. The character and adventures of Mūladeva. *Proceedings of the American Philosophical Society* 53: 616-648.

CAUDHARĪ, Gulābcandra 1973. *Jaina Sāhitya kā Bṛhad Itihās*, VI. Varāṇasī: Pārsva Vidyāśrama Śodh Saṃsthān.

COLLINS, Stephen 1998. *Nirvana and other Buddhist Felicities. Utopias of the Pali Imaginaire*. Cambridge: Cambridge University Press.

DUNDAS, Paul 1987-88. The tenth wonder: Domestication and reform in medieval Śvetāmbara Jainism. *Indologica Taurinensia* 14: 181-194.

—— 2002. Haribhadra on giving. *Journal of Indian Philosophy* 30: 1-44.

HALLISEY, Charles & Anne HANSON 1996. Narrative, sub-ethics and the moral life: Some evidence from Theravāda Buddhism. *Journal of Religious Ethics* 24: 305-328.

JAIN, B. K. 1983. Ethics and narrative literature in the daily life of a traditional Jain family of Agra during the nineteen thirties. In: *Proceedings* 1983: 175-182.

JAIN, Hiralal 1966. *Sugandhadaśamī Kathā*. (Jñanapīṭha Mūrtidevī Jaina Granthamālā, Apabhramsha, 6.) Calcutta: Bhāratīya Jñanapīṭha.

KULKARNI, V. M. 1994a. *A Treasury of Jain Tales*. Ahmedabad: Sharadaben Chimanbhai Educational Research Centre.

—— 1994b. Haribhadrasūri's Viṃśativiṃśikā: An approach. In N. N. Bhattacharyya (ed.), *Jainism and Prakrit in Ancient and Medieval India*: 129-132. Delhi: Manohar.

LEUMANN, Ernst 1998. *Kleine Schriften*. Ed. by N. Balbir. Stuttgart: Franz Steiner.

MALVANIA, Dalsukh 1983. On Bhadreśvarasūri's *Kahāvalī*. In *Proceedings* 1983: 77-95.

NARAYAN, Kirin. 1989. *Storytellers, Saints and Scoundrels. Folk Narrative in Hindu Religious Teaching*. Penn Press: University of Pennsylvania.

OBERLIES, Thomas 1996. Die Erzählungen von Kāmpilya-König Brahmadatta. Eine Untersuchung im Anschluss an Vorarbeiten von Ernst Leumann. *Berliner Indologische Studien* 9/10: 259-313.

OBEYESEKERE, Ranjini 1992. *Jewels of the Doctrine. Stories of the Saddharma Ratnāvaliya*. Delhi: Shri Satguru Publications.

PATTON, Laurie 1996. *Myth as Argument. The Bṛhaddevatā as Canonical Commentary*. Berlin: de Gruyter.

PFEIFFER, Martin 1994. *From Field to Plot. Locating Indian Narrative Traditions*. In: N. Balbir & J. K. Bautze (eds.), *Festschrift Klaus Bruhn*: 489-503. Reinbek: Verlag für Orientalistische Fachpublikationen.

Proceedings 1983 = *Proceedings of the International Symposium on Jaina Canonical and Narrative Literature*. Ed. by N. Balbir & C. Caillat. (Indologica Taurinensia, 11.) Torino : Edizioni Jollygrafica.

TATELMAN, Joel 2000. *The Glorious Deeds of Pūrṇa. A Translation and Study of the Pūrṇāvadāna*, Richmond: Curzon.

WARDER, A. K. 1992. *Indian Kāvya Literature*, VI. Delhi: Motilal Banarsidass.

Some Features of Āśādhara's *Sahasranāmastotra*

JEAN-PIERRE OSIER

THE *SAHASRANĀMASTOTRA* OUTSIDE JAINISM

Indian literature gives priority to hymns as expressions of homage to the divinities. Most of them are praises aiming at propitiating a particular god in order to obtain special favours. In this sense, a hymn is a kind of gift and obeys the law *do ut des*: the addressee is not always addressed by means of the vocative, but rather by means of the dative, for something (the praise) is given to him, for instance in the formulas *namas* X and so on. This form of dedication does not by principle exclude descriptive elements of the addressee, who is praised because he has such and such qualities; but they are instrumentalised by the mode of expression: within the praise. A quality is meant for itself, but it is not left unaffected by the rhetorical aim of the sentence where it is used. In itself the addressee can or could be different from what he looks like thanks to the magic words of the poet. It can be only a suspicion, but the shadow of a doubt is enough to cancel the reality of the exalted qualities. The hymns where the dative is used cannot be expected to express the authentic essence of the praised one; if they do so, it is by chance.

On the contrary, calling the gods by their names in the nominative case is not invoking them, but uncovering what they are in fact, independently of the speaker's feelings or opinions, even if one can by a simple addition substitute an innuendo verbal form to the name only: you are X or Y. But the real meaning of the nominal clause is not an interpellation, it is an affirmation: he (= the god) is X or Y, or X or Y is.

This grammatical possibility of praising the gods by the simple utterance of their names used in the nominative accounts for an encompassing fixed set of titles. Amongst them the 1008 names list (hereafter called *sahasranāmastotra*) is important. The number 1000 or 1008 was selected on account of its symbolic value, as signifying the wholeness of the divinity or of the being concerned: in the rituals one can find such a recourse to 1000 symbolic objects in order to give to the worshippers an image of the god. Thus the Śaiva *Rauravāgama* describes a ritual of the bath with 1009 vessels and the corresponding list of gods.[1] Whether the number is accurate or not, the symbolic value remains unchanged. It is possible to consider the *sahasranāmastotra* as an Indian literary micro-genre.

"Names-hymns" in the *Ṛgveda*

In Vedic times "names-hymns" only exist in an embryonic stage. Thus ṚV 1.89.10:

> *Aditir dyaur aditir antarikṣam*
> *aditir mātā sa pitā sa putraḥ*
> *viśve devā aditiḥ pañca janā*
> *aditir jātam aditir janitvam.*

Here the nominal sentence is used, but the sentence is clearly attributive. The nominal sentence rests on the following principles. The "rection" (*karman*), which depends on the verb, modifies the object by imposing the burden of an action proper to the subject. The use of the nominative case does not involve the subject in the actions which are attributed to it. However, the nominative case by itself cannot have the value of a sentence. By itself a name appears only as a name, not as a meaningful utterance, open to the distinc-

[1] Dagens & Barazer-Billoret 2000: 105-116.

tion of truth and falseness. In Sanskrit, despite "the centrality of verb and action"[2], the use of nominal sentences is a means to overcome this apparent difficulty: in the nominative case, a name can have the meaning of a sentence endowed with the epistemological values of true and false, because it involves an affirmation. This peculiar, but common use of the nominative and of the name gives a number of facilities to the poets when they praise the gods.

In the Vedic stanza quoted above, although the poet obviously enjoys identifying Aditi's attributes with the names *dyauḥ*, *antarikṣa* and so on, he does not "dare" to remove the subject/attribute distinctions and to simply enumerate *dyauḥ*, *antarikṣa* and so on. In fact by praising the Viśvedevāḥ, the poet does not aim at unveiling the gods' essence, but is asking the favour of a 100 years' life[3] for himself and for the *yajamāna*.

Sahasranāmastotra in the Epic period

In the *Anuśāsana-parvan* of the *Mahābhārata*, this "obstacle" is overcome. Hymns using the second person (*tvam* ...) as in the *Vana-parvan*, give place to the *sahasranāmastotra*s of Śiva[4] and Viṣṇu.[5]

---

[2] Deshpande 1991: 468.

[3] ṚV 1.89.2:

devānāṃ bhadrā sumatir ṛjūyatāṃ
devānāṃ rātir abhi no ni vartatām
devānāṃ sakhyam upa sedimā vayaṃ
devā na āyuḥ pra tirantu jīvase.

1.89.8-9:

bhadraṃ karṇebhiḥ śṛṇuyāma devā
bhadram paśyemākṣabhir yajatrāḥ
sthirair aṅgais taṣṭuvāṃsas tanūbhir
vy aśema devahitaṃ yad āyuḥ.
Śatam in nu śarado anti devā
Yatrā naś cakrā jarasaṃ tanūnām
Putrāso yatra pitaro bhavanti
mā no madhyā rīriṣatāyur gantoḥ.

[4] MBh 13.17.

[5] MBh 13.135.

A first list of 10,000 names is given to a *ṛṣi* called Taṇḍi by Śiva; the *ṛṣi* gives it to Upamanyu, and the latter to Kṛṣṇa in an abridged form.[6] He gives only one tenth of the names, viz. 1008 names, this latter number signifying a perfect totality. Despite the "absence" of interpellations or of attributive forms, the whole list is called *stavana*. As a teacher Upamanyu utters it loudly[7] to his listener. Presenting it to Kṛṣṇa, he calls it a meditation, an object of meditation, a knowledge, a *japya*[8] and a secret. This terminology gives a peculiar character to this form of praise: as the other hymns, the *sahasranāmastotra* aims at obtaining a favour for the praising person, but its main function is to provide knowledge under the forms of meditation and *japa*. Manu (2.85) favours the interiorised forms of sacrifice (*japa-yajña*) in comparison with the formal and exterior forms. From this point of view *japa* is neither an exactly mute contemplation of an object, nor its verbalisation, but an intermediate form, an association of a softly articulated word and of meditation. The Śiva *sahasranāmastotra* gives the uttering person a verbal aid to help him meditate upon the god he praises. So language is the tool for a form of meditation, which is not mere thinking without images or words. The list prevents the thought from wandering through the void of meaningless and objectless speculation: every name recalls to the worshipper's attention the necessity of being mindful of his mental and verbal acts. In later literature, beads and diagrams are described as a means of helping to strengthen this mental attitude.[9]

The *sahasranāmastotras* praise Śiva and Viṣṇu, and most of the great gods of the Hindu pantheon. In this sense, they constitute a kind of specific micro-genre which is still alive today. This persis-

---

[6] MBh 13.17-18.

[7] MBh 13.17-23: *nigadiṣye mahābāho stavānām uttamaṃ stavam.*

[8] MBh 13.17-18:
idam dhyānam idaṃ yogam idaṃ dhyeyam anuttamam |
idaṃ japyam idaṃ jñānaṃ rahasyam idam uttamam ||

[9] Dagens & Barazer-Billoret 2000: 87-104.

tence shows that these hymns are not a vestigial witness of an obsolete past; on the contrary, they play an important part in Indian religious life, giving rise to competitions in modern India.[10] Therefore they cannot be the property of Hindus only. Such an old literary genre should have its equivalent form in other Indian religions.

Sahasranāmastotra and Buddhism

Buddhism does not seem to be concerned with our topic. In the Pali canon, there are some *stutis*, such as the *Upālisutta*[11] which contain one hundred epithets applied to the Buddha, all in the genitive case. Later Mātṛceṭa's *Varṇārhavarṇastotra*[12] offers a whole collection of verses in which the poet expresses a personal homage to the Buddha as the addressee of the poem (in the dative). In the same way, the Khotanese *Jātakastava*[13] does not contain any praise which would be worth a comparison with the Hindu *sahasranāmastotra*. This micro-genre appears to be absent, but one must keep in mind that in spite of the iconographic trend to multiply the images of the Buddha (e.g., Halls of a Thousand Buddhas), the Buddhists perhaps never considered such a form of praise. Therefore they are not present in the competition.

THE JAIN TRADITION

On the contrary, the Jains never left the Indian battle-field and fought for their identity using the same weapons as their rivals. So they do not hesitate to give their own versions of Indian lore, rewriting the tales of Kṛṣṇa or Rāma: thus Vimalasūri's *Paumacariya* and Raviṣeṇa's *Padmacarita* are good witnesses to this method which led to a successful occupation of the field by the Jains. It is

---

[10] *The Hindu*, Dec. 12 2002 mentions a competition in Śrī Viṣṇu Sahasranāmam on the 15 and 22 December of the year 2002.

[11] *Majjhima-Nikāya* 1.386.

[12] Hartmann 1987.

[13] Dresden 1955, quoted by Lenz (2003: 95-97).

no matter of surprise to come across a Jain hymn praising the Tīrthaṃkaras in a composition which presents an obvious analogy with the corpus of the MBh, probably the first work to have included such hymns. The *sahasranāmastotra* of Jinasena's *Ādipurāṇa* can be viewed as providing a kind of answer to this challenge.

The *Ādipurāna* by Jinasena.

This Sanskrit poem (9th century) belongs to the Jain literary genre that has been named "Universal History", the first part of which is devoted to the life of the first Tīrthaṃkara, Ṛṣabha. As is well-known, Ṛṣabha is a kind of Prometheus who teaches all the arts to the first men of the cosmic cycle, from techniques to political art. But he is also the first ascetic and the first *siddha*. As such he is the first to conquer *sarvajñāna*, and, on the occasion of the universal meeting of all beings (*samavasaraṇa*), he deserves the first praises of Indra. These are of two kinds. The first kind[14] is personal: Indra as a grammatical subject (nominative case) addresses a long hymn of praise to the new Tīrthaṃkara. He himself defines the nature of *stuti*:

> Praise is the exaltation of merits and qualities; I who praise you, I am pious and clever; you are the matter of praise *par excellence*; the profit to come is the supreme bliss.[15]

According to this program, Indra describes Ṛṣabha's pure beauty at length, emphasising the physical features and particularly his optical and acoustic qualities (25.15-66). After this descriptive celebration, he pays homage (*namas*) to the new hero by giving him names which are known from Hindu mythology: Viṣṇu, Śiva.[16] These names have in fact a symbolic meaning: thus Ṛṣabha being *tri-*

---

[14] Jinasena, *Ādipurāṇa* 25.8-97.

[15] *Ādipurāṇa* 25.11:
stutiḥ puṇya-guṇotkīrtiḥ stotā bhavyaḥ prasannadhīḥ
niṣṭhitārtho bhavān stutyaḥ phalaṃ naiḥśreyasaṃ sukham.

[16] *Ādipurāṇa* 25.67-74.

purāri means he is the destructor of the three enemies (birth, death and old age),[17] but the allusion to Śiva is clear. However, Indra does not forget either the historical individuality to which he pays homage, or the specific Jain titles he deserves:[18] he is not praising an abstraction or an essence, but Ṛṣabha, the son of Nābhi, from the Ikṣvāku tribe.[19] Ṛṣabha is also a Jina and as such one who deserves praises which have their basis in the Jain doctrine: so Ṛṣabha is a *tāyin*,[20] a luminous one, and so on. Indra seems to perfectly understand the difficulties of his undertaking: the matter is peculiar because its subject, the Jina, has infinite qualities, and almost eludes a complete description, which was the main target of the worshipper. So Indra concludes this first hymn in these terms:

> The praise of your qualities is enough; they are infinite; by merely remembering you, we will pay you the proper worship.[21]

The mental recollection looks like a failure of the fulfilment of the original project: instead of the exalted celebration (*utkīrti*) of line 11, Indra contents himself and the worshippers with a much less ambitious expression which reminds of the efficiency of the name, and more precisely, of the proper name of the worshipped being (*tvām*) as a magic weapon, or a *mantra.*

Giving up a full exposition of the qualities in favour of a more economical formula would fit Hindu thought: nobody is able to articulate the essence of the Absolute. At the end of the verbal utterance a kind of silence is bound to begin. But from the Hindu point of view the simple worshipper is not oriented towards

---

[17] *Ādipurāṇa* 25.71.

[18] *Ādipurāṇa* 25.75-95.

[19] *Ādipurāṇa* 25.75.

[20] *Ādipurāṇa* 25.93:
namaḥ paramavijñāna namaḥ paramasaṃyama
namaḥ paramadṛgdṛṣṭaparamārthāya tāyine |

[21] *Ādipurāṇa* 25.98:
alam āstāṃ guṇastotram anantās tāvakā guṇāḥ
tvāṃ nāma smṛtimātreṇa paryupāsiṣāmahe.

omniscience. On the contrary, Jain thought has its basis in the possibility of a perfect (without remain) *omniscience*. In other words, names must express the essence of the Jina, not only names, but *all* the names. In MBh 13.17, Kṛṣṇa learned only one tenth of Śiva's names from Upamanyu. Thus the god kept his own secret or mystery. Just after introducing his restrictive remark, Indra offers a new method of worshipping Ṛṣabha:

> In order to successfully fulfil the desired aim, we have the intention to praise you, the *Lord of speeches*, who are accurately characterised by the well known 1008 names, and we will proceed to praise you with these 1008 names.[22]

The epithet Indra given to the Jina is not without link with the situation. In the *samavasaraṇa* context, Ṛṣabha is proclaiming the true doctrine with accurate words; so he is "Lord of speeches", in actuality and not metaphorically by mere emphasis. This feature can explain the existence of the 1008 names. They are not Indra's verbal creations, but belong to the real personality of Ṛṣabha whose *lakṣaṇa* they are. Therefore, unlike Upamanyu in front of Kṛṣṇa, Indra does not have to explain the origin of this exhaustive list. These names are inherent to Ṛṣabha without the mediation of a tradition. Thus uttering them is addressing the Jina, and praising him, considering the previous definition of the *stuti*. Moreover, listing the names of the Jina is also knowing him absolutely. The list with 1008 names is equivalent to the presentation of the Jina himself. In front of him, in the *samavasaraṇa*, the point is not very important, but in the daily context, it is essential for the monk or lay worshipper, who in this way becomes able to see how really the Jina is.

The first striking feature of the *Ādipurāṇa* list is the evident amount of lexemes it shares with the Śiva list. Thus for instance, by

---

[22] *Ādipurāṇa* 25.99:
prasiddhāṣṭa sahasreddhalakṣaṇaṃ tvāṃ girāṃ patim
nāmnām aṣṭasahasreṇa toṣṭumo 'bhīṣṭa-siddhaye.

comparing the first hundred names of each list, the reader will find that at least 40% of the terms appear in both sets of ten verses. Of course the third name, *Ṛṣabha*, does not imply the same person: in the *Ādipurāṇa* it is a proper name, in the MBh (13.135.2) it is only a descriptive name. This lexical community has a simple reason: the wish to respond to the rival Hindu list without introducing "foreign" technical terms. However the same words cannot have the same meaning: should this be the case, sectarian confusion would not be possible, since everybody would be able to understand precisely the nature of things by merely calling them by their names. But the fact that there are several different points of views, that these later ones find an expression in the same words, here the names, testifies to the contrary. From another point of view, the mere substitution of another lexicon does not provide a good way out: the adoption of a sectarian, more or less *esoteric* language would be a failure. Using the common language, Jinasena and the Jains refuse the easy way out. Language is not univocal, but plurivocal, ambiguous. The *syād-vāda* doctrine allows the understanding of the equivocal use of speech. In a way, Ṛṣabha could be (*syād*) a name fit for Śiva; in another way, it is the adequate name of the Tīrthaṃkara. It is easy to understand that on the very peculiar occasion of the *samavasaraṇa*, Indra, being in front of *Ṛṣabha*, has no problems with the verbal material he uses. But is everybody in any daily circumstance capable of such an understanding? The answer is of course negative.

A second feature follows from the latter conclusion. The Jina *sahasranāmastotra* is in bad need of a commentary. In the absence of a commentary, written or oral, the worshipper is in great danger of falling into a trap: namely heterodoxy, that is a false representation of the Jina or mere mechanical recitation, that is an exercise without any religious value. The second term of the alternative has to be softened: in fact a mere recitation is an act of worship and for instance the utterance or the remembrance of the *Pañcanamaskāra* is a powerful mantra which is able to save somebody in danger.[23] But, in this latter case, the auspicious formula has only an apotropaic value; it is not, according to the definition of a *stuti*, a representation of the Jina's qualities. On the contrary, in the former case, the *stuti* can be a mechanical one. It reaches its full value only if the meaning of the recited names is understood. Thus a commentary is necessary.

Here it is interesting to take note of the following fact: the Jains have strongly felt the necessity of creating a tight link between the names praised in the *stuti* and the explanation of their meaning. So, among the *Prakīrṇakas*, there is a small treatise, the *Vīrastava* "Hymn of praise to Mahāvīra".[24] In this composition, 26 names of *Vīra* are quoted, all of them in the nominative case, most of them later incorporated into the verses of the *sahasranāmastotra*:

> *aruha* (1), *arihanta* (2), *arahanta* (3), *deva* (4), *jiṇa* (5), *vīra* (6), *parama-kāruṇiya* (7) *savvaṇṇu* (8), *savvadarisī* (9), *pāraya* (10), *tikkālaviu* (11), *nāha* (12), *jaya vīyarāya* (13), *kevali* (14), *tihuyaṇaguru* (15), *savva* (16), *tihuyaṇavariṭṭha* (17), *bhayavaṃ* (18), *titthayara* (19) *tti ya sakkehiṃ-namaṃsiya* (20), *jiṇinda* (21), *sirivaddhamāṇa* (22), *hari* (23), *hara* (24), *kamalāsaṇa* (25), *pamuha* (?*buddha*)(26)....[25]

Immediately after this list come 37 verses which give one or several meanings to every name with the help of explicit clauses which are often based on etymologies. Thus this small composition is a good testimony to a *relatively* ancient feeling concerning the necessity of a link between the names and their exegetical meanings. By themselves, the names do have a power of evocation, but this power looks weak and is perhaps blind without the commentary which gives them their full meaning in a discursive form.

Today, Pannalal Jain, the translator of the *Ādipurāṇa* into Hindi, has fully understood this necessity for binding together names and explicative meanings. For every name of the Jina he gives in his

[23] Roth 1974: 5.

[24] *Paiṇṇayasuttāiṃ*, pp. 292-297.

[25] *Paiṇṇayasuttāiṃ*, p. 292.

translation the motivation for the designation so that the Hindi reader is able to see the name together with its orthodox interpretation.

This need for an interpretation is not a specific feature of the Jain *sahasranāmastotra*. The same need is felt in the same way in the Hindu context. For instance Śaṅkara has written a *bhāṣya* on the *Viṣṇusahasranāmastotra*. Thus a *stotra* with 1008 names and its interpretation are tightly bound together and have to be understood as the two complementary parts of a whole.

Āśādhara's *Jinasahasranāma*[26]

The *stuti* written by Āśādhara accompanied by the same author's commentary forms a case in point.

The circumstances of the recitation

In his *Anagāradharmāmṛta*, Āśādhara (12th century) clearly connects the genre of *sahasranāmastotra* and Jinasena's hymn. According to him, the names which build the matter of a *sahasranāmastotra* can be found in the *Ādipurāṇa* of which he quotes the first and the last verses in his commentary of 8.39.[27] But he does not follow Jinasena's method. Instead of embedding his own *sahasranāmastotra* into the dramaturgy of Ṛṣabha's *samavasaraṇa*, he rather follows Hemacandra's pattern (12th century). In the section of his *Triṣaṣṭiśalākāpuruṣacarita* devoted to Ṛṣabha, the *Śvetāmbara* monk describes Indra praising the Jina with *stuti*s on the occasion of his *samavasaraṇa*, but none of them takes the form of a *sahasranāmastotra*; the situation is the same for the 23 other Tīrthaṃkaras. However, Hemacandra composed an independent *sahasranāmastotra*.[28] The second verse gives indications about its

---

[26] In Jain 1954.

[27] *Tāni* [i.e. the names] *cārṣe pañcaviṃśatitame parvaṇi* [verses 100 and 217 of the *Ādipurāṇa* 25 are then quoted] *ity etena prabandhenoktāni pratipattavyāni*.

[28] Text in Jain 1954: 53-56.

recitation: just after getting up, the worshipper has to utter it every morning.[29] Without being a Canonical *āvaśyaka*, this *stuti* seems to belong, for the *Śvetāmbara* monk, to the *dinacaryā*. R. Williams (1963: 183) has underlined how much Āśādhara owes to Hemacandra when he puts emphasis on the *dinacaryā* in his *Sāgāradharmāmṛta*. Going to the temple is in fact going to a kind of daily *samavasaraṇa*, and, being in the temple, the worshipper has to represent the Jina before him. In this context the *stuti* with 1008 names could be a particularly appropriate device.

Some features of Āśādhara's hymn

Jinasena, Hemacandra and Āśādhara have composed three hymns with 1008 names. In spite of a similarity of inspiration (allowing the worshipper a means of purification), in spite of similarities in the formation of names (for instance *composita* beginning by *viśva°*, *jina°*, *mahā°* and so on), in spite even of a common vocabulary, they have their individual features and are good witnesses to the plasticity of this literary micro-genre. Of course this flexibility has nothing to do with the continuous invention which has been observed, for instance, by Whitney M. Kelting in her survey of the Jain *stavan*.[30] The micro-genre of the *sahasranāmastotra* has its obvious constraints: 1008 names, nominal clauses, sequences grounded on a phonic and semantic identity (concatenation), ideological, that is to say orthodox requirements, including last but not least a polemical goal. Nevertheless, the three authors have been able to compose original works which are far from repeating each other.

This is the case with Āśādhara's hymn which has an additional interest: it is accompanied by a commentary from the author himself.

---

[29] *Ata eva pratiprātaḥ samutthāya manīṣibhiḥ bhaktyāṣṭāgrasahasrārhannāmoccāro vidhīyate.*

[30] Kelting 2001.

1. ACQUAINTANCE WITH A SPECIFIC JAIN MYTHOLOGY

The Hindu *sahasranāmastotra*s include a lot of mythological features which the requirements of the genre reduce to a mere name or a nominal compound. Thus *bhasmaśayin,*[31] *umāpati*[32] are clear allusions to Śiva even if these names coexist with other less characteristic ones. It seems impossible in fact to separate the *stuti* from a set of legends and myths. This impossibility appears to be a universal principle ruling every kind of *stuti*.

> The Jains are acquainted with it, but they refer to their own mythology from which they extract specific legends and myths. Āśādhara gives the Jina several titles which come from the Jain lore and which are explained by the commentary.

Thus the Jina is *pañcakalyāṇa-pūjitaḥ* (verse 33). This name has a meaning only in the Jain context. *Kalyāṇa* refers to conception, birth, renunciation, enlightenment and final death.[33] But it applies to all the Jinas. Other titles allow a "historical" specification of the praised Jina, who is the first one, Ṛṣabha. He is *padmabhūḥ* (verse 35), a name which reminds of the epithet *padma-garbha* said of both Śiva and Viṣṇu,[34] but, in spite of this wink, this name alludes to legends of Ṛṣabha's birth narrated by the commentary: it means either that his mother's courtyard was adorned with lotuses, or that in his mother's womb there was a lotus created by his powers, upon which the wonderful child was sitting awaiting his birth.[35] In verse 36 the name *śacī-sṛṣṭa-praticchanda* refers to a replica (*pratikāya*) whom Indrāṇī creates and lays down on the side

[31] MBh 13.17.92.

[32] MBh 13.17.134.

[33] Jain 1954: 71: *pañcasu kalyāneṣu garbhāvatāra-janmābhiṣeka-niḥkramaṇa-jñāna-nirvāṇeṣu pūjitaḥ.*

[34] Respectively, MBh 13.17.103 and 13.135.51.

[35] Jain 1954: 71-72: *padmair upalakṣitā bhūr mātur aṅgaṇaṃ yasyeti. Athavā mātur udare svāmino divya-śaktyā kamalaṃ bhavati, tat-karṇikāyāṃ siṃhāsanaṃ bhavati tasmin siṃhāsane sthito garbharūpo bhagavān vṛddhiṃ yāti iti kāraṇāt padmabhūr bhagavān bhaṇyate.*

of the sleeping Marudevī in order to proceed to the bath of the real baby.[36]

These features concern particular legends of Ṛṣabha's birth. Others come both from the *samavasaraṇa* lore and from the Jain doctrine and they are mingled together. Thus from this latter point of view the Jina is *satya-vākyādhipa* (verse 49), "lord of those whose voice is true, i.e. the *Digambara* ascetics" an explanation which involves a sectarian doctrinal reference.[37] In the same way, the Jina is said *syād-vādin* (vs. 50), *sapta-bhaṅgi-vāc* (vs. 52), *apauruṣeyya-vāc* (vs. 52), the latter term being a loan from the Brahmanic lexicon particularly fit for characterising the eternity of the Veda. Ṛṣabha's voice also has many wonderful mythological aspects: it is *divya* (vs. 50), viz. "not human" (*amānuṣī*, comm.), *avyāhatārtha-vāc* (vs. 50), "without contradictions", *ardhamāga-dhi-yokti* (vs. 50), "speaking Ardhamagadhi":[38] half of the Jina's discourses are addressed to the people of Magadha, half to everyone, according to the commentary;[39] it is immaterial, since the lips do not move during utterance, *acaloṣṭha-vāc* (vs. 52). Last but not least, the voice is *a-varṇa-gīḥ* (vs. 53), literally "without articulated phonems".

Like Śiva or Viṣṇu, in their respective *sahasranāmastotra*s, Ṛṣabha receives the names which are given to a god. Is he really a god? From the point of view of the doctrine, he is not. Gods, and even Śakra, their lord, belong to a special destiny lower than the human one: a god cannot become *siddha* without going through human condition. Therefore a Jina is not a god. However, as a *sahasranāmastotra*'s addressee, he deserves the names which are

---

[36] Jain 1954: 72: *śacyā indraṇyā sṛṣṭo vikriyayā kṛtaḥ praticchandaḥ pratikāyo māyāmayabālako yasya sa tathoktaḥ.*

[37] Jain 1954: 78.

[38] The same voice is also *sarva-bhāṣā-maya-gīḥ* (verse 53), then speaking the languages of all countries, for made of these languages: *sarveṣāṃ bhāṣāmayī gīḥ* (Jain 1954: 81).

[39] Jain 1954: 79: *bhagavad-bhāṣāyā ardhaṃ magadha-deśa-bhāṣātmakaṃ ardhaṃ ca sarva-bhāṣātmakam.*

allotted to the gods in the homologous Hindu *stutis*. So Ṛṣabha is not only *īśvaraḥ*, but also *adhīśvaraḥ* (vs. 61). According to Āśādhara, this additional title means that he is *also* the lord of Indra and of the other gods.[40] The name *adhīśaḥ* (vs. 61, and comm..) points to the Jina's power over Hara, Hari, Hiraṇyagarbha and the rest of the gods. In Hinduism, worship of a divinity implies sacrifice, thus *hiṃsā par excellence*: being superior to the other gods, Ṛṣabha deserves such worship, free from *hiṃsā*. He is *yajñārha* (vs. 31), but *yajña* here means the *pūjā* accomplished by the gods who acknowledge his superiority. He is even *yajñāṅga*, part or expedient of the sacrifice, because, Āśādhara says, "without him there would be no *jīva* deserving *pūjā*".[41]

Behind most of these attributes lay Jain lore known by singers and listeners as much as concepts from the doctrine. Some of these epithets seem to have a meaning only within the Jain legends. While losing a great deal of meaning, they can or could nonetheless be understood without these references, while some others refer clearly to Hindu mythology. This remark applies especially to Āśādhara who shows a clear interest in what can be called *conscious assimilation* of heterodox names and concepts.

2. ASSIMILATION

According to R. Williams, "the Jain *pūjā* is manifestly one of Jainism's earliest conscious imitations of the Hindu world around".[42] Imitation supposes a difference between the original and its copies, as accurate as it can be. On the contrary assimilation implies a complete erasure of the differences: the other has become the same.

The first case is very simple and concerns only the Jain mythological field. Many of the names which have been already men-

---

[40] Jain 1954: 85: *adhika īśvaraḥ indrādīnām api prabhuḥ*. Other optional explanation with a pun on *a-dhi*: his power applies equally to unintelligent cattle.

[41] Jain 1954: 75: *yajñasya aṅgam abhyupāyaḥ, svāminaṃ vinā pūjyo jīvo na bhavatīti*. The neuter instead of the expected masculine is justified as an *āvīṣṭāliṅga* case.

[42] Williams 1963: 216.

tioned belong only to Ṛṣabha and give to Āśādhara's *stuti* a peculiar hue. But what about a new list such as verses 88-90 where one finds the *proper* names of the 24 Tīrthaṃkaras?[43] Āśādhara's commentary does not give an explanation for this uncommon attribution. The proper names are understood as common ones: so Ṛṣabha is such because he shines with the *dharma* which is characterised by virtuous *ahiṃsā*; Ajita is such because enemies such as desire and anger have never defeated him;[44] Vardhamāna owes his name to his *growing* knowledge and disgust for the world.[45] So these names can legitimately be attributed to Ṛṣabha whose qualifications they are. But, at the same time, they keep their meaning as proper names, and in this latter case they signify that the addressee of the hymn is all the Jinas, something like a timeless essence of the Jina which shines beyond these individual proper names. This interpretation is only a possibility, but it agrees with the following cases of assimilation, which rest on such a *witty* double meaning.

Verses 110-123 give the Jina the names of the main Indian *darśanas* and sometimes of their founders. Thus the Jina is *buddhaḥ* and *śākyaḥ* (vs. 110), *yogaḥ*, *vaiśeṣikaḥ*, *naiyāyikaḥ* and *sāṃkhyaḥ* (vs. 114), *kapilaḥ* (vs. 116), *mīmāṃsakaḥ* (vs. 121), *cārvakaḥ* (vs. 122), *saṃvid-advayin* (vs. 123). This almost exhaustive enumeration is not very startling: the Jains' analytic mind is well known and in the Śvetāmbara canon one can find many texts where Mahāvīra himself reflects upon all the philosophical schools and confronts their doctrines from a position of the true orthodoxy. In this latter case, of course, he neither *is* these heterodox theses, nor does

---

43 *Vṛṣabhas tadvat Ajitaḥ Saṃbhavaś cābhinandanaḥ*
munibhiḥ Sumatiḥ Padmaprabhaḥ proktaḥ Supārśvakaḥ
Candraprabhaḥ Puṣpadantaḥ Śitalaḥ Śreya-āhvayaḥ
Vāsupūjyaś ca Vimalo 'nantajid dharma ity api (89)
Śāntiḥ Kunthur Aro Malliḥ Suvrato Namir apy ataḥ
Nemiḥ Pārśvo Vardhamāno Mahāvīraḥ suvīrakaḥ (90).

44 Jain 1954: 99: *vṛṣeṇāhīṃsālakṣaṇopalakṣitena dharmeṇa bhāti, śobhate; na kenāpi kāmakrodhādinā śatruṇā jitaḥ ajitaḥ.*

45 Jain 1954: 102: *vardhate jñānena vairāgyena ca lakṣmyā dvividhayā vardhamānaḥ.*

he even share them, but being omniscient, he *knows* them. In Āśādhara's list, on the contrary, he *is* these heterodox views!

According to Āśādhara's commentary, "Buddha" means possessor of omniscience;[46] *śākyaḥ* means a man who has power (*śakaḥ*) and is the father of a Tīrthaṃkara who is called *śākyaḥ*[47] by a mere secondary initial *vṛddhi*. So Ṛṣabha is together the historical founder of Buddhism and the son of a powerful man, not a member of the *Śākya-gotra*, in spite of an obvious pun. The glosses of the names *sāṃkhyaḥ* and *kapilaḥ* go in the same direction and the pun is more evident: the former term receives a common definition and alludes to the capacity of calculating; by breaking the latter into its supposed elements (*kapi* + *lāti*),[48] being *kapila* reminds of the old Indian image of the mind (*mano markaṭaḥ*) unable to concentrate on a project or an object, like the monkey who springs without a cause from one branch to another, and also the idea of taming this animal's instability. But, simultaneously, the vicinity of *sāṃkhyaḥ* and *kapilaḥ* which are separated only by one name imposes the reference to the well known *darśana*, and this all the more since Kapila, being the first disciple of the heretic Marīcī, is a well known figure[49] in the Jain Universal History. Thus, Ṛṣabha is together the historical figure and the subject of the qualities Āśādhara's gloss gives him.

Assimilation, but also double meaning and use of puns, allows the integration of all the forms of thought into what can be called a kind of philosophic *encyclopaedia*. The list of 100 names (vss.110-123) is neither chaotic nor arbitrary as it could seem. Arbitrary are for instance alphabetic lists produced by no internal principle but mere juxtaposition. This is not the case here, because between

---

[46] Jain 1954: 119: *buddhiḥ kevala-jñāna-lakṣaṇā vidyate yasya.*

[47] Jain 1954: 119: *svamate śaknoti śakaḥ tīrthakṛt-pitā, śakasyāpatyaṃ pumān.*

[48] Jain 1954: 123: *kapir iva kapiḥ mano-markaṭaḥ, kapiṃ lāti viṣaya-kaṣāyeṣu gacchantaṃ lāti ātmani sthāpayati niścalīkaroti yo bhagavān tīrthakara-parama-devaḥ sa kapila ucyate.*

[49] Balbir 1993: 134.

these 100 names there is a powerful link which explains all these attributions, namely omniscience. Being *kevalajñānin*, the Tīrthaṃkara is the legitimate subject of all these names. If he was not constituted by the different erroneous thoughts, he would suffer this absence as an insufficiency in his own knowledge: so he would be inferior to his own attainment, which would be an internal contradiction! This is not the case, and in his mind knowledge forms a circle without any break: this is strictly speaking the definition of an encyclopaedia. In spite of a certain doxographic appearance, the "philosophical" section particularly underlines this aspect, which is equally present in the other sections of the *stotra* with 1008 names.

3. OPENNESS AND RELEVANCY

Most religions are based on the admission of a real discrepancy between the verbal expression of their principle (God, Absolute, and so on) and this principle itself. In Judaism the "explicit" Name (*shem ha-mephorash*) or Tetragrammaton is unfathomable, and the attributes of God are only a few (the 13 *middoth*); moreover, praising by increasing the number of the known names is explicitly forbidden.[50] This reticence about engaging in praise has its basis in the idea that God cannot be totally known. Islam admits 99 names of God without emphasising the possibility of a total knowledge of Allah by mere use of his names.[51] The Śiva's *sahasranāmastotra* of the MBh is given explicitly as a fraction, that is to say, one tenth of the real names of the god. The worshipper cannot uncover the whole essence of the god by a mere recitation of his names, a restriction which does not forbid envisioning the god by other means. All these attitudes rest on the awareness that language is not an adequate means of achieving the total penetration of the absolute. Thus these religious systems permit, with or without any reluctance, going beyond the bounds of explicit language and thought.

[50] *Talmud Bavli, Berakhoth* 33 b.

[51] Gimaret 1988. This book (p. 10) excludes the Sufi perspectives.

The Jain *sahasranāmastotras* follow another way: they think that the names given by the worshippers in these special hymns and in others can be appropriate to their supposed purpose because of their *relevancy*.

This concept can be understood by a reference to Śabara. For the *mīmāṃsaka*, in the case of an unperceived or an un-perceptible individual (for instance a god) who requires the use of a *proper* name, the equivalence between this and the named being is not the product of an artificial human denomination (*saṃjñā-kāraṇa*), but is eternal and without any human creator (*apauruṣeya*): as Śabara puts it, "the link between word and its object is not-human".[52] On the contrary, the Jains think that every form of knowledge proceeds from perception. On account of this principle, names stem from an empirical basis.[53] Links (*saṃbandha*) between names and beings can be either right or wrong: this is the human problem of heterodoxy and orthodoxy. Āśādhara gives to the Brahmanical *apauruṣeya* a new orthodox meaning in his gloss on the name *apauruṣeya-vāk-śāstā*: according to him, this name means that Ṛṣabha is teaching with magisterial authority the words of beings such as non humans, etc. (gods included) so that he alone is able to vouch for their truth.[54] By lack of such a warranty, many proper names have been applied wrongly to gods, animals and humans in Brahmanical mythology: this fact does not endanger the possible equivalence between names and things, but merely undermines the heterodox point of view. So the names are relevant when they are *produced* or *created* by agents who have the right view. These agents can be

---

[52] Śabara, *Śābarabhāṣya*, 1.1.5, quoted by M. Biardeau 1964: 166: *anupalabdhe ca devatādāv arthe 'narthakaṃ saṃjñā-kāraṇam aśakyaṃ ca | viśeṣān pratipattuṃ hi saṃjñāḥ kriyante viśeṣāṃś coddiśya | tad viśeṣeṣv ajñāyamāneṣu bhayam apy anavakḷptam | tasmād apauruṣeyaḥ śabdasyārthena saṃbandhaḥ.*

[53] The *nigodas* cannot be perceived, but they are derived by empirical inference from the necessity of avoiding an empty world.

[54] Verse 52, Jain 1954: 80: *apauruṣeyīṇām anādi-bhūtānāṃ vācāṃ śāstā guruḥ, athavā apauruṣeyīṇāṃ divyānāṃ vācāṃ śāstā.*

divine like Śakra, the main author of hymns to the Jinas in the Universal History; they can be human also, like Hemacandra or Āśādhara with their *stuti*s comprising 1008 names, or like the many anonymous ancient and modern creators of hymns (see Kelting 2001). The names they use are not relevant by themselves or on account of a putative eternal connection between words and things. Their relevancy has its basis in orthodoxy.

Thus, when correctly used, names are capable of signifying the essence of the Jina, imparting to it a total openness without any hidden remainder. There is nothing remarkable in this. The key here is the *ātman*. Between the Jinas, the *siddha*s and men, there is no difference of nature but only of degree in the scale of their spiritual development: the former enjoy their own *ātman* in its stainless purity, while on account of karmic stains the latter do not know their own *ātman*. However, between them a common language can be found. Even a flawed human being can understand the names of the *stuti*, because these names are attributes of an *ātman* like his own, without any change of essence. In this sense, *stuti*s composed of names allow the worshipper to know himself as he has to be, as an *ātman*, not as a mixture of *ātman* and body.

Finally this openness and relevancy of *sahasranāmastotra* discourse leads to an original view of this micro-genre. Aiming at purification, being inspired by devotion (*bhakti*), these *stuti*s look like a special kind of prayer: *special* because they do not use the personal form "You are…", the dative of the addressee and so on, but have an exclusive recourse to nominal clause. In view of these special features, the status of *apophasis* can be claimed for these *sahasranāmastotra*s. Aristotle distinguishes between clauses which use imperative or optative and apophasis, which uses only indicative.[55] Truth is not implied in the former, but is wholly involved in the latter: an apophasis is either true or false, an order or a praise can succeed or not, but without any relation with truth. Using 1008

[55] *De Interpretatione* 17 a 1-4.

nominal clauses, Jain *sahasranāmastotra*s build a kind of true, almost not-discursive (only a name, which builds a clause!) discourse on the essence of the Jina which they develop openly via the names. From this point of view, in spite of the repetitive appearance which is given by singing and music, these lists are not to be considered as mere litanies. In a litany, a conventional image is connected to a transcendent object; in the *stuti*s with 1008 names, there are no conventional images, but concepts which are at the same time subject and attribute by the virtue of the nominal clause, and, as such, do express the absolute character of the Jina.

4. Poetry and Restrained Emotion

Most Indian hymns are composed and recited in a rapture of emotion, with bhakti being the special concept which expresses the particular link between the worshipped and the worshipper. Bhakti generates the process of composition and recitation. Without it, the poem, whatever it might be, would be a fruitless and tedious litany.

The Jain poets understand *bhakti* as prompting religious inspiration. So, for instance, at the beginning of the *Bhaktāmarastotra* Mānatuṅga explains the importance of *bhakti* in the composition of the poem. Is it, he says, not quite contradictory and shameless, being without intelligence, to undertake praise of a being worshipped by the wise? A child only wishes to catch the reflexion of the moon in water.[56] However, Mānatuṅga takes up the challenge: induced by *bhakti*, he will undertake praise, being as unaware of his weakness as an antelope rushing against a lion to protect her fawns.[57] *Bhakti* simply impels him to become as talkative as the

---

[56] Kapadia 1932: 10, vs. 3:
buddhyā vināpi vibudhārcita-pādapīṭha
stotuṃ samudyata-matir vigata-trapo 'ham,
bālaṃ vihāya jala-saṃsthitam indu-bimbam
anyaḥ ka icchati janaḥ sahasā grahitum?

[57] Kapadia 1932: 15, vs. 5:
so 'haṃ tathāpi tava bhakti-vaśān munīśa
kartuṃ stavaṃ vigata-śaktir api pravṛttaḥ.

Indian cuckoo in spring.[58] These verses seem to rest on a mere rhetorical basis: *captatio benevolentiae* is their aim. But this interpretation overlooks the meaning of *bhakti*. This feeling involves a shared link between the addressee and the worshipper: the latter does not want only a result (here not financial reward) but the purification of his own mind; towards the former, he feels a kind of impulse which urges him to laud the object of his religious emotion. The first spring when the poem springs is not a thought, but an amorous feeling which legitimises the use of poetic similes.

All our *stuti*s with 1008 names are recited out of *bhakti*. Like Hemacandra[59] at the beginning of his hymn, Āśādhara addresses the Jina personally in verse 4 of the prologue of his hymn[60] and qualifies his main feeling by *bhakti*, a word he glosses twice by *anurāga*.[61] In *anurāga* there is indeed some *rāga*, a passion which stains the *ātman*. It is of course possible to explain this term by assimilation to the homologous Hindu feeling, but this explanation is extraneous. In fact, the Jain poet speaks about the feeling which ought to inspire the utterance of the names or, as it is explained, the dharma. The object of attachment changes the nature of the link: in the Hindu context an addressee who is addressed as *Thou*, a pronoun which emphasises the personal relationship, in the Jain context 1008 names which are by themselves quite independent of any utterance. The latter cannot awaken love, but rather a kind of vigi-

---

prītyātmavīryam avicārya mṛgo mṛgendraṃ
nābhyeti kiṃ nija-śiśoḥ paripālanārtham?

[58] Kapadia 1932: 17, vs. 6:
alpaśrutaṃ śrutavatāṃ parihāsa-dhāma
tvad-bhaktir eva mukharī-kurute balān mām
yat kokilaḥ kila madhau madhuraṃ virauti
tac-cāru-cūta-kalikā-nikaraikahetuḥ.

[59] Verse 2, quoted above in footnote 29.

[60] *Bhaktyā protsāryamāṇo 'pi dūraṃ śaktyā tiraskṛtaḥ*
tvāṃ nāmāṣṭasahasreṇa stutvātmānaṃ punāmy aham.

[61] Jain 1954: 57: *bhaktyā, ātmānurāgeṇa.* Verse 140 of the conclusion: *idam aṣṭottaraṃ nāmnāṃ sahasraṃ bhaktito 'rhatām ...* In the commentary (p. 139) *bhaktitaḥ* is explained as *parama-dharmānurāgeṇa.*

lance or attention in which understanding plays the main part. Understanding is not personal, egoistic: were it the case, it would be only opinion, not science. But understanding too has its own affective requirements: it needs taming of the passions and diverting them from their egoistic aims to the apprehension of the truth. So by this diversion or sublimation the *bhakta* becomes *attached* to the truth.

There is room for poetic feeling. The *stuti* with 1008 names is not only a didactic poem as, for instance, is the case with Samantabhadra's *Āptamīmāṃsā*. In spite of one personal verse,[62] this latter poem is rather a demonstration of the necessity of *kevalajñāna* and *kevalajñānin* by discursive proofs and reasoning. It never calls upon feeling, even in verse 6 which appears as a kind of conclusion, rather than an invocation or even a statement of praise: you the Jina are the one who fulfils the conditions of the problem, i.e. the possibility of knowing what is really true (verses 1-5). In the first two verses, Samantabhadra erases all the mythological elements which could nurture poetical inspiration, and aesthetic feeling: so *devāgama*, *nabhoyāna*, *cāmara*, and even possession of a divine body (*vigraha*).[63] Since his *kevalajñānin* has no personal story, not even a body, he can disappear from the demonstration of truth (verses 7-114), to become at last (verse 115) the victorious *yatipati* who has destroyed the *ekāntavādin* points of view. No room here for poetry, except in some very conventional similes of verse 115.

On the contrary, the *stuti* with 1008 names does not totally eradicate the poetical images: such is the case with Jain mythology. And even using expressions which he borrows from the Brahmanical lexicon, Āśādhara finds in them a subject matter on which he can lean to lead the feeling of the reader in the right direction. For instance, the Jina is *sarvagata* (verse 118), "pervasive": the image

---

[62] Ed. Nagin J. Shah, p. 5, vs. 6: *sa tvam evāsi nirdoṣo yukti-śāstrāvirodhi-vāk* । *avirodho yad iṣṭaṃ te prasiddhena na bādhyate.*

[63] Jaini 1979: 83-84.

directs the mind to the presence of God, particularly Viṣṇu, in everything, and poetic memory swarms with other images which distract the attention from the god to his "lodgings", like waters, ocean and so on. According to Āśādhara, pervasiveness means only immediate and universal intelligence of everything, that is omniscience.[64] Imagination cannot follow its own direction and fall into representations stained by passions, it must be held back for the benefit of simple knowledge and understanding which are closely akin to omniscience. The feelings which accompany imagination are compelled to proceed in the same direction: not to stains of passions, but to purity of knowledge. Could *bhakti* be proper to this variety of hymns – an attachment to the essence of the Jina in which, without being eradicated, emotions are diverted and curbed under the power of intelligence?

* * *

To sum up: A peculiarity of linguistic expression (the nominal clause in Sanskrit) and a philosophical feature (the reality of omniscience) give to a common form of praise a quite uncommon status: in the Jain *stuti*s with 1008 names, praise gives way to a total unveiling of the praised one, independent of any worldly interest, which could without any difficulty be assimilated to a mere act of contemplation, which is perfectly satisfactory, because it brings in itself its own satisfaction, that is to say, the discovery of the pure *ātman* by itself.

[64] Jain 1954: 125: *sarvaṃ paripūrṇaṃ gataṃ kevalajñānaṃ yasya, athavā jñānāpekṣayā, na tu pradeśāpekṣayā, sarvasminn loke 'loke ca gataḥ prāptaḥ.*

REFERENCES

Aristotle, *De Interpretatione*. Ed. by L. Minio-Paluello. Oxford: Oxford University Press.

Āśādhara, *Dharmāmṛta (Anagāra)*. Ed. with a Jñānadīpikā and Hindi translation by Pt. Kailash Chandra Shastri. 2nd edition, (Jnanapitha Murtidevi Jain Granthamala: Sanskrit Grantha, 46.) Delhi: Bharatiya Jnanpith, 1996.

Āśādhara, *Svopajña vivṛti yuta Jinasahasranāma*. With Hindi Translation and Introduction. With the commentary of Sruta Sagar Suri. Transl. & ed. by Pandit Hiralal Jain. (Jnanapitha Murtidevi Jain Granthamala, Sanskrit Grantha, 11.) Kashi: Bharatiya Jnanapitha, 1954.

BALBIR, Nalini 1993. *Āvaśyaka-Studien*, I: *Introduction générale et traductions*. (Alt- und Neu-Indische Studien, 45.1.) Stuttgart: Franz Steiner Verlag.

BIARDEAU, M. 1964. *Théorie de la connaissance et philosophie de la parole dans le brahmanisme classique*. Paris: Mouton.

DAGENS, B. & M.-L. BARAZER-BILLORET (ed. & transl.) 2000. *Le Rauravāgama, un traité de rituel et de doctrines śivaïtes*. Pondichéry: Institut français.

DESHPANDE, M. M. 1991. Prototypes in Pāṇinian syntax. *Journal of the American Oriental Society* 111.3: 465-480.

DRESDEN, M. J. 1955. *The Jātakastava or Praise of the Buddha's Former Lives*. (Transactions of the American Philosophical Society Held at Philadelphia for Promoting Useful Knowledge, 45.) Philadelphia: The American Philosophical Society.

GIMARET, D. 1988. *Les noms divins en islam. Exégèse lexicologique et théologique*. (Collection Patrimoines.) Paris: Cerf.

HARTMANN, J.-U. (ed. & transl.) 1987. *Das Varṇārhavarṇastotra des Mātṛceṭas*. (Sanskrittexte aus den Turfanfunden, 12; Abhandlungen der Akademie der Wissenschaften in Göttingen, 160.) Göttingen: Vandenhoeck & Ruprecht.

Hemacandra, *Triṣaṣṭiśalākāpuruṣacaritra*, I-VI. Transl. by Helen M. Johnson. Baroda: Oriental Institute, 1931-62.

Jain 1954: See Āśādhara.

JAINI, P. S. 1979. *The Jaina Path of Purification*. Delhi: Motilal Banarsidass.

Jinasena, *Ādipurāṇa*. Ed. by Pannalal Jain. (Jnanapitha Murtidevi Jain Granthamala: Sanskrit Grantha, 8.) Kashi: Bharatiya Jnanapitha, 1965.

KAPADIA, Hiralal Rasikdas (ed.) 1932. Mānātuṅga, *Bhaktāmara, Kalyāṇāmandira and Namiuṇa Stotra*. (Devchand Lalbhai Jain Pustakoddhar Fund Series, 79). Surat: Devchand Lālbhai Jain Fund, 1932.

KELTING, W. M. 2001. *Singing to the Jinas, Jain Laywomen Maṇḍal Singing and the Negotiations of Jain Devotion*. Oxford: Oxford University Press.

LENZ, T. 2003. *A New Version of the Gāndhārī Dharmapada and a Collection of Previous-Birth Stories*. (Gandhāran Buddhist Texts, 3.) Seattle: University of Washington.

Paiṇṇayasuttāiṃ. Ed. by Muni Punyavijaya & A. M. Bhojak. (Jaina Āgama Series, 17.1.) Bombay: Mahāvīra Jaina Vidyālaya, 1984.

ROTH, G., 1974. Notes on the Pañca-namokkāra-parama-maṅgala in Jain literature. *Brahmavidyā: The Adyar Library Bulletin Mahavira Jayanti Volume* 38: 1-18.

Samantabhadra, *Āptamīmāṃsā*. Ed. by Nagin J. Shah. Ahmedabad: Sanskrit-Sanskriti-Granthamala, 1999.

WILLIAMS, R. 1963. *Jaina Yoga*. London: Oxford University Press. [Reprint: Delhi: Motilal Banarsidass, 1983.]

Autobiographies of Jain Monks and Nuns in the 20th Century: A Preliminary Essay

NALINI BALBIR

Modern religious or spiritual autobiography in India is a type of autobiographical writing which has not yet received the attention it deserves. Yet autobiography of this nature is relevant in that it uncovers "lives that would otherwise remain marginal" (Arnold & Blackburn 2004: 14) because they represent "social segments whose voices are generally unheard" (ibid., p. 6), just like those of women and Dalits, to take only two instances of groups whose voices are being increasingly heard (examples in Arnold & Blackburn), thanks in part to the incentives of sociologists and anthropologists from India and the West. But religious autobiography (i.e. autobiographies of religious teachers) has started to arouse interest of late.[1]

The most famous instance in the sphere of Hinduism, *The Autobiography of a Yogi* by Paramahaṃsa Yogānanda, first published in

---

[1] This is not the place to enter into a general discussion of religious autobiography in India in the pre-modern period. Some poems of the *Thera-* and *Therī-gāthā*s can be read as spiritual autobiographic statements. The same holds true for sayings of the medieval Sants. But in style and contexts these texts are obviously very different from what I intend to deal with here. If autobiography is understood only in the narrow sense of writing about one's self in the first person, some parts of the *vijñaptipatra*s, which are made of fragmentary letters addressed by a Jain mendicant to his teacher who is residing in a distant place, also have to be mentioned. On the other hand, I am not certain whether the term "biography" (used by Jain 1999: 43) is proper when referring to *gurvāvalī*s and *paṭṭāvalī*s.

1946 and reprinted many times, is now available online free of charge,[2] and stands among the recommended readings for a course organized in an American University on "Writing Faith: Religious Biography and Autobiography".[3] The *Autobiography of an Indian Monk* by Shri Purohit Swami lesser known was first published in 1932 and reprinted in India in 1992. Very recently, Monika Horstmann, who is developing a project on this topic at Heidelberg University, published a spiritual autobiography originally written in Marwari by a lady saint named Banāsā.

Paramahaṃsa Yogānanda became a famous figure who in a sense introduced Hindu Yoga to America. He was supported by a wide infrastructure so that his autobiography became a bestseller and a classic. Purohit Swami was also in close contact with the West; he stayed at Oxford in the 1930s and was urged to write his "experiences" by the Irish poet W. B. Yeats (see below). Banāsā's impact, on the contrary, did not go further than her native region of Shekhavati.

Among (non Tibetan) recently published Buddhist autobiographies, *Journey of Mindfulness, The Autobiography of Bhante G.* (2003), by a Theravādin monk from Sri Lanka, Bhante Henepola Gunaratana, who was born in 1927 and settled in the United States in 1968, is also an interesting representative of the genre, because of the personality of its author, his eventful life, and the compelling style of the narrative from which emerges a complex individual increasingly striving for knowledge and learning, intensely involved in the world, and a pioneer in his own field.[4] These works will be

---

[2] http://www.crystalclarity.com/yogananda/index.html or http://www.gutenberg.org/etext/7452, etc.

[3] Prof. Douglas E. Cowen, The University of Missouri-Kansas City, Fall Semester 2003.

[4] For other life stories of Buddhist monks in South East Asia see some of the contributions in Schober 1997 and, even more, Tiyavanich 1997, which is a vibrant plaidoyer in favour of drawing on the rich resources of the numerous life stories of Thai forest monks, some of them autobiographical (see especially pp. 11-15).

used to various extents for the sake of comparison in the following pages.

To my knowledge, religious autobiographies from the Jain milieu have not yet attracted any attention beyond Jain circles. This essay is a preliminary attempt to review and discuss a few 20th-century representatives of this literary form. The narratives considered here are full-fledged books written by a single person in the first person. They differ from autobiographical fragments based on interviews conducted by anthropologists, who are, indeed, "among the primary users and theorizers of life histories" (Arnold & Blackburn 2004: 4), in order to document one or another aspect of Jainism, some of which are available in studies published in the last decades (Goonasekera 1986: 87ff.; Vallely 2002). On the other hand, the autobiographies examined here are seen as both genre *and* source:

> Despite the partial move away from the polished biographies and autobiographies of the "great and famous" toward the investigation of more marginalized and subaltern sections of society, for which few such literary self-narratives are available, historians of India have generally been inclined to consider life histories as *sources*, of varying degrees of utility and trustworthiness: they have seldom paused to consider them as *genres* worthy of systematic analysis (Arnold & Blackburn 2004: 3-4).

Ideally such an investigation should be based on a large, if not exhaustive, collection of texts in order to propose significant conclusions. This goal, however, is difficult to reach and, as it often happens in Jain studies, collecting the documents is a task in itself. Efforts in this direction led to the following observation: biographies written by monks' or nuns' monastic or lay disciples are rather numerous, being available either in the form of independent booklets or in the form of sketches included in Felicitation volumes, and have developed as a "new genre of Jain history".[5] Auto-

[5] Cort 1995: 494. See, among a large number of examples, *Śāsan samrāṭ: jīvana paricaya* (life of Vijayanemisūri, 1872-1949) written by Ramaṇlāl Cī. Shah, Hindi translation, Ahmedabad, 1999 (89 pages); *Jina śāsana ke samartha*

biographies appear to be much rarer. This simple fact is significant, as will be seen later.

The corpus which emerged for the present paper consists of the following three autobiographies, all written in Hindi:[6]

(1) The autobiography of the Śvetāmbara Muni Jinavijaya (27.1. 1888–3.6.1976) was published in two installments, in 1971 and 1976. The first part, entitled *Jinavijaya Jīvana Kathā*, covers the life of the author's father and grandfather and his own childhood up to the age of 15 (= 1902-03), when he ordained as a Sthānakavāsī monk. The second part, *Merī Jīvana prapañca kathā* "My extensive life-story", covers the six years of Muni Jinavijaya's life as a Sthānakavāsī monk, referring to events occurring between 1902-03 and 1908. The total number of about 300 pages corresponds to only 20 years of the long and eventful life of this uncommon figure. The rest of his life remains untold. In the next phase, he lived for 12 years as a Mūrtipūjaka monk.[7] Although he was always known as Muni, he then disrobed and devoted the rest of his life to scholarship, visiting Germany at the invitation of H. Jacobi for about one year and a half in 1928. He is best known for his energetic editorial activity. After reaching Shantiniketan and meeting Shri Bahadursinh Singhi, the Singhi Jain Series through which so many Jain works of all types were made known to the scholarly world was founded and developed thanks to the numerous editions provided

---

unnāyaka Ācārya Padmasāgarasūri, Koba, 2001 (60 pages); *Maṇḍalācārya śrī Kuśalacandrajī gaṇivara (jīvana caritra)* by Muni śrī Bhuvanacandrajī, Śrī Kaccha pradeśa Pārśvacandragaccha Jaina sangha, 1991 (in Gujarati); Miśrīlāl Jain, *Ātmaśilpī Ācāryaśrī Vidyāsāgara (jīvana-darśana)*, Ahmedabad, 2001 (in Hindi; Digambara monk).

[6] The translations given in this paper for Jinavijaya 1971, Jinavijaya 1976, Jñānamati 1984/1990 and Varṇī 1988/1997 are all by the writer. Note on transcription: in Hindi words the short *a* has been noted systematically, whether it would be actually pronounced or not.

[7] Changing from Sthānakavāsī groups to Mūrtipūjaka groups, and vice-versa, is not an uncommon phenomenon (see Jinavijaya 1976: 76 and 82, the well-known example of Ātmārām alias Āc. Vijayānandasūri and others into Flügel 2000: 80, n. 78) but still merits further investigation.

by Jinavijaya. A general outline of Jinavijaya's life until 1971 is given in the introduction to the first part of the autobiography (Jinavijaya 1971: ii-xvi; see also References below).

In many respects, the personality of Jinavijaya, his relation to the world and the style of his writing find an echo in Bhante Gunaratana's work. Both are gifted men with critical turns of mind, always looking for something better. They are strong personalities who are not easily tamed by the constraints of monastic life in the rural and somewhat backward contexts of India or Ceylon at the beginning of the 20th century, victims of internal monastic politics. They are men of changes, not keeping themselves secluded from the world where they live. Jinavijaya was the first 'soldier' of Gandhi after Gandhi had established the Gujarat Vidyapith (1920). He took part in the Salt march in Dandi (1930) and was put in jail. While in Sanchi with the Indian branch of the Mahabodhi Society (1955-56) Bhante Gunaratana was actively involved in teaching Buddhism to the newly converted Untouchables following Ambedkar's leadership (Gunaratana 2003: 137), while in the United States, his presence and teachings were a solace to Vietnamese refugees temporarily settled in refugee camps (Gunaratana 2003: 203-205). Both Jinavijaya and Bhante Gunaratana are independent and self-willed minds, creative and innovative figures in their respective fields. Both their books make fascinating reading in their own ways.

(2) *Merī smṛtiyāṃ*, "My memories", by Āryikā Jñānamati, published in two installments, in 1984 and 1990, covers the author's life up to 1990. Born in 1934, she is a prominent Digambara nun who took an active part in the development of Hastinapur (U.P.) as a Digambara Jain *tīrtha* of increasing importance in the last 15 to 20 years. She is closely associated with this place where she stays almost continuously. She was introduced to Western readers by Shântâ's book *The Unknown Pilgrims*, for she was the author's main source of information on Digambara *sādhvīs*.[8] She is the fe-

[8] Shântâ 1997: 678-683.

male voice in our corpus, although her specifically feminine side is not predominant in her narrative. It is her role as a leading nun that counts.

(3) *Merī Jīvana gāthā* , "My life song", by Kṣullaka Gaṇeśa Prasāda Varṇī (1875-1961), was published in two parts (in 1949 and 1960) and covers the author's life up to 1955-56. The author is a highly respected figure in the Digambara community and his autobiography is regarded as a significant contribution to Hindi literature. Varṇī qualifies for our corpus because he is a spiritual leader, although he is not a monk in the full sense of the term. He lived as a celibate devoted to study and learning until 1947 when he took the minor *dīkṣā* and was ordained as a *kṣullaka*. There are some points of contact between him and the now famous Banārasīdāsa, the Digambara layman who wrote the *Ardhakathānaka* (in 1641). Varṇī's autobiography, which reflects throughout the perspective of a preacher and of an indefatigable volunteer for the promotion of education, whose life is punctuated by extensive travels in Bundelkhand and the opening of new places to Jainism, has been extensively and interestingly used as a source permitting the "reconstruction" of the Digambara situation in North India, on a par with contemporary fieldwork, in an ethnographical perspective (Jain 1999: 50-82). It throws light on social stratification and castes (*jāti*) at the basic level of the *pancāyata*, on interplay between religious and lay groups, on the connection between practice and doctrine, and on the actual functioning of institutions and principles:

> It will be no exaggeration to say that his autobiography is mainly about the manner in which he collected financial resources in *dan* for the establishment of Jain schools throughout Bundelkhand (Jain 1999: 62).

The account of an activist's life, *Merī Jīvana Gāthā* is a sophisticated combination of network-creation and concern for spiritual matters.

Path without Destination was originally written in English (not in Hindi) by Satish Kumar, a leader in favour of world-peace and a guiding spirit behind ecological, spiritual, and educational ventures. Now residing in England, he is a border case in our corpus. The author, born in 1936 in Rajasthan in a *kṣatriya* family, was a Jain monk among the Terāpanthins between the ages of 9 and 17 (under the name Bhairavdan, cf. Goonasekera 1986: 108). The teachings of Vinoba Bhave and Gandhi in pre-Independence India, along with the disillusion caused by several aspects of monastic life, led him to escape with a friend, and disrobe. Hence his autobiography cannot be strictly considered on a par with the other texts, which have mendicants as their authors. The first two and a half chapters (Kumar 1999: 1-35), however, which are relevant in the present context (and have been extensively quoted with analysis in Goonasekera 1986: 108-113, 132-136, 141ff., 158ff., 190-196; again in Vallely 2002: 199-205), offer some structural similarities with the narrative of Jinavijaya's childhood. The death of the father leaves the mother alone with the child, opening opportunities for increased interactions with religious practice and teachers which leave strong imprints on the young mind. On the other hand, there is the wish to attract a promising intelligence to one's fold on the side of the monks, and the custom, quite common within the Terāpantha, to encourage child renunciation. First-hand insights into daily lay and religious practice resting on a fine sense of observation provide quasi-ethnographic data on the Jains' lives in this region at that point of time. It does so in a flowing style.

As has often been observed by specialists of the autobiographical genre, the writing of an autobiography is never considered obvious by its author. Reticence is the dominant attitude in the face of the awkwardness of the task.[9] The narrative itself is generally preceded by a preface, or a manifest, which sometimes amounts to

[9] See in general Arnold & Blackburn 2004: 15, 86, etc.; Gyatso 1998: 106; and Granoff 1994: 49-50 on Tārāśaṅkar Bandhyopādhyay (1898-1971) as a reluctant autobiographer.

a self-justification, in which the author announces his aim and outlines the scope of his undertaking. In the religious context, one more obstacle could be adduced: is the writing of an autobiography, which supposes that the individual is at the centre of the narrative, not in contradiction with the modesty or discretion expected from a mendicant, or even with the principles of the doctrine? Such an embarrassment was felt, for instance, by Purohit Swami after he had been encouraged by Yeats to relate his life. Yeats reports:

> I found afterwards that I had startled and shocked him, for an Indian monk who speaks of himself contradicts all tradition, but that after much examination of his conscience he came to the conclusion that those traditions were no longer binding, and that besides (...) a monk, a certain stage of initiation reached, is bound by nothing but the will of his Master (Yeats in Purohit Swami 1992: xiii).

The Theravāda Buddhist monk Bhante Gunaratana expresses his reticence no less clearly in the first lines of his Preface:

> Writing an autobiography might seem like an inappropriate exercise for a bhikkhu, a Buddhist monk, since we bhikkhus strive to eradicate the ego, not glorify it. Through meditation and mindfulness we want to let go of attachments and practice selflessness. Why then would I write a whole book about *me*?[10] (Gunaratana 2003: 7.)

Among the works of our corpus Jinavijaya's is the only one which includes such a rather detailed introduction written by himself.[11] The two other books (Āryikā Jñānamati and Varṇī) are preceded by interesting prefaces written by disciples where the problematic genesis of the autobiographies is addressed. It appears that none of the three authors considers autobiographical writing as self-evident and that the three works are the result of strong incentives or pressures coming from around them. These people feel that they have come into contact with an outstanding figure whose experiences

---

[10] For other instances of autobiographical reticence in the Buddhist context see Tiyavanich 1997: 13-14.

[11] Jinavijaya 1976: 1-9 (*kiṃcit prāstāvika*).

and achievements are new (Āryikā Jñānamati is considered as a nun of special intellectual value) or whom they feel they are unable to know thoroughly except through that individual's own revelations (Varṇī). Similarly Purohit Swami's or Bhante Gunaratana's autobiographies are consequences of encouragements from friends (W. B. Yeats) or disciples. In these two cases there is an additional element: the incentive comes when the Hindu master and the Buddhist monk are in the West (England and USA respectively).[12] They are exotic, intriguing and charismatic figures who bring with them new attitudes towards life. Apart from the ideas there are the individuals who arouse immense curiosity:

> We sat on for a couple of hours after lunch while the monk, in answer to my questions, told of his childhood, his life at the University, of spiritual forms that he had seen, of seven years' meditation in his house, of nine years' wandering with his begging-bowl. Presently I said: "The ideas of India have been expounded again and again, nor do we lack ideas of our own; discussion has been exhausted, but we lack experience. Write what you have just told us; keep out all philosophy, unless it interprets something seen or done." (Yeats in Purohit Swami 1992: xiii.)

Their spontaneity ("childlike" is an adjective applied by Yeats to Purohit Swami) is felt to be refreshing:

> Usually people want to know about meditation. (...) Sometimes, though, someone asks a question about my life: "How long have you been a monk?" "What was it like, growing up in Sri Lanka?" – "How do you maintain monastic discipline in this world full of temptations?" When I answer those kinds of questions, I tend to ramble. I tell stories about my life and people seem to enjoy them. The meditation hall, usually a silent place, fills with laughter. Often the students say, "Bhante, you should write your autobiography!" (Gunaratana 2003: 7.)

---

[12] Compare Vinod Sena in Purohit Swami 1992: xxxv: "It is interesting that both Purohit Swami and Yogananda were led to write their memoirs in order to bring the truths of yoga alive to western seekers." No less significant is the fact that Purohit Swami's autobiography was first written in English, and only much later translated into Marathi, the original language of the author (Vinod Sena in Purohit Swami 1992: xxxiii, n. 2: *Mi Ek Sanyasi*, translation by Mrs. Mrinalini Chitale, Bombay, 1987; reprint 1989).

The idea of Jinavijaya's undertaking, started when he was 84, similarly goes back to foreign interest while he was in the West. He narrates (Jinavijaya 1971: 2-4) how, invited to Hamburg in July-August 1928, he visited Walther Schubring's house, where the conversation turned to his earlier life. Schubring particularly liked Jinavijaya's accounts of his paternal grandfather's and father's deeds in 1857, and encouraged him to put this into writing in the form of a simple verse *praśasti* in Sanskrit. This resulted the next day in an eleven verse poem (reproduced with Hindi translation in Jinavijaya 1971: 4-6). Following Schubring's suggestion, Jinavijaya wrote it down again in fine script, and Schubring had it framed. Schubring explained to Jinavijaya that in Germany it was common for important scholars, poets, or writers to write a brief account of their own life to present to their friends and family, showing him some examples.

> This is the occasion which gave birth to the idea of putting to writing memories of my earlier life. But until I completed 80 years this idea did not materialize. (Jinavijaya 1971: 3.)

Not only is autobiographical writing not spontaneous. When pressed to this task, each of our authors in his own terms expresses his great reluctance and resists considerably before complying with the wish. Gaṇeśa Prasāda Varṇī avoids it as much as possible, mentioning the respect and humility owed to the great authorities of the past: how could he write about his life when Kundakunda and Samantabhadra have written nothing about their own? And what is there to be told in his own life?[13] The publication, however, of a 16-page biography by Pannalal Jain modifies his approach, for he finds that it is either inaccurate or pure praise (*stutivāda*) and has nothing of a life-account (*jīvana kī jhānkī*). Facing this dilemma – and additional pressure from a devotee who undertook a fast as a means of persuasion – Varṇī started writing his life-story, side by side with a commentary on the *Samayasāra*. The actual publication

[13] Varṇī 1988: 12 (Preface).

was preceded by a sort of oral test, in the form of public reading of some extracts of the work. Āryikā Jñānamati's and Muni Jinavijaya's autobiographies were written in two stages. The positive response offered by the readers to the first parts led the authors to continue their task.

In the case of the Digambara nun, Gaṇeśa Varṇī's book seems to have had a significant impact, and her own autobiography is presented as a feminine counterpart to it (Jñānamati 1984: 13). However, although the nun finally writes a continuation to the first part, she clearly expresses at the end of the 843 pages that she has written in a state of displeasure (and not in a state of self-praise),[14] a state which she had not experienced when writing any of her other books.

Jinavijaya wrote his autobiography as an old man in the evening of his long life.

> In the last two years, because well-known friends suggested so, on the one hand, and because I went on surveying the past of my life, various thoughts agitate my mind: through which incidents and situations did I have to go during the journey of such a long life? With what wish? When? In which task did I have to enter? On which road? How? Some memories are put to writing in the next pages for this satisfaction of the mind. (Jinavijaya 1971: 3-4.)

The feeling that the death is drawing near is thus a motivation, for memories and people come to mind and cannot be discarded as long as the mind works, but are bound to disappear with the death. Further, the introductory pages of the second part (written on 14 February 1976, five months before Jinavijaya's death) amount to a kind of confession or attempt to explain the events as being caused by personal factors depending on one's own nature, a feature which probably deserves to be noticed because it does not emerge in full light in our other accounts. This style is determined by the specificity of the monk's trajectory, as recalled earlier. His account is

---

[14] *Eka arucipūrṇa bhāva se hī likhā hai, svapraśaṃsā ke bhāva se nahīṃ* (Jñānamati 1990: 843).

thus intended "to relieve his unsettled mind" and to explain that his strong attraction towards change (*parivartana*), which he always equates with progress and which needs to be implemented as soon as it comes, is only responsible for the fact that he left some places or cut some ties, even though he was respected and honoured. He sees this justification is necessary since what he writes could be taken negatively by the Sthānakavāsīs. He also takes care to underline that the narrated facts refer to a specific historical context and a given period of time, and should not be viewed as eternal truths still valid 65 years later (Jinavijaya 1976: vi).

Bhante Gunaratana's preface reveals similar scruples together with an aspiration for truth, factors which distinguish autobiography from biography written by disciples, and Western from Oriental perception:

> I thought about the sometimes ugly truths of my life, and I worried. If I wrote about them honestly, I would be displaying my weaknesses, my shortcomings. But hiding the truth – well, that didn't feel right either. And furthermore, it seemed so un-monk-like to write about unpleasant conversations and situations that happened decades ago, to reveal people who were unkind to me, especially when many of them aren't around anymore to defend themselves. (...) People in Sri Lanka don't want to hear about a monk's mistakes or character flaws. They prefer to think of him as an exalted holy man to whom they can bow down in reverence. In the spiritual economy of Asian Buddhist monastics and laypeople, honoring a venerable bhikkhu by giving him gifts or supporting him brings spiritual merit. To find out that he is anything less than worthy would disturb a layperson's sense of order. But in Western culture, the truth is highly prized. So I couldn't tell my life story and leave out the bad parts; that would be a "sanitized" version and would perhaps be perceived as dishonest. And if I portrayed myself as having never struggled with difficulties and shortcomings, my story certainly wouldn't help anyone see the value of the Dhamma in dealing with life's slings and arrows. (Gunaratana 2003: 10.)

In other words, the writers consider autobiography to be a means to convey their own truth and their own perspectives, but they also see it as a secondary task, almost a waste of time, which cannot compete with their work done in connection with the scriptures.

Their lay-devotees, however, are inspired by autobiography as a manifestation of devotion, and see the result as equal to a *dharma-śāstra* (Varṇī) or to a historical composition (Jñānamati).[15] They feel that facts and thoughts drawn directly from the source in their integrity and authenticity should be preserved.

No direct statement is available in the texts on the sources or models of inspiration. However, the existence of influential autobiographies outside Jain circles could not have remained without any effect. Among them Mahatma Gandhi's *The Story of My Experiments with truth* has probably a special place because it inaugurated a kind of 20th century Indianized autobiography which has rendered invalid the following objections raised by one of Gandhi's friends and mentioned in the Introduction:

> What has set you on this adventure? Writing an autobiography is a practice peculiar to the west. I know of nobody in the East having written one, except among those who have come under Western influence.[16]

The works of our corpus share at least two common features with Gandhi's undertaking: their titles as well as their style of composition. None of the titles focuses directly on the individual himself, in that they eschew the use of the Hindi word *ātmakathā*,[17] but rather focus on external events in relation to the individual. Even the wording *merī smṛtiyāṃ* of Āryikā Jñānamati seems casual. Jinavijaya justifies his use of the term *prapañcakathā* (1976), which is a deliberate and significant choice, by referring to Siddharṣi's *Upamitibhavaprapañca-kathā*, and ascribes a technical spiritual meaning to the word: the detailed narrative of all external and internal manifestations of a soul in *saṃsāra* (Jinavijaya 1976: 1).[18] This

[15] Jñānamati 1990: 13 (Preface).

[16] Gandhi 1940: 3-4 [Mahatma Gandhi's *Autobiography*. Originally published in Gujarati in 2 volumes: vol. 1, 1927; vol. 2, 1929. Introduction by the author dated 1925. English translation in the form of a book published in 1940].

[17] For instance by Rajendra Prasad, the first President of India, for his autobiography published in 1946. A variant is *Ātmaparicaya*.

choice has an effect on the composition: a "connected account of the experiments" (to quote Gandhi's words)[19] in the form of mostly brief chapters written in a fluid and vivid style characterizes all the three Jain works in Hindi.[20]

Even if the influence of Western models cannot fully be ruled out, our three Jain autobiographies can be seen as entirely Indian products, unique in their individual conceptions. They do not seem to have been informed by Western influence. Co-authors or redactors may intervene, however, in the process of religious autobiographical writing: the goal is an authentic experience, but the account must be made accessible to readers unfamiliar with the subject, and, eventually, needs to be "cleaned" of didactic elements. Purohit Swami and Bhante Gunaratana offer parallel illustrations of the implication of a "second hand". The role of Jeanne Malmgren, an American journalist and a Buddhist, in Bhante Gunaratana's undertaking is difficult to appreciate in the absence of any explicit statement. The writing of Purohit Swami's autobiography, on the other hand, was explicitly guided by a European hand:

> [Purohit Swami] took my [= Yeats] advice and brought his book, chapter by chapter, to Sturge Moore for correction. Sturge Moore, one of our finest critics, would say: "You have told us too much of this, or too little of that; you must make us see that temple more clearly", or he would cross something out, or alter a word, helping him to master our European sense of form. (Yeats in Purohit Swami 1992: xiii.)

Primarily addressing foreign (western) audiences, the two books contain an additional element of elucidation (of concepts, of terms, of customs) absent from the three Jain autobiographies, which were meant for readers acquainted with Jain practice, and only for them.

---

[18] On the particular realization of autobiography in Siddharṣi's work see Granoff 1994: 36-39.

[19] Gandhi 1940: 4.

[20] The compositional pattern is similar in Purohit Swami's or Bhante Gunaratana's autobiographies.

As might be expected, the Jain religious autobiographies are punctuated by alternating peregrinations (*vihāra*) and stays at a single place during the rainy season. This constructs a precise geographical nexus. In contrast with the accounts by the Hindu yogis of their own careers (or with the Buddhist forest monks), which give a rather large place to miraculous feats, attainment of special powers, visions and remembrance of previous births, those of our Jain mendicants are generally matter of fact. They do not hide the shortcomings or difficulties met in various circumstances. The events they narrate may be remarkable, but they always keep to a human dimension. This is where the boundary line between biography written by a monk himself and biography written by disciples, meant as "praise" – *stutivāda* (see Varṇī above p. 152) and often hagiographical, appears to be drawn. Moreover, some of the modern religious biographies reveal an underlying structure that more or less reproduces the pattern of a Jina's career which is taken as the ideal model. In contrast, the corresponding autobiographies have a distinctly individual character and their authors do not seem to feel the need to go beyond their own specific experience, even if traditional literary stereotypes are not entirely absent. This is illustrated by the rather considerable place devoted to the narration of childhood as the time in life when the seeds of the future are sown. In contrast with traditional Jain religious autobiography, of which the *Taraṅgavaī – Die Nonne* – is the oldest and most complete example, or with the segments inserted in wider frames in the *Vasudevahiṇḍī* or the *Kuvalayamālā*,[21] the chronological limits within which the narrative is encompassed correspond to the individual's lifespan. The "dispersal of life by projection of it into history beyond" (it) so that it starts "before the cradle and past the grave",[22] and a narrative which expands over a stretch of rebirths are no longer possible (cf. Gyatso 1998: 107). Our samples suggest

[21] For autobiographical encounters in the Sanskrit rewriting of the *Kuvalayamālā* by Ratnaprabhasūri see Granoff 1994: 31-36.

[22] Houtman 1997: 326.

that a degree of rationality, positivism and historical verifiability is a necessary characteristic of modern Jain religious autobiographies, in tune with the orthodoxy that the authors, none of whom is an ordinary mendicant, are now expected to propagate, and in accordance with the historical context within which they were born. I agree with Cort's statement that "the traditional understanding of time and history is being discarded in favor of a progressive and positive view of time and history, more in tune with Western Enlightenment",[23] but am tempted to find that it applies better to religious autobiographies than to bio/hagiographies.

With their "commitment to the actual" these autobiographical accounts can be viewed as "a counterpoint to ethnography" emphasizing aspects of crucial importance in the Jain context. They show "the interplay between an individual and the micro social dimensions of his monastic community"[24] on the one hand, and modes of interaction with the outside world represented both by the Jain laity and the followers of other faiths. This is what I shall try to illustrate now.

Varṇī's account of his early youth throws light on the relationship between Vaiṣṇavas and Jains in a small town in Bundelkhand at the end of the 19th century. There is, indeed, "a fluidity of attitude towards religious identity" (Dundas 2002: 4-5) that is encouraged by the non-ghettoization of the habitat: Vaiṣṇava and Jain families stay in neighbouring houses; the house of Varṇī's parents, whose background is Vaiṣṇava, is located in front of the Jain temple. Similar situations were also common in Gujarat during this period, as shown by Gandhi's autobiography. However, this does not amount to a loss of religious identity. Otherwise one would be unable to understand the young Varṇī's radical reaction when he decided to adopt the Jain way of life. His first way to translate his conversion into act was a public refusal to eat from the hands of his mother or from people of his caste at a wedding. Later on, in a ra-

[23] Cort 1995: 494.

[24] All three quotations from Taylor 1997: 291.

ther impetuous letter to his mother and wife (whom he has married at the age of 18), he urged them to imitate his decision, threatening that otherwise he would refuse to see them again. The young man's headstrong rejection of former codes of social behaviour, which was wisely moderated by his Jain advisors, can be accounted for in part by the young convert's enthusiasm, but would be unlikely if the relationships between the two communities were not more complex than they generally appear. And the author's deep Jain convictions obviously influence the tonality of his narrative. They inform his positions on various social issues of the time, on which his opinion was often asked (access of untouchables to the Jain temples, Varṇī 1997: 83ff.; Jain 1999: 73; marriage of widows, Varṇī 1988: 83ff.). True and touching emotion pervades several passages which are more personal in nature. Such is the case when Varṇī can at last fulfill his longstanding wish of taking the full vow of celibacy (technically termed "the seventh *pratimā*"), because he has met the right person, Bābā Gokulacandrajī, a *tyāgī* who arouses instant devotion in his heart (Varṇī 1997: 180-181). Emotional outbursts are prevalent in the complex relationship between Varṇī and his spiritual mother, Bāījī (see below), and are fully evident in his account of her last months when, realizing that her end was not far away, she expresses the wish to take the last vow from Varṇī himself, whom she has always considered as a son, and when she narrates her own life vividly (Varṇī 1997: 302-310).

Āryikā Jñānamati's autobiography is probably the most ordinary account of our three Hindi sources in the sense that the author, born into a pious Jain family in Uttar Pradesh, follows a rather straight trajectory, and does not seem to go through any spiritual crisis or dissatisfaction with the monastic *milieu* during her life. Thus, after the initial urge for *vairāgya* and the ceremony of initiation into the Digambara order, first as a *kṣullikā*, then later with the higher status of an *āryikā* soon allowed to have her own group of nuns, which are dealt with in the first and second parts, the narrative mainly concentrates on the daily activities of a monastic life:

vihāra and *caturmāsa*, a number of pilgrimages from Rajasthan and Gujarat to the South of India, the various festivals or ceremonies which mark the religious calendar of the Digambaras, the initiation of new disciples or the writing of books (parts 3 and 4). The climax is reached in the fifth part, with the project to establish a scale replica of Jambūdvīpa in Hastinapur to incarnate the Jain cosmological conception, its successful achievement and the final admission of Hastinapur into the group of the best known Jain *tīrtha*s (part 6). The relevant pages amount to a chronicle of the events and a report on the subtle balance in the relationship between the nun as an inspiring figure and Jain lay patrons as well as political power, represented by Indira Gandhi, who participated in the inauguration of the monument in June 1982 (Jñānamati 1990: 587). The whole work provides a useful insight into Digambara "internal politics" in the second part of the 20th century, with precise information on persons, groups, difference of opinions, time and place (Jñānamati 1990: 141ff., 195 [*matabheda*], etc.), and can be usefully contrasted with Varṇī's reports for the earlier period of the century. The wide-spread use of dialogue helps to sustain interest and makes lively reading.

The first part of Jinavijaya's narrative provides precious insights into life in rural Rajasthan. Born in the village of Rūpāhelī in Mewar, the young Kiśanalāla/Kiśanasiṃha's care rested primarily in the hands of his mother (who affectionately called him Raṇamalla/Riṇamal). His father, a *kṣatriya*, was employed far away and dies when the child was 10. Until this age, the child was totally illiterate. In this context, religious figures who interact closely with the population play a determining yet ambiguous role. Those with whom Kiśanalāla's family were in daily contact were Jain *yati*s. Their qualifications and characteristics emerge from various incidents in the youth's life. The first one he meets, Yati Devīhaṃsa, had been called to his house for his medical abilities when Kiśanalāla's father fell ill. The itinerant *yati*'s reputation in the medical field had already been confirmed after he had been called on purpose and settled in an old *upāśraya* in order to successfully cure the Ṭhākur of Rūpāhelī, who had earlier tried other cures in vain (Jinavijaya 1971: 50ff.). Kiśanalāla's father's health improved for a time, but, despite the *yati*'s good care, he did not survive long after. Insight is given into the way the *yati*s themselves prepare the specific vegetal remedies they prescribe, or how they otherwise procure them. It was in such circumstances that the young child had the opportunity to taste for the first time the juice of fresh oranges, an exotic treat which had been brought from Ajmer by the *yati* himself for his father (p. 56). The medical knowledge of the *yati*s is a recurring feature in the narrative. On another occasion, one of them successfully cured a rash (p. 84). Later on, the prospect of becoming a competent and reputed *vaidya* was offered as an incentive to convince the young Kiśanalāla to become a *yati* (p. 163; below). *Yati*s are expert in astrology and palmistry; this helps them to see that Kiśanalāla will have a brilliant future. They also play the role of teachers, in the absence of any organized educational system in isolated villages. When he came regularly to the house to cure and look after Kiśanalāla's father, Yati Devīhaṃsa had a chance to observe the child, to assess him and to become convinced of his promising future. He decided to take the boy's education into his own hands. The child thus spent most of the time with this first guru, who had profoundly impressed him at first sight:

> The *yati* was tall and strongly built. His face was very peaceful and profound. He had a large nose and wide eyes. He had long white hair like silk thread which hung on his neck, white moustaches and a resounding voice. He spoke very softly and was humorous. As soon as I saw him an unmanifested feeling of devotion towards him was anchored in my mind. (Jinavijaya 1971: 53.)

Beside learning the alphabet, the child had to learn basic Jain formulae (*namaskāra-mantra*) by heart. He also mastered Sanskrit grammar (through the *Kātantra vyākaraṇa*), Jain hymns, and Sanskrit verses from the *Cāṇakya Nīti* (Jinavijaya 1971: 58-59). But the guru's death following an accidental fall left the young boy to his own devices.

*Yati*s are not necessarily wanderers or celibates. While travelling with his guru, the young Kiśanalāla met a certain Dhanacanda Yati who had a small family. In addition to his old mother and a sister of advanced age, a widow with a small child lived in his house, probably as his wife (Jinavijaya 1971: 72). Another *yati*, Jñānacanda, was married to the daughter of a *yati* from a neighbouring town (p. 132). They were not without possessions either, and were significant actors in economic life. Kiśanalāla's guru receives either money or goods in exchange for his medical treatments, although he does not ask for anything (p. 60). These supports are used for helping others during a severe famine: the bread Kiśanalāla's mother makes out of flour received by the guru serves to feed several poor people. Moreover, *yati*s have some land under their authority. At a later stage, Kiśanalāla was made to work in the fields looked after by Dhanacanda Yati (p. 79), a rather money-minded person who refused to send him back to his mother after the guru's death, for fear that he would have to give back some money. On another occasion, Kiśanalāla's path crossed that of Yati Jñānacanda from Maṇḍapyā (near Ratlam) and he stayed with him for some time, again working in the fields all day long. Kiśanalāla had ample opportunity to get acquainted with this man:

> He did not like to work in the field himself, nor did he like to get the work done by his wife. He had a strong liking for singing and playing music, on which he usually spent two or three hours a day at home. He did not act like a lot of *yati*s who make special business out of remedies and alcohol. He was very fond of playing cards, therefore he used to sit at home with two or three persons and play. He also liked to play chess. But he played only when some good person would come to play with him. At about 3 or 4 o'clock he used to smoke hemp (*bhāṃg*).[25] (Jinavijaya 1971: 138.)

---

[25] For another description of the *yati*s' pleasures (eating betel, *pān*, for instance, see Jinavijaya 1971: 77).

*Yati*s are central actors of Jain religious life, being invited, for instance, to commemorative meals where they receive good food and money (pp. 77, 83). When Yati Jñānacanda was entrusted with the task of consecrating (*pratiṣṭhā*) a new temple and required the collaboration of other colleagues, he called upon the young Kiśanalāla: as a learned person with perfect pronunciation, he was an asset, and could be taught the sacred texts (*maṅgala-pāṭha* and *śānti-pāṭha*) to be recited in such circumstances (p. 141). The boy was then made to wear a *yati*'s clothes, covering his body with a sheet and keeping his head uncovered (p. 142). He was sent to collect alms (*gocarī*), uttering for the first time the word *dharmalābha* at the door of a Sheth's house (p. 142), receiving his share of the *honorarium*, and leading the life of a *yati*, without being one formally (p. 144, 145). He trained himself to read the *Kalpasūtra* aloud on the following Paryushan through an old manuscript of this work in mixed Gujarati and Rajasthani (pp. 145, 147).

During the rainy season, *yati*s are invited by local communities to stay with them. Yati Jñānacanda and Kiśanalāla set out for Gujarat (p. 150). Bad as well as good surprises waited for them. There was no place for them to stay when they arrived at Bāriyā, because another *yati* had already been invited (p. 151)! But they learned that at Badanāvar a new temple was under construction, and that the place was in need of a *yati* for the celebration of Paryushan. Yati Jñānacanda, who was acquainted with the local lay community, sent Kiśanalāla on a new path of his destiny on which he fared alone. He became the religious reference for the Jains who used to visit the temple. For the first time, he was offered a printed copy of the *Kalpasūtra* to read (p. 154), and he organized regular reading sessions under his supervision at a layman's house (p. 155).

Thus *yati*s are different from proper monks (*sādhu*, *muni*), although they share with them some practices such as begging alms or staying in one place during the rainy season. Kiśanalāla had been in close contact with several *yati*s, but when the laypeople of Badanāvar want to take him to attend the function celebrating the breaking of a 52 days' fast by a Jain monk, he was eager to go, writing

> I had never properly seen a Jain monk so far. When I was in Bāneṇ two or three monks had come for one or two days, but I never came in contact with them. (Jinavijaya 1971: 156.)[26]

Hence his great curiosity towards their way of life, which was a totally new thing for him (p. 158). The difference in religious culture is for him a matter of surprise as well: asked by the leading monk to recite something, Kiśanalāla recited the *Saṃsāradavānala-stuti*. The monk did not know the text because this hymn is a part of Śvetāmbara Mūrtipūjaka liturgy and has no place in Sthānakavāsī recitation (p. 160). The relations between the two categories – *yati*s and *sādhu*s – are complex and unfriendly. When Kiśanalāla, who had come into contact with Sthānakavāsī monks (p. 158ff.), was tempted to join their fold, he was discouraged by Yati Jñānacanda in rather strong terms:

> We, *yati*s, are opposed to this group (*sampradāya*) because they are extremely opposed to the building of temples, the main component of Jainism, to the worship or installation of Jina images, and to the celebration of festivals in connection with these images. They neither go to temples nor accept festivals nor accomplish any pilgrimage to Shatrunjaya, Girnar, Abu, Kesariyanath, etc. Their thoughts and behaviour are very different from ours. They never bathe, nor wash themselves and always wear dirty clothes. They wear a strip of cloth over their mouths, and do several similar things, that you will not like. The strong desire you have for knowledge will never be fulfilled by staying with them. They do not read our old books at all. Among us *yati*s there are very big residences, the leaders of which are very big scholars. You have not yet seen any of these places, and you have not travelled to Shatrunjaya and other sacred places. In these places and in cities like Ahmedabad there are hundreds of temples, and several schools where

[26] Compare Jain 1999: 53 about the picture emerging from Varṇī's autobiography: "Finally, a feature of utmost importance for Digambar Jain social organization in Bundelkhand is the presence in this region of Jain teachers and scholars (pandits) who form a significant intermediate layer between the munis and the laity. In fact MJG [=*Merī Jīvana Gāthā*] in its 700 odd pages contains only one or two references to munis."

> *yati*s' disciples also study. There are wealthy Jains who take big groups of people for pilgrimages, and invite very learned *yati*s. They also invite *śrī-pūjya*s, worship them in great pomp and offer them presents of several hundred rupees, shawls, etc. I want you to stay with an important *yati* and want to take care of your education. (...) By taking initiation with this monk you will not gain anything good. By staying in the *yati* fold you will be able to learn well and by staying with a *yati* of good reputation in the medical field, you will gain good medical knowledge, and you will earn thousands of rupees in the future. Your lamented teacher Devīhaṃsajī was famous and important owners, like Sheth Sāhukāra and others, were his devotees. You too will be able to earn the same fame. If you become a monk in this group there will be no progress in your life. They always go on foot taking their luggage with them. Every six months they pull out their hair with their own hands. They read only certain Jain *sūtra*s and they just recite to people *ḍhāla*s, *copāī*s and other works in vernaculars. They do not read works in Sanskrit at all. They wander in places where there are laypeople to honour them. They never go to assemblies, festivals, etc., and nobody invites them either. They just spend time in ascetic practices such as fasts, for which during the rainy season a lot of people – villagers at that – meet them, bow to them, and so on. (Jinavijaya 1971: 162-164.)

In vain: the experience of the foregoing years has aroused a feeling of detachment towards the world in the young boy's heart. His decision could not be changed (p. 164). Preparations for a grand *dīkṣā* were being made, despite opposition from local brahmins whose relations with Jains were tense, and the future monk received the insignia of his new status (p. 167). The first part of the autobiography ends with this event, which took place in V.S. 1959 (= 1902) in Digṭhāṇa, a village of Malwa.

Jain *yati*s and monks, however, were not the only ones to have been attracted by Kiśanalāla's sparkling and promising intelligence. After his guru's death and before living in proximity to Yati Jñānacanda, there was a Śaivite *intermède* to which the narrative gives a prominent place (Jinavijaya 1971, chapter 7: 84-130). An encounter with a brahmin during a stay in Bāṇeṇ (p. 80) and a visit to a religious festival in his company were the starting points for this adventure, in which Kiśanalāla, initiated into Yogi Khākhī Bābā's fold, temporarily became Kiśana Bhairava (p. 94) and was destined to become his Śaiva guru's successor. He was instructed thus:

> You will have to get your head shaven. You will have to cover the whole of your body with ashes of cow-dung (*bhabhūta*). You will wear only a loin-cloth, and keep iron tongs in your hand. You will have to take bath three times a day and worship the gods morning and evening. (Jinavijaya 1971: 93; see also p. 96.)

After initiation he was worshipped by devotees, but the hidden falsehood of the situation (he was not a brahmin as his friend had claimed) caused a pervading feeling of guilt (p. 102). The child, however, was overcome by other impressions, such as the enduring impression of the first time he drank out of a silver glass handed over to him by his new guru (p. 103). Provision was made for his education through a Brahmin pandit who taught him Sanskrit grammar, and also Śaiva chanting (*Mahīmnastotra*; Jinavijaya 1971: 113-114).

This chapter offers insight into life in a Śaiva monastery in Ujjain (p. 115ff.), its economic organization, and internal politics. After the pandit's departure, Kiśana Bhairava was disappointed by the ignorance of his companions, their lack of interest for anything other than food, sleep, tobacco and excursions (p. 120). The lack of any intellectual perspective led him to think of other possibilities, and aroused nostalgia for the Jain *yati*s, who, on the whole, seemed to him more cultured people (p. 125). Ongoing fights with a rival gang of ascetics were an additional danger. The guru encouraged the disciple to run away, with the help of his brahmin friend. He removed all traces of his Śaiva past through a bath: "This is how I became the old Kiśanalāla" (p. 130). It was as a Śaiva ascetic that Jinavijaya experienced for the first time the hardships of monastic life (p. 106).

The second part of the autobiography paints a picture of monastic life in the Sthānakavāsī tradition of Dharmadāsa to which the new monk belonged (*hamārā Dharmadāsajī kā sampradāya*, Jinavijaya 1976: 79). It reports on the first All India Sthānakavāsī

Conference which took place at Morvi in 1906 (Jinavijaya 1976: 79ff.),[27] and depicts the outside world as a permanent temptation for the young monk driven by an inexhaustible thirst for knowledge, in contrast with the closed universe of the monks and their rules. The autobiography of Jinavijaya as a young Sthānakavāsī monk follows a progressive path. In the beginning,

> there was some agitation in the mind, but to let enter looseness (*śithilatā*) in the respect of the rules was deemed a cause of karmic bondage. After two or three years of observation of the rules such reactions became more and more solid. At that time there was no opening in the mind for the incoming of other thoughts or reactions. (Jinavijaya 1976: 19.)

At the end of the book, Jinavijaya leaves the dwelling-place of his group during the night and gives up the Sthānakavāsī robe. Although analytical statements such as the one just quoted are relatively rare, the simple juxtaposition of the episodes, without any comment on the part of the narrator, is sufficient to convey the impression that the balance is rather fragile and always on the verge of breaking: for instance, when the author tells how he participated in a magnificent procession and then returned to his lodging where he simply went back to his daily activities (Jinavijaya 1976: 22).

This crisis gives a dramatic touch to the whole text. Weakness is not the problem, although it could have been one as for example for those who are unable to tolerate the difficulty of the regular plucking out of the hair (Jinavijaya 1976: 34), and although the rigorous character of the rules is never hidden.[28] A vivid and sober account of the extremely difficult journey of the monastic group through dense jungles and steep mountains, under the guidance of a tribal man, devoid of all picturesque or romanticism but instructive for the way some rules are liable to slight adjustments in adverse circumstances,[29] is sufficient to show that the hardships of monastic

[27] Flügel 2000: 81.

[28] Jinavijaya 1976: 44f., 47 (in case of illness).

life were not a factor in the young monk's *mal être*. The cause of Jinavijaya's dissatisfaction was a gradual critical examination in which a realization of the inanity of certain monastic practices and the pressure of outside events combined and led Jinavijaya to leave the order.

Each time the monastic group settled in a dwelling-place (*sthānaka*) for the rainy season, Jinavijaya reports how his teacher undertook a continuous fast of 50 to 60 days. This was deemed an extraordinary achievement by the local communities who rushed in order to visit the monk. At one point, however, the rush decreased considerably, for another monk was doing even better in the neighbourhood (Jinavijaya 1976: 86). To Jinavijaya's eyes, this competition in fasting only underlined the fact that fast was intended more as a means to attract attention to oneself or to gain a reputation rather than to annihilate bad karmas. He could not accept that this was the purpose of a monastic life.

On the other hand, his autobiography is punctuated by successive encounters which, as he writes, "sowed a seed" (*bījāropaṇa*) in his mind and were sources of a knowledge which could not be gained within the inner circle, and inspired new questions.[30] These meetings took place in the context of laymen's visits to the monks at the *sthānaka*. Whether they were young boys who receive school education, Bhandarkar on an archaeological tour in the town of Dhar (Jinavijaya 1976: 15ff.), or a school-teacher, they aroused his curiosity towards subjects such as paleography, history, geography or mathematics, that were totally unknown in the closed monastic context of the time. The spatial environment had a similar effect: the location of the *sthānaka*s in the heart of cities provided opportunities to be in contact with sights of things unknown: a car, a rail-

---

[29] Jinavijaya 1976: 51 (step over vegetation, drink water out of a river) and 54ff.

[30] Encounters with people who contribute to a decisive turn to his life also punctuate Bhante Gunaratana's narrative and progress: see for instance the meeting with Venerable Saddhatissa (Gunaratana 2003: 130-131).

way line and its trains, or even a temple converted into a mosque or a Muslim procession, which his teacher allowed him to investigate more closely. But curiosity transformed itself into doubt under the influence of external eyes: a school-teacher bringing a newspaper (a totally new object) and information on contemporary issues or about the new ideas professed by Lokamanya Tilak in the context of agitation against British rule (Jinavijaya 1976: 69), a Hindu female ascetic whose reactions to the Jain way of life are thought-provoking (p. 71ff.), or a young Jain student who opens the monk's mind to geography and physics in a way completely new for him, contrasting them with traditional cosmological Jain teachings (p. 78). At this stage however, the determining factor comes from the Jain community itself in the form of Ātmārām's works and life (pp. 87-89).[31] His works inspired Jinavijaya's interest in Jain images and temples (of which he had obviously very little idea) and stimulated his enduring taste for archaeology and ancient culture (later on he was known as *purātattvācārya*). Ātmārām's life and his books provided a pattern for imitation

> In this way, after reading these books of Āc. Ātmārām my mind started to be strongly impressed by his science and profound knowledge. I read his works several times during these two months. I started thinking that I should increase my knowledge by staying in the service of such a scholar (p. 89).

First a Sthānakavāsī in Panjab, Ātmārām turned to the Tapāgaccha, taking with him a whole group of monks, precisely in order to be exposed to more knowledge. A fact that encouraged Jinavijaya to think that he would better be able to quench his thirst for knowledge and learning among the Mūrtipūjakas than among the Sthānakavāsīs was that among the latter he could not find any monk who could read Sanskrit. Finally Jinavijaya escaped by night, relinquishing his Sthānakavāsī insignia and again exchanging his monastic robe for old clothes – all that after having explained his

---

[31] Ātmārām, the Sthānakavāsī name of Ācārya Vijayānandasūri (1836-1896), a significant Jain reformer; see Flügel 2000: 79 and n. 77.

state of mind in a short letter left for his teacher to read (p. 93). Both parts of Jinavijaya's autobiography thus show the constraints of Jainism as lived within small monastic groups prevailingly active in rural areas.

At various levels, the three autobiographies show how the scriptures of the mendicants' own tradition inform their lives. This feature is especially striking because the three authors are widely read scholars who ascribe a high value to knowledge and understanding of texts. Further, all three have played a significant role in the development of education within the Jain community by establishing several institutions.

Jinavijaya's account provides interesting critical information about the mendicant's curriculum and the differences in the use of scriptures by the Sthānakavāsīs and the Mūrtipūjakas. The role of the *Dasaveyāliya* as a fundamental source of learning, emphasized by the common typology of the Śvetāmbara Āgamas where it stands as one of the *Mūlasūtras*, is confirmed. After initiation, the first five verses of the work,[32] which form a kind of *maṅgala* and contain the essentials of a behaviour of detachment with regard to the daily task of collecting alms (simile of the bee which collects *rasa* from the flowers without hurting them), are the first thing to be learnt by heart, after which the whole work is progressively committed to memory. Its place in the curriculum of a beginner seems to have been dictated by practical considerations: it has a reasonable size, and, even more importantly, it has a direct connection with monastic life and ethics. This is explicitly acknowledged:

> According to the tradition of the Jain monk, every newly ordained person must read precisely this canonical work where all the main rules which have to be observed in the life of a Jain monk are depicted (Jinavijaya 1976: 6).

But this does not mean that the monk learns Prakrit as such. The question of the study of languages and the medium through which

[32] Their famous beginning is: *dhammo mangalam ukkaṭṭhaṃ, ahiṃsā saṃjamo tavo.*

the scriptures and technical terms are known was an important issue in Jinavijaya's eyes. With a tinge of bitterness he reports how it was only much later that he came to know of the existence of Haribhadra's Sanskrit commentary on the *Dasaveyāliya*. More generally, at several places he regrets that among the Sthānakavāsīs texts were explained only in vernacular languages (*lokabhāṣā*), and that monks were content with reading *ṭabos* (Rajasthani or Gujarati word-to-word glosses) or *ḍhāla*s, *copāī*s, *rāsa*s, etc., (Jinavijaya 1976: 85, 87 § 2 end), i.e. literary forms which developed in the vernacular languages and are either narrative texts or simplified exposés of the doctrine. No provision was made to learn Sanskrit or Prakrit. The monk contrasts this with the situation among the Mūrtipūjakas, where the study of short independent Prakrit treatises was a part of the basic curriculum, and acquainted the monks with the doctrine through this language. The texts included the *Jīvavicāra*, the *Navatattva-prakaraṇa* and the *(Covīsa)daṇḍaka* (Jinavijaya 1976: 7), which are still among works meant to inculcate the fundamental principles and the Jain conception of the universe.

Such views amount to a hierarchized picture of the languages used by the Jains, granting the vernaculars a lower status as if they were meant for laypeople or for those who are not properly educated, while classing Prakrit and Sanskrit as scholarly languages, to be learnt and transmitted by the monks. On the other hand, it implies that the Sthānakavāsīs deprive themselves of an important body of valuable works as result of their conception of the authenticity of the scriptures: since they only recognize the Canonical works as authoritative and reject the others as being "very late" (Jinavijaya 1976: 7), the monk is left either with the *Dasaveyāliya*, the *Uttarajjhāyā*, the *Āyāranga*, etc., or with the paraphrases and rewritings in the vernaculars. Further, restrictions also concern the material conditions and objects for the transmission of learning. The relation to printed documents is problematic when it comes to Jain scriptures. The young Jinavijaya reports with some enthusiasm about the first time he came into contact with an edition of two Jain canonical books (Jinavijaya 1976: 87). On the other hand, he expresses his regret that his superior felt no interest whatsoever when a layman brought him the "first English translation of *Uttarādhyayana* and *Kalpasūtra*, by a German scholar, – i.e. Jacobi – containing an introduction demonstrating that Jainism is not to be confused with Buddhism" (Jinavijaya 1976: 23-24). Texts were learned through manuscripts kept by the monks and copied by them (p. 18). But the question of the instruments of writing was also crucial. Using and keeping pens and pencils was forbidden. The only permitted instruments were reeds with black ink, which was liquefied every morning with a few drops of water brought by laymen. In the meantime the only solution was to wait, so that the copy went at a rather slow pace. To use directly the ink available in the market was impossible, and not even considered (Jinavijaya 1976: 18-19).

The scriptures themselves do not feature into Jinavijaya's account or his style of writing. The situation is different with our two other texts. Gaṇeśa Varṇī's autobiography, in particular, is "full of interludes on Jain doctrine, (...) sermonizing passages" (Jain 1999: 52). It is replete with quotations from various Digambara works, especially those authored by or ascribed to Kundakunda which form the expected background. For instance, the narration of the fasting unto death of Varṇī's spiritual mother shows the actual impact of texts both on the mind of the dying and on the surrounding people. In accordance with normative texts, where listening to edifying stories or various verses is prescribed as a support in the penance, the dying person herself asks for the reading of verses from the *Samayasāra*, from the *Śāntisamādhimaraṇa* or from Svāmi Kārttikeya's *Anuprekṣā*. When her strength decreases, only these two works remain. The *Anuprekṣā* on "absence of refuge" (*aśaraṇa*) is again quoted by Varṇī himself as a kind of comfort after death has occurred (Varṇī 1988: 313-315).[33] The effect of texts on the attraction towards Jainism of both Varṇī and his father is also documented. Thus a reading of the Jain *Padmapurāṇa* is presented as being responsible for the fact that Varṇī, as a child of 10, adopted a lifelong renunciation of eating at night. The young boy relates the experience to his Jain teacher in clear terms:

> In front of my house there was a Jain temple, where there was a sermon on (Jain) *Purāṇa*s. It was after hearing it that my faith went to this religion precisely. In the *Padmapurāṇa* the marvelous story of the excellent Rāma is told. It is this story which seems true to me. In the *Rāmāyaṇa* it is told that Rāvaṇa was a *rākṣasa* and Hanumān a monkey. I don't believe in that. From now on I shall not go to the (Hindu) temple. You are my teacher. Please do not insist that I believe otherwise. (Varṇī 1988: 2.)

The confrontation between Hindu and Jain traditions of the story of Rāma as experienced by this child brings a reaction which reminds one of statements made by Jain authors about their motivation to write *Rāmāyaṇa*s different from the Hindu versions. As for the future Āryikā Jñānamati, her desire for renunciation was nourished by the religious texts her mother read and invited her to read, causing her spontaneous attraction towards the children's games to gradually disappear in favour of such readings. The heroes of Jain *kathā*-literature function as models of inspiration, as do their staging in plays (Jñānamati 1990: 2ff.). She describes one book as having a specific importance, namely Padmanandin's *Pañcaviṃśati*. Her mother had received a copy in her dowry from her own father, and she studied it every day (Jñānamati 1990: 7-8). This Sanskrit collection of 26 short verse-treatises on various topics pertaining to ethics, which also includes two hymns, is indeed known to have enjoyed a vast popularity among Digambara circles all over India.[34]

---

[33] For two other accounts of *samādhimaraṇa* see Varṇī 1997: 348-350 (Ācārya Namisāgara, in 1956) and 351-353 (Kṣullaka Sambhavasāgara).

It is not really surprising to see the decisive role of the *ṇamokār mantra* on Varṇī's father who became strongly partial towards Jainism after this formula helped him in circumstances which do not sound unfamiliar: as he was crossing a dense forest with goods from his shop he met a tiger and a tigress face to face, but they passed to one side after he had recited the mantra. On a later occasion, in 1923, Varṇī as a student connected the extremely good result he got in an exam with the recitation of the *Sahasranāma* he had performed in the morning, very likely the *Jinasahasranāma* of Jinasena, and the corresponding section of the autobiography has the title "The extraordinary power of the *Sahasranāma*".[35] Such accounts evidence the performative role of different categories of scriptures and the close connection between scriptures and individual development in daily contexts. There is no reason to question the "sincerity" of the cases where a mantra and a hymn are ascribed a kind of magical power, if this issue is at all relevant. They could suggest that the literary counterparts of such occurrences, which are well attested in the case of the *namaskāra*-formula, the saving effect of which has become a stereotyped motif, are a transposition of such beliefs, or, on the contrary, that the autobiographical accounts are inspired by literary sources and models. On the other hand, the role of a key person of the family in the transmission of Jain values and texts is equally underlined:

[34] For the sake of comparison see the experience of Purohit Swami as a child: "I enjoyed listening to the addresses given by our family priest in a neighbouring temple. He always invoked the authority of the great epics, *Mahabharata*, the *Devi-Bhagavata*, the *Ramayana*, the *Geeta*, and I, though understanding little else, was deeply interested in all the narratives. (...) Thus the foundations of my faith were laid on the admiration of my eyes, ears and heart; and soul danced with body with an ease and naturalness like that of the changing seasons." (Purohit Swami 1992: 12; 13.) The future Bhante Gunaratana identified himself with Culapanthaka, a young boy of Buddha's time who aspired to become a monk (Gunaratana 2003: 36). Later on, when his turn to teach arrived, the taste for stories was still as strong in him (p. 81, stories from the Dhammapada commentary; p. 101: story about the Buddha and Devadatta).

[35] *Sahasranāma kā adbhuta prabhāva* (Varṇī 1988: 100-101).

from mother to daughter in the case of Jñānamati, from father to son in the case of Varṇī.

What type of "self" emerges from these autobiographical writings? All of them narrate outer events at a quick pace, moving forward in brief chapters or paragraphs. Jinavijaya's and Āryikā Jñānamati's works in particular are hardly discursive. Reflective breaks or analyses are minimal. In several of its pages the Digambara nun's text amounts to a report. All three Hindi accounts depict the individual within a network of other lives, in active conjunction and interaction with their lives, constructing the picture of a "self-in-society" (Arnold & Blackburn 2004: 19). Although introspection or psychological (or even less psychoanalytical) explanations of the writer's behaviour and private secrets are far from prevalent, the mere chain of events told in a matter of fact, albeit lively and compelling, fashion has a strong impact on the reader and discloses strong personalities.[36] What was convincingly written of the recollections of Thai forest monks applies here too:

> When a monk travels alone across a forest, wet and cold and hungry, maybe sick or lonely, he tells us. When he feels overwhelmed or uplifted by events and encounters, he reports it. He does so not self-indulgently or sentimentally but in a plain, matter-of-fact, and unforgettable voice – a voice that we do

---

[36] This is true of Bhante Gunaratana's and Purohit Swami's accounts as well. On the latter see Yeats's reaction, comparing the Irish protestant Lady Gregory's *Visions and Beliefs* with the Hindu monk: "These visionaries, memories, fragments, were eccentric, alien, shut off, as it were, under the plate glass of a museum; I had found something of what I wanted but not all, the explanatory intellect had disappeared. When Shri Purohit Swami described his journey up to those seven thousand steps at Mount Girnar, that creaking bed, that sound of patterns in the little old half-forgotten temple, and fitted everything into an ancient discipline, a philosophy that satisfied the intellect, I found all I wanted" (Purohit Swami 1992: xiv). Also compare Kaviraj (in Arnold & Blackburn 2004: 95) about Sibnath Sastri, "a major Brahmo intellectual in late-nineteenth-century Calcutta": (His autobiography) "is written artlessly, without any attempt to bring in literary skills or subtlety. Religious issues and crises are reported, but Sastri never adopts the tone of introspective intimacy, never reports the states of his consciousness psychologically. His text is strikingly unemotional and unpsychological".

> not hear in any administrative or scholar monk's biography. (Tiyavanich 1997: 13.)

Jinavijaya's life, in particular, is characterized by a plurality of successive identities – as the disciple of a Jain *yati*, as the disciple of a Śaivite *yogi*, as a Sthānakavāsī monk, as a Mūrtipūjaka monk, as a disrobed monk. In real chronology, these identities are conflicting and even incompatible with each other. This is why, even in the first part of the autobiography which covers the author's life as a child up to the age of 15, they have to be hidden from the various people encountered. In several cases, the young boy had to keep them secret, not revealing anything about himself to those he successively met. He worried about what others might say about him (Jinavijaya 1971: 112, 159). Thus it would not be justified to say that these monks or nuns do not give away anything of themselves. It is clear, however, that in contrast with Hindu autobiographies written by *bhaktas* (e.g., Banāsā: Horstmann 2003), the spiritual experience (*anubhav*) of the individual occupies an extremely limited part, to say the least.[37] Perhaps unexpectedly, the account of Varṇī (who is not strictly speaking a monk) is the most spiritually oriented of our corpus. Not to speak of Tibetan "secret autobiographies" (cf. Gyatso 1998), from which our three samples are extremely far.

To conclude: I hope to have shown that religious autobiographical material can enrich our view of Jain practice and the transmission of scriptures and history of the communities during the 20th century, and that this material can be viewed as a valuable counterpart to traditional narratives or ethnographic data. Jain religious autobiographies (like their Hindu or Buddhist counterparts) were composed by prominent monastic figures, rather than ordinary followers, partly because an autobiographical project is the outcome of external pressure from people feeling admiration

[37] For other differences between Jain and Vedāntic autobiographical accounts see Granoff 1994: 47-48.

and respect. The object of their discourse is the individual, acting within a complex social network of lay and religious groups. Hence emphasis is placed on outer events rather than on inner spiritual life, but in fact the two support each other. The person of flesh, bone, mind and heart emerges in its reactions to the events as a full human being, in balanced presentations which do not conform to any set pattern and are not modelled upon the paradigm of the Tīrthaṃkaras' lives. Sincerity and authenticity are aimed at and are perceptible. This is the basic difference with biographies written by disciples which are close to hagiographies and tend to eliminate controversial aspects.

REFERENCES

Primary sources

Non Jain modern religious autobiographies:

Banasa [1896-1957], *A Spiritual Autobiography*. Translated and introduced by Monika Horstmann. Wiesbaden: Harrassowitz Verlag, 2003.

Bhante Henepola Gunaratana [b. 1927], *Journey to Mindfulness. The Autobiography of Bhante G.* With Jeanne Malmgren. Boston: Wisdom Publications, 2003.

Paramahamsa Yogananda [1893-1952], *The Autobiography of a Yogi*. First ed.: New York: Philosophical Library, 1946.

Shri Purohit Swami [1882-1940/42], *The Autobiography of an Indian Monk*. With an introduction by W. B. Yeats and edited with an essay on the author by Vinod Sena. Delhi: Munshiram Manoharlal, 1992. (Originally published in 1932 as *An Indian Monk, His Life and Adventures*. London: MacMillan and Co.)

20th-century autobiographies of Jain monks and nuns:

Muni Jinavijaya [1888-1976]

Jinavijaya 1971: *Jinavijaya Jīvana Kathā, arthāt Muni Jinavijaya dvārā likhita apnī jīvana kahānī*. Bhūmikā svarūpa-prārambhika bhāga. grāma Rupāhelī meṃ Muni Jinavijayajī dvārā nirmita Mahātmā Gāndhī smṛti mandira antargata Rājakumārī bāla mandira ke hitārtha prakāśita, Vi. Saṃ. 2028 – 1971 Ī. san., xvi+200 p. [Autobiography proper pp. 1-169; letters and annotations pp. 169-200; 500 copies were printed; the copy theoretically available at the L.D. Institute of Indology, Ahmedabad, is missing; therefore a photocopy of the copy available at the Library of Congress had to be ordered; shelfmark: BL 1373.J56 A34 HIND].

Jinavijaya 1976: *Merī Jīvana Prapañca Kathā. Muni Jinavijaya likhita 'Jīvana Kathā' kā uttara bhāga Sthānakavāsī sampradāya kā jīvanānubhava.* Canderiyā, Chittorgarh, Rajasthan: Sarvodaya Sādhanā Āśrama, 1976, ix+93 p. [250 copies were printed].

For convenient information on Jinavijaya's life in English see also B. M. Singhi, "Muni Jinvijayaji: A Life-long Researcher." *Jain Journal* 11.1, July 1976: 1-5; No. 24 Pura Tattva Acharya Shri Jinvijayaji on www.jaina.org/education_material/ jain legends.

Āryikā Jñānamati(jī) [b. 1934; see Shântâ 1997: 678-683]

Jñānamati 1990: *Merī Smṛtiyāṃ*. Hastinapur. First part published in 1984, 172 p.; full version (including the first part) published in 1990, 843 p.

Gaṇeśa Prasāda Varṇī [1874-1961]

Varṇī 1988, 1997: *Merī Jīvana Gāthā*. Varanasi: Śrī Gaṇeśa Varṇī Digambara Jaina Saṃsthāna. Published in two parts (1st ed. 1949 and 1960). The editions used here are, for the first part, fifth ed., 1988, 436 p.; for the second part, third ed., 1997, 366 p.

For information on G. P. Varṇī's life in English see also No. 13 Saint Shree Ganeshprasadji Varni on www.jaina.org/education_material/jain legends and Jain 1999: 50ff. which includes analyses of several accounts.

Satish Kumar [b. 1936; known as Bhairavdan during his monkhood among the Terāpanthīs]

Kumar 1999: *Path without Destination. An Autobiography*. Eagle Brook, New York: William Morrow & Co., 1999. (First published in Great Britain in 1992 as *No Destination*; earlier published in 1978 in the United States.)

Secondary Sources

ARNOLD, David & Stuart BLACKBURN 2004. *Telling Lives in India. Biography, Autobiography, and Life History*. Bloomington: Indiana University Press – Permanent Black.

CORT, John E. 1995. Genres of Jain history. *Journal of Indian Philosophy* 23: 469-506.

DUNDAS, Paul 2002. *The Jains*. (Library of Religious Beliefs and Practices.) 2nd edition. London: Routledge.

FLÜGEL, Peter 2000. Protestantische und Post-Protestantische Jaina-Reformbewegungen. Zur Geschichte und Organisation der Sthānakavāsī I. *Berliner Indologische Studien* 13/14: 37-103.

GANDHI, M. K. 1940. *An Autobiography or The Story of My Experiments with Truth*. Translated from the original in Gujarati by Mahadev Desai. Ahmedabad: Navajivan Publishing House.

GOONASEKERA, Ratna 1986. *Renunciation and Monasticism among the Jainas of India*. PhD, University of California, San Diego.

GRANOFF, Phyllis 1994. This was my life: Autobiographical narrative and renunciation in medieval Jainism. *Annals of the Bhandarkar Oriental Research Institute* 75: 25-50.

GYATSO, Janet 1998. *Apparitions of the Self (The Secret Autobiographies of a Tibetan Visionary)*. Princeton: Princeton University Press. [Reprint: Delhi: Motilal Banarsidass, 2001.]

HOUTMAN, Gustaaf 1997. The biography of modern Burmese Buddhist meditation master U Ba Khin: Life before the cradle and past the grave. In: Schober 1997: 310-344.

JAIN, Ravindra K. 1999. *The Universe as Audience. Metaphor and Community among the Jains of North India*. Shimla: Indian Institute of Advanced Study.

SHÂNTÂ, N. 1997. *The Unknown Pilgrims: The Voice of the Sādhvīs. The History, Spirituality and Life of the Jaina Women Ascetics*. (Sri Garib Dass Oriental Series, 219.) Delhi: Shri Satguru Publications. [Originally published in French: *La voie Jaina*. Paris: O.E.I.L., 1985.]

SCHOBER, Juliane (ed.) 1997. *Sacred Biography in the Buddhist Tradition of South and Southeast Asia*. (National Foreign Language Center Technical Reports.) Honolulu: University of Hawaii Press. [Reprint: Delhi: Motilal Banarsidass, 2002.]

TAYLOR, James L. 1997. The textualization of a monastic tradition: Forest monks, lineage, and the biographical process. In: Schober 1997: 289-309.

TIYAVANICH, Kamala 1997. *Forest Recollections. Wandering Monks in Twentieth-century Thailand*. Honolulu: University of Hawaii Press. [South East Asia edition: Chiang Mai: Silkworm Books.]

VALLELY, Anne 2002. *Guardians of the Transcendent. An Ethnography of a Jain Ascetic Community*. Toronto: University of Toronto Press.

The Unknown Loṅkā Tradition and the Cultural Unconscious

PETER FLÜGEL

In the last two decades, the main focus of Jaina research has shifted from the effectively a-historical exploration of the language, content and form of the Śvetāmbara canon in particular, to the historical and anthropological investigation of "strategies of transmission" of tradition, including "canonisation" and "transformation" (Bruhn 1987: 107f.). The guiding question in this research is how to conceptualise the relationship between continuity and change within the "Jaina tradition" (Carrithers 1990: 142). The investigation of this question became imperative after the philological deconstruction of earlier notions of a Jaina "ur-canon" and the "dogmatic immutability" of the Jaina doctrine (Bruhn 1987: 104, 107), as a consequence of which even the core principles of "true Jainism" (Dundas 1993: 253) and the term "Jaina" itself (Flügel 2005: 2-5) became problematic.

THE PRESENT IN THE PAST

In current academic studies, the history of the Jaina tradition is predominately presented as an interactive process between texts and practices through time (Cort 1990: 59). The emphasis is on the continuity of canonical histories, monastic traditions, and religious properties,[1] which offer alternative points of connection for the for-

[1] See the empirical studies on Jain laity in Carrithers & Humphrey 1991.

mation of variable group identities. In this model, scripture,[2] lineal descent, and the direct link to a charismatic teacher function as alternative sources of authority and legitimation as Granoff (1991: 76f.; 1993: 315), Dundas (1993: 250), Qvarnström (1998: 33f., 46) and Balbir (2003a: 267-269) have shown in their studies of late medieval Jaina sectarian traditions. Practice is not seen anymore as a mere enactment of rules, but also as an impetus for re-interpretation of rules or for the creation of new rules. Examples of such processes are particularly visible in the context of sectarian rivalry "expressing the stiffening of group identity, rather than the persevering of an archaic tradition" (Balbir 2003a: 267). Neither textual traditions nor descent constructs are now seen as static, despite the fact that innovations are within the Jaina tradition commonly introduced as "views well-rooted in the scriptural tradition" (Balbir 2003a: 263).

Although earlier views of the unchanging nature of the principal features of Jainism are being replaced by this new approach, the dominant lines of influence still run from the past to the present, from text to practice. Yet, with growing historical and ethnographical information, it seems both possible and necessary to reverse the perspective. After all, in any situation, the choice is not whether to obey or to disobey transmitted rules, but which rule to obey, as the anthropologists M. Gluckman and E. Leach both noted.[3] In the Jaina context, this is a truism. The amorphous nature of the canonical scriptures alone, not to mention the commentaries and imports from non-Jain traditions, forces strategies of selection and reduction of complexity on everyone who refers to them, even disregarding instrumental interests. The question is not whether to obey or to disobey the scriptures, but which scripture to obey, and how to interpret it.

---

[2] Used in a wider sense, including commentary, and ritual literature.

[3] See Bloch 1989: 5; Bourdieu 1992: 53. See also Carrithers' (2000: 834) investigation of eclecticism or "polytropy" in the Jain tradition.

W. C. Smith's (1962/1991: 168) concept of "cumulative tradition" already highlighted that "a tradition" presents itself not as an entity but as "a growing congeries of items" of diverse nature, which is only "unified in the conceptual mind, by processes of conceptual abstraction". J. Assmann's (2000: 39f.) notion of "cultural memory" covers similar ground. Yet, it puts less emphasis on processes of conscious transmission and re-vitalisation of a tradition through the faith of individual participants, as Smith's notion does, or the selective instrumentalisation of the past through the "connective memory" of particular groups, as current reconstructions of Jaina sectarian histories do, but focuses on the latent function of the entire "archive" (Derrida) of the amorphous "cultural unconscious". In Assmann's view, the interesting aspects of "cultural memory" are the forgotten, ignored, obsolete, hidden, excluded, suppressed or disrespected elements of a tradition, which are still accessible but unutilised and therefore "freely at one's disposal".[4] The term "cultural memory" is wider than the term "tradition", which in its restricted sense refers to a consciously constructed instrumentalisation of the past in terms of present needs and interests. Though inspired by Freud's notions of repression and latency, the "cultural unconscious" in this sense must be distinguished both from inferred processes of "unconscious thought" and "deep motivations" (Goonasekere 1986: 7), and from spheres of value within the realm of ideology which are not systematically expressed (Laidlaw 1985: 51f.), and in this sense "unconscious" (Cort 1990: 60). It overlaps, however, with the sphere of pre-

[4] Assmann 2000: 34. His definition contrasts "cultural memory", based primarily on the medium of writing, with "communicative memory", the social aspect of individual memory, and with "collective" and "connective memory", which is primarily ritually constituted: "Das kulturelle Gedächtnis umfasst im Gegensatz zum kommunikativen Gedächtnis das Uralte, Abgelegte, Ausgelagerte und im Gegensatz zum kollektiven und Bindungsgedächtnis das Nichtinstrumentalisierbare, Häretische, Subversive, Abgespaltene" (p. 41). He uses the term "unconscious transmission" (p. 40).

conscious habits, dispositions and practices (Bourdieu 1992: 52ff.) in a yet to be explored way.

In this article, I will utilise this perspective for the analysis of the modern historiography of Loṅkā and the Loṅkāgaccha, by focusing on processes of canonisation and repression of memory, and on techniques of selective citation and re-combination of transmitted elements of the Jain tradition[5] through which authority was claimed both by Loṅkā and his successors and by modern authors who tried to establish Loṅkā as an ancestral figure for competing factions of the aniconic Jaina tradition, which Loṅkā is said to have founded on the basis of the scriptures alone. I will first explore the ways in which the teachings of Loṅkā and the Loṅkāgaccha tradition have been depicted in modern literature, and how the scant information on Loṅkā was compiled and redacted by different interested parties, and then turn to some of the texts which have been attributed to Loṅkā himself to delimit the scope of his influence on the still existing but ignored Loṅkāgaccha tradition, which has lost all memory of its own past and on the Sthānakavāsī and Terāpanth traditions. I am not trying to solve the presently unanswerable question of the accuracy of the transmitted historical knowledge on Loṅkā's biography and beliefs but will focus primarily on the analysis of the effective history (*Wirkungsgeschichte*) of his ideas.[6]

THE UNKNOWN LOṄKĀ

The true nature of the biography and teachings of Loṅkā is still disputed within the Jaina tradition, even now, more than five hundred

---

[5] "Source quotations play an essential part in the demonstration" (Balbir 2003a: 263). Important in this context is J. Leslie's distinction between authority and meaning (Leslie 2003: 74f.). Pioneering works on the use of quotations (*uddharaṇa*) in the Jaina scriptures itself are the *Berliner Konkordanz* of K. Bruhn and C. B. Tripathi, and the recent publication of K. K. Jain (2003). The re-combination of elements always involves aspects of creative invention.

[6] See Gadamer 1990: 305ff.; also Bruhn 1981: 18; 1987: 111; Gombrich 1988: 21. For an analysis of the institutional conditions of this history see also Flügel 2000; 2003a; forthcoming (c).

years after his death.[7] It is commonly accepted that Luṅkā or Loṅkā[8] was a layman who lived in Gujarāt sometime between 1415-1489. Because of his access to the Śvetāmbara scriptures, he was able to articulate a powerful, text-based critique of the laxity, *śithilācāra*, of contemporary Jaina mendicants, and to reject the prevailing practice of image-worship as "uncanonical", since, in his view, it was predicated on violence and attachment to property.[9] No consensus exists, however, on the nature of Loṅkā's influence on the formation of the aniconic mendicant traditions which emerged in the aftermath of his protest: the Loṅkāgaccha tradition,[10] which was founded by Bhāṇā in the 1470s, and the Sthānakavāsī traditions, which were established in the early 17th century by different groups of dissenting *sādhu*s of the Loṅkāgaccha who objected to the re-emergence of image-worship within the tradition. Due to a lack of reliable sources,[11] nothing certain can be said at present

---

[7] On the history of research of the aniconic Śvetāmbara traditions see Flügel 2000: 40-46; Jain & Kumār 2003: 109-115.

[8] Hastīmal (1995: 765) criticises that he is variously called *Luṃpaka* (from *luṭerā*, thief) or *luṅgā* (from *luccā*, scoundrel), etc., by his opponents, rather than by his real name. Weber (1882: 807f.) and Mālvaṇiyā (1965: 185) interpret *luṃpaka* as the Sanskrit translation of *luṃkā (lauṃkā)*, the "breaker" or "destroyer" of (the worship of) images, the creator of ruins. The real name of "Loṅkā" remains unknown. The first text which mentions "Śāh" as the family name seems to be the *Loṅkāśāha Siloko*, written in Saṃvat 1600 (1543/4) by the Loṅkāgaccha *yati* Keśavaṛṣi.

[9] Mūrtipūjaka scholars such as Devagupta Sūri (1016 CE) of the Upakeśagaccha defined injury to living beings committed during the construction of temples and in the preparation of *pūjā* with flowers, fruits and water as a form of unavoidable or occupational violence (*ārambhajā hiṃsā*) (Williams 1983: 66). Digambaras additionally use the term *udyogī hiṃsā*, violence that is connected with a purposeful (religious) action.

[10] Originally: "Jinamata".

[11] Apart from Deśāī's ground-breaking survey of Gujarātī literature (1926-44), only two studies of an exploratory character are available to date on the meagre surviving textual material of the Loṅkāgaccha *yati*s: Ālamśāh Khān 1965, and particularly Muni Kāntisāgara 1965. Judging on the basis of these sources, it appears that most texts of the Loṅkāgaccha traditions are poems or songs of a hagiographic or biographical nature. Given their chronological precedence, it seems that the surviving Loṅkāgaccha *paṭṭāvalī*s, published by Hastīmal (1968),

about the biography of Loṅkā, and even less about the early leaders of the Loṅkāgaccha, although this may change in due course.[12]

The dearth of historical sources is a consequence both of the long-standing suppression of all but the most basic information concerning Loṅkā by his opponents,[13] and of the lack of interest in the creation and transmission of literature by the followers of Loṅkā, who evidently were more concerned with the preservation of his basic ideas (*Sinnpflege*) than of the texts (*Textpflege*).[14] Emptied of historical memory, the modern image of Loṅkā can be painted in almost any colour, like contours on a white canvas. By the beginning of the 20th century, Loṅkā was revered as an ancestral figure not only by the Loṅkāgaccha traditions, but also by the rival Sthānakavāsī and Terāpanth traditions; each claiming to manifest his teaching in its purest form. The premise of this contest, that religious authority is conveyed not only by proper conduct in accordance with the prescriptions of the scriptures (*siddhānta*) but also by either lineal or direct spiritual descent (*paramparā*) from a prestigious ancestor,[15] was not entirely new in the aniconic tradition.[16] In addition to Mahāvīra, Loṅkā is mentioned as a source of

---

were composed on the basis of such earlier sources. See Flügel 2003a: 180f. Jñānsundar (1936: 27) rightly complained that the "unreliable" (*apramāṇika*) *paṭṭāvalī*s of the Loṅkāgacchas do not contain any information on the doctrine of Loṅkā or the Loṅkāgacchas nor on their forms of organisation.

[12] The surviving biographical sources on the Loṅkāgaccha ascetics have not yet been studied.

[13] The early Loṅkāgaccha traditiond were opposed by local Mūrtipūjaka and Sthānakavāsī rivals, and to a lesser extent by Digambaras. References to Loṅkā were, literally, erased from the few surviving manuscripts which could have been attributed to him (see picture on p. 278). Even today, Mūrtipūjaka libraries are often instructed by the *ācārya*s of their tradition not to permit access to materials relating to Loṅkā.

[14] See Assmann 1987 for the terms *Sinnpflege* and *Textpflege*.

[15] As Dundas (1993: 253) pointed out, the Terāpanth did initially not refer to any predecessors and has still not published an official *paṭṭāvalī* which constructs a direct line of succession back to Mahāvīra or another Tīrthaṅkara. In this respect, the Terāpanthīs present themselves as direct disciples of Mahāvīra, like the Śramaṇasaṅgha. See Bhaṇḍārī 1937: 96; Flügel 2003a: 194ff.

[16] See Balbir 2003a: 268f.

authority in almost all surviving old *paṭṭāvalī*s of the Loṅkāgaccha and Sthānakavāsī traditions. However, although they are amongst the earliest written documents of the tradition, the oldest Sthānakavāsī *paṭṭāvalī*s cannot be dated much earlier than the beginning of the 19th century.[17] Before the modern Jaina revival in the second half of the 19th century, the institutional structures of the aniconic traditions were very rudimentary and, within the five main lines of tradition, in a state of permanent flux. Instead of *paṭṭāvalī*s, which trace the succession of group leaders, the dominant descent constructs were *gurvāvalī*s, that is lists which trace the *guru-śiṣya* lineages, as documented in the colophons of the oldest surviving manuscripts which contain mostly biographical poems and songs.[18] It seems, the perceived need for group organisation and ideological integration through elaborate descent constructs emerged in the Sthānakavāsī tradition only when, facing extinction under conditions of colonial domination, Hindu nationalism and sectarian rivalry, the quest for organisation, reform and competitive re-appropriation of the past had gained a new momentum.[19]

At the time, the sectarian struggle over the definition of the cultural memory of Loṅkā was particularly intense between the Sthānakavāsīs and the reformed "Saṃvegī" Tapāgaccha Mūrtipūjakas. For the Mūrtipūjakas (and the Digambaras) Loṅkā continued to be the prototypical heretic and one of the greatest threats to the survival of their own tradition. In an intriguing role-reversal, the Sthānakavāsīs and the Mūrtipūjakas re-enacted the ideological struggle between Loṅkā (and the Loṅkāgaccha) and his Mūrtipūjaka opponents in the 15th century. Yet, the agenda had signifi-

[17] Cf. Hastīmal 1968. The fact that the chronologies are relatively young may be seen as confirmation for the general view that the Sthānakavāsī *muni* Jeṭhmal was the first to invoke Loṅkā as the *dharmaguru* of his tradition in 1808. See *infra*.

[18] On the form and function of *paṭṭāvalī*s and *gurvāvalī*s see Flügel 2003a: 177-196.

[19] Purification of the *saṅgha* was already an established motive for institution building in the Śvetāmbara tradition.

cantly changed. At stake was not only the justification of image-worship on the part of the Mūrtipūjakas, but also the quest for legitimacy of a wide variety of new monastic orders and sectarian traditions which, by now, derived their religious identity directly from the layman Loṅkā – either through descent constructs or through the acceptance of his interpretation of the scriptures. At the centre of the controversies were idiosyncratic points of the customary law, *sāmācārī* or *maryādā*, of the monastic traditions[20] which are at the heart of the aniconic sects.[21] Monastic customary law is multidimensional in both form and content. Usually it is transmitted in the form of hand-written lists of proclamations (*bol*) in vernacular prose, often only comprising quotes from the scriptures with or without commentary, but also in form of poems or question-and-answer texts (*praśnottara*). It regulates not only the conduct, but also the doctrinal outlook, organisation and liturgy of a particular group of mendicants.[22] As such, it provides a crucial link between doctrine and practice, scripture and community, and is prone to processes of canonisation.[23] A crucial point of contention between the Sthānakavāsī and the Mūrtipūjaka traditions was whether Loṅkā himself formulated a list of instructions which led to the formation of the Loṅkāgaccha, what exactly these instructions were, and how they related to the customs of the various contemporary Sthānakavāsī traditions. Currently, no records are

[20] According to Dundas (1993: 248), one of the principal critics of the Loṅkā tradition, the Mūrtipūjaka monk Dharmasāgara, rejected in his *Pravacana-parīkṣā* the arbitrary basis of customary law with the remark that if custom were an acceptable criterion then even the views of the Loṅkāgaccha would be acceptable. Jñānsundar (1936: 182) also distinguishes between the Jaina *ājñā* and Loṅkā's *maryādā* in order to devalue the latter. On the Jain *maryādā* literature see Flügel 2003b.

[21] The foci for processes of identity formation of the image-worshipping sects are both mendicant orders and temples.

[22] Balbir (2003a: 259; 2003b: 53) stresses the difference between "ethics" and "abstract ideas and concepts".

[23] On the problem of canonisation in the Jaina context see Bruhn 1987: 106.

known on disputes about Loṅkā's teachings amongst Sthānakavāsīs and members of the Loṅkāgaccha.

The key question, to what extent the prescribed[24] customary practices of the different aniconic traditions (and those of the Mūrtipūjakas) actually coincided with canonical prescriptions, triggered a series of heated disputes, which peaked in the 1930s, at the height of the nationalist and religious revivalist movements in India. At the time, the Śvetāmbara revivalist movements competed vigorously with one another and with Hindu revivalist groups, such as the aniconic Ārya Samāj of Svāmī Dayānand Sarasvatī (1824-1883),[25] and with Christian missionaries for support amongst the adherents of the traditional Jaina communities. Particularly virulent were the written exchanges between Sthānakavāsī mendicants and ex-Sthānakavāsī Mūrtipūjaka monks from the Pañjāb and Rājasthān, such as the polemicists Muni Buddhivijay (Būṭerāy) (1807-1882),[26] Ācārya Ātmārām (Vijayānand Sūri) (1837-1897)[27] and his Gujarāt-

---

[24] Observed behaviour of individual monks was generally not the key point of criticism.

[25] See for instance Dayānand's polemic against the Jains (1882/1908: 439ff.), which Śāstrī (1915) has also written about, the responses scattered throughout Ātmārām's work (1882/1906: 1-162, etc.), and a text of the Sthānakavāsī *sādhvī* Pārvatī (1905b), who attacked Dayānand's notions of god (*īśvara*) and *karma* based on the belief in liberation through transmigration. A vivid description of the exchanges from 1874 onwards can be found in P. L. Jain 1913/1923: 38ff. & II, 102-111. Farquhar (1915: 104) surmised that Dayānand's inexplicable rejection of image-worship was influenced by the Sthānakavāsī example in his native Morvī state in Gujarāt.

[26] See Būṭerāy 1878. He was in 1831 initiated into the Sthānakavāsī Jīvarāja Malūkacandra Sampradāya in the Pañjāb. See Upādhyāya Ātmārām 1914: 57, n.; Duggar 1989: 338; Flügel 2000: 80, n. 78.

[27] He was born in the Kṣatriya family of the soldier Gaṇeścandra Kapūr in the village Laharā in the Zīrā Tahasīl near Phīrozpur in the Pañjāb. After coming in close contact with Osvāl Sthānakavāsī Jains, he was initiated on 5.12.1853 (1910 *mṛgasār śukla* 5) by the Sthānakavāsī *muni* Jīvaṇrām (Jīvaṇmal), who probably belonged to the Jīvarāja Gaṅgarāma tradition. In 1874, he was re-initiated by the Mūrtipūjaka *ācārya* Buddhivijay (the ex-Sthānakavāsī monk Būṭerāy) in Gujarāt, and was given the name "Vijayānanda" when he became a *sūri* on 1.12.1886 (1943 *mṛgasār śukla* 5). See Ātmārām 1900a: 72f.; Vallabhvijay 1902: 33-85; 1996: 4ff.; Flügel 2000: 60 (n. 42), 79. Further details on his group affiliations

born disciple Muni Vallabhvijay (1870-1953), who were amongst the driving forces of the revival of the upright (*saṃvegī*) tradition of the Mūrtipūjaka Tapāgaccha in Gujarāt, which had to re-establish itself almost from scratch.[28] One of the fiercest critics of the aniconic tradition in the 20th century, the (ex-Sthānakavāsī) Mūrtipūjaka *muni* Jñānsundar (1936: 131ff.), born in 1880 in Rajasthan,[29] who attempted to revive the Upakeśagaccha, has argued that contemporary Sthānakavāsī intellectuals such as Ācārya Amolakṛṣi (1877-1936),[30] Vāḍilāl Moṭīlāl Śāh (1878-1931), Muni Maṇilāl (1849-1932?),[31] and Muni Saubhāgyacandra "Santabāḷa" (died 1981),[32] who invoked Loṅkā's critique of image-worship both in their innovative historiography of Loṅkā and in their polemics against the Mūrtipūjakas, had deliberately fabricated (*kalpita*) an artificial portrait of Loṅkā as their common spiritual ancestor to promote the unification of the multiple strands of their divided tra-

before leaving the Sthānakavāsīs, which are not entirely clear in his official biographies, have been highlighted in Mohanlāl Jain's polemic *Durvādī Mukha-Capeṭikā* (1892), which was summarised by P. L. Jain 1913/1923: 246-249. Accordingly, Ātmārām left his guru Jīvaṇmal already in 1863 to study in Āgrā with Muni Ratnacandra of the Manoharadāsa Sampradāya. Thereafter, he returned to the Pañjāb and joined the Pañjāb Lavjīṛṣi Sampradāya of Ācārya Amarsiṅha. In Vallabhvijay's biography (1902: 52) it appears that despite his physical separation, Ātmārām did not formally cut his link with Jīvaṇmal.

[28] See Cort 2001: 46.

[29] See the biographies by S. M. Jain (1929) and Guṇsundar (1938).

[30] See his monumental work *Jaina Tattva Prakāś* which was composed in 1903. The title of this not openly polemical text alludes to Ātmārām's *Jaina Tattva Ādarśa*. See also *Grantha Karttā kā Saṅkṣipt Jīvan Vṛttānta by Kalyāṇmal Corādiyā* in Amolakṛṣi 1908/1920: 3.

[31] His dates 1849-1932, cited in sources of the Līmbḍī Nānī Pakṣ, are probably wrong, since he was still a young man in a photo published by Amarvijay 1908: 77f. Maṇilāl's 1934 work was criticised by the Annual General Meeting of the AISJC in Ahmedabad in 19.5.1936 as "insufficient", because of its incompleteness and lack of proof. See *Jaina Prakāśa* 17.5.1936, p. 342, in Jñānsundar 1936: 16, n.

[32] Saubhāgyacandra "Santabāḷa" had publicised his views already in 1935 in the journal *Jaina Prakāśa*, the mouthpiece of the All India Sthānakavāsī Conference, and probably earlier in a book called *Viśvavaṃdya Prabhu Mahāvīr* (Ed. Ghīrajlāl Ṭokarśī Śāh), which is listed in Maṇilāl's bibliography (1934).

dition.[33] According to Jñānsundar, who perceived a unified Sthānakavāsī Śramaṇasaṅgha as a threat to the revival of the Mūrtipūjaka tradition, there was not a shred of evidence for Loṅkā's instructions to his followers in the literature of Loṅkāgaccha, the Sthānakavāsīs and the Terāpanthīs, except for one unspecific reference to Loṅkā's *upadeśa* in a Loṅkāgaccha text which was composed thirty-eight or forty-six years after Loṅkā's death and could, in his view, therefore not be trusted.[34]

The critique of the "lack of evidence" in the Sthānakavāsi literature on Loṅkā is a modern *topos* of the Mūrtipūjaka *praśnottara* literature. It was already articulated by Ātmārām (1884/1903) and repeated again by Jñānsundar (1936: 97) and Śeṭh (1962: 342), to name but a few. Proof and evidence (*pramāṇa*) are long-established criteria in Jaina scholasticism. However, the increasing influence of European historicism and academic jargon on modern Jaina vernacular historiographies cannot be underestimated.[35] The Jainas encountered the power of "scientific truth" and of historical "facts and figures" first in the colonial courts of law in the 19th century.[36] Its rhetoric quickly filtered into their internal sectarian and communal disputes soon after the introduction of the printing press and of modern means of communication and transportation which transformed Indian intellectual culture. Almost all printed

[33] For details see Flügel 2000; 2003a.

[34] *Dayādharma Caupāī* 11. The word *upadeśa* can also refer to Loṅkā's famous conversion of Lakhamsī which took place before the creation of the Loṅkā order. It is true that no details or references are offered by V. M. Śāh (1909: 49ff.) or Saubhāgyacandra (1939: 77ff.). Jñānsundar (1936: 136) writes that there is also no evidence in Jeṭhmal's (1930) work *Samakitsār*: *un meṃ in bātoṃ kā iśārā tak bhī nahīṃ kiyā hai.* However, on page 14f. of this text a *praśnottara* of fifty-two questions which are attributed to Loṅkā is published in Hindī, though no references to the original Ms. are given. The questions correspond to a list of fifty-four questions in a 17th-century text (K) attributed to Loṅkā which was published by Mālvaṇiyā (1963a: 80-82; 1964: 381).

[35] See Cort 1995: 471, 491-494.

[36] See for instance the report of Śāh (1909: 79) on the use of the courts to settle doctrinal disputes in 1822.

vernacular texts on Loṅkā profess to be interested in history and often use scientific jargon. This does not mean that the texts are products of a scientific attitude, in the sense of Max Weber's *Wissenschaft als Beruf*, with at least a notional commitment towards objectivity. Most vernacular historiographies to date are partisan and often polemical works which explicitly aim at influencing the present through one-sided re-constructions and reinterpretations of the past.[37] To its credit, the new Jaina historiography has unearthed numerous important historical documents. Its authors also reflect on the method of writing history itself, but often only to discredit the work of opponents as "unreliable".

As Jñānsundar (1936: 7) rightly observed, the interest of the Sthānakavāsīs in Loṅkā seems to be greatest during periods of expansion, crisis and change. Whenever "Sthānakavāsīs" feel the need to assert their common doctrinal heritage and the need for institutional integration, both Loṅkā and the common opposition against image-worship are brought into play. And whenever the "Mūrtipūjaka" tradition as a whole comes under attack, it usually retaliates in kind. In this way the antagonism generates a sense of self-identity in both traditions and contributes to their social integration. Underlying the antagonism between the previously socially insignificant denominational super-categories such as "Mūrtipūjaka" and "Sthānakavāsi", incorporating several "sub-"sects, is the struggle over the definition of the "essence" of "true Jainism" (understood in the manner of the new book oriented *Religionswissenschaft*) under the banner of "Jain" unity. At stake was the ideological self-definition and thus political positioning of the entire "Jain community" at a time of the emergence of Jain religious nationalism.[38]

---

[37] *Lokāśāh ke yug se lekar āj tak kisī bhī vidvān sthānakavāsī muni ne athvā gṛhastha ne viśuddha itihās ke dṛṣtikoṇ se kuch likhā ho, vah mere dekhne meṃ nahīṃ āyā. ... praśasti tathā guṇānuvād hī adhik hai – itihās us meṃ nahīṃ hai* (Mālvaṇiyā 1964: 365). The same is true for histories of Loṅkā by followers of other sectarian traditions.

[38] Flügel 2005; forthcoming (b).

ESSENCE OF RIGHT BELIEF

The Loṅkāgaccha tradition still exists today in small pockets in Gujarāt.[39] Yet, the contemporary followers of the Loṅkāgaccha remember nothing of Loṅkā or his teachings anymore, and have only the vaguest idea of the recent history of their tradition. Not even Loṅkā's name is mentioned in their few idiosyncratic rituals. With two negligible exceptions,[40] most of the modern texts on Loṅkā have been produced by Sthānakavāsī, Terāpanthī and Mūrtipūjaka mendicants and lay intellectuals. It appears that the first Sthānakavāsī text which explicitly sought support in Loṅkā's teachings was Muni Jeṭhmal's celebrated anti-Mūrtipūjaka polemic *Samakita-sāra*, essence of right belief. The original Gujarātī text was prepared by several unnamed Sthānakavāsī lay followers, sometime after the religious debate (*śāstrārtha*) in which Jeṭhmal reportedly used the published arguments,[41] and printed in 1882 in Rājkoṭ by Śeṭh Nemicand Hīrācand Koṭhārī from Goṇḍal in Saurāṣṭra.[42] Two further Gujarātī editions were published in the following decades, and one revised Hindī edition of two parts in 1930[43] (with the translation of the original text forming part one).[44] The way in which this work was created offers insights into the strategies through

[39] Flügel, forthcoming (c). The term *gaccha* can mean school, monastic order or sect.

[40] I have found only two histories of Loṅkā in the Loṅkāgaccha *upāśraya*s, Bagasarāvāḷā 1894, and P. T. Śāh 2001. Both texts are derivative and do not add anything new on Loṅkā. The second text relies largely on Vāṅā 1976.

[41] *Usī carcā kā sārāṃś, anekoṃ jijñāsu sadgṛhastha ke āgraha se, pustakākār ke rūp meṃ ḍhāl diyā gayā* (Pratham Bhāg kī Bhūmikā, in Jeṭhmal 1930: 4).

[42] Ātmārām 1903: 289; Vallabhvijay 1909: 14; *Bhūmikā* in Jeṭhmal 1930: 10.

[43] Without access to the first three editions it is impossible to clearly identify different layers of commentary which may have been added to the original text in the published version of 1930.

[44] V. M. Śāh (1909: 79) mentions a documentation of the counter-arguments of the Mūrtipūjakas, *Ḍhuṇḍhakmat Khaṇḍan Rās* by Muni Uttamvijay which was unavailable to me. Johannes Klatt's *Jaina Onomastikon*, III, p. 1281, mentions another polemical text of this author: *Dhundhiā no rāsado* (Ahmadābād: Nāran Kṛṣṇarām, 1869).

which the effective history of a tradition is created and re-created, and suggests that an investigation of parallels in the history of the transmission of knowledge in the Jaina tradition may yield materials for an understanding of processes of identity-formation through the work of canonisation outside the canon, which have not yet been investigated.[45] First of all, Jeṭhmal was not the author of the published work. At the time, it was generally not considered appropriate for Sthānakavāsī *muni*s to publish books under their own name, because of the violence of the printing press and because of the implicit promotion of egotism. Instead, lay-followers published lecture notes of the *pravacana*s of their gurus. In its prefaces and introductions, the text is described as a synopsis of the arguments used by Jeṭhmal in a public debate with the Tapāgaccha *saṃvegī muni*s Vīrvijay and Yaśovijay on doctrinal differences which divided their religious traditions.[46]

The debate took place in Ahmedabad, either in 1808/9 (Saṃvat 1865)[47] or 1821/2 (Saṃvat 1878).[48] It was triggered by a communal dispute. According to Śāh (1909: 78f.), Sthānakavāsī mendicants were proselytising at the time in the town. In response, the locally dominant Mūrtipūjaka laity threatened to excommunicate all Sthānakavāsīs from their castes (*jñātī*). In order to help his beleaguered co-religionists in this situation, Ācārya Prāg from the Sthānakavāsī Dariyāpūrī Sampradāya travelled from his abode in the village of Visalapura outside Ahmedabad to the Tabīā Poḷ in the Sāraṅgapura district of the city centre. He stayed in Gulābcand Hīracand's house

[45] On strategies of canonisation in the Jaina context see Bruhn 1987: 107, etc. To my knowledge, the term "secondary canonisation" was first used by Glasenapp (1925). The term "work of canonisation" was introduced by Assmann (1987: 19). For further studies on processes of canonisation in South Asia see Dalmia, Malinar & Christof 2003.

[46] Jñānsundar 1936: 15 suggests that Jeṭhmal developed his arguments on the basis of a text called *Vivāha Cūliyā Sūtra*, which was unavailable to me.

[47] Jñānsundar (1936: 15, 293) argued that the debate itself took place in Saṃvat 1865, because Jeṭhmal was already dead in Saṃvat 1878 (he does not give any information as to which Jeṭhmal he identified).

[48] V. M. Śāh 1909: 78f.

and also imparted religious instruction to the families of Gīrdhar Śaṅkar, Pānācand Jhavercand, Rāycand Jhavercand, Khīmcand Jhavercand, and others, who, in turn, helped him to spread his word. In order to end the ensuing quarrels between Sthānakavāsīs and Mūrtipūjakas, both parties went to court. To educate themselves about the Jaina religion, the judges invited *muni*s from both sides as expert witnesses. For Prāg's side the learned Muni Jeṭhmal, apparently a *suśiṣya* of Muni Rūpcand of the Bhūdhar Dharmadāsa Sampradāya in Rājasthān,[49] was present, together with twenty-seven other *muni*s;[50] and for the Mandirmārgīs Muni Vīrvijay together with Yaśovijay and several monks and scholars (*śāstrī*) came to the court. According to "someone's" notes (*yādī*) of the court-proceedings, the judgement of 1878 *pauṣ śukla* 13 (6.1. 1822)[51] apparently favoured the arguments of Jeṭhmal's side – described as *cetanapūjaka*s, worshippers of living consciousness, in contrast to the *mūrtipūjaka*s, worshippers of images – although in their respective literatures both sides claimed victory.[52]

Although there is no conclusive evidence, the timing of the belated publication was almost certainly related to the publication of what is probably the first polemic against the Sthānakavāsīs in

---

[49] Preface, in Jeṭhmal 1930: 4. Seṭh (1970: 1112, n. 1) writes that Jeṭhmal temporarily belonged to the orders of Ācārya Jaymal and of the Terāpanth *ācārya* Bhikṣu respectively. Other sources say that he worked under the directive of Ācārya Amarasiṅha (Flügel 2003a: 237).

[50] Reportedly, twenty-five monks from Rājasthān were present, plus two monks from Prāg's group, and apparently Muni Mul (Mūḷ?) from the Sāyalā Sampradāya in Gujarāt who is said to have supported Muni Jeṭhmal from the Palanpur Sampradāya (Maṇilāl 1934: 227f.). This points to a concerted effort on the side of the Sthānakavāsīs, which may have required them to take recourse to Loṅkā to find a common platform.

[51] Some sources say: 1878 *phālgun śukla* 1 (22.2.1822). The case is mentioned in V. M. Śāh 1909: 78f.; Maṇilāl 1934: 192f., 198f., 228; Jñānsundar 1936: 7, 15, 293; Candanākumārī 1964: 150, 192; Hastīmal 1971: 138f. See Flügel 2000: 68, n. 54 and 79, n. 77; 2003a: 237.

[52] Only the *mūrtipūjak ono parājay thayo – cetanapūjak ono jay thayo*; and *jeṭho rīkh āvyore, kāgaḷ vāṃcī rarī; pustak bahu lāvyore, gāḍuṃ ek bharī* (in V. M. Śāh 1909: 79). Jñānsundar 1936: 15 simply states Jeṭhmal's defeat (*hār*).

print[53] in Ātmārām's (1881/1954, II: 539f.) work *Jainatattvādarśa* which appeared in Bhāvnagar in Saṃvat 1937. After his separation from and excommunication by the Sthānakavāsī Ācārya Amarasiṅha (1805-1881) of the Pañjāb Lavjīṛṣi Sampradāya and his re-initiation into the Tapāgaccha in Saṃvat 1932 (1875/6) in Ahmedabad, the ex-Sthānakavāsī *muni* Ātmārām (Vijayānanda Sūri) contributed much to the Mūrtipūjaka revival in Gujarāt and in the Pañjāb. To revive the "Sanātan Jaina Dharma"[54] by attracting more followers, Ātmārām started a vigorous pro-image-worship campaign, which he had already instigated in his later years as a Sthānakavāsī monk, during which he criticised many of the contemporary practices of the Sthānakavāsīs. One of the points of contention before he left was that Ācārya Amarasiṅha did not answer twenty-one "legitimate" questions which were put to him in Saṃvat 1925 (1868) by certain Sthānakavāsī *śrāvaka*s from Dillī.[55] Amarasiṅha and his successor Ācārya Sohanlāl (1846-1936) of the Lavjīṛṣi tradition were the dominant Sthānakavāsī monks in his native Pañjāb at the time, and the main targets of his critique. After Ātmārām's excommunication and the publication of his *Jainatattvādarśa*, Sohanlāl sent – on request of Amarasiṅha[56] – a *praśnottara* of one hundred questions[57] to Ātmārām in Saṃvat 1938 *caitra śukla* 5 (4.4.1881), to which Ātmārām instantly replied in Saṃvat 1938 *caitra śukla* 7 (6.4.1881), without receiving a response.[58] Shortly thereafter, it seems, in Saṃvat 1938 (1882)[59]

---

[53] *yah lok to sarva jainmat se viparīt calanevāle hai* (Ātmārām 1954, II: 540).

[54] Ātmārām 1900a: 72.

[55] Vallabhvijay 1891: 131f. The first question asked for the *paṭṭāvalī* of all *ācārya*s beginning with Mahāvīra, which apparently did not exist in this Sthānakavāsī tradition at the time: 1. *śrī mahāvīr svāmī se lekar āj tak pāṭānupāṭ kaun se ācārya hue unoṃ ke nām likhne* (p. 131).

[56] In Vallabhvijay 1891: 72-82.

[57] On the *śataka* format see Balbir 2003a; 2003b.

[58] Published by Vallabhvijay 1891: 83-125.

[59] Generally, the South Indian calendar applies in Gujarāt, therefore Saṃvat 1938 must be 1882, not 1881.

the polemical *Samakitsār* appeared in print with its sustained attack on *mūrtipūjā* and a long list of questions to the Mandirmārgīs. Immediately after receiving a copy of this book from a Sthānakavāsī layman in Delhi, Ātmārām (1884/1903) composed an equally polemical point-for-point reply under the title *Samyaktva Śalyoddhāra*, removal of the thorns from right belief,[60] and the work *Ajñāna Timira Bhāskara* (1888/1906), radiant darkness of ignorance, in which both the Ārya Samāj and the Ḍhūṇḍhiyās are systematically criticised.[61] This triggered a long series of tit-for-tat exchanges between leading mendicants (and laity) of the two (three) traditions, which subsided somewhat only after Indian Independence in 1949, though the conflict is still smouldering and can re-erupt at any time.

Of particular interest for us is the role of "Loṅkā" in this debate. Ātmārām's sharp criticism of the "heresy" (*nihnava*) of the "*Ḍhūṇḍhiyās*" was provoked by Jeṭhmal's (1930: 1-9) construction of a contrast between "the path of compassion" (*dayā mārga*) and non-violence of the tradition of Loṅkā (in its Sthānakavāsī manifestation),[62] and "the path of violence" (*hiṃsā mārga*) of the Mūrtipūjaka *saṃvegī* mendicants, which were addressed as "yellow-clad pseudo-ascetics" (*pītāmbar bheṣadhārī*). As a synonym of *dayā mārga*, Jeṭhmal used the term *mokṣa mārga*, and compared the path of salvation of the Sthānakavāsīs, which he derived directly from

---

[60] *Ḍhūṃḍhīye hī hiṃsādharmī haiṃ aur dayā kā yathārtha svarūp nahīṃ samajhte haiṃ* (Ātmārām 1903: 289). There are many texts in the Jaina *bhaṇḍāras* with titles such as *Samakit Sār Praśnottar Pacchīsī Sajjhāy* (L.D. Institute Ms. No. 4734 etc.) which may contain information on earlier exchanges between exponents of the two traditions.

[61] The title alluded to Dayānand's book *Timir Bhāskar Jvālāprasād* (cf. P. L. Jain 1913/1923: 41). The work addressed the view of the two main rivals of Ātmārām in the Pañjāb. It was composed in two parts between 1882-85 in Ambālā, and first published in Bhāvnagar in 1888. Ātmārām's deliberation on the beliefs of the Christians, *Īsāī Mat Samīkṣā*, was published posthumously in the year 1900. See Kiraṇyaśāstrī 1999, Pariśiṣṭ I.

[62] Jeṭhmal 1930: 9f. does not use the word "Sthānakavāsī", but refers directly to Loṅkā and his "true mendicant path": *lokā gaccha-sādhu mārga hī saccā hai* (p. 3)

Loṅkā, with the dual concern of the Mūrtipūjakas (and Digambaras) with salvation and with material well-being (*kuśaliyā darśana*).[63] The Mūrtipūjakas are spreading lies, he argued, because they convey to their followers the illusion that salvation can be reached through *pūjā*, while preventing them from reading the truth in the scriptures.[64]

In his long list of rejoinders, of which only the *Samyaktva Śalyoddhāra* and the *Ajñāna Timira Bhāskara* seem to have been published during his lifetime, Ātmārām (1903; 1908)[65] highlighted Jeṭhmal's "misspellings" and "misunderstandings" of the scriptures, and furnished descriptions of the lax conduct of contemporary Ḍhūṇḍhaka mendicants. In his view, the Sthānakavāsīs generally did not observe the canonical prescriptions, and thus truly formed a religion of violence: *ḍhūṇḍhiye hiṃsā dharmī haim.*[66] In his critique of Jeṭhmal's account, Ātmārām (1903: 7f.) categorically stated that everything that "Jūṭhmal" wrote about Loṅkā's beliefs as the source of the Sthānakavāsī doctrines was a "self-imagined fabricated lie". In accordance with the conventions of the *praśnottara* genre,[67] he backed his claim with selected citations

---

[63] Two realms of value in the Mūrtipūjaka tradition are also identified by Cort 2001.

[64] In contrast to other Mūrtipūjaka *ācāryas*, Ātmārām opposed the publication of the scriptures. He permitted both *sādhus* and laity to read the *sūtras* only in the presence of a guru who could explain the meaning of the text, and prevented access to certain texts to women. See for instance Malukcand 1908: 182f.

[65] See also his answers to Sohanlāl in Vallabhvijay 1891: 83-125.

[66] Ātmārām 1903: 289. It is not entirely clear whether Ātmārām attacks both observed behaviour and customary law in this section. Since he does not address any particular order, though he may have had the Lavjīṛṣi Amarasiṅha Sampradāya in mind, his criticism is too vague to be considered in detail.

[67] In her discussion of the Kharataragaccha monk Samayasundara's (1553-1645) *Sāmācārī Śataka* of 1616, whose second section (and probably other points as well) is devoted entirely to the critique of "the Sthānakavāsīs" (probably the Loṅkāgaccha traditions, but since the canon of "thirty-two" is criticised in points 38 and 47 the Sthānakavāsī Jīvarāja may have been addressed), Balbir (2003a: 255, 257; 2003b: 56f.) argues that it was the conflict between Loṅkā and the Mūrtipūjakas which lead to the development of the *praśnottara* genre which reflects the formal features of oral debates. In her view it is the "tendency to

from the canon and from the writings of the Sthānakavāsī tradition itself.[68] Information on the true historical origin (*kharī utpatti*) of the "Ḍhūṇḍhak Panth",[69] he argued, can be found in two other Sthānakavāsī texts which he summarised in a few pages: Hīrakalaś-muni's *Kumati Vidhvaṃsana Caupāī*, quatrain on the destruction of stupidity, and the *Ḍhuṇḍhak Paṭṭāvalī* of Amolakcand of the Pañjāb Amarasiṅha Sampradāya.

Although the furnished information on the lines of succession is rudimentary,[70] Ātmārām's version of the "actual history" contrasts favourably with the account offered by Jeṭhmal[71] in the style of "localised" versions of Jaina "universal history", i.e. the history of great beings or *mahāpuruṣas*, and doctrinal "cosmological history".[72] In his first verse, Jeṭhmal (1930: 1) wrote, *śrī dayā dharma phailā aur bhasma graha utarā jiskā vistār*, effectively arguing –

---

stress divergencies" and the lack of "any global organising principle" which distinguishes the genre from the merely "literary" question-answer formats used in the canon, though the method of citing "authentic" written texts in the debates between the late medieval sectarian traditions (see Granoff 1993) seems to be the principal difference: "such works are meant to discuss specific points that gave birth to different opinions within different Jain circles by referring to scriptures, with the idea to settle them according to the view in force within the order to which the author belongs" (Balbir 2003a: 256).

[68] *Jeṭhmal meṃ jo luṃpakmat kī utpatti likhī hai bilkul jhūṭhī aur svakapol kalpit hai* (Ātmārām 1903: 11).

[69] Ātmārām 1954, II: 537 derives the term *Ḍhūṇḍhiya* or *Ḍhūṇḍhaka*, polemically from *Ḍhūṇḍha*, or ruin. The Sthānakavāsī themselves derive *Ḍhūṇḍhiya* from *Ḍhūṇṛhiya* or *Ḍhūṇṛhaka*, or seeker. See for instance Hastīmal 1995: 769.

[70] Cf. Flügel 2000; 2003a; Jain & Kumār 2003.

[71] Jñānsundar 1936: 29 used the same method of critique backed with more evidence of this kind in his rejoinder to the later Sthānakavāsī *itihāsa* literature.

[72] Bruhn 1983: 37 defines Jaina universal history in terms of "a definite mythological subject, the history of the sixty-three great men". Cort 1995: 473 coined the loosely defined term "localised history" to describe similar narrative structures, focusing on great personalities, etc., within particular sectarian traditions. For the present purpose – the analysis of "historical narratives of great beings" – both definitions are too specific, and do not account for the cosmological themes in Jaina historical narratives. I would suggest to see "universal history", as defined by Bruhn, as a term which mediates between "chronological" and "cosmological history".

as Devṛṣi's commentary explains – that Loṅkā's revival of "true Jainism" in the year Saṃvat 1531, exactly two thousand years after Mahāvīra's death, was predicted already by the canonical *Jina-cariya* 129-131, which says that after a two thousand year period during which

> there will not be paid much respect and honour to the śramaṇas, the Nirgrantha monks and nuns (...) when the great [Bhasma] Graha, &c., leaves that natal asterism [of Mahāvīra], there will be paid much respect and honour to the śramaṇas, the Nirgrantha monks and nuns for an era of two-thousand years (KS 130f.).

This somewhat optimistic version of Jaina cosmological history, which allows for progressive intervals within the generally predicted decline, contrasts however with other passages in the scriptures. In his rejoinder, Ātmārām (1903: 4) cited the famous section Viy 20.8.4 in which Mahāvīra predicted that his teaching will survive for at least 21,000 years after his death. The same argument had previously been used by the 16th-century founders of two Sthānakavāsī orders, Lava and Dharmadāsa, against the followers of the Loṅkāgaccha and the Ekal Pātriyāpanth, who indeed seem to have favoured the *Jinacaritra* passage, to which Jeṭhmal had reverted without fear of sanction, because the Loṅkāgaccha was already in terminal decline, and no competition for the Sthānakavāsīs anymore.[73] Since there is no independent criterion for judging which of the two versions is more authentic (even historical precedence would not solve the issue) any choice between them is a matter of personal preference and of sectarian interests. However, due to his correspondence with European scholars such as Hoernle[74] and the presence of his representative V. R. Gāndhī at the first Parliament of World Religions in Chicago in 1893, Ātmārām's writings were widely read outside India, and significantly influenced the image of the Jaina community projected by the first

---

[73] Flügel 2000: 72f.

[74] Ātmārām 1916.

generations of modern Indologists. Jeṭhmal's text, by contrast, circulated only within the literary elite of the Sthānakavāsīs and Mūrtipūjakas. Thus, only the Mūrtipūjaka depiction entered European textbooks on Jainism.

The second round of the dispute was fought on behalf of Sohanlāl and Ātmārām between the Sthānakavāsī *mahāsatī* "Jainācārya"[75] Pārvatī Devī (1854-1939) from the Amarasiṅha Sampradāya and Ātmārām's disciple and future *ācārya* Muni Vallabhvijay (1870-1954). Pārvatī Devī was a remarkable Jaina nun[76] who on the 28.12. 1872 (1929 *mārgaśīrṣa kṛṣṇa* 13) in Delhi changed from the Manoharadāsa Sampradāya of Ācārya Ratnacandra (died 1864)[77] to the Pañjāb Lavjīṛṣi tradition of Ācārya Amarsiṅha (1805-1881).[78] According to Sarlā (1991: 299), she chose a less restrictive group in order to be able to preach in public, to publish books, and to wander alone.[79] Her official biography by P. L. Jain (1913/1923: 30), however, informs us that she joined the Amarsiṃha Sampradāya because its mendicants followed the scriptures more closely. Pārvatī Devī's pamphlet *Jñāna Dīpikā* (Lāhaur 1889), a critique of the *Jainatattvādarśa*,[80] and Muni Vallabhvijay's (1891: 9-71) reply,

---

[75] Book cover Pārvatī 1905b. "*Ācārya*" is here used as a honorific title.

[76] According to Vallabhvijay's often polemical remarks on her biography (1891: 6-11), she was born in an Agravāl *baniyā* family of the village Luhāra near Āgrā, took *dīkṣā* from her teachers Muni Kuṃvarsena and Sādhvī Hīrāṃ of Ratnacandra's Sthānakavāsī Manoharadāsa Sampradāya on the 6.4.1867 (1924 *caitra śukla* 2). Kuṃvarsena did not follow Ratnacandra's command (*ājñā*) and separated himself later together with his disciples. Pārvatī's official biographer P. L. Jain (1913/1923) confirms her basic biodata. He relates the interesting detail that her father's brother followed the Digambara tradition, and her father the Sthānakavāsī tradition of Ratnacand's disciple Kuṃvarsena (p. 5).

[77] Vallabhvijay 1902: 46.

[78] Vallabhvijay 1891: 8 notes that the disputes between Pārvatī and Ātmārām, who left the Sthānakavāsīs in 1874, caused great discordance between the Jaina traditions in the Pañjāb: *pañjāb meṃ ākar bahut Jaina dharma kī nindā karāvegā.*

[79] Her texts are published in the *praśnottara* format, and are probably based on protocols of oral conversations with her lay followers.

[80] The contents can be inferred from Vallabhvijay's response (1891: 9-71). I have not been able to locate a copy of this or any other text mentioned in the

Gappa Dīpikā,[81] re-ignited the debate in the Pañjāb which was again conducted in the form of *praśnottara*s, in which for instance the difference between the thirty-one Āgamas which were allegedly accepted by Loṅkā and the thirty-two Āgamas of the Sthānakavāsīs was questioned by Vallabhvijay (1891: 130f.), who dismissed Pārvatī's book as a "work of sin" which calls for an atonement (*prāyaścitta*) since, in accordance with the rules of the scriptures, no *sādhvī* before her had ever written a book nor spoken in the assembly of men.[82] Vallabhvijay was, in turn, repudiated by an anonymous [?] pamphlet called *Gappa Dīpikā Samīr kā Gappa* and Paṇḍit Jiyālāl Jain's (1893) *Carcā Candroday Bhāg Tisrā*. According to Vallabhvijay's (1909: 14-18) chronology of the exchanges between 1881-1909,[83] in response to Vallabhvijay, Ācārya Sohanlāl wrote *Draupadīpūjā Khaṇḍan* (Amṛtsar),[84] Muni Ṛṣirāj *Satyārtha Sāgara* (Pune), and an unnamed author *Saṃvegīmat Sāguphā*

---

following which is not listed in the bibliography. Further books of Pārvatī, which were inaccessible to me, are *Jaina Dharma ke Dās Niyam* (1889), *Go Rakṣā kā Upadeś* (1900), *Kuvyasan Niṣedh* (1915), *Mukti Nirṇay Prakāś* (1916), *Śrīmad Bhagavān Nemināth Rājīmatījī kā Jīvan Caritra* (1918), *Brahmacarya Vidhi* (1919), and *Vairāgya Prakāś* (1930). Further criticisms of Ātmārām, whom she met personally for the first time in 1863 in Āgrā, are summarised in P. L. Jain 1913/1923: 32-37, 249f., 278-283, II: 47-50, 71f. They concern issues such as the initiation of five year old children, or the habit of Ātmārām's mendicants of taking baths, which are defended in the *Jainatattvādarśa*, and in particular the "misrepresentation" of the Sthānakavāsī tradition in the last section of this book.

[81] The title of Vallabhvijay's *Ḍhuṇḍhak-hita-śikṣā Apanām Gappa-dīpikā-samīr* (1891) alludes also to V. M. Śāh's *Hita-śikṣā*. Vallabhvijay quotes extensively from Ātmārām. His authorship of the work, as well as the attribution of the authorship of "Vijayrājendra Sūri's" *Caturtha Stuti Kuyukti Nirṇay Chedan Kuṭhār* to Vallabhvijay's disciple Dhanvijay, has been disputed by J. Jain (1893: 6f.), in response to the polemical attribution of Pārvatī's book to an anonymous Brāhmaṇ.

[82] Vallabhvijay 1909: 1f.

[83] With details supplemented from other sources.

[84] The critique of image worship in the manner of Draupadī, who apparently only at her wedding under special circumstances venerated images, is a *topos* of the aniconic Jaina literature. See for instance L 7; Jeṭhmal 1930: 84-112. Compare: "The Story of Draupadi" in: Nagendra K. Singh (ed.), *Encyclopaedia of Jainism*, Vol. 22, pp. 5931-5945. New Delhi: Anmol Publications, 2001.

(Ambālā); which was countered by an unnamed author's text *Jahālat Ḍhuṇḍhiyā* (Ambālā). Three further Sthānakavāsī pamphlets, *Kāgahans Nirṇay* (Ambālā), *Manta kī Bahsa Pūjerāṃ* of Kanīyālāl (Paṭayālā), and *Samyaktva athavā Dharma no Darvājo* by V. M. Śāh (Ahmedabad), were countered by Muni Amarvijay's *Dharma nā Darvājā Jovā nī Diśā*, which in turn was criticised by a text published in Ahmadabad, *Kamalprabhā*. The response to Mahāsatī Pārvatī's *Satyārtha-Candrodaya-Jain* (Lāhaur: Lālā Meharcand, 1904) on the "stupid" worship of "lifeless objects" (*jaṛ pūjā*)[85] and on the *nikṣepas*[86] was Muni Amarvijay's (1908) *Ḍhūṇḍhak-Hṛday-Netrāñjanaṃ athavā Satyārtha-Candrodayāṣṭakaṃ*; and in response to the Sthānakavāsī pamphlet *Iśatahār-Amarāvatī*, an unnamed Mūrtipūjaka author wrote *Ḍhuṇḍhakpol Amarāvatī*, which was countered by the texts *Khulāsāpol Saṃvegīyāṃ* (Amṛtsar), Muni Ratnacand's *Saṃvegīmat Mardan* (Amṛtsar), and *Śāstrārtha Nābhā* (Ambālā). The last Mūrtipūjaka text on Vallabhvijay's list is *Ḍhuṇḍhakmat Parājay* (Ātmānand Jain Sabhā Pañjāb 1909) which gives information on the judgement of Mahārāja Hīrāsiṃha Bahādur of Paṭayālā in favour of Vallabhvijay in a debate with Sohanlāl on the scriptural foundations of their respective views in

[85] Like most topics of the sectarian debate, the issue was already addressed by Loṅkā, and discussed for instance in Samayasundara's *Sāmācārī Śataka* 40 (Balbir 2003a: 260). However, like Ātmārām (Vijayānandsūri), Pārvatī (1905b) was also engaged in an ideological battle against the "Āryyās", i.e. the Ārya Samāj.

[86] See Jeṭhmal's (1930) critique of the interpretation of the *nikṣepa* doctrine by the *hiṃsādharmī*, i.e. the image-worshippers. The Mūrtipūjaka tradition treats the four principal analytical standpoints, or *nikṣepa* (*nāma*, *dravya*, *sthāpana*, *bhāva*), as equivalent, whereas the Sthānakavāsī or *dayādharmī* tradition gives priority to the *bhāva nikṣepa*: *anuyogadvāra sūtra meṃ 4 nikṣepa kahe haiṃ yah to satya hai par cāroṃ hī nikṣepa vandanīk nahīṃ kahe. ek bhāv nikṣepa vandanīk kahā hai* (Jeṭhmal 1930: 54). The principal reply was formulated by Muni Ātmārām (1884/1908), who in turn was criticised by Mahāsatī Pārvatī (1905a) in her work *Satyārtha Candrodaya Jaina*, which was rejected in Muni Amarvijay's *Ḍhūṇḍhak Hṛday Netrāñjanaṃ athavā Satyārtha Candrodayāṣṭakaṃ* (1908). An early Digambara critique of this view can be found in the *Sūryaprakāśa* of the year 1825. See Dundas 2001: 67, n. 44. For short summaries of Pārvatī's debates with Digambara laity see P. L. Jain 1913/1923.

5.2.1904.[87] It was followed by seven Sthānakavāsī responses, some of which are reprinted and criticised in the collection edited by Muni Amarvijay (1908): *Pītāmbarī Parājay* (Amṛtsar), Muni Rāmcandra's *Amṛtsar Saṃgraha* (Mumbaī), the *stavan* of Muni Mādhav *Taraṅgiṇī Dvitīya Taraṅg* (Āgrā 1908), Muni Saubhāgmal's *Vividh Ratna Prakāś* (Pune), Muni Kundanmal's *Pragaṭ Jaina Pītāmbarī Mūrtipūjakoṃ kā Mithyātva* (1908),[88] and his *Ātmārām Saṃvegī kī Karttūt, Ātmārām kī Ādat kā Namūnā* (n.d.), and finally V. M. Śāh's (1909) *Sādhumārgī Jaina Dharmānuyāyīoe Jāṇvā Jog Keṭalīk Aitihāsik Noṃdh*, a key text for the modern Sthānakavāsī unification movement, which attracted much critical response from the Mūrtipūjakas, not least from Vallabhvijay (1909),[89] Ujamcand (1909), and Jñānsundar (1936: 247ff.), because it again referred to Loṅkā as the common forefather of all Sthānakavāsīs and thereby started a new round of debates.[90]

HISTORICAL NOTES

V. M. Śāh (1878-1931) was the first layperson to make an important intellectual contribution to the study of Loṅkā's legacy for the Sthānakavāsīs,[91] and the first Sthānakavāsī to collect some of the available though "untrustworthy" *paṭṭāvalī*s in order to tentatively reconstruct, in the manner of Ātmārām, an accurate history of the entire Sthānakavāsī tradition.[92] He was also a prime mover

---

[87] Note that many pamphlets of the Mūrtipūjaka monks have been published under Ātmārām's name even after his death. See footnote 81.

[88] Kundanmal belonged to the Raghunātha Sampradāya.

[89] He described it as a "work of deceit". See V. M. Śāh's reply (1925: 3f.).

[90] Muni [Ācārya] Amolakṛṣi's *Śāstroddhār Mīmāṃsā* (1920), an addendum to his Āgama edition is also a key text for the Sthānakavāsī revival. It contains a few pages on Loṅkā (pp. 57-60) and sustained a criticism of the Mūrtipūjakas and Digambaras. I only recently gained access to this book.

[91] The Mūrtipūjaka layman Lālā Jayadayāl's *Ḍhūṇḍhak Mat Samīkṣā* (n.d.) must have been published in the Pañjāb sometime before 1908.

[92] Śāh 1909: 5 singles out the *paṭṭāvalī*s of the Darīyāpurī Sampradāya, the Pañjāb (Lavjīṛṣi) Sampradāya and of the Mūrtipūjaka "Vijaya" and "Sāgara"

behind the creation of the *All India Sthānakavāsī Jaina Conference* (AISJC) of the Sthānakavāsī laity in February 1906 in Morvī,[93] and publicised in his 1909 book for the first time the idea of creating a unified order of all Sthānakavāsī mendicants. Although Loṅkā was a layman, it was he alone who could serve as a common ancestor, because the Sthānakavāsī tradition was founded not by one but by several different ex-Loṅkāgaccha mendicants, who initially shared little more than the rejection of image-worship and the criticism of "lax conduct" of the Loṅkāgaccha *yati*s. After their creation between c. 1628-1668, the original five Sthānakavāsī mendicant traditions quickly split into numerous sub-groups which developed different customs and began to struggle with one another, until the AISJC finally called for an end of all "internal" antagonism. Conflicts between mendicant orders were divisive for the Sthānakavāsī laity as well and obstructed aim of the AISJC leadership to assert the political influence of Sthānakavāsī representatives on a national platform. From 1906 onwards, the AISJC, like the competing Conferences of the Digambaras and Mūrtipūjakas which were established in 1893 and 1902 respectively, held regular meetings on an all-India basis to prepare the ground for the first *mahāsammelan*, or great assembly, of representatives of all Sthānakavāsī mendicant traditions, which was finally held in 1933 in Ajmer.

Before the assembly congregated, a fourth edition of the *Samakitsār*, which was also the first Hindī edition, was published in 1930 under the auspices of *the Akhil Bhāratīya Sthānakavāsī Jaina Conference* after years of careful preparation of the translation by Muni Devṛṣi (1872-1942), who in 1936 succeeded Ācārya Amolakṛṣi (1877-1936) – one of the most influential Sthānakavāsī monks at the time who was the first to publish a printed edition and

---

Śākhā (which treated the Sādhumārgī and Loṅkagacchī as "*sammūrcchima*") for their untrustworthiness, but exempts the Cha Koṭī Saṅgha (Līmbḍī Nānī Pakṣa) *paṭṭāvalī*.

[93] On the significance of V. M. Śāh and the text *Aitihāsik Noṃdh* see Flügel 2000; 2003a.

Hindī translation of the Sthānakavāsī Āgamas – as the leader of the Mālvā Ṛṣi Sampradāy. The plan was to make the ideas of Loṅkā available to everyone, in the national language of India, and to create a sense of unity amongst the Sthānakavāsī mendicants in opposition to the Mūrtipūjakas in particular. In this context, the author of the *Samakit Śalyoddhāra* became again a useful target. One of the three anonymous introductions to the *Samakitsār*[94] accused the "stubborn mischief maker" Ātmārām in an *ad hominem* attack for not understanding the substance of *samakita* (*samyaktva*), right belief, nor practising it, as his violent use of language testified. As proof for Ātmārām's wrongdoing, the following passage of the *Dasaveyāliya* is cited:

> When he notices that [a monk] who has mastered the Āyāra and the [Viyāha-]Pannatti [and] who is studying the Diṭṭhivāya, makes a mistake in speaking, he should not mock him. (DVS 8.49).[95]

In other words, Ātmārām was chided for not seriously criticising the principles of the Sthānakavāsīs, which are beyond reproach, but only the lax conduct of individual ascetics, and in so doing harmed himself due to the aggressive style of his attack. The impressive *Loṅkāśāh* [sic!] *Jaina Gurukul*, which was built by the AISJC in 1951 in Sādaṛī as a fitting venue for the 1952 *mahāsammelan*, at which the Śramaṇasaṅgha was formally founded, still stocks dozens of copies of this edition of the *Samakitsār*,[96] which demonstrates the key role the text played during the constituent phase of the Śramaṇasaṅgha, both as a symbol of the doctrinal unity of the Sthānakavāsīs and as a common reference source for arguments against the Mūrtipūjakas.

---

[94] Written either by Devṛṣi or, more likely, by one of the editors of the book in Jeṭhmal 1930: 11-19.

[95] Schubring's translation. Original cited in Jeṭhmal 1930: 18.

[96] The Hindī edition of the *Śrīlāljī Mahārāj kā Sacitra Jīvancaritra* which was composed by Durlabh T. Jhauharī (1922/23), one of the principal leaders of the Sthānakavāsī laity at the time, is the only other text which is available in huge quantities.

The Ajmer *sammelan* identified the problem of harmonising the different *maryādā*s of the Sthānakavāsī *sampradāya*s as one of the prime obstacles for the planned formation of a unified Śramaṇa-saṅgha. Another obstacle was the lack of a common origin and lineage. One year after this momentous meeting, the first important study of the history of the Sthānakavāsī tradition as a whole appeared in print: the *Śrī Jaina Dharm ano Prācīn Saṅkṣipt Itihās ane Prabhu Vīr Paṭṭāvalī* by Muni Maṇilāl (1934) of the Līmbḍī Nānī Pakṣa.[97] The text contains a long chapter on the "great reformer" Loṅkā Śāh,[98] in which Maṇilāl – with debatable success – attempted for the first time to resolve the contradictions between the transmitted biographies of Loṅkā in order to clearly establish the historical links between Loṅkā and the various Sthānakavāsī lineages, which are subsequently described in the book. Maṇilāl unearthed much new material,[99] particularly on the Gujarātī traditions, and produced the first comprehensive work on the aniconic traditions, as far as his (not clearly referenced) sources permitted.[100] His work was nevertheless criticised by the General Annual Meeting of the AISJC on the 10.5.1936 for its "incomplete" nature because it does not give a sufficient account of the Ajmer *sammelan*, and probably also because it does not provide much evidence on the Sthānaka-

---

[97] Reprinted photos of Maṇilāl and Pārvatī Devī are mocked as "suitable evidence" for the "aniconic" credentials of the Sthānakavāsīs in Amarvijay 1908: 77f.

[98] Maṇilāl 1934: 157-178. See also the chapter on the Loṅkāgaccha, pp. 179-186. There is no evidence in the oldest sources that Loṅkā's family name was Śāh, though this is commonly assumed in modern literature.

[99] For instance, the Tapāgaccha *muni* Kāntivijay's *Ath Loṅkāśāh nuṃ Jīvan*, which he published in its entirety at the beginning of the chapter on Loṅkā (Maṇilāl 1934: 161f.). For a critique of this text and its influence on Maṇilāl see Jñānsundar 1936: 9ff.

[100] Deśāī 1926-44, III: 2204 mentions that Maṇilāl edited the *paṭṭāvalī*s on which the published work is based in Saṃvat 1941. Śeṭh 1962: 342 quotes an additional book of Maṇilāl, *Prabhuvīr Paṭṭāvalī māṃ Loṅkāśāh nuṃ Jīvan-caritra*. I was unable to trace these works; nor Jīvaṇlāl Kālīdās Vorā's (ed.) *Jaindharma Darpaṇ* of Saṃvat 1942 which, according to Deśāī, also contains *paṭṭāvalī*s of the aniconic traditions.

vāsī traditions in North India.[101] Jñānsundar (1936: 16), whose own publication *Śrīmad Lauṅkāśāh* responded critically to the renewed Sthānakavāsī interest in Loṅkā, did not fail to mention this.

After the Ajmer *sammelan*, the role of Loṅkā as a "founding father" was made more prominent within the Sthānakavāsī movement, and for the first time entire books were devoted to the depiction of his religious reforms. The most widely read account of Loṅkā at the time was the *Dharmaprāṇ-Loṅkāśāh (Krānti no Yuga-sṛṣṭā)*, by the social reformer Muni Saubhāgyacandra "Santabāḷa" (1939) of the Līmbḍī Moṭī Pakṣa. It was apparently written already in the 1920s and first published in the journal *Sthānakavāsī Jain*, founded in Ahmedabad Pañcabhāī nī Poḷ in 1932,[102] and between 10.11.1935–13.1.1936 re-published in Gujarātī in the form of a series of articles in the journal *Jaina Prakāśa*, the mouthpiece of the AISJC. The text contains few references, although Deśāī's work is mentioned. In the same year (1935), the Sthānakavāsīs celebrated "Loṅkāśāh's birthday"[103] with a national poetry festival in the Rājasthān town Sojat Road. The festival was organised by "Marudhar Keśarī" Mantrī Muni Miśrīmal (1891-1984) of the Raghunātha Sampradāya, a fervent advocate of reform (*kṣetra viśuddhi*) and of the unification of all Sthānakavāsī traditions (Editors, in Miśrīmal 1936: 1), whose speech at the regional *sammelan* of the Sthānakavāsī *sādhu*s [sic!] on the 10.3.1932 in the town of Pālī, on the necessity to strengthen the influence of the Sthānakavāsīs "in the world", is now celebrated as one of the pivotal moments of the unification movement.[104] At the time, no "reliable" biography of Loṅkā was available in Hindī, apart from the 1925 translation of V. M. Śāh's (1909) pioneering work. In 1936, Miśrīmal therefore

---

[101] My earlier statement that Maṇilāl's work was declared as the official history of the AISJC has to be corrected. See Flügel 2000: 41. The Līmbḍī Nānī Pakṣa, to which Maṇilāl belonged, never joined the Śramaṇasaṅgha.

[102] I have not been able to trace early editions of this journal.

[103] The historical date is disputed, but the Sthānakavāsīs declared *kārtik śukla* 15 to be Loṅkā's birthday.

[104] Miśrīmal, in Surāṇā 1976: 217f.

published in Hindī a book entitled *Dharmavīr Loṅkāśāh*. This work relies mostly on V. M. Śāh, Maṇilāl, and Saubhāgyacandra, but also uses two newly discovered sources: a "Prācīn Paṭṭāvalī"[105] which he found in the Jaitāraṇ Bhaṇḍār, and a "few leafs" from the Loṅkāgaccha Upāśray in Kuraḍāyā.[106] It was followed in 1941 by a versified biography called *Krāntikārī Vīr Loṅkāśāh* in 1941, and in 1946 by a short collection of *dohā*s and *ḍhāl*s, biographical poems, called *Vīr Loṅkāśāh*. Saubhāgyacandra's and Miśrīmal's works spread the new Sthānakavāsī "standard portrait" of Loṅkā throughout the north Indian Jaina world. However, both books contain, if at all, only general references and no critical evaluation of the available sources. Their "scientific" value was therefore dismissed not only by Muni Jñānsundar (1936) in his evidence-based critique of the contemporary Sthānakavāsī historiography, but even by the Sthānakavāsī *muni* Suśīlkumār (1959: g), who further disagreed with Saubhāgyacandra's "extreme" (*ativāda*) interest in social reform.

A doctrinal response to Mūrtipūjaka criticisms was formulated in the book *Loṅkāśāh Mat-Samarthan*, "Confirmation of Loṅkā's belief", whose revised version was published in 1939.[107] It is one of four works which were published by Ratanlāl Ḍośī of Sailānā (M.P.) in the 1930s and 1940s to defend key Sthānakavāsī doctrines and practices, such as the rejection of *mūrtipūjā* and the permanent use of the *mukhavastrikā* (which Loṅkā reportedly never wore). Ḍośī was a leading lay intellectual of the orthodox Jñānagaccha and a personal devotee of its *ācārya* Samarthamal (1898-1972), who was opposed to the unification of all Sthānakavāsī traditions. In the work *Loṅkāśāh Mat-Samarthan* he compiled textual evidence from the Śvetāmbara canon in support of the propo-

---

[105] This may be the same text that was published in the collection of Hastīmal 1968.

[106] Miśrīmal 1936: 64.

[107] The published text has a complex history of translation from Hindī to Gujarātī (first edition) and back again.

sition that image worship is uncanonical, which he associated with the name of Loṅkā in a general way. Kesarīcand Bhaṇḍārī's (1938: 92) widely circulated *Sthānakavāsī Jaina Itihās* – one of the first books with the 20th-century self-description "Sthānakavāsī" in the title[108] – also refers to "Ḍośī's (1939) text for authoritative doctrinal arguments. However, this work does not contain any references to Loṅkā's writings, for which no direct evidence existed at the time. The conventional counter-arguments of the Mūrtipūjakas against the "lying *sampradāyavādīs*" – the aniconic traditions – who undermine the "unity" of the Jaina *dharma* were repeated several decades later in the works of the Mūrtipūjaka layman Nagīndās Girdharlāl Śeṭh, *Mūl Jaina Dharma ane Hāl nā Sampradāyo* (1962), *Sthānakavāsī Jaino nuṃ Dharma Kartavya* (1963), and *Loṅkaśāh ane Dharmacarcā* (1964). Whereas Ḍośī worked on the premise that the Sthānakavāsīs continue Loṅkā's doctrinal tradition, Śeṭh (1962: 342) reiterated Jñānsundar's (1936: 171ff.) verdict that the followers of the Loṅkāgaccha and the Sthānakavāsīs are historical enemies. To this purpose, he cites the depiction of Loṅkā in early Mūrtipūjaka and Loṅkāgaccha sources,[109] published by Jñānsundar (1936: 234-240) and Deśāī (1926-44, II-III: 1931-1944), which had been entirely ignored by the Sthānakavāsī commentary literature until the 1960s.

SIXTY-NINE STATEMENTS

Before the publication of two old manuscripts of the Loṅkāgaccha tradition in 1936 by Jñānsundar (1936: 234-240), "Loṅkā's" beliefs

---

[108] In isolated form, the word "*sthānakavāsī*" occurs reportedly much earlier (Suśīlkumār 1959: 427), but even Upādhyāya Ātmārām (1942: 12, cf. 16), who devoted an entire article on the history of the word *sthānakavāsī* to prove that the principal Sthānakavāsīs are the *mokṣa*-seeking *bhāva sthānakavāsīs* not the *dravya sthānakavāsīs* (*sthānake bhāvasaṃyamādirūpe samyakcāritre vasati tacchīla iti sthānakavāsī*), did not cite earlier examples of its modern use as a self-description. John E. Cort mentioned to me that the word is used in a polemical Mūrtipūjaka text of the late 18th century.

[109] Śeṭh 1962: 344-383.

were only indirectly known through the early polemics of his Mūrtipūjaka and Digambara opponents. The earliest known sources for the views of Loṅkā written by his own followers are the *Dayādharma Caupāī*, composed by the Loṅkāgaccha "*yatī*" (monk or lay-ascetic) Bhānucandra in Saṃvat 1587 (1521/2),[110] and the *Loṅkāśāha Siloko*, written in Saṃvat 1600 (1543/4) by the Loṅkāgaccha *yati* Keśavarṣi.[111] However, they were not widely circulated and had no notable impact. The oldest dated texts on the Loṅkā-tradition were written by their Mūrtipūjaka opponents. The *Asūtranirākaraṇa Batrīśī* of Muni Bīkā was written in Saṃvat 1527 (1470/1),[112] the *Luṅkāmata Pratibodha Kulak* was written by an anonymous author in Saṃvat 1530 (1473/4),[113] the *Siddhānta Caupāī* of Muni Lāvaṇyasamay in Saṃvat 1543 (1486/7),[114] and the short *Siddhānta Sāroddhāra* [*Caupāī*] of Upādhyāya Kamalsaṃyam of the Kharataragaccha in Saṃvat 1544 (1487/8).[115] A text that has often been cited by Sthānakavāsīs is the *Ath Loṅkāśāh nuṃ Jīvan* (ALJ), composed in Pāṭaṇ in Saṃvat 1636 (1579/60) by the Tapāgaccha *muni* Kāntivijay.[116] Apart from a short passage in

---

[110] Published by Jñānsundar (1936: 234-237) who located the Ms. in the Lābhasundarajī Jñāna Bhaṇḍāra.

[111] Published in a Bombay paper on the 18.7.1936, and republished by Jñānsundar (1936: 238-240). For bibliographic references of early Loṅkāgaccha sources see Deśāī 1926-44; Flügel 2003a: 219-222.

[112] A manuscript of the Gokulbhāī Nānī Saṃgraha in Rājkoṭ was published by Desāī in *Jaina Yuga* (Bhādrapad 1985 – Kārtak 1986): 99-100 (reprint in Koṭhārī 2001: 501-503) and reprinted by Jñānsundar 1936: 230-233. For further bibliographic information on the following texts see Flügel 2003a: 230-233.

[113] Ms. No. 5837, L.D. Institute, Ahmedabad, published with a Hindī translation in Hastīmal 1995: 642-646.

[114] A manuscript of the Jñānbhaṇḍār in Pāṭaṇ was published by Desāī (reprint in Koṭhārī 2001: 486-499) and reprinted by Jñānsundar 1936: 209-227.

[115] A manuscript of the Jñānbhaṇḍār in Pāṭaṇ was published by Desāī in *Jaina Yuga* 1.2 (Vaiśākh-Jeṭh 1986): 339-349 (reprint in Koṭhārī 2001: 499-500) and reprinted by Jñānsundar 1936: 228f.

[116] Published in Maṇilāl 1934: 161f.; Hastīmal 1995: 752-759, Hindī summary by Jñānsundar 1936: 9f. A copy of one original Ms., which was with Yati Sundar of the Kacch Nānī Pakṣa, has been given to Ācārya Hastīmal 1995: 751.

Ācārya Ratnanandī's *Bhadrabāhu Caritra* vv. 155-163 of Saṃvat 1625 (1568/9), the only presently known Digambara critiques of Loṅkā are the *Loṅkāmata Nirākaraṇa Caupāī* of Sumatikīrti-sūri which was written almost a century after Loṅkā's death, in Saṃvat 1627 (1570/1),[117] and the *Sata Prābhṛta Mokṣa Prābhṛta Ṭīkā* (pp. 305f.) of Bhaṭṭāraka Śrutasāgara.[118] Most of these and similar texts are still difficult to access and have therefore not been properly studied. The only early sources on Loṅkā which were widely accessible in the 19th and early 20th centuries were short passages in Dharmasāgara's *Pravacana Parīkṣā* of 1572 (Saṃvat 1629) and his *Tapāgaccha Paṭṭāvalī Sūtraṃ* of 1589/1590 (Saṃvat 1646).[119]

The first published text which was directly attributed to Loṅkā himself was the *Loṅkejī kī Huṇḍī* (A), or *Ath Huṇḍī Lūṅkārī Likhyate*, which contains sixty-nine doctrinal assertions (*bol*). The printed text is based on a manuscript that was reportedly found in the Sarūpacanda Rāmacanda Upāśrāya in Jaitāraṇ, a town in southern Rājasthān which was a centre of the Loṅkāgaccha Nānī Pakṣa until the beginning of the 20th century. It was first published by K. S. Caudharī (1936?: 338-430) in a book called *Jin Jñān Ratnākar*, together with the original *sūtra* texts, which are summarised by "Loṅkā's *bol*s", an interpretation of their meaning (*bhāvārtha*) in Hindī, and several versified Rājasthānī commentaries in the *ḍhāl*, *dohā* and *soraṭhā* meters which were composed in 1926 in Jaypur by Gulābcand (Luṇiyā?), a devotee of the Terāpanth *ācārya* Kālūgaṇi (1877-1936), who may have discovered the original

---

[117] Ms. Bīkāner Bṛhata Jñānabhaṇḍāra, Dānasāgara Saṃgraha No. 72. Padmanabh S. Jaini is currently publishing a book on the anonymous Digambara text *Cauryāṃsī Bol* which contains extensive criticism of the "Loṅkā" tradition.

[118] The text is mentioned in Mahāprajña 2000: 7. The followers of Loṅkā are apparently accused by the author to be materialists and atheists, because they rejected the veneration of (protector) gods. It must be identical with the author's commentary to "Kundakunda's" Pāhuḍas in the *Ṣaṭprābhṛtādisaṃgraha*, which according to Schubring 1957: 559, describes the followers of Launka as "Pseudo-Śvetāmbaras" (*śvetāmbarābhāsa*) and as "sinful wrong believers" (*pāpiṣṭhā mithyādṛṣṭayaḥ*) because they reject images.

[119] Published in Darśanavijaya 1933: 41-119.

manuscript.[120] The *bol*s were published in a slightly different form and without any commentary by Āñcaliyā (1937: 120-128). Although Kālūgaṇi's oral explanations clearly informed Gulābcand's work,[121] no written commentary on Loṅkā's ideas has ever been created by any Terāpanth *ācārya*.[122] The present Terāpanth *ācārya* Mahāprajña (2000: 6) always cites the *Loṅkejī kī Huṇḍī* as an authoritative source on Loṅkā's teachings.

Like the famous *ṭabos* (*ṭabbā*) of the Sthānakavāsī *ācārya* Dharmasiṅha (1599-1671) and of other, anonymous, authors – vernacular texts which offer rudimentary word-for-word translations of the Prakrit Jaina Āgamas without regard to their syntax – "Loṅkā's *bol*s" were, it seems, deliberately disseminated by the lay disciples of Ācārya Kālūgaṇi and his successor Ācārya Tulsī in order to establish an easy access to the "essential teachings" of the Āgamas in a language which everyone could understand.[123] This was important, since, with few exceptions, Sanskrit and Prakrit scholarship was all but lost in the Jaina mendicant traditions in the early 19th century, and did not exist at all within the aniconic traditions before the Jaina revival in the late 19th century.[124] Even

---

[120] No further information is available on the original Ms.

[121] *huṇḍī jahe Loṅkā taṇī, acche purātan teha,*
tiṇmeṃ āgam sākṣi thī, bol unhattar jeha. (1)
sakal suguṇ śir sehrā, śrī kālū gaṇi rāy,
tāsu pasāye gulāb kahe, dohā rūp banāya. (3)
(Gulābcand, in Caudharī 1936?: 338, cf. 428f.).

[122] Information from Muni Navratnamala, 12.8.2004, who also stated that according to Terāpanth sources, Loṅkā's original *Huṇḍī* (or rather the Ms.?) was written in Saṃvat 1583.

[123] See Dundas 1996: 74 on Jayācārya's Rājasthānī translation of Abhayadeva Sūri's 11th-century Sanskrit commentary on the *Viyāhapannatti*, and Budhmal 2001: 419 on the introduction of the study of the Sanskrit commentaries into the monastic curriculum of the Terāpanth by Kālūgaṇi.

[124] A standard critique of Ācārya Bhikṣu, even from the Sthānakavāsīs who were subject to the same criticism, was that he "had no knowledge of Sanskrit and Prakrit" (Muni Rajyash, in Nair 1970: iii). See already the complaints of Jñānsundar 1936: 97, and Mālvaṇiyā 1964: 378 cited in Dundas 2002: 247 and 250, on the lack of learning of the followers of the aniconic tradition in general,

in 1936, few Terāpanthī ascetics knew Sanskrit and Prakrit. Another reason for the publication of the text must have been the desire to legitimate the Terāpanth doctrine, which had been the target of critique from all other Jaina sects, with direct reference to Loṅkā, who was accepted as an authoritative reference point within the Sthānakavāsī movement.

It remains doubtful whether this text can really be attributed to Loṅkā. In contrast to other texts attributed to him (see *infra*), the cited passages from the primary literature contain not a single quote from the commentary literature, only citations from the Āgamas,[125] together with the explanations (*bol*) of "Loṅkā" in a quasi-stenographic Rājasthānī-Hindī mix (which indicates that these are not Loṅkā's own words), and of Gulābcand in both Rājasthānī and Hindī. The citations are so skilfully woven together that the resulting text does not assume the form of a casuistic list of unconnected points, but reads like a coherently constructed argument.[126]

---

which prevented them from understanding the Ardhamāgadhī canon itself and the Sanskrit commentary; though Mālvaṇiyā excluded Loṅkā himself from this verdict, in view of his extensive citations from the canon. Jñānsundar (1936: 63-5, 109) and most Mūrtipūjakas credit Pārśvacandra Sūri of the Pārśvacandra-gaccha for the "translation" of the Aṅgas into Gujarātī, whereas the Sthānakavāsī tradition refers to Dharmasiṅha as the author of the first *ṭabo*s. See Flügel 2000: 62; 2003a: 195.

[125] 1. Sūy(agaḍa) 1.12.16, 2. Uvav(āiya) 2.19, 3. Viy(āhapannatti) 7.2 (294b), 4. DVS (Dasaveyāliya) 4.12, 5. Utt(arajjhāyā) 28.29, 6. DVS 4.10, 7. Viy 8.6, 8. Sūy 1.1.2.4, 9. DVS 7.48, 10. Pannavaṇā 22, 11. DVS 5.1.92, 12. Āyāra 1.8.4.13, 13. Sūy 1.1.2.14, 14. Uvav 2.20, 15. Utt 28.31, 16. Utt 36.260, 17. Uvav 2.20, 18. Āyāra 1.2.6.5, 19. Aṇuogaddārāīṃ 7 [?], 20. Sūy 1.6.7, 21. Sūy 1.9.1, 22. Sūy 1.1.4.10, 23. Sūy 1.10.3, 24. Utt 4.8, 25. DVS 1.1, 26. Nis(īha) 11.81, 27. Nis 11.91, 28. Nis 15.74f., 29. Nis 16.13f., 30. Nis 17.223, 31. Nis 11.11, 32. Nis 17.224, 33. Nis 8.12, 34. Nis 8.13, 35. Sūy 1.11.20, 36. Utt 20.44, 37. Pannavaṇā 11, 38. Dasāsuyakkhandha 9.9, 39. Sūy 1.10.15, 40. DVS 7.1, 41. Sūy 1.12.5, 42. Āyāra 1.6.4.1, 43. Āyāra 1.2.2, 44. Āyāra 1.5.6.1, 45. Uvav 2.19, 46. Utt 31.3, 47. Sūy 1.3.4.6-7, 48. Nis 12.1-2, 49. Āyāra 1.4.4.1f., 50. Utt 14.12, 51. Uvav 2.21, 52. DVS 6.19 [not: "6.21"], 53. DVS 4.[10], 54. Nis 4.22, 55. Utt 10.15, 56. Utt 21.24, 57. Nis 13.42-45, 58. Nis 12.17, 59. Ṭhāṇa 2.3.6, 60. Ṭhāṇa 2.1.25, 61. Ṭhāṇa 2.1.25, 62. Utt 28.36, 63. Utt 23.63, 64. Āyāra 1.4.2.1, 65. DVS 9.4.4, 66. Āyāra 1.1.7 [not: "1.2.4"], 67. Uvav 2.34, 68. Uvav (*samavasaraṇa adhikār meṃ*, four types of meditation), 69. DVS 7.47.

Moreover, the content of the text corresponds entirely with the views of the Terāpanthīs at the time.[127] It focuses almost exclusively on the principles of proper monastic conduct,[128] as taught by the *kevalins*,[129] the condemnation of non-believers, heresies (*niṇhava*),[130] pseudo-monks,[131] on the strict distinction between the standards for the Jaina householder and the mendicant,[132] and on the prescribed atonements for transgressions.[133] It seems that indirectly the credentials of the Sthānakavāsī *dayā-dāna* theory are also deliberately undermined through the condemnation of the accumulation of good karma through gift-giving and acts of compassion, etc.[134] Instead, the priority of knowledge over compassion is em-

---

[126] In this respect, it contrasts with many *maryādā* lists. See Mette 1974: 4f.; Flügel 2003a: 17.

[127] That is, before the reforms of Ācārya Tulsī (1914-1997) after 1949.

[128] Nos. 5-6, 10, 15, 22-25, 55, 62, 64-66, 68.

[129] Nos. 1, 11-14, 17-18, 20-21.

[130] Nos. 2, 8, 16, 41, 45, 50, 63.

[131] Nos. 3, 9-13.

[132] Nos. 39, 58-61, 67.

[133] Thirteen points are concerned with *prāyaścitta*s as outlined in the *Nisīha*, whereas not one of the *bol*s of L, LH, and LTC deal with atonements. This, and the absence of any discussion of image-worship, indicates that the sixty-nine *bol*s are probably the creation of a (Terāpanth) monk rather than a layman such as Lonkā.

[134] Nos. 6, 7, 36, 46-49, 55. An exception is No. 35: *je ya dāṇaṃ pasaṃsanti, vaham icchanti pāṇiṇaṃ; je ya ṇaṃ paḍisehanti, vitticcheyaṃ karanti te* – "Those who praise the gift, are accessory to the killing of beings; those who forbid it, deprive (others) of the means of subsistence" (Sūy 1.11.20, Jacobi's translation). This passage has been associated with the Sthānakavāsī *muni* Jaymal's defence against Bhīkhaṇ's famous critique of the value of gift giving for the purpose of accumulating *puṇya* (Seṭh 1970: 1004). It does not come as a surprise, then, that different interpretations of the Prakrit original are offered: "Lonkā's *bol*" explains the verse as follows: *sāvadya dāna kī praśansā kare tiṇa ne prāṇī jīvāṃ ko badha bañchaṇhāro kahyo* (in Caudharī 1936?: 376). Gulābcand's *dohā* says:

> *do sāṃsārika dāna rī, kare praśansā koya;*
> *badha bañche kāya nūṃ, sūyagaḍānge joya (128).*
> *adhyayana igyārahvāṃ ne viṣai, bīsmī gāthā māṃhi;*
> *niṣedhiyāṃ varttamān meṃ, vṛtti cheda kahāhi (129)*
> (Caudharī 1936?: 376f.).

phasised, and that giving "pure gifts" to a mendicant does not lead to accumulating good karma but to the destruction of karma.[135] In contrast to the available indirect evidence on Loṅkā's teachings, there is no discussion of image-worship at all. It therefore remains doubtful whether the text, which has apparently not been commented upon by any author, is the product of Loṅkā; despite the fact that it also contains some of the most well known of "Loṅkā's" quotations from the canon.[136] Thus, by publishing a hitherto unknown text confirming their own views, together with a Terāpanth commentary, the Terāpanthīs could implicitly claim Loṅkā as their own predecessor while challenging the assertion of the Sthānakavāsīs to be Loṅkā's only legitimate successors.[137]

OUR HISTORY

The appropriation of Loṅkā by the Sthānakavāsīs was explicit and on quite a different scale. It culminated in the period after the creation of the unified Śramaṇasaṅgha under the rule of only one *ācārya*, which was accomplished after forty-six years of preparation at the *mahāsammelan* in 1952 at the *Loṅkāśāh Jaina Gurukul* in Sāḍaṛī. The Gujarātī Sthānakavāsī *sampradāya*s refused to join the new organisation, which was dominated by Hindī-speaking

---

The *sorṭhā* finally objects to "Loṅkā's" insertion of the word *sāvadya*, blameful, in front of the word *dāna*, because it is not in the original text: *sāvadya śabda nahīṃ pāṭha meṃ, samuccai dān kaheha re* (p. 377). In order to explain the meaning, two types of gifts are distinguished: *supātra dāna* and *kupātra dāna*, and Viy 8.6.1 (No. 7. in the list of *bol*s) is invoked which states that a gift of pure food to a worthy recipient (a pure monk) is a pure gift (*śuddha dāna*) "which brings about the annihilation of *karman*", rather than the influx of *puṇya* (which is *pāpa* from the "absolute" point of view that is favoured by the Terāpanth).

[135] Nos. 6-7, 8, 55.

[136] Nos. 5, 22-25. See *infra*.

[137] The method of legitimising a particular sectarian interpretation of the canon by constructing a selective list of "authoritative" citations is not unusual (Balbir 2003a: 272). Today, it can be found for instance in the unpublished *Sāmācārī* of the Sthānakavāsī Kacch Āṭh Koṭī Nānī Pakṣa (personal communication by Ācārya Rāghav).

mendicants. This may have been one of the reasons why, in the decade after the constituent assembly of the Śramaṇasaṅgha, two official histories of the Sthānakavāsī tradition in Hindī were commissioned by the Śramaṇasaṅgha *ācārya* Ānandṛṣi and the AISJC respectively to put the significance of the new organisation into a historical perspective.[138] The resulting publications are Muni Suśīlkumār's (1959) *Jainadharma kā Itihās* (*Pramukhataḥ Śrī Śvetāmbara Sthānakavāsī Jainadharma kā Itihās*) and Sādhvī Candanākumārī's (1964) *Hamārā Itihās: Sthānakavāsī Śramaṇ-Sāṃskṛtik Paramparā kā Paricāyak*. Both works built on earlier standard histories of the Sthānakavāsī tradition, but did not make use of the published old sources on Loṅkā.[139] Suśīlkumār (1959: g) mentions that his work was initially based on an unpublished manuscript of Saubhāgyacandra "Santabāḷa", which was handed to him by the AISJC. Since he saw no historical value in the manuscript, he wrote an entirely new text on the basis of information from leading mendicant scholars and of unspecified historical sources from Bīkāner, which were made available to him by Agarcand Nāhaṭā in 1957, two years after he started his work.[140] Candanākumārī's book is to a large extent based on Suśīlkumār's text and offers a crisp summary of the historical literature of the Sthānakavāsīs at the time, but without providing any references.[141] Both texts contain extensive sections on Loṅkā, on the Sthānakavāsī-dominated "Loṅkāśāha Yuga" and on the "Saṅgha Yuga" which begins, according to Suśīlkumār (1959: 2), with the foundation of the Śramaṇasaṅgha in

---

[138] See Flügel 2000; 2003a.

[139] See also Jain & Kumār's (2003: 109) critique.

[140] Suśīlkumār (1959: N) received advice from Ācārya Ānandṛṣi, Upādhyāy Hastīmal, Upādhyāy Amarmuni, Muni Pyārcand, and "Marudhar Keśarī" Miśrīmal, i.e. from the Śramaṇasaṅgha *munis* who had the greatest interest and expertise in the study of history.

[141] She received advice from Ācārya Ānandṛṣi, Upādhyāy Hastīmal, Upādhyāy Amarmuni, Pravartak Pannālāl, "Marudhar Keśarī" Miśrīmal, Muni Ambālāl, Muni Puṣkarmuni, and Muni Padmacandra (Prakāśakīya, in Candanākumārī 1964: 9).

1952.[142] And both emphasise the differences between the Loṅkāgaccha "*yatis*", whose tradition is characterised as negligible "after the 15th century", and the Sthānakavāsī "*sādhus*". Candanākumārī (1964: 105) contends that (in the view of the leading mendicants of the Śramaṇasaṅgha) the Sthānakavāsī traditions are the true followers of Loṅkā's doctrine (*siddhānta*) – if not his direct lineal successors.[143] In support of this view, she points to the common lay practice of *dharmadhyāna* in the *sthānakas*, which she interprets as a replication of the ancient institution of the *poṣadhaśālā*; which, according to early Mūrtipūjaka sources, Loṅkā himself is said to have rejected.[144] Both authors employ various strategies to bypass the conventional Mūrtipūjaka emphasis on the importance of a continuous teacher lineage for the transmission of the "authentic" Jaina tradition.[145] Rather than attempting to construct lists of succession in the form of a single *paṭṭāvalī*, which is generally not acceptable within the Sthānakavāsī movement due to the continuing existence of competing lineages or sub-groups with independent histories, the texts present chronological lists of important historical personalities in the Sthānakavāsi tradition.[146] They begin their respective narratives with Ṛṣabha, not with Mahāvīra, whose ancestry is generally favoured: In the work of Bhaṇḍārī (1938: 85-87), who ignored the Loṅkāgaccha tradition entirely, though not Loṅkā him-

[142] Suśīlkumār 1959: 2 distinguishes five eras: 1. Ādi Yuga (pre 500 before V.S.), 2. Mahāvīra Yuga (500 before V.S. – 2nd century before V.S.), 3. Bhadrabāhu Yuga (2nd century before V.S. – 16th century V.S.). 4. Luṅkāśāha Yuga (16th century V.S. – 2007 V.S.), 5. Saṅgha Yuga (2007 V.S. – today). See Flügel 2000: 43, n. 11 for other emic periodisations of the Jaina history.

[143] *vartamān meṃ pracalit śvetāmbar sthānakavāsī jain-samāj Loṅkāgacch kī vartamānkālīn kaṛī hai. isī samāj meṃ hameṃ āj sahī rūp meṃ śrī Loṅkāśāh-siddhānta ke darśan hote haiṃ* (Candanākumārī 1964: 105).

[144] See the sources published by Jñānsundar 1936.

[145] Cf. Dundas 1996: 79.

[146] The idea for this procedure evidently stems from Ācārya Javāharlāl (1875-1943) whose arguments were rejected at the Ajmer *sammelan* in 1933. See Flügel 2003a: 195. On the incompatibility of many Sthānakavāsī *paṭṭāvalīs* see Ātmārām 1884/1908: 8-11; Vallabhvijay 1891: 67-70; V. M. Śāh 1909: 96ff., 103f.; Jñānsundar 1936: 296-300.

self, it is asserted that "only the Sthānakavāsī *sādhu*s are Mahāvīra's true disciples".[147] The opening pages of Bhaṇḍārī's book suggest that the only reason for including the *tīrthaṅkara*s of the "Ādi Yuga" (Suśīlkumār) in a "historical" account is to prove the *ancienneté* of the Jaina tradition *vis à vis* the competing Hindu and Buddhist traditions.

Instead of lists of succession, the concept of a common Sthānakavāsī "culture" (*saṃskṛti*) is invoked – which figures in the title of Canadanākumārī's book – with an emphasis on common scriptures and doctrinal principles. The Śramaṇasaṅgha has also a common code of conduct (*sāmācārī*);[148] but no common rituals and liturgy, which remain different amongst the constituent *sampradāya*s.[149] The "Varddhamāna" Śramaṇasaṅgha has not been able to construct a single official *paṭṭāvalī*, because no consensus could be established amongst the leading monks as to which names should be selected. Instead, it produces *abhinandana grantha*s for eminent mendicants within the tradition. These texts comprise *paṭṭāvalī*s of the respective sub-tradition of a particular monk or nun, but not of the united Śramaṇasaṅgha as a whole.

Accordingly, Suśīlkumār and Candanākumārī present the history of the Sthānakavāsī tradition as a chronology of great individuals and their disciples, not as the history of a single lineage of succession going back to Mahāvīra, Pārśva or even Ṛṣabha, as preferred by the constituent sub-groups. Although their contents cannot be described as "mythological", the narrative form of the texts – the chronology of the deeds of selected great beings – represents a spectrum of compromises between the chronological history of modern historiography and the *paṭṭāvalī*s and *gurvāvalī*s on the one hand, and of the cosmologically informed Sthānakavāsī universal

---

[147] *phakat sthānakavāsī sādhuja mahāvīr nā sācā śiṣya che* (Bhaṇḍārī 1938: 96).

[148] AISJC 1987: 71ff. See Flügel 2003a: 195f.; forthcoming (a).

[149] Cf. Cort's definition of *gaccha*s = *sampradāya*s as "units, defining the boundaries within one can ritually interact" (Cort 1991: 662).

histories *à la* Jeṭhmal on the other.[150] As such, the peculiar combinations of history (without source references) and legend reflect the particular problems of legitimation of the Śramaṇasaṅgha.

An extreme example of a new Sthānakavāsī universal history is Ācārya Ghāsīlāl's (1983)[151] Sanskrit [sic!] poem *Śrī Loṅkāśāha Caritam*, which associates Loṅkā and the Sthānakavāsīs, taken together, directly with Mahāvīrā and Gautama,[152] without mentioning any structures of mediation. His *mahākāvya*, he concedes, is based on hearsay or oral (*jabānī*) history for which, as the editor Muni Kanhaiyālāl notes in his introduction, no trustworthy evidence exists.[153] Kanhaiyālāl's remarks show that a century of debate on "factual history" has generated a critical awareness within the Jaina tradition that even the questionable attempts of attributing all common doctrinal features of the "Sthānakavāsī" tradition, such as the rejection of image-worship, the "ur-canon" of thirty-two texts, and the permanent wearing of a *mukhavastrikā*, to the legendary founding father Loṅkā, utilise the toolkits of legend, historiography and canonisation.[154] The age-old method of excluding and including, compiling and re-compiling, of picking-and-choosing – and inventing – authoritative references from the amorphous sediments of the preserved tradition to legitimise contemporary preferences, has, to a certain extent, become self-reflective.[155]

---

[150] The texts are not stifled by formalism, whose significance for other genres of the Jaina literature was highlighted by Bruhn 1981: 36. Only the information on the "great beings" after Loṅkā can claim some historical credibility.

[151] Ghāsīlāl (1884-1973) originally belonged to the Sādhumārgī tradition, which left the Śramaṇasaṅgha in the 1950s. He was apparently made an *ācārya* by Ācārya Javāharlāl in 1933, but left when Gaṇeśīlāl became leader, and founded his own splinter group, which does not exist today. See his disciple Kanhaiyālāl's *Bhūmikā*, in Ghāsīlāl 1983: 5f.; personal communication of Umeśmuni 13.10.2002.

[152] Ghāsīlāl 1983: 2f.

[153] Kanhaiyālāl's *Bhūmikā*, in Ghāsīlāl 1983: 12.

[154] See Bruhn 1987: 107, 111f., also for the term "canon of research".

[155] Although history writing as such was not always an issue, the "delicate balance between objectivity and in-depth analysis ... and aggressivity" is nothing

THE DISCOVERY OF LOṄKĀ'S SCRIPTURES

Thus far, our cursory review of the development of the pivotal role of Loṅkā in the new Sthānakavāsī historiography has shown that received models of "chronological" and "cosmological" history both informed the modern portraits of Loṅkā. Features of the two models were creatively mixed during the modern period of revival of the Jaina tradition, which consciously distinguished itself from earlier epochs through an increasing concern with verifiable "facts" as a principal source of legitimation. In the context of renewed sectarian rivalry, the analysis of vernacular Jain sources – which Schubring (1944: vi) saw as the next important step in the history of Jaina research – has started in India earlier than elsewhere. Methodical research was nevertheless largely confined to the post-independence period, probably benefiting from a slight easing of the overt sectarian tensions within the Jaina tradition.[156]

After more than one hundred years of inquiry, historical sources on Loṅkā and the Loṅkāgaccha from within the aniconic tradition are still extremely rare.[157] The same can be said of critical scholarship of the tradition. The first manuscripts composed by early Loṅkāgaccha *yati*s were discovered and described by Deśāī (1931) in Part II of his ground-breaking study *Gūrjar Kavio*. Two further

---

new in Jaina religious discourse as Balbir 2003a: 259, 268 has shown with regard to the 16th-century Kharataragaccha monk Samayasundara. Both "canonisation" and "creeping change" and the "reconstruction of history from the point of view of the present" are founded in one-sided interests, strategies of exclusion and inclusion, and in polemics. The contrast between "canonical interest" and "historical interest" proposed by Assmann (1987: 15) is therefore not as sharp in practice as the conceptual distinction suggests.

[156] Several factors are responsible for this. Some explicit agreements were made between leading *ācārya*s to discourage the production and distribution of violently polemical pamphlets which can harm the public image of Jainism as a whole. Overt attacks and *ad hominem* denunciations are therefore nowadays largely confined to intra-sectarian politics. Another factor was the accomplishment of the unification of most Sthānakavāsī traditions, and the end of the main period of institutional reform.

[157] There are also hardly any sources concerning the founders of the Sthānakavāsī traditions.

texts (see *infra*) were published by Jñānsundar (1936: 234-240), who was the first monk to emphatically emphasise that only the study of historical sources itself can provide a more reliable picture of Loṅkā's life and work. Detailed information on Loṅkāgaccha (and Sthānakavāsī) *paṭṭāvalī*s – in addition to the unreferenced materials provided by Ātmārām (1884/1903) and Vallabhvijay (1891), Śāh (1909) and Maṇilāl (1934), and others – was published in Part III of Deśāī's (1944: 2205-2222) work. Further historical materials on the Loṅkā tradition, such as *gurvāvalī*s, *paṭṭāvalī*s, historical poems and lists of *bol*s,[158] were unearthed by the next generation of Jaina scholars in the 1950s and 1960s, in particular by Bhanvarlāl Nāhaṭā (1957), Agarcand Nāhaṭā (1958; 1964; 1966, etc.), Dalsukhbhāī Mālvaṇiyā (1963a; 1963b; 1964; 1965), and Ācārya Hastīmal (1968), who revolutionised the historiography of the aniconic Jaina tradition (see *infra*). Most of these authors contributed to the *Muni Śrī Hajārīmal Smṛti Granth*, edited by Śobhācandra Bhārill (1965), which contains further important articles on the literature of the Loṅkāgaccha tradition by Muni Kāntisāgar (1965) and Ālamśāh Khān (1965).[159] Particularly significant for future research was Ācārya Hastīmal's (1968) compilation *Paṭṭāvalī Prabandh Saṅgrah*, which made the oldest surviving *paṭṭāvalī*s of the Loṅkāgaccha traditions and the North Indian Sthānakavāsī traditions available for the first time. This fertile period of historical research, during which almost every Sthānakavāsī tradition investigated its own history in order to construct its own *paṭṭāvalī*, culminated in Hastīmal's (1987/1995) synopsis of most of the available material on Loṅkā in the fourth volume of his monumental work *Jaina Dharma kā Maulik Itihās*, after which only the book by Duggar (1989) furnished new information on the extinct lineages of the Loṅkāgaccha in the Pañjāb.

While the outlines of the structure of differentiation of the mendicant lineages of the aniconic tradition became clearly visible by

---

[158] See Nahar 1918: 38, etc. for short inscriptions of the Loṅkāgaccha.

[159] Another widely read article on Loṅkā was written by K. L. Nāhaṭā (1968).

the end of the 1960s, the teachings of Loṅkā, and the doctrinal and organisational differences between Loṅkā and the Loṅkāgaccha traditions, and the Sthānakavāsī traditions remained almost unknown – and to a large extent still are. The answers to these questions hinge on the credibility of the sources on Loṅkā's teachings, in particular Loṅkā's own writings – which probably neither Jñānsundar (1936: 97) nor his adversaries had known – since no traces of the rules and regulations of the various Loṅkāgaccha traditions, whose practices differed from Loṅkā's own, had ever been discovered.

In a series of path-breaking articles, D. D. Mālvaṇiyā (1963a, 1963b, 1964, 1965) identified for the first time two manuscripts in the Puṇyavijay collection at the L.D. Institute in Ahmedabad which, in his view, can clearly be attributed to Loṅkā himself. The publication of this discovery changed the entire discourse on Loṅkā. The authenticity of the texts is now accepted within the aniconic tradition itself. They are the only documents which were published by the followers of the Loṅkāgaccha itself (Vārīā's 1976 modern Gujarātī translation, in P. T. Śāh 2001), together with summaries of Hastīmal's (1968) collection of Loṅkāgaccha *paṭṭāvalī*s. But Mālvaṇiyā's claim has not remained unchallenged, especially by Mūrtipūjaka authors.

The manuscripts can be attributed to Loṅkā in terms of their contents,[160] which clearly relate to the beliefs of Loṅkā or the Loṅkā tradition, and because both of the two key texts mention "Luṅkā" or the "Luṅkāmatī" at the end;[161] though Loṅkā's name has been deliberately cut out at two places at the beginning and at the end of the Ms. *Luṅkā nā Saddahiyā ane Kariyā Aṭhāvan Bol*, as Mālva-

---

[160] *ukt donoṃ partiyoṃ kā sīdhā sambandh lokāśāh se avaśya hai. kyoṃki lokāśāh ke mat ko, unkī vicārdhārā ko usmeṃ spaṣṭ rūp meṃ prastut kiyā gayā hai* (Mālvaṇiyā 1964: 366).

[161] *e sarva Luṅkāmatī nī yukti chai* (*Luṅkā nī Huṇḍī 34 Bol*) (L.D. Institute Ms. No. 4121). The early sources always use the term *mata*, doctrine or sect, and never *gaccha*, order, sect or school, as a designation of the Loṅkā tradition.

ṇiyā (1964: 381) has pointed out.[162] Mālvaṇiyā (1964: 366, 1965: 188) believed that Loṅkā was either the author of these texts, or that the texts have been written under his instruction, since his opponents would have used the Sanskrit term Luṃpaka for Luṅkā, although no final proof has been furnished yet. Śeṭh (1964: 54) disputed Mālvaṇiyā's argument and attributed both texts to the Sthānakavāsī *ācārya* Dharmasiṅha. His views were comprehensively rejected by Hastīmal (1995: 759-789)[163] because of the "lack of proof", and with reference to Pārśvacandra Sūri's[164] text *Lūṅkāe Pechela 13 Praśna ane Tenā Uttarī*, which cites Loṅkā's questions concerning image-worship: why should *vandana* be performed to non-living entities, why are *sādhus* not allowed to perform *dravya pūjā*, etc.[165] This 16th-century text is now routinely referred to as a significant source for Loṅkā's views, which indirectly confirms the authenticity of the disputed texts.[166]

---

[162] *iti ... Luṅkā nā saddahiyā anaī Luṅkā nā kariyā aṭhāvana bola anaī tehanuṃ vicāra likhauṃ chai. śubhaṃ bhavatu sramaṇasaṅghāya, śrī* (L.D. Institute Ms. No. 2989). Mālvaṇiyā's view is still vigorously opposed by orthodox followers of the Mūrtipūjaka tradition, who point out that the manuscript had been tampered with. Even today, many Mūrtipūjaka libraries, such as the Kailāśasāgarasūri Jñān Mandir of the Śrī Mahāvīr Jaina Ārādhana Kendra in Kobā, restrict access to texts of the aniconic tradition which criticise Mūrtipūjaka practices.

[163] Hastīmal (1995: 759ff.) disproved Śeṭh's (1964: 43) "sectarian" view that Loṅkā had only a few followers with citations from the Tapāgaccha *paṭṭāvalīs*, and that his views were *adharmik* (Śeṭh 1964: 46) and that he had no knowledge of Ardhamāgadhī (p. 25) with Āgama citations from Loṅkā's *Aṭṭhāvan Bol*.

[164] The founder of the Pārśvacandragaccha.

[165] The thirteen questions, a selection of the longer text (L.D. Institute Mss. No. 24466, 30565), were published by Hastīmal (1995: 694f.) and re-published by Jain and Kumār (2003: 539-541), who also rendered the text into Hindī (Jain & Kumār 2003: 115-117).

[166] Jain & Kumār 2003: 115-117. Hastīmal 1995: 762 also refers to Pārśvacandrasūri's *Sthāpanā Pañcāśikā*, which was not accessible to me.

LOṄKĀ'S FIFTY-EIGHT PROCLAMATIONS

The first manuscript attributed to "Loṅkā", No. 2989, has been dated by Mālvaṇiyā (1964: 381) to the 17th century CE. It contains three texts which, judging on the evidence of the handwriting and the format of the texts, must have been written by three different individuals. The main text, *Luṅkā nā Saddahiyā ane Luṅkā nā Kariyā Aṭhāvana Bolo* (L), "Loṅkā's beliefs and fifty-eight assertions created by Loṅkā",[167] has Loṅkā's name in its title. It is clearly the oldest text of the three. The text is framed by an untitled index of the fifty-eight topics at the beginning of the Ms., and at the end by a list of fifty-four questions to unnamed opponents, which is generally referred to as *Keha nī Paramparā Chai* (K), "Whose tradition is this?", in the secondary literature. Both of these supplementary texts, the index and the *praśnottara* text, must have been added sometime after the completion of the core text, which is the only document of "Loṅkā" which contains not just questions to opponents, but also positive doctrinal statements.[168] The main text (L) consists largely of selected quotations (*uddharaṇa*) from the Śvetāmbara scriptures, on both ethical and abstract doctrinal issues concerning Jaina mendicants as well as laity, and renditions of their meaning in Old Gujarātī. At the beginning of the text the citations form a logical sequence on *samyaktva* which can be read as an entirely new text on the "essence" of the Jaina scriptures, although many subsequent statements take the form of questions and can be attributed to the *praśnottara* genre. The method of weaving selected citations together to form a new text is not fundamentally

[167] The original text was published for the first time by Mālvaṇiyā (1963a), then together with a modern Gujarātī translation by Vāṇā (1976), and again by Hastīmal (1995: 655-693). A Gujarātī summary of this text has been published by P. T. Śāh (2001), and a Hindī rendition by Jain and Kumār (2003: 124-139), who also re-published the version by Hastīmal and a copy of an unspecified hand-written manuscript of the text in an appendix (Jain & Kumār 2003: 503-537).

[168] Only a future comparison of different manuscripts can establish whether K is always presented in conjunction with L.

different from the method of compilation of the Āgamas themselves. Loṅkā's work can therefore be interpreted as a case of secondary canonisation, since many of his tenets are still reflected in the Sthānakavāsī literature, although their original handwritten sources are either lost or hidden away. There are, as Bruhn (1987: 106) has indicated, many examples of canonisation outside the canon in the Jain tradition; and generally the post-canonical literatures achieve a higher degree of closure than the canon itself; which Schubring (1910: 63) pointedly described as a "chaos of atoms". Considering its form, content and function, it would be misleading to classify Loṅkā's *siddhānta* as an instance of a mere literature of use (*Gebrauchsliteratur*),[169] that is as an *ad hoc* composition, since, *de facto*, Loṅkā's teachings established an entirely new doctrinal school within the Jaina tradition.

The text starts with *Āyāra* 1.4.1, the precursor of the later *ahiṃsā vrata*, which uses the term *dayāiṃ dharma*, or law of compassion, to describe the law of non-violence. *Āyāra* 1.4.2.3-6 is then cited in the second statement which comprises the rejection of the negation of this proposition: many Brāhmaṇas and Śramaṇas say that there is nothing wrong in injuring living beings, but this is not true because all living beings fear pain. The third *bol* cites *Āyāra* 1.4.2.1-2 which describes the necessity to discriminate between actions which cause the influx (*āsrava*) of karma and actions which destroy karma (*nirjarā*). The fourth and fifth *bol*s establish the importance of the law of compassion (non-violence) as the sole path to liberation (*Sūyagaḍa* 17), by contrasting it to violence, which produces only suffering (*Sūyagaḍa* 18). *Bol* 6 and 7 use for the first time more than one citation within a sustained argument, and leave the monastic sphere behind in order to apply the basic

[169] Cf. Bruhn 1981: 18. In her *4th Annual Lecture on Jainism* at the London School of Oriental and African Studies on the 17.3.2004, "Thoughts on the meaning and the role of the Śvetāmbara canon in the history of Jainism", Nalini Balbir introduced the term "canon of use" which can be usefully applied in this case; though the difference between a primary and secondary canon is merely a matter of degree.

principles of *bol* 1-5 "with discrimination" to the case of image-worship.[170] Point 6 establishes that unavoidable violence committed in the course of the prescribed duties of a monk, such as crossing a river, must be counteracted through atonements (*prāyaścitta*), and asks why the same rule is not applied to the image worship of the laity. *Bol* 7 argues that "according to the scriptures (*siddhānta*)" the path of liberation (*mokṣamārga*) cannot be entered through image worship, since it only produces worldly gratification (*phal*). Any other interpretation is "opposed to the scriptures" (*sūtra viruddha*). *Bol* 8 states that liberation can only be accomplished by observing the five *mahāvrata*s, the *gupti*s and *samiti*s on the level of the mendicants, and the *bārah vrata*, and the *ṣaḍāvaśyaka* rituals, etc., on the level of the laity, but not through image-worship, which most of the remaining *bol*s address.

Mālvaṇiyā (1964: 382) classified the contents of L into three broad categories: *samyaktva* and *mithyātva;*[171] the inauthenticity of the commentary literature; and the problems associated with *mūrti-pūjā*,[172] such as image-making and installation, *prasāda*, the *sthāpanā nikṣepa*, and the term *caitya* (Pkt. *ceiya*).[173] Other categories could be created, for instance concerning the prominent issues of *tīrtha yātrā*,[174] lay or mendicant practices (generally all points concerning image-worship imply lay conduct), or assertions addressing particular opponents, such as in L 30 (Āgamikagaccha's rejection of *pūjā* with flowers) or L 26, which questions the scriptural basis for the dispute between the view of the A(ñ)calagaccha (and Kaḍuāgaccha) that only the laity can perform *pratiṣṭhā*s and other Mūrtipūjaka sects which regard the performance of this ceremony

---

[170] Most *praśnottara* texts address issues in the religious life "of the mendicant as well as of the layman" (Balbir 2003a: 259), which reflects the prevalence of "fourfold", etc., sectarian forms of organisation.

[171] L 1-9, 17, 20-21, 40-52, 54-55, 58.

[172] L 7-16, 18-19, 22-32, 34-39, 42, 53, 56.

[173] L 57.

[174] L 53 points to the inner journey advocated by Viy 18.10.4 for instance.

as a prerogative of the mendicants.[175] Only one statement (No. 27) explicitly refers to the Digambaras, asking where in the scriptures the issue of the naked representation of *tīrthaṅkaras* is discussed, which is controversial between Digambaras and Śvetāmbaras.

The analysis of the contents and exegetical procedures employed by the author of this text requires a separate study. A cursory view shows that all selected texts belong to the canonical literature (of thirty-two scriptures), though no new classification of the Āgamas is offered. Mālvaṇiyā (1964: 378) argued that Loṅkā only rejected those passages in the commentaries which are not in agreement with the scriptures, which made the creation of a new canon unnecessary.[176] He suggested that the various canons of the aniconic traditions were products of the early Loṅkāgaccha and Sthānakavāsī traditions.[177] These are open questions. The commentary literature – which the author of L evidently knew – is expli-

---

[175] Balbir 2003b: 57 refers to "some inscriptions" as evidence for the view that A(ñ)calgaccha mendicants "take help from *ācāryas* belonging to other groups" for *pratiṣṭhā*.

[176] Mālvaṇiyā 1964: 377 cites the key passage of Loṅkā's texts, and asks what harm there is to accept the commentaries which are in agreement with the *sūtras*: *'niryukti, bhāṣya, cūrṇī, vṛtti aur ṭīkāoṃ meṃ jo sūtra viruddha bāteṃ haiṃ, unheṃ pramāṇ kaise mānā jā saktā hai?' lekin jinkā siddhānta sūtroṃ ke sāth meṃ mel baiṭh jātā hai, unheṃ pramāṇ mānne meṃ kyā hāni hai*? He suggests that, judging on the basis of the two Mss., Loṅkā himself must have been of this view (Mālvaṇiyā 1964: 378).

[177] According to Dharmasāgara's *Pravacanaparīkṣā*, in Mālvaṇiyā 1964: 378, some of Loṅkā's followers accepted twenty-seven scriptures, and others twenty-nine. Earlier Loṅkāgaccha sources, such as Bhānucandra's *Dayādharma Caupāī*, already mention the Loṅkāgaccha canon of thirty-two scriptures, though the canon of thirty-two may have originated with the Sthānakavāsī *ācārya* Jīvarāja. The modern association of a canon of thirty-one with Loṅkā seems to go back to Ātmārām 1881/1954, II: 519; 1888/1906: 204; in Vallabhvijay 1891: 131. Ātmārām wrote that the *Vavahāra* was added by the Sthānakavāsīs, whereas Jñānsundar (1936: 106) argued that it was the "*Āvaśyaka Sūtra*". Suśīlkumār (1959: 395, 431f.) tells us that the Sthānakavāsī *ācārya* Jīvarāja (died ca. 1641) created the present canon of thirty-two scriptures. Mālvaṇiyā (1964: 378f.) also believes that it was created after the emergence of the Sthānakavāsīs, because in all cases only thirty-two are mentioned in the later literature. See Flügel 2000: 49, n. 18 and 59, n. 38.

citly rejected in L 41, with reference to additional insertions concerning image worship which cannot be found in the original text, and in L 57, which argues that the elaboration of exceptions (*apavāda*) of the prescriptions of the Āgamas in the commentary literature[178] opens the door to laxity. However, the claim that Loṅkā rejected the entire Śvetāmbara commentary literature in the name of a "fundamentalist scriptural literalism",[179] seems too broad, since all aniconic traditions accept the "philological commentary", while rejecting the "canonical commentary", which while explaining the meaning of the scriptures also mediates creatively between the closed canon and the openness of the world.[180]

If L was really composed by Loṅkā, and there are more arguments in favour than against this assumption, then there can be no doubt that he propagated the necessity for the mendicants to observe the five *mahāvrata*s, and for the laity to observe the twelve lay vows (which include the *poṣadha vrata*), the *āvaśyaka* rituals (*sāmāyika*, *caturviṃśatistava* etc.), and to support the ascetics with offerings of food, *upāśraya*s, etc., if they wish to reap the fruit of salvation (*mokṣa nāṃ phal*).[181] He rejected, however, all rituals which are predicated on violence (against flowers and fruits, water, fire, etc.). The claim by his early Mūrtipūjaka opponents,[182] which Jñānsundar (1936: 98ff.) and Śeṭh (1964) cited in support of their

---

178 For instance, in the *Āvassaya Nijjutti* or the *Bṛhatkalpabhāṣya*.

179 Dharmasāgara, in Dundas 1996: 74; 2002: 62. See also Mālvaṇiyā's (1964: 376) critique of the "hard" (*dṛṛh*) dogmatism of the Sthānakavāsīs, who in his view do not tolerate differences of opinion.

180 The terms are from Assmann 1987: 13f.

181 ... *tathā śrāvaka naiṃ bāra vrata pālyā nāṃ phal śrī uvavāī upāṅga tathā sāmāiya cauvīsatthao ityādi āvaśyaka nāṃ phal ānuyogadvāra madhye, tathā śrāvaka naiṃ ju sādhu cāritrīā vandanīka chaiṃ tu sādh unai vāṃdyā nāṃ phal, tathā sādhu nī paryupāsti kīdhā nāṃ phal tathā annā pāṇī dīdhā nāṃ phal tathā upāśraya dīdhā nāṃ phal, tathā vastra pātra dīdhā nāṃ phal ityādi* (L 8).

182 See the *Asūtranirākaraṇa Batrīśī* of Muni Bīkā of 1470/1, the *Siddhānta Caupāī* of Muni Lāvaṇyasamay of 1486/7, and the *Siddhānta Sāroddhāra* of Upādhyāya Kamalsaṃyam of the Kharataragaccha in 1487/8. The *Loṅkāśāha Siloko* vv. 13-15 of 1543/4 by the Loṅkāgaccha *yati* Keśavṛṣi also contains similar statements, which is difficult to explain.

own views, that Loṅkā had rejected the standard Jaina *sāmāyika*, *pratikramaṇa*, *poṣadha*, *dāna* etc. rituals entirely,[183] is neither confirmed by the two published manuscripts of "Loṅkā", nor by his "thirteen questions".[184] The *Dayādharma Caupāī* vv. 15-19 of 1521/2 of the Loṅkāgaccha *yati* Bhānucandra[185] explicitly mentions the practice of two *sāmāyika*s (in the morning and evening), one-day *poṣadha*, *pratikramaṇa* (not without taking a vow), *pratyākhyāna*, *dāna* to restrained individuals, *bhāva pūjā* (but not *dravya pūjā*), and the belief in thirty-two Āgamas (v. 19) within his own group;[186] Jñānsundar (1936: 237, n. 1) explains this away as the result of a post-Loṅkā reform, and further argued that no such lay rites could have been practised before probably Bhāṇā introduced them, because the *śrāvaka pratikramaṇa* is not part of the *Āvaśyaka Sūtra* (*Niryukti*) amongst the thirty-two accepted Āgamas, and because it is known that both Loṅkā and Kaḍuā were householders who rejected the *sāmāyika* (Jñānsundar 1936: 105-107). Yet, the statement that Kaḍuā was "also" against the *sāmāyika* is obviously fabricated, since several points of Kaḍuā's *Niyamāvalī* demand its performance.[187] Without taking note of Jñānsundar's writings,

---

[183] Jñānsundar 1936: 29, 97, App. 3; Mālvaṇiyā 1964: 367f.; Dundas 2002: 248.

[184] *kintu Loṅkāśāh ke 58 bolom evaṃ 13 praśnoṃ ādi meṃ kahīṃ koī ek bhī aisā śabda nahīṃ. ... Loṅkāśāh ke virodha meṃ likhane vāle vidvānoṃ ke dvārā kiye gaye ullekhoṃ meṃ sthān-sthān par is prakār ke tathyoṃ kī andekhī dṛṣṭigocar hotī hai* (Hastīmal 1995: 751, cf. 759-789).

[185] *sāmāika ṭālaiṃ be bāra, parva pare posaha parihār,*
paḍikkamaṇuṃ bina vrata na karaiṃ, paccakhāṇai kima āgāra dharaiṃ (17).
ṭālai asaṃyati naiṃ dāna, bhāva pūjā thī rūḍau jñāna,
dravya pūjā navi kahī jinarāja, dharma nāmaiṃ hiṃsāi akāja (18).
sūtra batīsa sācā saddahyā, samatā bhāve sādhu kahyā,
siri Luṅkā no sācco dharma, bhrame paṛiyā na lahai marma (19)
(Bhānucandra, in Jñānsundar 1936: 236).

[186] This is evidently the first reference to the thirty-two Āgamas in the Jaina literature, which points to a pre-Sthānakavāsī origin of this classification.

[187] Dundas 1999: 22. Jñānsundar 1936: 327 also cites Kaḍuā's list, but comments on the relevant point 4 (point 6 in Dundas' list) that Kaḍuā may have included it in the list to distinguish himself on paper from Loṅkā: *śāyad lauṃkā-*

Mālvaṇiyā (1964: 367f.) merely mentions that the difference of opinion between Loṅkā and the Mūrtipūjakas over these issues developed only when in Saṃvat 1544 Loṅkā met Lakhamsī, who became his first associate. But Hastīmal (1995: 786-788) points out that nowhere in Loṅkā's own writings is *sāmāyika*, *poṣadha*, *pratikramaṇa*, *pratyākhyāna* or *dāna* rejected in principle. What is rejected is the manner in which these rituals are performed or not performed, for instance the ostentatious giving of gold and money in the context of *pratiṣṭhā*, etc., rituals. He also notices that there is no mentioning of any opposition to *sāmāyika*, *pratikramaṇa*, *poṣadha*, etc. in the report on the meeting between Bhāṇā and Kaḍuā in Saṃvat 1539 in the *Kaḍuvāmat Paṭṭāvalī* (*Paṭṭāvalī Parāga Saṃgraha*, p. 483), which would have recorded a debate between the two if Bhāṇā had indeed not practiced these rituals which Kaḍuā himself observed.[188]

Another controversial issue is whether Loṅkāgaccha mendicants observed the *mahāvrata*s, or whether they were *yati*s in the modern sense of half-ascetics from the outset; as apparently the Kaḍuāgaccha ascetics were, though this remains doubtful (Klatt 1888: 58f.; Dundas 1999: 21, cf. 30, n. 11). Modern commentators such as V. M. Śāh (1909: 49f.), Jñānsundar (1936: 97ff.), and Mālvaṇiyā (1964: 367-369), who stressed the difference between Loṅkāgaccha "*yati*s" and Sthānakavāsī "*sādhu*s", expressed the opinion (backed by the reports of the Mūrtipūjakas Dharmasāgara and Kamalsaṃyam) that the first leader of the Loṅkāgaccha, Bhāṇā, was known for not observing the *mahāvrata*s and for not wearing the dress of a *sādhu*.[189] He therefore must have been a *yati*, i.e. neither a householder nor a monk; which would turn the Sthā-

---

śāh ne sāmāyik ko bhī asvīkār kiyā thā, isī lie kaḍuāśāh ko yah niyam banānā karā ho (p. 327, n. 4).

[188] Hastīmal 1995: 750 also points to the absence of any polemic along these lines in critique of Loṅkā in the Digambara *muni* Ratnanandī's *Bhadrabāhu Caritra* 158-163 of Saṃvat 1625.

[189] A different picture is painted in the much younger *Vinaycandrajī-kṛt Paṭṭāvalī*, published by Hastīmal (1968: 141).

nakavāsī mendicants into the first truly *pañca-mahāvratī* ascetics of the aniconic tradition. If this is indeed true, then already the practices of the earliest Loṅkāgaccha ascetics would not have corresponded with the principles of Loṅkā, as articulated in L.

L ends with the statement that *mokṣa* can only be reached through the practice of protecting life (*jīvadayā*),[190] even now [sic!] and in future by everyone, as stated in the *Sūyagaḍa*:

> O ye monks, the virtuous (Jinas) that have been and will be, the followers of the law of Kaśyapa, they all have commended these virtues. Do not kill living beings in the threefold way, being intent on your spiritual welfare and abstaining from sins. In this way numberless men have reached perfection [*siddhā*], and others, who live now, and who are to come, (will reach it) (Sūy 1.2.3.20-21, translated by Jacobi).

Loṅkā's main ("*ekānta*")[191] focus was the doctrine of *dayā dharma*, or the law of compassion.[192] His interpretation of *jīvadayā* is, however, restricted to practising abstinence from violence in general, and does not explicitly recommend an active intervention into the world for the saving of life, as advocated today by most Sthānakavāsī traditions. Since L presents such practices as an aspect of worldly conduct, but not of the *mokṣamārga*, this text could be cited in favour of Ācārya Bhikṣu's interpretation of the dividing

---

[190] *jīvadayāiṃ karī mokṣa puhatā* (L 58).

[191] L 46. See Mālvaṇiyā's (1964: 373-375) critique of the "one-sidedness" of Loṅkā's *niścaya-naya* approach, which does not take into account practical considerations of religious instruction for beginners: *dharma kī jo sādhana 13veṃ guṇasthāna se 14veṃ guṇasthāna meṃ jāne ke lie hotī hai, vahī sādhanā pratham guṇasthāna vāle ke lie bhī āvaśyak hai – is prakār kā āgrah karne se sāmānya vyakti ko dharma ke mārga par kaise lāyā jā saktā hai? sādhanā ke mārga par is prakār ekānta āgrah se kām nahīṃ caltā. kyoṃki sabhī sādhakoṃ kī yogyatā samān nahīṃ ho saktī.* This critique echoes the standard criticisms of the views of the Terāpanth *ācārya* Bhikṣu. The additional criticism, directed at the Sthānakavāsīs, that their emphasis on *dayā* unduly neglects the importance of knowledge is, partly, polemical: *sthānakavāsī paramparā jñān-śūnya ban gaī* (Mālvaṇiyā 1964: 376).

[192] See L 17 for a lengthy list of citations from the Āgamas using the term *dayā* in defence of his choice of catchphrase.

line between *laukika* and *lokottara dharma*, though his controversial equation of *puṇya* and *pāpa*, from the *niścaya* point of view, is not discussed in the text.[193] Notably, the text does not reject religious property per se, but declares the gift of *upāśraya*s (= *sthānaka*s) to the mendicants (*sādhu*) as a religious act.

LOṄKĀ'S THIRTY-FOUR PROCLAMATIONS

The second manuscript, No. 4121, contains only one text, *Luṅkā nī Huṇḍī 34 Bol* (=LH), Loṅkā's list of thirty-four assertions,[194] which gives thirty-three examples from the commentaries for significant deviations from the scriptures under the label of *apavāda*, or exception. The statements No. 1-25 criticise various points of the *Niśītha Cūrṇī*, which cannot be found in the *Nisīha*, No. 26 does the same for the *Uttarādhyayana Vṛtti*, No. 27 for the *Vyavahāra Vṛtti*, Nos. 28-33 for the *Āvaśyaka Niryukti*, and the last section for the *Prajñāpanā Vṛtti*. The underlying ordering principle of the diverse list of topics is the reference to the five *mahāvrata*s. More than one example is given for excuses for the exceptional use of violence in self-defence (Nos. 1, 22, 26); for the violation of the vow on non-possession (Nos. 3, 4); for the violation of the vow of not taking what is not given (Nos. 2, 18, 28, 29); for the violation of the vow of celibacy (Nos. 14, 15, 23);[195] and for using living objects such as water, fire, earth, food, plants, etc., in various contexts. Because the text focuses only on explicit discrepancies between canonical and

---

[193] Cf. Mālvaṇiyā 1964: 373f., and Jain and Kumār's (2003: 140) summary of the text, which would also support this interpretation.

[194] Mālvaṇiyā 1964: 382 cites the text as *Luṅkā nī Huṇḍī 33 Bol*. It was however published with an explanation in Hindī under the title *Cauṃtīs Bol* (34 assertions) by Hastīmal (1995: 648-655), and re-published under the same title by Jain and Kumār (2003: 499-503), who also give a summary in Hindī (Jain & Kumār 2003: 120-124). The numerical difference can be explained by the fact that Mālvaṇiyā did not count *bol* No. 34, because it contains only the general statement that only on the basis of the scriptures progress can be achieved.

[195] See U. P. Shah 1955b for an inscription documenting historical cases.

post-canonical monastic law, and on the use of *prāyaścitta*s for normalising transgressions (No. 23), image-worship is not mentioned at all, and neither are issues of contemporary practice. Interestingly, both the *Vavahāra* and the *Āvassaya Sutta* are implicitly referred to, which are often cited in the modern secondary literature as the two texts whose canonical status may have been disputed between the early Loṅkāgaccha and the Sthānakavāsī traditions.[196]

LOṄKĀ'S FIFTY-FOUR QUESTIONS TO THE IMAGE-WORSHIPPERS

The fifty-four rhetorical questions *Whose tradition is that?* (*Te Keha nī Paramparā Chai*?),[197] which are appended to the *Aṭhāvan Bol* in the L.D. Institute Ms. 2989, effectively ask (like some of the *Aṭhāvan Bol*s) whether any of the listed practices (not beliefs), which must have been prevalent amongst the image-worshipping Jaina traditions of the time, are backed up by the "root" scriptures.[198] Since the answer is assumed to be "no" in all cases, the main function of the questions is to provide summary criticism of the key shortcomings of the addressees of these questions, which in accordance with the etiquette of the *praśnottara* genre are not explicitly mentioned. Fifty-two almost identical questions which were attributed to Loṅkā were published in Hindī in the fourth edition of Muni Jeṭhmal's (1930: 14f.) polemical work *Samakitasāra*.[199] The content of this slightly shorter list overlaps to a large

---

[196] See Flügel 2000: 18.

[197] The text was first published by Mālvaṇiyā (1963a: 80-82), and reprinted in Hastīmal 1995: 691-693, and from Hastīmal's publication (without an indication of the original source) in Jain & Kumār 2003: 537-539. A Hindī summary can also be found in Jain & Kumār 2003: 118-120.

[198] See Samayasundara's question "What are the textual references for such and such a rite, usage, etc.?" in his *Sāmācārī Śataka* cited by Balbir 2003a: 267.

[199] Fourth edition with Hindī translation by Muni Devṛṣi (1872-1929), who became the *ācārya* of the Sthānakavāsī Mālvā Ṛṣi Sampradāya after Amolakṛṣi's death, and was the predecessor of Ānandṛṣi (1901-1963), the second *ācārya* of

extent with K, but comprises some extra questions, which points to the existence of other recensions which are yet to be unearthed, or to later interpolations.[200] The original text (K) can be translated as follows:

> The tradition is written. Someone says, Śrī Vīra's tradition says this. Where is that?[201]
>
> 1. To cause images to be made and to be installed (*maṇḍāvai*) in the house, whose tradition is that?[202] To buy male and female disciples (*celā-celī*), whose tradition is that?[203]
> 2. To give initiation to small children, whose tradition is that?[204]
> 3. To change the name (to give a different name at the time of initiation), whose tradition is that?
> 4. To cause the ear to be extended (*vadhārai*), whose tradition is that?[205]
> 5. To venerate (*viharai*) the forgiving *guru* (in the presence of symbols), whose tradition is that?[206]

---

the Śramaṇasaṅgha in which the Mālvā Ṛṣi Sampradāya was incorporated in 1952. See Flügel 2000: 70, n. 62.

[200] Jeṭhmal 1930: 14 has as question No. 6: *ghoṛā, rath, bail, ḍolī meṃ baiṭhte ho*. – To sit on a horse, chariot, bullock (-cart) or litter carried by porters; No. 8: *ghar jākar kalpa sūtra paṛhte ho*. – To read the *Kalpa Sūtra* after going to a house; No. 12: *rassī ḍore dete ho*. – To give strings of rope (as blessings); No. 13: *mantra, jantra, jhāṛ phūk karte ho*. – To perform *mantra*, *yantra*, exorcism; 14. *pustak, pātare becte ho*. – To sell leafs of a book (to sell knowledge); 15. *māl uṛāte ho*. – To indulge in property; 25. *ṭīp likhā rupaye lete ho*. – To take money for writing documents; 29. *tapasyā karākar paise lete ho*. – To accept money after performing a fast; 45. *mor piñch ke ḍaṇḍāsaṇ rakhte ho*. – To keep a peacock feather staff (Digambara style); 46. *strī kā saṅghaṭṭā karte ho*. – To keep the company of women; 49. *kapṛe dhulāte ho*. – To cause clothes to be washed. These are standard complaints against "domesticated" Jain mendicants.

[201] On the uses of written texts in earlier medieval Jaina debates see Granoff 1993, and also Dundas 1996. On the role of written texts for the "protestant" Jaina reform movements see Flügel 2000: 38, 46.

[202] Jain and Kumār (2003: 118) have *ghar meṃ pratimā banavāne yā citrit karavāne*. This sentence appears in Jeṭhmal 1930: 14 as No. 24: *māṇḍvī karāte ho*.

[203] This sentence has only been published in Hindī in Jeṭhmal 1930: 14. It is not related to the first sentence of point 1, and should have been listed separately. The laxities of (some) medieval Mūrtipūjaka mendicants are well documented in an inscription published by U. P. Shah 1955b.

[204] On *bāl dīkṣā* see Balbir 2001.

[205] Or "split". On ascetics piercing their ears see Wujastyk 1984.

6. To amuse oneself (*viharai*)[207] sitting in the householder's house, whose tradition is that?

7. To go every day to the same house (for food), whose tradition is that?[208]

8. To ask (someone) to take a bath, whose tradition is that?[209]

9. To make use (*prajumjai*) of the secret of astrology, whose tradition is that?

10. To tell the future, whose tradition is that?[210]

11. To cause a reception to be held at the time of entering into a town, whose tradition is that?

12. To consecrate sweets, whose tradition is that?

13. To cause the worship of religious books, whose tradition is that?

14. To cause the performance of *saṅghapūjā*, whose tradition is that?[211]

---

[206] The word *khamāsamāsaṇu* refers to the *vandanā* ritual to the *kṣamāśramaṇa*, which begins with the words *icchāmi khamā-samaṇo vandiuṃ* – I desire to venerate you forgiving monk, which Mūrtipūjaka ascetics (and laity) also perform in front of symbolic objects representing the *guru*, such as the *sthāpanācārya*, and in front of statues (*caitya vandanā*). See Leumann 1934: 7-10; Williams 1983: 199-203; Cort 2001: 65. The sentence is interpreted by Jain and Kumār (2003: 118) as: "*khamāsaṇā guru ko diyā jātā haim, dev ko nahīṃ*". The issue is also addressed in Samayasundara's *Sāmācārī Śataka* 1 etc. (Balbir 2003a: 261).

[207] Also: to spend time.

[208] A common mistake, known in the scriptures as *nitya-piṇḍa* or *nitiya-piṇḍa*.

[209] Jain and Kumār (2003: 118) have: *snān karne kā kahanā aur snān karnā.* – To ask (someone) to take a bath and to take a bath. LH 19 criticises that the *Niśītha Cūrṇī* permits taking a bath under certain circumstances, although the scriptures prohibit it unequivocally for mendicants. The question may also address the obligatory practice of image-worshipping lay Jainas to take a bath before entering the temple in order to "purify" themselves outwardly. See Williams 1983: 221, and Laidlaw 1995: 273 on the "incongruence between purity in *puja* and purity in asceticism".

[210] In Rājasthānī (R.) *kalavāṃṇī*, means "dirty water" (Lālas 1986-87: 208). The question may thus alternatively refer to *sacitta* water that is left over from the ablutions of the ascetics and/or images, and distributed as a sacred object, or to "raw" water used at certain ritual consecrations. Cf. Williams 1983: 224. Jain and Kumār (2003: 118) have *kalavānī karke dete haiṃ.*

[211] There are two uses of the term: (1) The prime recipients of the *saṅghapūjā*, which Williams 1983: 166 described as a "later development", are the mendicants, who during an annual ceremony (at the end of *paryuṣaṇa*) receive at once "blankets, cloth, needles, thread, staves, almsbowls, *rajoharaṇa*s, and other objects useful to an ascetic". Jeṭhmal 1930: 14 (question No. 18) uses the expression "to extract" (*nikalnā*) the *saṅghapūjā*. (2) The "worship of the congrega-

15. To perform installation ceremonies (of idols), whose tradition is that?[212]

16. To give books during *paryuṣaṇa*, whose tradition is that?[213]

17. And to sell pilgrimages, whose tradition is that?[214]

18. And to give a certain amount,[215] whose tradition is that?

19. And to bind garlands made of vegetation to arched gateways, whose tradition is that?

20. To keep specially prepared food (*ādhākarma*) for the ascetics in the *poṣadhaśālā*,[216] whose tradition is that?[217]

---

tion" may also involve "giving every participant at some public religious function a small amount of money (usually a one-rupee coin) and a red forehead mark as a token of respect" (Cort 2001: 150). *Saṅghapūjā* is, for instance, performed in connection with the visit of prominent ascetics to the residence of a householder. The host invites his family and friends to participate in this event and prepares *kunkum* for auspicious *tilaka*s on the fronts of their heads and distributes money to each visitor after the monk or nun has left – a kind of *prasāda* (personal communication K. Śeṭh).

[212] This question reflects L 26. The A(ñ)calagaccha did/does not allow this for its own mendicants. See Balbir 2003b: 57.

[213] Jeṭhmal 1930: 14 understands this as: *paryuṣaṇ meṃ pothī, de rātra jāgaraṇ karāte*. – To cause night watches to be done to books given out during *paryuṣaṇ*. Loṅkā thus may have rejected the veneration of books as objects. Often, manuscripts are copied or books printed in honour of deceased parents, whose names are mentioned in the introductory sections of a text, and then offered to the mendicants during *paryuṣaṇa*. The objection may also have been directed against the payments for something that has been produced especially for the mendicants, or, more likely, against motivating the laity to auction the privilege of taking the *Kalpa Sūtra* home for one night.

[214] For allocating the honour of leading specific rituals, auctions (*bolī*) are routinely held in many Jaina traditions. In the question, the practiçe of bidding for the privilege of leading the *saṅgha yātrā* as a *caitya paripāṭī* is addressed. Williams 1983: 234 indirectly confirms Loṅkā's suspicion. He writes: "The *tīrtha-yātrā* seems to be a later development".

[215] The contextual meaning of *mātra* is unclear here. It could mean measure, a certain amount of money, etc. Jain and Kumār (2003: 118) interpret the half-sentence as: *mātrā (prasravaṇ) dene*, *prasravaṇa* meaning flow, outflow.

[216] *posāliṃ*; see R. *posāla*, S. *pāṭhaśālā*. The *poṣadhaśālā* is a special room that is used for the collective performance of a one-day fast, or *poṣadha*, during which the practising laity imitates the lifestyle of the ascetics. A variety of fasts can be performed. Because not all of them require the complete renunciation of all nourishment, food and drink may be brought to the *poṣadhaśālā* from home (Yaśovijay, in Williams 1983: 145). Since *poṣadha* does not involve performing an almsround, only specially prepared food can be eaten. Therefore, Loṅkā must have disagreed with eating food at all during *poṣadha*, apparently in agreement

21. To create the impression of the importance of the scriptures but not reading them, whose tradition is that?[218]

22. To cause decorative pavilions (for images) to be constructed, whose tradition is that?[219]

23. To cause the fast in the name of[220] "Gautama" to be performed, whose tradition is that?

24. To cause the "Saṃsāratāraṇa" (vow to be taken), whose tradition is that?[221]

25. To cause the "Candanabālā" fast to be performed, whose tradition is that?[222]

26. To cause the "ladder of gold and silver" (*sonā rūpā nī nīsaraṇī*) to be created, whose tradition is that?[223]

---

with the A(ñ)calagaccha and the Kāḍuāgaccha, but in contrast with the Tapāgaccha and Kharataragaccha (Samayasundara) at the time (cf. Balbir 2003b: 60).

[217] *Ādhākarma* is discussed in L 21 as well.

[218] Loṅkā advocated open access to the scriptures.

[219] The word *māṇḍavī* (H. *maṇḍapa*) can also signify a temple, or the entrance hall of a temple.

[220] Literally, the sound or echo (*paṛagho*, G. *paḍaghī*). Jeṭhmal 1930: 46-52 lists fifteen practices opposed to the scriptures (*sūtra*) which the *hiṃsā dharmī*, i.e. the image-worshippers, associate with the name of Gautama. Vāriā 1976: 129 explains the question as: *gautam paḍaghā nuṃ tap karāve che*. Jain and Kumār (2003: 119) read the word *paṛagho* as *pratipadā* (*paṛvā*) – the first day of the lunar fortnight. Though Jeṭhmal does not mention this, the question may also refer to the *sūrimantra* (cf. Dundas 1998) which is addressed explicitly in questions 45 and 46, or, more likely, to Gautama's invocation during the annual *pūjā* of the account books at Dīpāvalī (cf. Cort 2001: 168-70).

[221] *Saṃsāra-tāraṇa* means literally "to cross the ocean of existence". John Cort informed me that this practice is listed as a fast in the Tapāgaccha monk Jinendravijaygaṇi's *Taporatna Mahodadhi* (Lākhāvāḷa-Śāntipuri: Harṣapuṣpāmṛta Jaina Granthamālā 101, 1982) which is based on the Kharataragaccha *ācārya* Vardhamāna's 15th-century *Ācāradinakara*. Jeṭhmal 1930: 14 speaks of the *Saṃsāra-tāraṇa* "*telā*", i.e. a continuous three-day fast. Most, if not all, of the practices mentioned in questions Nos. 24-27 are likely to be special fasts, which involve auctions of the meritorious act of giving the first drink and food to a *tapasvin(ī)* to conclude, or "break", the fast (*pāraṇa*).

[222] This fast takes four days: three one-day fasts (*upavāsa*), followed by one day eating only one meal (*ekāsana*) with or without practising *āyambila* (to eat only one unsalted cereal). Both the privilege of the first feeding of the *tapasvī/n(ī)* on day four, and of the first feeding at the time of the breaking of the fast on day five are auctioned (Kelting 2001: 46). For the story of Candanā see Shāntā 1997: 122-128.

27. To cause the "Lākhā Paḍavi" to be performed, whose tradition is that?[224]

28. To cause gifts to be given (*ḍhovarāvai*) to celebrate the end of a fast (*ūṃjamaṇā*), whose tradition is that?[225]

29. To cause the *pūjā* to be recited,[226] whose tradition is that?

30. To cause the "Aśoka-tree" (*āso vṛkṣa*) to be supported (*bharavāī*),[227] whose tradition is that?[228]

31. To cause the eightfold bath (*aṭṭhottarī snātra*) to be performed, whose tradition is that?[229]

---

[223] This is probably another fast involving public auctions. Alternatively, the question may or may not refer to one of the following practices: (a) a ladder of gold is often given by grandsons to grandfathers; (b) ladders are often used to reach a large statue for *pūjā* (personal communication K. Śeṭh).

[224] John Cort suggested to me, this may refer to the *lakṣa pratipada* fast (G. *lākhī paḍavo*), which is listed in modern Gujarātī Jaina compilations of fasts.

[225] G. *ujamaṇuṃ*, R. *ujamaṇau*, *ujavaṇau*, a celebration at the end of a fast, involving donations of money to the fasting person(s). Jain and Kumār (2003: 119) translate *ūṃjamaṇā* as "*udyāpana*", which signifies the concluding ceremony or the dedication of a temple on completion. The meaning of the word *ḍhovarāvai* (? S. *ḍhauk*, P. *ḍhovaṇa*, to offer, to give gifts) is not entirely clear. It may generally refer to celebrations. Jeṭhmal 1930: 15 has "*ḍhurāna*".

[226] Or to be sung (*pāḍhāī*).

[227] The Hindī verb *bharvāī* or *bharvāna*, to have something filled, makes less sense here than the Rājasthānī verb *bharvāī*, to carry, nurture, maintain, or pay for.

[228] Mahāvīra renounced the world under an Aśoka-tree; which is also one of the twelve symbols of the *arihantas*. The tree is associated with the worship of portable Jina images, and is believed to have wish-fulfilling powers. Models of it are often installed on the roofs of temples (Jain & Fischer 1978, II: 3, 7f., 24, Plate XIIb). The *aśoka vṛkṣa* is also listed as a fast in Jinendravijaygaṇi's *Taporatna Mahodadhi*, the breaking of which was possibly auctioned off in various ritual contexts (personal communication of John Cort). The word *bharavāi* could refer to an auction as well. Kanubhāī Śeṭh (personal communication 7.7.2003) informs me that the expression may also point to a decorative curtain with a tree motif (though it seems unlikely). These curtains are made with gold and silver inlays to adorn the wall behind the seat of a monk. Today, they are called *choḍa*, a small tree or shrub. They contain the name of the donor, his family members, and the name of the inspiring monk or nun. After being used as an adornment, they are later venerated in the house of the donor. Sometimes sixteen or eighteen curtains of this type are requested to be made, to be presented to women who have performed a long fast.

[229] This question refers back to L 35, which questions the canonical basis of the "upper eight" (Skt. *aṣṭottarī*, Pkt. *aṭṭhottarī*) ritual of installation of images,

32. To cause fresh rice and fresh fruit to be offered in front of an image, whose tradition is that?[230]

33. To put sandalwood powder[231] on the head of laymen and laywomen, whose tradition is that?

34. To be involved[232] in the search for possessions, whose tradition is that?[233]

35. To cause the laity to offer a head tax (*pāīṃ mūṇḍaka*) before ascending a hill (pilgrimage site), whose tradition is that?[234]

36. To place garlands (on persons or idols), whose tradition is that?[235]

37. To permit laymen and laywomen to walk together (during pilgrimages) by foot, whose tradition is that?[236]

38. To cause the "Nāndi"[237] to be erected, whose tradition is that?

39. To cause foot prints (shrines) (*padīka cāṃka*) to be built, whose tradition is that?

40. To put powder (*bhūko*) into the water, whose tradition is that?[238]

---

which includes the use of fire in *āratī*, the rite of throwing "living" salt into the fire, etc.

[230] This was also rejected by the A(ñ)calagaccha. See Balbir 2003b: 60. Since image-worship is rejected *per se*, this point is redundant, and may have been imported simply to add more venom to the attack.

[231] S. *vāsakṣepa*, colloquial *vāskṣep* or *vāskep*, to sprinkle with scented powder. Mūrtipūjaka ascetics charge sandalwood powder with *mantra*s and sprinkle it on the heads of their devotees to transfer their blessings-*cum*-spiritual energy to them.

[232] *bāṃdhai*, H. *baṃdhnā*.

[233] An alternative reading would be: "To set a limit (for individual laymen) in their search for possessions". Jain and Kumār (2003: 119) interpret the meaning of the passage as *upadhi ādi poṭaliyoṃ meṃ bāṃdhte haiṃ* – to tie up/bring together property etc. in small parcels.

[234] The religious legitimacy of the pilgrimage sites of Śatruñjaya, Girnār, Ābū, etc., and *tīrtha*s other than the *caturvidhasaṅgha* is questioned for instance in L 36, L 38, L 39, L 41, L 44.

[235] The privilege of giving garlands, for instance for the successful performers of the *upadhāna tapa*, is also auctioned off amongst Mūrtipūjakas.

[236] Samayasundara, in Balbir 2003a: 260, similarly questioned the co-wandering of monks and nuns, which is still practised within the Tapāgaccha.

[237] The questioned issue is not clear. Maybe the word *nāndi* refers to the *nandīśvara-paṭa* which is venerated in the context of the *nandīśvara* fast (U. P. Shah 1955a: 121; Williams 1983: 232; Jain & Fischer 1978, II: 19). It could also (though unlikely) refer to the bull *Nandin*, who is associated with Śiva, or to an inauguration involving praise of the gods (*nāndī*).

41. To cause worship (*vāndaṇā*) to be offered, whose tradition is that?[239]

42. To move the broom (*oghā*) (in front of the idols), whose tradition is that?[240]

43. To keep the *deva dravya*, whose tradition is that?[241]

44. To wear a long covering garment (*pacheṛī*) down to the feet, whose tradition is that?[242]

45. To accept the *sūrimantra*, whose tradition is that?[243]

---

[238] G. *bhūko* or *bhūkā*, powder, is related to R. *bhūkau* (Lālas 1986-87: 296). The question addresses a common form of water sterilisation amongst the Jainas through "killing" *sacitta* water by adding a different living substance such as lime powder (*cūnā*). Hastīmal 1995: 693 transcribes the original *bhūko* as *bhūṃkā*. Jain and Kumār (2003: 119) interpret *bhūṃkā* as G. *thūṃka* or H. *thūka*, saliva, spittle. The issue of *cūrṇa*, or powder, is also addressed in Samayasundara's *Sāmācārī Śataka* 37 etc. (Balbir 2003a: 261).

[239] The sentence apparently means: "to cause veneration to be given (to an ascetic or image)", since R. *vāndaṇau* (*bāndaṇau*) is equivalent to S. *vandana*, to worship. Jain and Kumār (2003: 119) translate *vāndaṇā dirāvai* as *bāṃdhanā dilānā* – to cause someone to give an oath (to bind him/herself). They derive *vāndaṇā* from S. *bandhana*, to bind, R. *bāṃdhaṇau*. Cf. Lālas 1986-87: 194f.

[240] Jain and Kumār (2003: 119) render the words *oghā phervai chai* as *āśīrvād svarūp kisī par oghā phernā*. Loṅkā apparently did not use an *oghā* at all (Mālvaṇiyā 1964: 369).

[241] The donations given "to the gods" should only be used for the maintenance of the temples, etc. Jeṭhmal 1930: 15 has as question No. 44: *gāṃṭh meṃ paisā rakhte ho*. – To keep money in the pocket.

[242] To wear a long *pacchevaṛī* (P. *pacchāga*) is considered wasteful. It seems, Loṅkā himself used one almsbowl (*pātra*), one loincloth (*colapaṭṭāka*) and one short *pacchevaṛī* (*cādar*) (L D. Institute Ms. No. 2328, in Mālvaṇiyā 1964: 369). He rejected the *oghā*, *muhapattī*, *kambala*, and *daṇḍa*. See Mālvaṇiyā 1964: 369; he cites Ghelārṣi, a contemporary of Loṅkā, who reportedly (L.D. Institute Ms. No. 7588, question 86) asked him in which *sūtra* it is written to wear a *colapaṭṭa*, or loincloth: *āp jaisā colpaṭṭak pahante haiṃ, vaisā kis sūtra meṃ likhā haī*?. From this, it can be deduced that the ascetics at the time did not wear a *colapaṭṭa*; though *colapaṭṭa*s are mentioned in the canon (Viy 8.6.2 (374), etc.). Jñānsundar (1936: 173f.) writes that in the 20th century (?) Loṅkāgaccha ascetics wore *colapaṭṭaka*s and *caddar*s (*cādar*), but in a slightly different form than the Sthānakavāsīs. In contrast to the Sthānakavāsīs, they did not wear a *muhapattī* permanently, but carried an *oghā*, *kambal*, and *daṇḍa*, etc. I have never seen any evidence of a Loṅkāgaccha *yati* carrying a *daṇḍa* though of *oghā* and *kambal*.

[243] For the tantric cult of the *sūrimantra* in the Mūrtipūjaka tradition see Dundas 1998: 36-46. He points out that it is not used by the Sthānakavāsīs because they claim "during the fifth century C.E. there occurred a major inter-

46. To recite the *sūrimantra* every day, whose tradition is that?[244]

47. To shine in starched[245] (white clothes), whose bright tradition is that?

48. To cause the "Bairakanhai" fast to be performed during *paryuṣaṇa*, whose tradition is that?[246]

49. To cause a waterpot (*ghaḍūlā*) to be made, whose tradition is that?[247]

50. To cause the *āyambila olī* fast to be performed together with the *siddhacakra* (*pūjā*), whose tradition is that?[248]

51. To hold a ceremony of mourning (*ūṭhamaṇuṃ*)[249] after the death of an ascetic, whose tradition is that?

52. To cause the swinging of the images (of the fourteen dreams of Mahāvīra's mother) to be performed, whose tradition is that?[250]

---

ruption of the teacher lineage through which the formula was transmitted" (Dundas 1998: 36).

[244] The *mantra* was recited to acquire mystical powers, and in order to strengthen the commitment to the particular lineage.

[245] Jain and Kumār (2003: 119) translate the expression *kalapaṛā* with the Hindī word *kalaf*, starch.

[246] Jain and Kumār (2003: 120) identify this fast as the *vajra-kṛṣṇa* (*vaira-kannai*), or black thunderbolt-fast. No further information is given.

[247] G. *ghaḍūlo*, small pitcher, water pot. Pots and bowls should be produced by the ascetics themselves. K. Śeṭh informs me that the question may point to welcoming celebrations for ascetics (*nāgara praveśa*) performed by women with auspicious water pots on their heads, for which see the photo on the dustjacket of Cort 2001. The Hindī rendition of Jain & Kumār 2003: 120 reads: *jhaḍūle karvānā* (*bāl utarvānā*), i.e. to cause the hair to be shaved (R. *jhaḍūlau* signifies the hair of a newly born child). Jaina ascetics should pluck their hair or have it plucked by another ascetic.

[248] For a description of this ritual, which comprises the use of flowers and fruit and the veneration of images and gods, see Jain & Fischer 1978, II: 2-4; Cort 2001: 162f. Jain and Kumār (2003: 120) have: *siddhacakra ke āyambīl kī bolī karvānā*, to cause the auction of the *siddhacakra āyambila* fast to be done, which must have been one of the main objections implied by the question.

[249] In Rājasthānī, *uṭhāvaṇau* denotes collective mourning. In the case of ascetics, this is the *guṇānuvāda sabhā*, the auspicious praise of the deceased ascetic. A special carpet is used in this context.

[250] This ritual is performed by the Mūrtipūjaka Jaina laity on the fifth day of *paryuṣaṇa*, which is called Mahāvīra Jayanti, though the actual birthday of Mahāvīra falls on an earlier date in the year. For details of this ritual, which is performed for well-being and involves extensive bidding for ritual acts, see Cort 2001: 154-7, who also cites earlier literature.

53. To create a decorated table (*thavaṇī*) in front of the feet (of an ascetic or an image),[251] whose tradition is that?

54. To perform the *pratikramaṇa* on the fourth day (of the second lunar fortnight) of *paryuṣaṇa*, whose tradition is that?[252]

Notably, the questions are addressed to a Jaina mendicant, not to the laity, and imply a mendicant perspective. The basic question, whether any of the fifty-four listed beliefs and practices corresponds to the teachings of the root scriptures seems, at first sight, to reflect an attitude of a-temporal lay-inspired scriptural literalism which deliberately ignores the commentary traditions of the teachers of the mendicant lineages.[253] However, a closer view reveals that Loṅkā may not have rejected commentaries per se, especially not those (such as the later vernacular *ṭabo*s) which merely explain the meaning of the *sūtra*s themselves, but only commentaries or parts of commentaries whose contents do not correspond at all to the teachings of the root scriptures. Mālvaṇiyā 1964: 377f. argued that this interpretation is supported by the fact that the two Mss. which have been attributed to Loṅkā make use of all available Jaina scriptures and commentaries. Further evidence for a positive attitude toward the commentaries in the aniconic Jaina tradition can be found in the published Sthānakavāsī and Terāpanth Āgama editions which make explicit use of all commentaries in order to establish the literal meaning of the *sūtra*s themselves, though some modern monks, such as Upādhyāya Amarmuni, argue that because of their condensed nature the *sūtra*s are intrinsically polyvalent and can therefore only be interpreted symbolically.[254] In contrast to

---

[251] Jain and Kumār (2003: 120) use the word *gavalī* (*uṃbaṇī*) for *ṭhavaṇī*.

[252] This refers to the practices of the Tapāgaccha and the Kharataragaccha to perform the final *saṃvatsarī pratikramaṇa* not, like most Jaina traditions, on *bhādrapad śukla* 5 but already on *bhādrapad śukla* 4, apparently following the advice of Kālakācārya (cf. Jacobi 1880). In contrast to Loṅkā, Kaḍuā seems to have accepted "the general practice established by Kālakācārya" (in Dundas 1999: 22), but not the A(ñ)calagaccha (Balbir 2003b: 59).

[253] Dundas 1996: 74, 89f.

Mālvaṇīya's view that the canon of thirty-two was codified after the emergence of the Sthānakavāsī orders, there is evidence that Loṅkā himself advocated for a restricted canon of thirty-two scriptures in Bhānucandra's *Dayādharma Caupāī* v. 19 of 1521/2, though, if Mālvaṇīya's source Dharmasāgara's *Pravacanaparīkṣā* of 1572/3 can be believed, it had not been canonised one hundred years later. According to Kāpaḍiā (1941/2000: 38, 53), even the current Mūrtipūjaka classification of forty-five scriptures emerged sometime after the 14th century. The construction of alternative Āgama classifications in the late medieval period thus appears to be generally a product of sectarian politics, predicated on the emergence of a new style of text-oriented critique in "reformed" *gaccha*s and *gaṇa*s.

The fifty-four questions are *de facto* commentaries themselves, whose contents have in parts been canonised in the aniconic tradition. Their rhetoric may be literalist and fundamentalist, but they function as means of innovation and of canonisation, since they censure certain customary practices which back them up, while favouring others which are not explicitly mentioned. The fluidity of the usage of textual allusions is illustrated by Loṅkā's objection to child initiation (K2) which contradicts the canonical *Vavahāra* 10.16f.,[255] and by the fact that the equally rejected custom of changing names at the point of initiation (K3) is nowadays practiced by several Sthānakavāsī traditions,[256] and by the Terāpanthīs. Since much of the meaning of the fifty-four questions is contextual and implicit, their interpretation must remain tentative. However, the collection and analysis of similar lists from the same period, as studied by Dundas (1999) and Balbir (2003a; 2003b), may in future

---

[254] See Flügel 2003a: 162, n. 49; 195, n. 140; 196, n. 145. Dundas (1996: 80, 83, 86) has discussed similar remarks of Abhayadeva, Prabhācandra and Dharmasāgara.

[255] Schubring 1935/2000: 250; Balbir 2001: 154. Amongst the Śvetāmbara sects, only the Śramaṇasaṅgha rejects child initiation.

[256] Amongst the Sādhumārgīs only women change their names. The empirical situation is complex.

produce a clearer view of the sectarian faultlines in the 15th and 16th centuries.

LOṄKĀ'S TEACHINGS ACCORDING TO MODERN STHĀNAKAVĀSĪ SOURCES[257]

With the publications of Mālvaṇiyā and Hastīmal, in particular, fruitful comparisons between the early beliefs and customs of different aniconic traditions are rendered possible for the first time. Of special interest is the reconstruction of the early development of the Loṅkāgaccha for which still hardly any evidence exists. For the present investigation of the effective history of Loṅkā the comparison between "Loṅkā's" writings and versions of his teachings transmitted within the Sthānakavāsī tradition is important, as are preliminary observations on the differences between the customary law (*maryādā*) of the early Sthānakavāsī traditions and "Loṅkā's" proclamations.

To my knowledge, in addition to the paraphrases in Jeṭhmal (1930), only two texts are currently available on Loṅkā's rules in the Sthānakavāsī secondary literature. One was published by Sādhvī Candanākumārī (1964: 102)[258] and the other by Gulābacanda Nānacanda Seṭh (1970: 703f.).[259] This is somewhat surprising, given the importance of Loṅkā as the founder of the aniconic Jaina traditions. However, a recent survey by the present writer has shown that most of the ancient sources of the comparatively sparse literary output of the aniconic traditions before the 20th century has either been lost or not been catalogued or used. Even the writings of the founders of the Sthānakavāsī traditions have not been pre-

[257] Original source not cited in Candanākumārī 1964: 102; Prakāścandra 1998: 31.

[258] It is possible that Candanākumārī extracted the rules from the book by Suśīlkumār (1959), which was one the main sources for her work. I cannot disconfirm this, since several pages of the chapter on Loṅkā are missing in my own xerox-copy of Suśīlkumār's text.

[259] The texts were also published in Flügel 2000: 52; 2003a: 233.

served in their original form. It is therefore not surprising that no literary traces of the debates between the followers of the Loṅkā traditions and the Sthānakavāsī (and Terāpanth) traditions have been discovered to date.[260] Candanākumārī (1964: 102) writes that several manuscripts of the regulations (*niyama*) which Loṅkā himself composed for the Loṅkāgaccha mendicants (*sādhu-sansthā*) can be readily found in old Jaina libraries. She therefore decided to publish only a selection of eleven particularly "useful" rules in summary form in Hindī under the title *Loṅkāgaccha kī Sāmācārī* (LS).[261] Without acknowledgement of the source, her list was republished in Gujarātī by Muni Prakāścandra (1998: 31) of the Līmbḍī Moṭī Pakṣa.

The code of conduct of the Loṅkāgaccha[262]

1. Only the Sanskrit commentaries (*ṭīkā*) which agree with the scriptures are acceptable as authoritative.
2. One should live a steadfast disciplined life in agreement with the scriptures.
3. From the point of view of religion "image-worship" is not in agreement with the scriptures.
4. Genuine, pure vegetarian food can be accepted from every family [caste].
5. It is not necessary for anyone to set up the symbols of the monastic order (*sthāpanācārya*) [for worship].[263]
6. During the vows of *upavāsa*,[264] etc., absolutely all types of lifeless (*prāsuka*) water can be accepted.

---

[260] Flügel 2000; 2003a; forthcoming (c).

[261] *prācīn śāstra-bhaṇḍāroṃ meṃ in niyamoṃ ke anek patra prāpta hote haiṃ. un sabhī niyamoṃ kā likhnā yahāṃ āvaśyak nahīṃ hai. un meṃ se kuch upayogī niyam jānkārī ke lie yahāṃ diye jā rahe haiṃ* (Candanākumārī 1964: 102).

[262] Translated by the author.

[263] The A(ñ)calagaccha allowed its use only for mendicants, not for the laity as most Mūrtipūjaka traditions. See Balbir 2003b: 59f.

[264] The word *upavāsa* signifies either fasting in general, or a specific thirty-six-hour fast (Pkt. *cauttha bhatta*, Skt. *caturtha-bhakta*) without any food, but with or without drink. I have preferred the more specific meaning in all translations, since the *upavāsa* performed in the context of *poṣadha* is addressed, though often fasting in general may have been the intended meaning in a particular case.

7. The one-day fast (*upavāsa*) can even be performed on days other than the lunar holy days (*parva-tithi*).[265]

8. There is no need for monks to practise the skills of *mantra-tantra* and *yantra*, etc.

9. Laymen can beg, but cannot receive religious gifts (*dāna*).

10. To give gifts (*dāna*) to the poor due to the feeling of compassion is not a sin (*pāpa*), but rather the cause of merit (*puṇya*).

11. There is no need to keep a staff (*daṇḍa*).[266]

If this list was indeed composed on the basis of primary literature, then the information must have been selected from all the texts that have been attributed to Loṅkā to date. The critique of the validity of the Jaina commentary literature in point one, for instance, is mainly discussed in the *Loṅkā nī Huṇḍī 34 Bol*, and the *locus classicus* of Loṅkā's critique of image worship is the text *Luṅkā nī Aṭhāvan Bol*. Candanākumārī's method of extraction and her utilitarian criterion of "contemporary relevance" offers a glimpse into the rational of the strategies of selection, exegesis and transmission of chosen elements of the doctrinal tradition and of the customary law within the aniconic Jaina mendicant traditions.

A second Sthānakavāsī source for the rules and regulations of Loṅkā was published by Gulābcand Nāncand Seṭh (1970: 703f.), a poet who was hired to write down the results of the extensive historical research of Muni Cauthmal (died 1951) on the life of Ācārya Jaymal, which was completed by the *muni*s Cāndmal (1908-1968), Jītmal and Lālcand, who in 1964 split from the Śramaṇasaṅgha in protest against the controversial institutional

---

[265] This rule is identical with one of the stipulations of Kaḍuā (KS 7); though Jñānsundar 1936: 327, n. 5 expressed the opposite view. The point was rejected by the A(ñ)calagaccha and the Kharataragaccha (Samayasundara), but accepted by the Tapāgaccha (Balbir 2003b: 59). Dundas 1999: 22 understands the meaning of rule KS 7 slightly differently – that "the *poṣadha* fast can be celebrated when it does not fall on an observance day (*parvan*)".

[266] The prototype must be LH 22, which criticises the *Niśītha Cūrṇi*'s permission for using an *acitta* staff for purposes of self-defence, which contradicts the *Niśītha* 5 itself.

reforms of Ācārya Ānandṛṣi, and founded the independent Dharmadāsa Jayamala Sampradāya.[267] The bulky text, entitled *Jaydhvaj*, was published with the aim of strengthening the sectarian identity of the newly established tradition. The publication was supported by the influential Ācārya Hastīmal, who in 1968 also separated himself from the Śramaṇasaṅgha to re-establish the Ratnavaṃśa as an independent order. Hastīmal (1968) had already published a collection of *paṭṭāvalī*s of the Loṅkāgaccha tradition and of the Sthānakavāsīs, and systematically researched the history of the aniconic Jaina tradition during the following two decades.[268] The following twenty points (LN) which Seṭh attributes to Loṅkā have been summarised by him in Hindī without any reference to the original source. The introductory sentence only mentions that Loṅkā prepared this *sāmācārī* in Saṃvat 1531 (1474/5 CE) in order to prevent the rise of *śithilācāra*, or laxity, amongst the *sādhu*s of Bhāṇā's newly created Loṅkāgaccha:[269]

1. Even without having completed the *upadhāna* fast one can study the scripture.[270]
2. From the point of view of religion, worshipping the Jina image is not in the forty-five scriptures.

---

[267] Varddhamāna Sthānakavāsī Jaina Śrāvaka Saṅgha Jaypur 1964; Flügel 2003a: 164-168; forthcoming (a).

[268] See Hastīmal 1968; 1971; 1987/1995, and his collection of Mss. in the Lāl Bhavan Sthānak in Jaypur.

[269] Translation by the author.

[270] The *upadhāna tapa* is a special, extended (usually thirty-five or forty-seven day long) collective *poṣadha*, a collective fast-*cum*-study exercise which, according to Cort 2001: 137, has been first described in the 7th-century *Mahānisīha* 3.3.15-3.36.1. At the end of the programme, which demands image-worship three times a day, "each lay faster takes a garland of flowers used in temple worship and puts it over the head of the mendicant leader". Dundas 1999: 22 cites the stipulation of Loṅkā's younger contemporary, Kaḍuā, that "One should not perform garlanding (*mālāropaṇa*) at the end of *Upadhāna Tapas*", which he interprets as the ceremony of the "lay votary being garlanded by the presiding monk" (Dundas 1999: 30, n. 21). The objection expressed in the text that is attributed to Loṅkā addresses another aspect of *upadhāna*, i.e. that one is not allowed to study without a prior fast.

3. Apart from the root aphorism (*sūtra*), the scripture (*āgama*) and the root teaching (*śāstra*), joined together with the Sanskrit commentaries (*ṭīkā*), other scripture and Sanskrit commentary is not to be believed in any respect.

4. It is forbidden to practice magical skills (*vidyā*).

5. The fast day (*poṣadha*) [and the] ritual of repentance (*pratikramaṇa*) is performed according to individual custom.

6. Apart from *cāturmāsa*, one can also use a seat (*pāṭa*) [during the rest of the year].[271]

7. One should not keep a staff.

8. One can possess books.[272]

9. Paying attention to genuineness and purity, one can collect alms from every family.

10. A layperson (*śrāvaka*) can also perform the almsround (*gocarī*).

11. A layperson (*śrāvaka*) cannot accept a religious gift (*dāna*).

12. During fasting (*upavāsa pratyākhyāna*) one can take lifeless whey (*āch*) of buttermilk.[273]

13. *Poṣadha* can even be performed without practising a one-day fast.[274]

---

[271] The meaning of this statement is not entirely clear, though there is a certain resonance with point 6 in Dharmadāsa's critique of Lava (in Seṭh 1970: 368, n.) on the use of seats, which are unnecessary luxuries, even outside of *cāturmāsa*. The printed text has the word *pāṭakā*, which may be a corruption of S. *pāṭaka*, part of a village, which would make even less sense.

[272] The issue of the possession of books is touched upon in a different context in K 16 on the distribution of books during *paryuṣaṇa*. It was also a point of contention between the "bookish" Dharmasiṅha and Lava, who rejected the possession of books. See *Pracīn Paṭṭāvālī* in Hastīmal 1968: 186-192.

[273] Cf. Dharmadāsa's critique of Dharmasiṅha, who apparently upheld Loṅkā's rule, in Seṭh 1970: 369, n.: *upavās meṃ chāch kī āch pīnī nahīṃ*. – One should not drink the whey of buttermilk during a fast. The Sthānakavāsī traditions of Raghunāth (Dharmadāsa Sampradāya), Amarsiṅha, Dīpcand, Malūkcand (Jīvarāja Sampradāya), Khetsī and Khemsī (Hara Sampradāya) also touched on this issue in a common decree of 1753 whose wording is, however, not entirely intelligible: 2. *tapasyā meṃ telā uparānt dhovaṇ tathā āch aur chāch kī āch pīnī nahīṃ. pī lī jāye to ādhe tap kā prāyaścit* (Seṭh 1970: 919f.; cf. Flügel 2003a: 237f.). The Terāpanth mendicants, which emerged from the Dharmadāsa traditions as well, however, use *āch* during fasts: "When they undertake long fasts they take, if available, the greenish water floating on boiled whey, after the thicker portion of the boiled whey has settled down, otherwise they take boiled water only" (Chopra 1945: 27, n.).

[274] Even in the *Śrāvakācāra*s of the image worshippers, *poṣadha* is not identical with *poṣadhopavāsa*. See Williams 1983: 142f. on the four spheres of appli-

14. A one-day fast (*upavāsa*) can even be performed on days other than the lunar holy days (*tithi parva*).

15. One can take the vow of a one-day fast together (in a group).

16. One should not enumerate the auspicious days (*kalyāṇaka*) amongst the lunar days (*tithi*).[275]

17. The day on which one takes a milk product, on that day one should not use hard (*dvidala* grains).[276]

18. It is not necessary to set up a *sthāpanācārya*.

19. Within forty-eight minutes (*do gharī*) life is generated in waste water (*dhovana*).[277]

20. From a religious understanding, to give a gift (*dāna*) to an unworthy one (*apātra*) must be violence (to give to a poor person out of compassion is not the cause of the fault of one-sidedness (*ekānta pāpa*)).[278]

---

cation of the *poṣadha* vow. The issue is also addressed in Samayasundara's *Sāmācārī Śataka* 25, 29 which accepts this practice (Balbir 2003a: 260), as did the Tapāgaccha, but not the A(ñ)calagaccha (Balbir 2003b: 60).

[275] Cf. L 22. For another debate concerning the *kalyāṇakas*, in Samayasundara, see Balbir 2003a: 263ff.

[276] Soft food made of milk, such as yoghurt, and hard food made of grains that are (under their skin) split into two parts (S. *dvidala*) should not be eaten on the same day. The rule is identical with one of the stipulations of Kaḍuā (KS 8 citing the *Bṛhatkalpabhāṣya*); though Jñānsundar (1936: 327, n. 6) expressed the view that Loṅkā permitted the use of *dvidala*. It is also mentioned in the lists of forbidden food (*abhakṣya*) in the medieval *Śrāvakācāra* texts under the name *ghola-vaṭāka*, buttermilk in tiny lumps (Williams 1983: 110f.). Here, *dvidala* are described as "pulses which when ground yield no oil". They should not be consumed because they contain many micro-organisms; in particular not in combination with milk products "for in this latter instance it is the combination of sour food and milk-product which curdles the milk product and thus results in the generation of innumerable organisms" (Cort 1989: 271). The issue is also addressed in Samayasundara's *Sāmācārī Śataka* 7 (Balbir 2003a: 261).

[277] It is believed that new micro-organisms develop in lifeless water after forty-eight minutes. *Dhovana* (P. *dhovaṇa*) water has been used by Jaina ascetics from the outset (see AS 2.1.7.7-9, DVS 5.1.75-79, 5.1.47-55), although some Jaina traditions insist nowadays that only boiled water is acceptable (see Sūy 1.2.2.18, 1.2.2.20, DVS 5.2.22). Often *dhovana* water is filtered and thus kept much longer than forty-eight minutes.

[278] This rule is oriented towards a layperson. It resonates with the debate on the nature of the pure gift (*dāna*) between the Sthānakavāsīs Raghunāth and Jaymal on the one hand and the founder of the Terāpanth, Bhīkhan (Bhikṣu), on the other. The Terāpanthīs argued that for the seeker of salvation, the imperative to get rid of all *karma* is authoritative. Giving for reasons of compassion is counter-

The list overlaps to a great extent with Candanākumārī's, and may indeed have served as the immediate source for Candanākumārī's selection of useful points. In many cases the wording is almost identical. Another indication is that Seṭh's list is much more detailed, and must have been available to Candanākumārī, because it was apparently composed by Muni Cauthmal, who died in 1951, although it was published much later.[279] It is an intriguing but currently unanswerable question whether all of these rules go back to Loṅkā, or Bhāṇā, or whether at least some of these rules have been created by subsequent Loṅkāgaccha or Sthānakavāsī writers. Rule 2 states wrongly that worshipping images is not mentioned in the "forty-five" scriptures.

LOṄKĀ AND KAḌUĀ

As indicated in the footnotes, most, but not all, points of the two largely overlapping lists concur with topics of "Loṅkā's" texts L, LH and K, and can be said to be historically akin to Loṅkā's teachings. However, certain points, particularly on gift giving and *jīvadayā* (see *infra*), seem to be later additions,[280] while many of the more intricate points in Loṅkā's texts have been left out altogether.

---

productive, and thus a form of violence against the self, because it contributes to the accumulation of more *karma*, i.e. *puṇya*. The Sthānakavāsīs argued that compassionate giving, even to a non-ascetic or to a bad ascetic, is nevertheless a religious act, since both the relative point of view (*vyavahāra naya*) of conventional morality and the absolute point of view (*niścaya naya*) of the *karma* theory are part of religion. See Flügel 1995-95: 123f.; 2000: 96, n. 107. The statement in the "Loṅkā's" *sāmācārī* supports both Bhikṣu's view, which is based exclusively on the *niścaya naya*, and Raghunāth's belief that the more fundamental Jaina principle of non-onesidedness (*anekāntavāda*) supports the ethics of compassionate help, because it is predicated on the irreducible complementarity of the absolute and the conventional point of view.

[279] I asked Candanākumārī personally which sources she used for this list, but she said she could not remember anymore.

[280] LN 6 (using a seat) and LN 8 (possession of books) touch on issues which were controversial between Dharmasiṅha, Lava and Dharmadāsa. See Flügel 2000; forthcoming (b).

Although the wording sometimes differs, the contents of Candanākumārī's list (LS) are entirely covered by Seṭh's list,[281] which confirms its derivative nature. The two lists have only few issues in common with the reported *maryādās* of three of the founders of the Sthānakavāsī tradition, Dharmasiṅha, Lava, and Dharmadāsa.[282] But many points mirror Kaḍuā's rules, which were, as Jñānsundar (1936: 327, n. 4, etc.) suspected, probably formulated in contradistinction to Loṅkā's rules or vice versa. Though they differ in certain details, many of the transmitted rules of Loṅkā and Kaḍuā address similar issues. The main common topics are "ascetic"[283] rituals for the laity, such as the *pratikramaṇa*, *sāmāyika*, *upadhāna*, and *poṣadha*, which is often discussed in connection with the *upavāsa* fast. However, because both authors discuss many areas of monastic conduct as well, which do not overlap, it cannot be inferred from this that the followers of either Loṅkā and/or Kaḍuā were advanced householders, or *yati*s, and not mendicants. If the two Sthānakavāsī lists are considered together ("Loṅkā's" writings), the following picture emerges with regard to the lay rituals:

Both Loṅkā and Kaḍuā advocated the performance of the *pratikramaṇa* ritual, according to individual (LN 5) and group custom, not scripture (there are no *pratikramaṇa* texts in the Āgamas). However, Loṅkā (K 58) determined that, in accordance with the scriptures, the *saṃvatsarī pratikramaṇa* should be performed on the 5th *bhadrapāda*, not on the 4th *bhadrapāda* as Kaḍuā (following the Tapāgaccha custom) prescribed (KS 4). Contrary to the scriptures, Kaḍuā also fixed the *pākṣika pratikramaṇa* for the 14th of every lunar fortnight, not for the 15th (KS 3), and additionally adopted the *tristuti* formula (KS 11), which has been introduced by the Āgamikagaccha into the *pratikramaṇa*.[284]

---

[281] LS 8 (*mantra-tantra*) and LN 4 (*vidyā*) cover similar ground, as does future telling and astrology which "Loṅkā" criticised for instance in K 9, K 10.

[282] Seṭh 1970: 368, n. & 369, n. See Flügel, forthcoming (b).

[283] "Ascetic" rather than "symbolic" or reflective rituals such as *pūjā*.

[284] See Dundas 1999: 30, n. 23.

Loṅkā (K 8) and Kaḍuā (KS 6) also agreed that the *sāmāyika* should be performed repeatedly. But only Kaḍuā asserted that the laity should use a *muhapattī* during the ritual (KS 5), and should recite the *īryāpathika ā locanā* after the first *sāmāyika* (KS 15).

The *poṣadha* is the topic of many points. It is usually discussed together with the topic of the one-day-fast (*upavāsa*).[285] Both Loṅkā (LS 7) and Kaḍuā (KS 7) determined that *poṣadha* can be performed repeatedly according to individual preference (LN 5), even outside the *parvan* days, on which it is obligatory.[286] However, Kaḍuā (KS 13) prohibited the consumption of all food or water during the fast (*upavāsa*), whereas Loṅkā permitted the use of all types of lifeless water, and of the whey (*āch*) of buttermilk, the use of which was/is prohibited in many Sthānakavāsī traditions.[287] Kaḍuā stressed particularly that women can also perform *poṣadha* (KS 11). Loṅkā emphasised that one *upavāsa* can be performed together in a group (LN 15).

The statements KS 11 and LN 15 may refer to the collective *upadhāna* fast as well. The *upadhāna* is an extended *poṣadha* (*cum* study) exercise, that was propagated by Loṅkā and Kaḍuā, who both however rejected the ceremonial garlanding of the *tapasvīn*s with flowers at the end of the fast (K 36, KS 9), as performed by the Mūrtipūjakas. At the time, the *upadhāna* must have been performed either with or without studying, otherwise Loṅkā would not have highlighted that one can study the scripture "even without having completed the *upadhāna* fast" (LN 1); although his rule

---

[285] In the *Śrāvakācāra* literature of the image-worshipping traditions, which Williams (1983: 142) studied, *poṣadha* usually means "the fast on the *parvan* day". The term *poṣadhopavāsa* therefore appears to be "etymologically tautological", though other interpretations of *poṣadha* can be found as well, such as "that which strengthens or fattens the religious life" (YŚ 3.85) or "the supreme mendicant" (Cāritrasundar).

[286] Jñānsundar 1936: 327, n. 5 deliberately misunderstands the respective rules.

[287] See footnote 273.

may also reflect customary prohibitions for studying certain texts without prior fasting.

The principal difference between Kaḍuā and Loṅkā, according to the lists published by Seṭh and Candanākumārī, was that Kaḍuā, who assumed an intermediary position between Loṅkā and the Mūrtipūjakas (especially the dominant Tapāgaccha), also propagated image-worship (KS 1, KS 20),[288] though rejecting the installation (*pratiṣṭhā*) of images by monks rather than laity (KS 2). Kaḍuā also advocated the veneration of the *sthāpanācārya* (KS 10), which Loṅkā rejected as a "worship of dead objects" (LS 5, LN 18). These differences can be explained in terms of fundamentally different attitudes to the scriptures, because Kaḍuā accepted the authority of the post-canonical calendar,[289] and maybe (though there is no evidence) defined the auspicious days (*kalyāṇaka*) as moon days (*tithi*) which Loṅkā explicitly criticised (since this would artificially reduce the number of fast days) (LN 16), and commentaries such as the *Āvaśyaka Cūrṇī* (KS 13, KS 15) or the *Bṛhatkalpa-bhāṣya* (KS 8) which Loṅkā had rejected (L 57, LS 1),[290] though both referred to the "seniors" of the canon as the main source for monastic conduct (KS 18).[291]

CONCLUSION: REMARKS ON COMPASSIONATE GIVING

One of the most controversial issues in the aniconic Jaina tradition is the question of the origins of the so-called *dāna-dayā* theory, the doctrine of the religious value of the protection of life through charity and active compassionate help, not only to Jainas but to all living beings. Under Ācārya Bhikṣu, the Terāpanth tradition split from the Sthānakavāsī Dharmadāsa Raghunātha Sampradāya because it believed that such actions contributed only to the accumu-

---

[288] Image-worship is also a traditional ingredient of the *upadhāna*.

[289] See Jñānsundar 1936: 328, n. 2; Dundas 1999: 31, n. 31.

[290] Dundas 1999: 31, n. 31.

[291] Dundas 1999: 31, n. 30.

lation of *puṇya*, but nothing to the reduction of the overall karmic load. From the absolute point of view (*niścaya naya*), therefore, compassionate help is an impediment to ultimate salvation, and in this sense a sin (*pāpa*). The Terāpanthīs tend to claim that Loṅkā already rejected the *dāna-dayā* theories of the Mūrtipūjakas and Sthānakavāsīs, and that they are presently the only aniconic tradition which still pursues Loṅkā's neo-orthodox point of view. It seems that the text *Loṅkejī kī Huṇḍī* was published deliberately by the Terāpanth tradition in the mid-1930s, when the sectarian disputes within the Jaina community peaked, to prove this point. By contrast, many contemporary Sthānakavāsīs believe that Loṅkā was the originator of their own interpretation of the *dāna-dayā* theory, which promotes merit-making through *dāna* for financing *gośālās* rather than temples, although Jñānsundar (1936: 210, n. 1) and other critics of the aniconic tradition argued, with reference to early Mūrtipūjaka polemics against Loṅkā, that it must have been one of the early leaders of the Loṅkāgaccha who introduced this doctrine, since Loṅkā rejected the religious merit of gift giving altogether (for purposes other than sustaining the subsistence of worthy mendicants), though L commends the sponsorship of *upāśrayas*.[292] At the same time, most modern commentators underline that Loṅkā himself was not an initiated monk, and that even the early Loṅkāgaccha ascetics may have been *yatis*, half-ascetics in the modern sense, rather than *sādhus* and *sādhvīs*, and thus must have stood with one foot in the world.[293] This remains an open question, although Loṅkā's own writings suggest that Loṅkā himself was vigorously opposed to a semi-ascetic lifestyle (L8 and LH whose structure is informed by the *mahāvratas*). The example of contemporary Digambara *bhaṭṭārakas*[294] indicates that even *yatis*

---

[292] See L 23 and DC 18 for the distinction between worthy (*yogya*) and unworthy mendicants.

[293] See for instance V. M. Śāh 1909: 54, 65; Jñānsundar 1936: 105; Suśīlkumār 1959: 426; Mālvaṇiyā 1964: 368.

[294] Johārāpurkar in Shāntā 1985: 186, n. 99; Flügel 2006: 382, n. 190.

tend to be *pañca-mahāvratis*, they simply do not observe the rules strictly, or interpret them slightly differently, not unlike the *aṇuvratas* for the laity.

Of particular interest in this context are the three statements concerning compassionate gift giving (*dāna-dayā*) in the two Sthānakavāsī summaries of "Loṅkā's" teachings, LS and LN. For these statements, no equivalent assertions can be found in "Loṅkā's" texts L, LH, and K, which use *dayā dharma* and *jīva dayā* merely as synonyms of *ahiṃsā dharma*.[295] The rules LS 4 = LN 9 describe in a straightforward way that a renouncer can collect food from all families, without regard to caste and class, if the food and the manner of giving correspond to the canonical rules.[296] This contrasts both with the rule No. 75 of *101 Bol* of the Kaḍuāgaccha which prohibits the renouncers to visit houses of followers of the Loṅkāgaccha,[297] and with the Mūrtipūjaka preference for *vaṇik* (*vāṇiyā*) households as expressed in rule No. 2 of the *Paĩtīs Bol* (PB) of 1526/7 of the Mūrtipūjaka reformer Ācārya Ānandvīmalsūri (1490-1539).[298] The texts ascribed to Loṅkā himself remain silent on this point.

Rules LS 9 = LN 10+LN 11 are more puzzling. They state that "a layperson" can perform *gocarī* in the manner of an ascetic, but cannot receive *dāna* in the manner of an ascetic. How can this be understood? The use of the term *gocarī* rules out non-religious contexts of begging which are addressed in LS 10. The most likely explanation points to the definition of the intermediary stages between householder and mendicant, since the religious status of Loṅkā and the Loṅkāgaccha ascetics was disputed from the beginning in the literature. In the eleventh *pratimā*, or stage of spiritual

---

[295] See for instance L 17, which lists several passages from the canon where the word *dayā* occurs.

[296] The same conviction is expressed by the contemporary Loṅkāgaccha laity, though no universally recognised *yatis* exist anymore.

[297] In Jñānsundar 1936: 333.

[298] *keval vaṇik jāti ke viraktoṃ ko hī śramaṇ-śramaṇī dharma meṃ dīkṣā karnā, anya jāti ke logoṃ ko nahīṃ* (PB 2, in Hastīmal 1995: 582).

progress for the laity, a lay person should renounce all business of the world, has the head shaven, is clad in a mendicant's garment, carries a broom (*rajoharaṇa*), and a begging bowl (*pātra*), and performs the begging round, though technically not in the same manner as a monk (Williams 1983: 178-180). This means that although a layperson who took the vow of the eleventh *pratimā* performs the almsround in exactly the same way as a mendicant, technically s/he does not qualify for being a worthy receiver (*supātra*) for a religious gift (*dāna*) which generates a destruction of karma (and the accumulation of *puṇya karma*) on the part of the giver.

The rules concerning giving must have been created or selected from an unmentioned source by the Sthānakavāsīs to clearly demarcate the status of a properly initiated mendicant from an advanced householder or (Loṅkāgaccha) *yati*.[299] A material gift can, after all, also become a means of material enrichment. This explanation corresponds well to LN 20, which is addressed not to the receiver but to the giver. The first part states: "From a religious understanding, to give a gift (*dāna*) to an unworthy one (*apātra*) must be violence". This statement coincides with the conventional view presented in the Āgamas and in the Śrāvakācāra literature.[300] However, rather than representing the summary of a statement of "Loṅkā", the second part of the assertion (in brackets) seems to introduce a new argument, which lends support to the dominant Sthānakavāsī position in the debate with the Terāpanthīs on the nature of the pure gift (*śuddha dāna*), seen from the transcendent (*niścaya*) and conventional (*vyavahāra*) perspectives: "to give to a

---

[299] As in the case of Digambara *bhaṭṭāraka*s, only few *yati*s existed in the Loṅkāgaccha traditions between the 17th and 21th centuries, often only single individuals without disciples who were in charge of the property and religious ceremonies of a particular *gaccha*.

[300] See Williams 1983: 152 for the difference between a *kupātra*, a poor person of a more or less righteous lifestyle but wrong belief, and an *apātra*, a person devoid of all good qualities. Both are normally not considered worthy recipients of religious gifts in the *Śrāvakācāra* literature, nor are adherents of non-Jain traditions. See Viy 8.6.

poor person out of compassion is not the cause of the fault of one-sidedness" (*ekānta pāpa*).[301] In contrast to the first part of LN 20, the equivalent formulation LS 10 in the list of Candanākumārī is not entirely consistent with the previous rules on giving, by eliminating the brackets and by using the unqualified term *dāna*[302] for the compassionate giving to the "poor" (*garīb*), while avoiding the doctrinal term *kupātra*: "To give gifts (*dāna*) to the poor due to the feeling of compassion is not a sin (*pāpa*), but rather the cause of merit (*puṇya*)". This interpretation contrasts both with the Terāpanth distinction between *lokottara dāna* and *laukika dāna* and with the conventional Sthānakavāsī interpretation of religious charity, which also stresses the suboptimal, if sometimes acceptable, character of giving to a *kupātra* or *apātra*. Given the subsequent life-course of the author Candanākumārī, the founder of the reformist Vīrāyatan group of nuns who engage in social work in the manner of Christian nuns,[303] it must be assumed that the word *dāna* was used intentionally in an unqualified form. It should be interesting to trace the origins of this belief in *anukampādāna*, a concept which is mentioned already in the canonical texts *Ṭhāṇa* 10.475 and *Viyāhapannatti* 304b but re-projected and attributed to Loṅkā within the Sthānakavāsī traditions which now regard it as their own distinctive teaching. The contemporary Loṅkāgaccha tradition itself has lost all written sources and retains no cultural memory anymore on the doctrinal views of Loṅkā or the earlier Loṅkāgaccha *ācārya*s.

---

[301] The reasons for interpreting *anukampādāna* to a *kupātra* or *apātra* as an acceptable and even meritorious act are discussed by Puṣkarmuni (1977: 504).

[302] Ṭhāṇa 10.97 distinguishes between ten forms of *dāna* only one of which is called *dharmadāna*.

[303] See Flügel, forthcoming (b).

REFERENCES

Primary Sources

A = *Loṅkejī kī Huṇḍī*, of Loṅkā [?]. (Reportedly based on a Rājasthānī Ms. of Saṃvat 1830 in the Rūpacanda Rāmacanda Upāśraya, Jaitāraṇa.) With a *dohā*-style commentary of Gulābcand (Luṇiyā?), written in Jaypur in 1926. Published in Caudharī 1936?: 338-430. A corrupted version of the Rājasthānī root text has been published under the title *Ath Huṇḍī Lūṅkārī Likhyate* in Āñcaliyā 1937: 120-128.

AB = *Asūtranirākaraṇ Batrīśī*, of the Mūrtipūjaka Muni Bīkā. Ca. Saṃvat 1527 (1470/1). Published in Jñānsundar 1936, Appendix 1, pp. 230-233; Koṭhārī 2001: 500-503.

ALJ = *Ath Loṅkāśāh nuṃ Jīvan*, of the Tapāgaccha Muni Kāntivijaya. Written in Pāṭaṇ in Saṃvat 1636 (1579/60). Published in Maṇilāl 1934: 161f.; Hastīmal 1995: 752-759.

DC = *Dayādharma Caupāī*, of the Lauṃkāgacchīya Yati Bhānucandra. Saṃvat 1587 (1521/22). Published in Jñānsundar 1936, Appendix 2, pp. 234-237.

DVS = *Dasaveyāliya* (*Daśavaikālika Sūtra*), of Ārya Sayyaṃbhava. Edited by Ernst Leumann. And translated, with introduction and notes, by Walther Schubring. Ahmedabad: The Managers of the Sheth Anandji Kalianji, 1932. (Reprinted in: *Kleine Schriften* (ed. Klaus Bruhn): 109-248. Wiesbaden: Franz Steiner, 1977.) – *Arya Sayyanbhava's Daśavaikālika Sūtra*. Translation and Notes by Kastur Chand Lalwani. Delhi: Motilal Banarsidass, 1973.

J = *Jinacariya*. Translated by Hermann Jacobi as *Lives of the Jinas*. In: Sacred Books of the East, 22 (1884): 217-285.

K = *Keha nī Paramparā Chaī?*, of Loṅkā [?]. Ms. No. 2989, L.D. Institute, Ahmedabad. A Hindī variation is published in Jeṭhmal 1930: 14f. The original is published in: Mālvaṇiyā 1963a: 80-82; Vāṅā 1976: 127-130 with a Gujarātī translation; Hastīmal 1995: 691-693; reprinted in Jain & Kumār 2003: 537-539, with a Hindī translation pp. 118-120.

KS = "*Kaḍuā-Mat kī Sāmācārī*", on the basis of Śāh Kalyāṇavijaya's Kaṭukamat Paṭṭāvalī. Saṃvat 1684 (1628/9). Translated by Dundas 1999: 21f. A slightly different extract was published by Muni Jñānsundar (1936: 326-336) under the title *Kaḍuā-Mat Paṭṭāvalī kā Sār*.

L = *Luṅkā nā Aṭhāvana Bolo*, of Loṅkā [?]. Ms. No. 2989, L.D. Institute, Ahmedabad. See also Mss. No. 19224 and 19225, Oriental Institute, Baroda; Ms. Rājagranthāsāra, Prācya Vidyāpīṭha, Śāhajāpura (photographic reproduction in: Jain & Kumār 2003, Pariśiṣṭa). Ms. No.

2989, L.D. Institute, published by Mālvaṇiyā 1963a: 52-82; Vārīā 1976: 1-127, with a Gujarātī translation; Hastīmal 1995: 655-691; reprinted in Jain & Kumār 2003: 403-537 with a Hindī summary pp. 124-139.

LH = *Luṅkā nī Huṇḍī Cauṃtīs Bol*, of Loṅkā [?]. Ms. No. 4121, L.D. Institute, Ahmedabad. Extract (*Loṅkāśāh ke Cauṃtīs Bol*) in Hastīmal, 1995: 648-655; reprinted in Jain & Kumār 2003: 499-503, with a Hindī summary pp. 120-123.

LN = "*Loṅkā's Niyamāvalī*". In Gulābcand Nāncand Seṭh 1970: 703f.

LP = *Loṅkāgacchīya Paṭṭāvalī* (Bābu Puraṇcandjī Nahār no Bhaṇḍār). In Koṭhārī 2001: 405-407. (First published in the Jain Śvetāmbara Conference Herald, April-June 1918, 169-171).

LS = *Loṅkāgaccha kī Sāmācārī*. In Candanākumārī 1964: 102.

LTC = *Luṅkā nū 13 nī Carcā*, of Pārśvacandrasūri of the Pārśvacandragaccha. Ca. 16th century CE. Mss. No. 24466, 30565, L.D. Institute, Ahmedabad. Extract (*Luṅkāe Pūchela 13 Praśna ane tenā Uttaro*) in Hastīmal 1995: 694f.; reprinted in: Jain & Kumār 2003: 439-441, with a Hindī translation pp. 115-117.

PB = *Paiṃtīs Bol*, of the Mūrtipūjaka Ācārya Ānandvīmalsūri. Saṃvat 1583 (1526/7). Published in Hastīmal 1995: 582-584.

PP = *Pravacanaparīkṣā*, of Upādhyāya Dharmasāgara, 1572/3. Surat: Ṛṣabhadeva Keśaramalajī Śvetāmbara Saṃstha, 1937.

SC = *Siddhānta Caupāī*, of the Mūrtipūjaka Muni Lāvaṇyasamaya. Saṃvat 1543 Kārtik śukla aṣṭamī (5.11.1486/7). Published in Jñānsundar 1936, Appendix 1, pp. 209-227; Koṭhārī 2001: 486-499.

SS = *Siddhānta Sāroddhāra* [*Caupāī*], of the Kharataragaccha Upādhyāy Śrī Kamalsaṃyam. Saṃvat 1544 [1487]. Published in Jñānsundar 1936, Appendix 1, pp. 228f; Koṭhārī 2001: 499-500.

Sūy = *Sūyagaḍa (Sūtrakṛtāṅga Sūtra)*. Translated by Hermann Jacobi. In: Sacred Books of the East, 45 (1895): 233-435.

TPS = *Tapāgaccha Paṭṭāvalī Sūtraṃ*, of Dharmasāgara. Saṃvat 1646 [1589/90]. Published in Darśanavijaya 1933: 41-119.

Viy = *Viyāhapannatti (Bhagavaī). The Fifth Anga of the Jaina Canon*. Introduction, Critical Analysis, Commentary & Indexes. Brugge: Rijksuniversiteit de Gent, 1970.

Ṭhāṇa = *Ṭhāṇa (Sthānāṅga)*. Mūla Pāṭha, Saṃskṛta Chāyā, Hindī Anuvāda tathā Ṭippaṇa. Vācana Pramukha: Ācārya Tulsī. Sampādak-Vivecaka: Muni Nathmal. Lāḍnūn: Jaina Viśva Bhāratī, 1976.

YŚ = *Yogaśāstra of Hemacandra. A Twelfth Century Handbook on Śvetāmbara Jainism*. Translated by Olle Qvarnström. (Harvard Oriental Series, 61.) Cambridge, Mass.: Harvard University Press, 2002.

Secondary Sources

AISJC = Akhil Bhāratīya Sthānakavāsī Jaina Kānfrens (ed.), *Akhil Bhāratvarṣīya Vardhamān Sthānakavāsī Jaina Śramaṇ Saṅghīya Samācārī.* Compiled by Saubhāgyamuni "Kumud". Dillī: Akhil Bhāratīya Varddhamaṇ Sthānakavāsī Jaina Kānfrens, 1987.

AMARVIJAY, Muni (ed.) 1908. *"Ḍhūṇḍhak Hṛday Netrāñjanaṃ" athavā "Satyārtha Candrodayāṣṭakam".* Amadāvād: Śrī Satyavijay Priṇṭing Pres māṃ, Śā. Sāñkulcand Harīlāle Chāṣyuṃ.

AMOLAKṚṢI, Muni [Ācārya] 1908/1920. *Jaina Tattva Prakāś.* Duliya: Amola Jñānālaya. (Fourth edition, Ahmednagar 1920.)

—— 1920. *Śāstroddhara Mīmāṃsā.* Sākandarābād: Jaina Śāstroddhara Mudrālaya.

ĀÑCALIYĀ, Dhansukhdās Hīrālāl (ed.) 1937. *Śiśu Hit Śikṣa.* Gaṅgāśahar: Dhansukhdās Hīrālāl Āñcaliyā.

ASSMANN, Jan 1987. Kanon und Zensur als kultursoziologische Kategorien. In: Aleida & Jan Assman (eds.), *Kanon und Zensur. Beiträge zur Archäologie der literarischen Kommunikation,* II: 100-112. München: Wilhelm Fink.

—— 2000. *Religion und kulturelles Gedächtnis.* München: C. H. Beck. (English version: *Cultural Memory. Ten Studies.* Transl. by R. Livingstone. Stanford: Stanford University Press, 2006.)

Ātmānand Jain Sabhā Pañjāb 1909. *"Ḍhūṇḍhakmat Parājay arthāt Phaislā Śāstrārthanāmā" tathā "Phaislā Samānā Ilākā Mahārājā Paṭiyālā".* Lahaur: Ātmānand Jain Sabhā Pañjāb kī Ājñā se Ātmānand Pustak Pracār Maṇḍal ke Janral Sakreṭarī Ajmer ke Seṭh Hīrācandjī Secetī ne Chapdhāyā. (Tṛtīyā Vṛtti. Lahaur: Jasvantrāy Jaini, 1906.)

ĀTMĀRĀM, Ācārya (Vijayānanda Sūri) 1881/1954. *Jainatattvādarśa.* Bhāg 1 & 2. Ed. Banārsīdās Jain. Pañcam Saṃskaraṇ. Bambaī: Śrī Ātmānand Jaina Sabhā.

—— 1884/1903. *Śrī Samyaktva Śalyoddhāra.* Third edition. Hindustānī translation of the Gujarātī original. Lahore: Śrī Ātmānand Jaina Sabhā Pañjāb.

—— 1884/1908. *Śrī Samyaktva Śalyoddhāra Dohā Ḍhūṇḍhak Mat ke Śalya ko Dūrakare Niradhāra Satya Nāmaim Grantha kā Samākita Śalyoddhāra.* Dillī: Ātmānand Jain Pustak Pracār Maṇḍal.

—— 1888/1906. *Ajñāna-timira-bhāskara.* Bhāvnagar: Jaina Dharma Hitecchu Sabhā. (With the exception of the Prastāvanā to the 1st edition, cited after the 2nd edition of the Jaina Ātmānand Sabhā in Bhāvnagar, 1906).

ĀTMĀRĀM, Ācārya [1888-90] 1916. *Praśnottara-saṃgraha (Śrīmad-Vijayānanda-Sūrīśvarāj (Ātmārāmjī) Mahārājajī Kalkattā Esīāṭīk Sosāiṭī nā Sekreṭarī Ḍaṃkṭar Hornla nā Praśno nā āpelā Uttaro)*. Bhāvnagar: Jaina Ātmānand Sabhā Taraph thī Bhāvsār Gāṇḍālāl Māncand.

—— 1893/1900a. *Jainamata Vṛkṣa*. Second revised edition. Ed. Muni Vallabhvijay. Amadāvād: Śrī Ātmārām Jaina Sabhā Pañjāb.

—— 1895/1902. *Tattvanirṇayaprāsāda: 36 Stambha*. Samśodhankarttā: Muni Vallabh Vijay. Prasiddhakarttā: Amarcand P. Parmār. Mumbaī: Induprakāś Jāīṭasṭāṃk Kaṃ. Lī. meṃ chāpkar prasiddha kiyā.

—— 1900b. *Īsāī Mat Samīkṣā*. Bambaī: Jaina Jñāna Prasārak Maṇḍal.

ĀTMĀRĀM, Upādhyāy 1914. *Śrīmad Jainācārya Śrī 1008 Amarasiṅha kā Jīvan Caritra*. Lāhaur: Pañjāb Ekāntomīkal Yantrālay.

—— 1942. *Sthānakavāsī*. Ludhiyānā: Lālā Valāyatī Rām Kastūrī Lāl Jain.

BAGASARĀVĀḶĀ, Rāma Deva Maḍīā 1894. *Loṅkāgacchotpatti ane Mahārāja Śrīpūjya Bhaṭṭāraka Kalyāṇa Candrajī Surīśvarjī nuṃ Jīvana Caritra*. Mumbaī Ghī Royal Prīṇṭiṅg Pres Bāhārakoṭa Bhājīpālā Len. (Reprinted with additions as *Loṅkāgacchotpatti ane Upāśraya nā Praṇetā Pūjya Ācārya Śrī Kalyāṇacandrajī Sūriśvarjī nuṃ Jīvana Caritra*. Mumbaī: Śrī Mumbaī Loṅkāgaccha Jaina Saṅgha. Upāśraya nā Śatābdi Mahotsava Prasaṅge Sabhāsado ne Bheṭa, 11.3.2001.)

BALBIR, Nalini 1993. *Āvaśyaka-Studien*, I: *Introduction générale et traductions*. (Alt- und Neuindische Studien, 45.1.) Stuttgart: Franz Steiner Verlag.

—— 2001. La question de l'ordination des enfants en milieu jaina. In: Christine Chojnacki (ed.), *Les âges de la vie dans le monde Indien*: 153-182. Paris: Diffusion de Boccard.

—— 2002/2003a. Samayasundara's Sāmācārī-Śataka. In: Piotr Balcerowicz (ed.), *Caturaranayacakram. Essays in Jaina Philosophy and Religion*: 253-277. (First Indian edition: Delhi: Motilal Banarsidass.)

—— 2003b. The A(ñ)calagaccha viewed from inside and from outside. In: Olle Qvarnström (ed.), *Jainism and Early Buddhism. Essays in Honor of Padmanabh S. Jaini*: 47-77. Fremont: Asian Humanities Press.

BHAṆḌĀRĪ, Kesarīcand 1938. *Sthānakavāsī Jaina Itihās*. Amadāvād: Śrī Sthānakavāsī Jaina Kāryālay.

BHĀRILL, Śobhācandra (ed.) 1965. *Muni Śrī Hajārīmal Smṛti Granth*. Byāvar: Muni Śrī Hajārīmal Smṛti Granth Prakāśan Samiti.

BLOCH, Maurice. 1977/1989. The past and the present in the present. In: *Ritual, History and Power. Selected Papers in Anthropology*: 1-18. London: The Athlone Press.

BOURDIEU, Pierre 1980/1992. *The Logic of Practice*. Translated by Richard Nice. London: Polity Press.

BRUHN, Klaus 1981. Āvaśyaka-Studies I. In: Klaus Bruhn & Albrecht Wezler (eds.), *Studien zum Jainismus und Buddhismus* (Gedenkschrift für Ludwig Alsdorf): 11-49. Universität Hamburg: Steiner Verlag.

—— 1983. Repetition in Jain narrative literature. *Indologica Taurinensia* 11: 27-75.

—— 1987. Das Kanonproblem bei den Jainas. In: Aleida & Jan Assmann (eds.), *Kanon und Zensur. Beiträge zur Archäologie der literarischen Kommunikation*, II: 100-112. München: Wilhelm Fink.

BUDHMAL, Muni. *Terāpanth kā Itihās. Dvitīya Khaṇḍ.* Saṃpādak: Muni Sumeramal 'Sudarśan' & Muni Mohanlāl 'Śārdūl'. Calcutta: Jain Śvetāmbar Terāpanth Mahāsabhā Prakāśan, 2001.

BŪṬERĀY, Muni 1878. *Muhapatti Viṣe Cārcā.* Racnār Śuddha Mārg nā Rāgī Śrī Būṭerāyjī Mahārāj Temnā Carītra Sāthe. Amadāvād: Māṇekcok āgal Kāgadīol nā sāme Śā. Hīrābhāi Puñjāsānā Makān māṃ Amadāvād Ṭāims Pres māṃ Kālīdās Sāṅkalcand chāpī prasiddha karī.

CANDANĀKUMĀRĪ, Mahāsatī 1964. *Hamārā Itihās. Sthānakavāsī Śramaṇ-Sāṃskṛtik Paramparā kā Paricāyak.* Sampādak: Ācārya Śrī Amṛtkumār. Ahmadnagar: Śrī Tilok Ratna Sthānakavāsī Jaina Dhārmik Parīkṣā Borḍ.

CARRITHERS, Michael 1990. Jainism and Buddhism as enduring historical streams. *Journal of the Anthropological Society of Oxford* 21.2: 141-163.

—— 2000, On polytropy: Or the natural condition of spiritual cosmopolitanism in India: The Digambar Jain case. *Modern Asian Studies* 34.4: 831-861.

CARRITHERS, Michael & Caroline HUMPHREY (eds.) 1991. *The Assembly of Listeners. Jains in Society.* Cambridge: Cambridge University Press.

CAUDHARĪ, Kastūrcand Sūrajmal (ed.) 1936? *Jinjñān Ratnākar.* Kalkattā: Mahāland Bayed "Osvāl Pres".

CHOPRA, Chogmal 1937/1945. *A Short History of the Terapanthi Sect of the Swetambar Jains and its Tenets.* 4th Edition. Calcutta: Sri Jain Swetamber Terapanthi Sabha.

CORT, John E. 1989. *Liberation and Wellbeing. A Study of the Mūrtipūjak Jains of North Gujarat.* Ph.D. dissertation, Harvard University.

—— 1990. Models of and for the study of the Jains. *Method & Theory in the Study of Religion* 2.1: 42-71.

—— 1991. The Śvetāmbar Mūrtipūjak Jain mendicant. *Man (N.S.)* 26: 651-671.

—— 1995. Genres of Jain history. *Journal of Indian Philosophy* 23: 469-506.

CORT, John E. 2001. *Jains in the World. Religious Values and Ideology in India*. New York: Oxford University Press.

DALMIA, Vasudha, Angelika MALINAR & Martin CHRISTOF (eds.) 2001/2003. *Charisma & Canon. Essays on the Religious History of the Indian Subcontinent*. Delhi: Oxford University Press.

DARŚANAVIJAYA, Muni (col.) 1933. *Paṭṭāvalī Samuccayaḥ*. Prathamo Bhāgaḥ. Vīramgām: Cāritra Smārak Granthamālā. (Reprinted by the Jinaśāsana Ārādhanā Ṭrusṭ in Mumbaī in 1996.)

DAYANAND Sarasvati, Svami 1882/1908. *Satyartha Prakash*. Translated into English by Durga Prasad. Lahore: Virjanand Press.

DEŚĀĪ, Mohanlāl Dalīcand 1926-44. *Jaina Gūrjar Kavio*. Mumbaī: Jaina Śvetāmbara Conference Office (Second edition: Sampādak: Jayant Koṭhārī. Bhāg 1-5. Mumbaī: Śrī Mahāvīra Jaina Vidyalaya, 1988.)

ḌOŚĪ, Ratanlāl 1939. *Loṅkāśāh Mat-Samarthan*. Hindī Anuvād. Jodhpur: Jaina Ratna Pustakālay. (Hindī translation of Jīvaṇlāl Bhāī's Gujarātī translation of lost Hindī original revised by the author.) (Reprint Byāvar: Akhil Bhāratīya Sudharma Jaina Saṃskṛti Rakṣak Saṅgh, Jodhpur, 2002.)

DUGGAR, Hīrālāl 1989. *Madhya Eśiyā aur Pañjāb meṃ Jainadharma*. Dillī: Jaina Prācīn Sāhitya Prakāśan Mandir.

DUNDAS, Paul 1993. The marginal monk and the true tīrtha. In: Rudy Smet & Kenji Watanabe (eds.), *Jain Studies in Honour of Jozef Deleu*: 237-259. Tokyo: Hon-no-Tomosha.

—— 1996. Somnolent sūtras: Scriptural commentary in Śvetāmbara Jainism. *Journal of Indian Philosophy* 24: 73-101.

—— 1998. Becoming Gautama: Mantra and history in Śvetāmbara Jainism. In: John E. Cort (ed.), *Open Boundaries. Jain Communities and Culture in Indian History*: 31-52. Albany: SUNY.

—— 1999. Jainism without monks? The case of Kaḍuā Śāh. In: N. K. Wagle & O. Qvarnström (eds.), *Approaches to Jain Studies. Philosophy, Logic, Rituals and Symbols*: 19-35. Toronto: University of Toronto, Center for South Asian Studies.

—— 2001. History in future mode: A nineteenth century Digambara Jain prophetic text. In: Jayendra Soni (ed.), *Vasantagauravam. Essays in Jainism*: 51-72. Mumbai: Vakils, Feffer & Simons.

—— 2002. *The Jains*. Second revised edition. London: Routledge.

FARQUHAR, J. N. 1915. *Modern Religious Movements in India*. New York: Macmillan.

FLÜGEL, Peter 1995-96. The ritual circle of the Terāpanth Śvetāmbara Jains. *Bulletin d'Études Indiennes* 13: 117-176.

FLÜGEL, Peter 2000. Protestantische und Post-Protestantische Jaina-Reformbewegungen: Zur Geschichte und Organisation der Sthānakavāsī I. *Berliner Indologische Studien* 13/14: 37-103.

—— 2003a. Protestantische und Post-Protestantische Jaina-Reformbewegungen: Zur Geschichte und Organisation der Sthānakavāsī II. *Berliner Indologische Studien* 15/16/17: 149-240. (Also published on line: http://eprints.soas.ac.uk/view/subjects/1500.html).

—— 2003b. The codes of conduct of the Terāpanth Samaṇ order. *South Asia Research* 23.1: 7-53.

—— 2005. The invention of Jainism: A short history of Jaina studies. *Journal of Jaina Studies* (Kyoto) 11: 1-19. (Also: *International Journal of Jain Studies* 1, http://www.soas.ac.uk/ijjs).

——, forthcoming (a). Protestantische und Post-Protestantische Jaina-Reformbewegungen: Zur Geschichte und Organisation der Sthānakavāsī III. *Berliner Indologische Studien* 18.

——, forthcoming (b). Protestantische und Post-Protestantische Jaina-Reformbewegungen: Zur Geschichte und Organisation der Sthānakavāsī IV.

——, forthcoming (c). The Loṅkāgaccha revisited. Paper presented at the 12th World Sanskrit Conference in Helsinki, July 2003, and at the 6th Jaina Studies Workshop at SOAS, March 2004.

GADAMER, Hans-Georg 1960/1990. *Wahrheit und Methode. Grundzüge einer philosophischen Hermeneutik*. Tübingen: J.C.B. Mohr (Paul Siebeck).

GHĀSĪLĀL, Ācārya 1983. *Śrī Loṃkāśāha Caritam*. Niyojaka: Muni Kanhaiyālāl. Ahmadāvād: Akhila Bhāratīya Śvetāmbara Sthānakavāsī Jaina Śāstradvāra Samiti Pramukha Baladevabhāī Ḍosābhāī Paṭel.

GLASENAPP, H. von. 1925. *Der Jainismus – Eine Indische Erlösungsreligion*. (Kultur und Weltanschauung, 1.) Berlin: A. Hager.

GOMBRICH, Richard 1988. *Theravāda Buddhism. A Social History from Ancient Benares to Modern Colombo*. London: Routledge & Kegan Paul.

GOONASEKERE, Ratna Sunilsantha Abhayawardana 1986. *Renunciation and Monasticism among the Jainas of India*. Ph.D. dissertation. San Diego: University of California.

GRANOFF, Phyllis 1991. The politics of religious biography: The biography of Balibhadra the Usurper. *Bulletin d'Études Indiennes* 9: 75-91.

—— 1993. Going by the Book: The role of written texts in medieval Jain sectarian conflicts. In: R. Smet & K. Watanabe (eds.), *Jain Studies in Honour of Jozef Deleu*: 315-338. Tokyo: Hon-no-Tomosha.

GUṆSUNDAR, Muni 1938. *Ādarś Jñān. Śrīmān Jñānsundarjī Mahārāj Sāhib kā Ādarś-Jīvan*. Bhāg 1-2. Jodhpur (?).

HASTĪMAL, Ācārya 1968. *Paṭṭāvalī Prabandh Saṅgrah*. Ed. Narendra Bhanawat. Jaypur: Jaina Itihāsa Nirmāṇ Samiti.

—— 1971. *Jaina Ācārya Caritāvalī (Jaina Ācārya Paramparā kā Kāvyabaddha Rūpa)*. Ed. Gajasiṅha Rāṭhoṛ. Jaypur: Jaina Itihās Samiti.

—— 1987/1995. *Jaina Dharma kā Maulik Itihās*, IV. Jaypur: Jaina Itihās Samiti.

JACOBI, Hermann 1880. Das Kālakācārya-Kathānakam. *Zeitschrift der Deutschen Morgenländischen Gesellschaft* 34: 247-298.

JAIN, Jiyālāl 1893. *Carcā Candroday Bhāg Tisrā*. Ahmadāvād: Yuniyan Priṇṭiṅg.

JAIN, Jyotindra & Eberhard FISCHER 1978. *Jaina Iconography*, I-II. Leiden: E.J. Brill.

JAIN, Kamleś Kumār 2003. *Jaina Uddharaṇa Kośa*. Bhāg I. Dillī: Bhogīlāl Leharcand Bhāratīya Saṃskṛti Saṃsthān.

JAIN, Mohanlāl 1892. *Durvād Mukh-Capeṭikā*. Lāhaur: Eṅglo Saṃskṛt Yantrālay.

JAIN, Pannālāl L. 1913/1923. *Jainācārya Śrī 1008 Śrīmatī Pārvatījī ke Jīvan Caritra*. Pratham Bhāg & Dvitīya Bhāg. Hindī Anuvād: Dayācandra Jain. Lāhaur: Candra Lakhanpāl. (1st Edition in Urdū.)

JAIN, Sāgarmal & Vijay KUMĀR 2003. *Sthānakavāsī Jaina Paramparā kā Itihās*. Vārāṇasī: Pārśvanāth Vidyāpīṭh.

JAIN, Śrīnāth Modī 1929. *Muni Śrī Jñānsundarjī*. Jodhpur: Rājasthān Sundar Sāhitya Sadan.

JAYDAYĀL, Lālā, n.d. *Ḍhuṇḍhak Mat Samīkṣā*. (Photocopy without bibliographic references.)

JEṬHMAL, Muni 1882/1930. *Samakit-Sār I-II*. Prabodhak: Tapasvīrāj Śrī Devjīṛṣi. Prakāśak: Śrīmān Sardārmal Pugaliā, Nāgpur, Śrīmān Ratanlāl Pīrcand Pārasevanī evam Barār Jaina Śrīmān. Caturtha Saṃskaraṇ. Hindī Anuvād: Rastabcand. Ratlām: Jainoday Pustak Prakāśak Samiti.

JHAUHARĪ, Durlabh Trībhuvan. 1922/1923. *Śrīlāljī Mahārāj kā Sacitra Jīvancaritra*. Morvī-Jaipur: Durlabh Trībhuvan Jhauharī.

JÑĀNSUNDAR, Muni 1936. *Śrīmad Lauṃkāśāh*. Phalodī: Śrī Jñān Puṣpamālā.

KĀNTISĀGAR, Muni 1965. Śrī Loṅkāśāh kī Paramparā aur uskā Ajñāt Sāhitya. In: Śobhācandra Bhārill (ed.), *Muni Śrī Hajārīmal Smṛti Granth*: 214-253. Byāvar: Muni Śrī Hajārīmal Smṛti Granth Prakāśan Samiti.

KĀPAḌIĀ, Hīrālāl Rasikdās. *A History of the Canonical Literature of the Jainas*. Surat: Hiralal Rasikdas Kapadia, 1941. (Reprint: Ahmedabad: Shree Shwetambar Murtipujak Jaina Boarding, 2000.)

KELTING, Mary Whitney 2001. *Singing to the Jinas. Jain Laywomen, Maṇḍal Singing, and the Negotiations of Jain Devotion*. Oxford: Oxford University Press.

KHĀN, Ālamśāh 1965. Loṅkāgaccha kī Sāhitya-Sevā. In: Śobhācandra Bhārill (ed.), *Muni Śrī Hajārīmal Smṛti Granth*: 203-213. Byāvar: Muni Śrī Hajārīmal Smṛti Granth Prakāśan Samiti.

KIRAṆYAŚĀSTRĪ, Mahārāj 1999. *Śrī Vijayānandjī ke Vāḍam kā Vihaṅgāvalokaṇa*. Baṛaudā: Mahilā Jaina Upāśray.

KLATT, Johannes 1888. Eine apokryphe Paṭṭāvalī der Jainas. In: *Festgruss an Otto von Böhtlingk zum Doktor-Jubiläum 3. Februar 1888 von seinen Freunden*: 54-59. Stuttgart: W. Kohlhammer.

—— *Onomasticon*. Bound copy. 8 vols. Hamburg: Institut für Indologie und Tibetologie.

KOṬHĀRĪ, Jayant 2001. *Prācīn Madhyakālīn Sāhitya Samgraha* (Mohanlāl Dalīcand Desāī Sampādit Laghukṛti Saṃgraha). Ahmedabad: L.D. Institute of Indology. [See AB, LP, SC and SS under Primary sources.]

KUNDANMAL, Muni 1908. *Pragaṭ Jain Pītāmbarī Mūrtipūjakoṃ kā Mithyātva. Amarāvatī. Mūlcand Jugrāj.* (The short *stavan* is reprinted in Amarvijay 1908: 34-36.)

——, n.d. *Ātmārām Saṃvegī kī Karttūt, Ātmārām kī Ādāt kā Namūnā.* Ambālā: Paṇḍit Bhīmasena.

LAIDLAW, James 1985. Profit, salvation and profitable saints. *Cambridge Anthropology* 9.3: 50-70.

—— 1995. *Riches and Renunciation. Religion, Economy, and Society among the Jains*. Oxford: Clarendon Press.

LĀLAS, Padmaśrī Sītārām (ed.) 1986-87. *Rājasthānī-Hindī Saṅkṣipt Śabda Koś*, I-II. Rājasthān Purātan Granthamālā. Prabandh Sampādak: Padmadhar Pāṭhak. Jodhpur: Rājasthān Prācyavidyā Pratiṣṭhān.

LESLIE, Julia 2003. *Authority and Meaning in Indian Religions. Hinduism and the Case of Vālmīki*. Hants: Ashgate.

LEUMANN, Ernst 1934. *Übersicht über die Āvaśyaka Literatur*. Aus dem Nachlass herausgegeben von Walther Schubring. (Alt- und Neuindische Studien, 4.) Hamburg: De Gruyter.

MĀDHAV, Muni 1908. *Taraṅgiṇī Dvitīyā Taraṅg*. Āgrā. (Reprinted in Amarvijay 1908: 31-34.)

MAHĀPRAJÑA, Ācārya 2000. *Jainism and Its Philosophical Foundations*. New Delhi: Anmol Publications.

MALUKCAND, Anūpcand 1908. *"Praśnottara-ratna-cintāmaṇī" aur "Aṭhārah Dūṣaṇa-nivāraka"*. Ahmadābād: Rāy Bahādur Bābu Buddhasiṅghjī.

MĀLVAṆIYĀ, Dalsukhbhāī 1963a. Śrī Loṅkāśāh nī ek Kṛti. *Svādhyāya* 2.1: 50-82.

—— 1963b. Śrī Lokāśāh ane temnā Mat. *Svādhyāya* 2.2: 143-155.

—— 1964. Lokāśāh aur unkī Vicār-Dhārā. In: Vijay Muni Śāstri & Harīśaṅkar Śarmā (eds.), *Gurudev Śrī Ratna Muni Smṛti-Granth*: 365-383. Āgrā: Gurudev Smṛti Granth Prakāśak Samiti.

—— 1965. Loṅkāśāh Mat kī Do Pothiyāṃ. In: Śobhācandra Bhārill (ed.), *Muni Śrī Hajārīmal Smṛti Granth*: 184-188. Byāvar: Muni Śrī Hajārīmal Smṛti Granth Prakāśan Samiti.

MAṆILĀL, Muni 1934. *Śrī Jaina Dharma no Prācīn Saṅkṣipt Itihās ane Prabhu Vīr Paṭṭāvalī*. Amadāvād: Jīvaṇlāl Chaganlāl Saṅghvī.

METTE, Adelheid 1974. *Piṇḍ'esaṇā. Das Kapitel der Oha-Nijjutti über den Bettelgang übersetzt und kommentiert*. Wiesbaden: Franz Steiner.

MIŚRĪMAL, Mantrī Muni "Marudhar Kesarī" 1936. *Dharmavīr Loṅkāśāh*. Ṭāṇṭoṭī/Ajmer: Jaina Śvetāmbara Sthānakavāsī Sakal Śrī Saṅgh Ṭāṇṭoṭī.

—— 1941. *Krāntikārī Vīr Loṅkāśāh*. Jodhpur Sṭeṭ: Jaina Buddhavīr Smārak Maṇḍal.

—— 1946. *Vīr Loṅkāśāh*. Prakāśak: Śāh Mukancand Nemīcand Bahorā Jain. Jodhpur: Jaina Buddhavīr Smārak Maṇḍal.

NAHAR, Puran Chand. 1918/1983. *Jaina Inscriptions*. Delhi: Indian Book Gallery.

NĀHAṬĀ, Agarcand 1958. Kaḍuā Mat kī Mānyatāoṃ par Prakāś. *Jaina Bhāratī* 6.2: 19f.

—— 1964. Uttarārdha Gaccha. *Jaina Bhāratī* 12.9.

—— 1966. Nāgorī Loṅkāgaccha ke Sthāpak Hīrāsāh aur Rūpcand. *Jinavāṇī* 15: 2-4.

—— 1968. Bhūmikā. In: Ācārya Hastīmal, *Paṭṭāvalī Prabandh Saṅgrah* (Ed. Narendra Bhanawat): 33-39. Jaypur: Jaina Itihāsa Nirmāṇ Samiti.

NĀHAṬĀ, Bhanvarlāl 1957. Luṅkāśāh aur unke Anuyāyī. In: Agarcand Nāhaṭā et al. (eds.), *Śrīmad Rājendrasūri Smārak Granth*: 470-477. Āhora tathā Bāgarā (Mārvāṛ): Śrī Saudharmabṛhattapāgacchīya Jaina Śvetāmbara Śrī Saṅgh.

NĀHAṬĀ, Kuṃvar Lālcandra "Taruṇ". 1968. Lauṃkāśāh: Vyaktitva aur Vicār. In: Śobhācandra Bhārill (ed.), *Marudhar Kesarī Muni Miśrīmaljī Mahārāj Abhinandan Granth*: 159-168. Jodhpur: Marudhar Kesarī Abhinandan Granth Prakāśan Samiti.

NAIR, V. G. 1970. *Jainism and Terehpanthism*. Bangalore: Shri Adinath Jain Svetambar Temple, 1970.

PĀRVATĪ, Mahāsatī 1905a. *"Satyārtha-Candroday Jaina" arthāt "Mithyātva Timir-Nāśak". Jis ko Sanātan Satya Jaina Dharmopadeśikā Bāl Brahmacāriṇī Jainâryyājī Śrī Mahāsatī Pārvatījī ne banāyā.* Lāhaur: Lālā Meharcandra Lakṣmīdās Śrāvak.

—— 1905b. *"Samyaktva Sūryoday Jaina" arthāt "Mithyātva Timir Nāśak". Jis ko Jainācāryya Pañjābī Śrī 1008 Śrī Parampūjya Amarasiṅhajī kī Sampradāya meṃ Sanātan Satya Jaina Dharmopadeśikā Bāl Brahmacāriṇī Jainācāryyājī Śrīmat Śrī 1008 Satījī Śrī Pārvatījī ne banāyā.* Hośiārpur: Lālā Kṛpārām Koṭūmal Śrāvak. (Second edition: Rohtak: Jyotrām Seṭh kī Dharmapatnī Lā. Śerasiṅha.)

PRAKĀŚCANDRA, Muni 1998. *Ā Che Aṇagār Amārā.* Mumbaī: Śrī Naval Sāhitya Prakāśan Maṇḍal.

PUṢKARMUNI, Upādhyāy 1977. *Jain Dharma meṃ Dān. Ek Samīkṣātmak Adhyayan.* Sampādak: Devendramuni & Śrīcand Surānā 'Sarat'. Agra: Śrī Tārakguru Jaina Granthālay.

QVARNSTRÖM, Olle 1998. Stability and adaptability: A Jain strategy for survival and growth. *Indo-Iranian Journal* 41: 33-55.

ŚĀH, Pravinçand Tulsīdās 2001. *Dharma Priya Krāntivīr Lokāśāh nuṃ Jīvan Caritra (Saṅkṣep).* Mumbaī: Śrī Mumbaī Loṅkāgaccha Jaina Saṅgha.

ŚĀH, Vāḍīlāl Motīlāl 1909. *Śrī Sādhumārgī Jaina Dharmānuyāyīoe Jāṇvā Jog Keṭalīk Aitihāsik Noṃdh.* Amadāvād: "Jaina Samācār".

—— 1925. *Aitihāsik Noṃdh.* Hindī Anuvād, Mulatānmal Hīrācand Dhārīvāl. Ratan Rāypur C. P.: Jaina Pāṭhśālā ke Sahāya Tīrth.

SARLĀ, Sādhvī 1991. Sthānakvāsī Pañjāb Sampradāy kī Pramukha Sādhviyāṃ. [Extract of: Sādhanā Path kī Amar Sāhikā.] In: Hīrābāī Boradiyā, *Jainadharma kī Pramukh Sādhviyāṃ evaṃ Mahilāeṃ*: 298-304. Sampādak: Sāgarmal Jain. Vārāṇasī: Pārśvanāth Vidyāśram Śodha Saṃsthān.

ŚĀSTRĪ, Hansrāj 1915. *Svāmī Dayānand aur Jainadharma.* Gopipura/Surat: Paṇḍit Hansrāj Śāstrī.

SAUBHĀGYACANDRA, Muni "Santabāḷa" 1939. *Dharmaprāṇ-Loṅkāśāh (Krānti no Yugasṛṣṭā).* Amadāvād: Sthānakavāsī Jaina Kāryālay. (First published in *Jaina Prakāś* 1935.)

SCHUBRING, Walther 1935/2000. *Die Lehre der Jainas. Nach der alten Quellen dargestellt.* (Grundriss der Indo-Arischen Philologie und Altertumskunde, 3.7.) Berlin: Walter De Gruyter & Co. [Cited after the English translation: *The Doctrine of the Jainas. Described after the Old Sources.* Transl. Wolfgang Beurlen. 3rd English edition. Delhi: Motilal Banarsidass.]

—— 1944. *Die Jaina-Handschriften der Preussischen Staatsbibliothek.* Leipzig: Otto Harrassowitz.

SCHUBRING, Walther 1957. Kundakunda echt und unecht. *Zeitschrift der Deutschen Morgenländischen Gesellschaft* 107: 537-574.

SEṬH, Gulābcand Nāncand 1970. *Jaydhvaj. Pūjya Ācārya Jaymaljī Mahārāj kā Jīvan Caritra*. Madrās: Jaydhvaj Prakāśan Samiti.

ŚEṬH, Nagīndās Girdharlāl 1962. *Mūḷ Jaina Dharma ane Hāl nā Sampradāyo*. Mumbaī: Jaina Siddhānta Sabhā.

—— (ed.) 1963. *Sthānakavāsī Jaino nuṃ Dharma Kartavya*. Satya Dharma Samāj vā Icchanāra ne Māṭe Ja. Jaina Siddhānta Granthamāḷā Aṅko 49 Mo. Mumbaī: Jaina Siddhānta Sabhā (Rajīsṭarḍ) nī Vatī Śeṭh Nagīndās Girdharlāl. [Includes chapters 7-13 and 22-26 of Śeṭh's Mūḷ Jaina Dharma ane Hāl nā Sampradāyo: E Pustak māṃ nā Ahīṃ Umerelā Mūrti ne Lagtā Prakaraṇo.]

—— 1964. *Loṅkāśāh ane Dharmacarcā*.

SHAH, Umakant Premanand 1955a. *Studies in Jaina Art*. Varanasi: Pārśvanātha Vidyāpīṭha.

—— 1955b. A forgotten chapter in the history of the Svetambara Jaina church, or, a documentary epigraph from Mount Satrunjaya. *Journal of the Asiatic Society of Bombay* 30: 100-113.

SHĀNTĀ, N. 1985/1997. *La voie Jaina. histoire, spiritualité, vie des ascètes pèlerines de l'Inde*. Paris: O.E.I.L. (English version: *The Unknown Pilgrims. The Voice of the Sādhvīs: The History, Spirituality and Life of the Jaina Women Ascetics*. Transl. by M. Rogers. (Sri Garib Dass Oriental Series, 219.) Delhi: Shri Satguru Publications, 1997.)

SMITH, Wilfred Cantwell. 1962/1991. *The Meaning and End of Religion*. Minneapolis: Fortress Press.

SURĀNĀ, Śrīcand "Saras" 1976. *Mahāprajña Pravartak Śrī Pannālāljī Mahārāj. Jīvan, Vyaktitva aur Kṛtitva*. Vijaynagar/Rājasthān: Śrī Prajña Jaina Smārak Samiti.

SUŚĪLKUMĀR, Ācārya 1959. *Jainadharma kā Itihās* (*Pramukhtaṛ Śrī Śvetāmbara Sthānakavāsī Jainadharma kā Itihās*). Kalkattā: Samyag Jñān-Mandir.

UJAMCAND, Rikhabcand (Mumbaī) 1909. *Sthānakavāsī Sādhumārgī Satyatā Ūpar Kuhāḍo. Urphe. Bhī. Vāḍīlāl-kṛt Aitihāsik Khoṭī Noṃdh Upar Ṭīkā*. Bhāg 1. Amadāvād: Eṅglo Varnākyular Prinṭīṅg.

VALLABHVIJAY, Muni (ed.) 1891. *Ḍhuṇḍrak-hita-śikṣā Apanām Gappa-dīpikā-samīr*. Amadāvād: Śrī Jainadharma Prasārak Sanā. Nāvnagar.

—— 1902. Tapāgaccha Ācārya Śrīmad Vijayānandasūriśvarjī Prasiddha nām Ātmārāmjī Mahārājjī Jainī Sādhu kā Janmacaritra. In: Ācārya Ātmārām (Vijayānanda Sūri), *Tattvanirṇayaprāsāda: 36 Stambha*: 33-83. Samśodhankarttā: Muni Vallabh Vijay. Prasiddhakarttā: Amarcand P. Parmār. Mumbaī: Induprakāś Jāīṭasṭāṃk Kaṃ. Lī. meṃ Chāpkar Prasiddha kiyā.

—— 1909. *Javābdāvā. Jain Samācār Ḍhūṇḍhak Patrādhipati kī Pūkār kā Javāb*. Written in Pālaṇpur, Gujarāt. Lāhaur: Jasvantrāy Jaini.

—— 1996. *Navyug Nirmātā (Nyāyāmbhonidhi Ācārya Śrīmad Vijayānand Sūri (Ātmārāmjī) Mahārāj kī Jīvan Gāthā)*. Dvitīya Saṃskaraṇ. Pāvāgaḍh Tīrtha: Vijayānand Sūri Sāhitya Prakāśan Phāuṇḍeśan.

Varddhamāna Sthānakavāsī Jaina Śrāvaka Saṅgha, Jaypur (ed.) 1964. *Ajmer Śikhar Sammelan meṃ Saṃśodhit evaṃ Pārit – Varddhamān Sthānakavāsī Jaina Śramaṇ Saṅgh ke Prastāv, Vidhān evaṃ Sāmācārī.* Jaypur: Mantrī, Varddhamāna Sthānakavāsī Jaina Śrāvaka Saṅgha.

VĀRĪĀ, Ratanśī 1976. *Dharma Prāṇ Śrī Loṅkāśāh nā Aṭṭhāvan Bol*. Jāmnagar: Lālbāg (Ratanśī Vārīā).

WEBER, Albrecht 1882. Über den Kupakshakauçikāditya des Dharmasāgara. Streitschrift eines orthodoxen Jaina, vom Jahre 1573. In: *Sitzungsberichte der Königlich Preussischen Akademie der Wissenschaften zu Berlin* 37: 793-814.

WILLIAMS, Ronald. 1963/1983: *Jaina Yoga. A Survey of the Medieval Śrāvakācāras*. London: Oxford University Press.

WUJASTYK, Dominik 1984. The spikes in the ears of an ascetic: an illustrated tale in Brahmanism and Jainism. *Oriental Art (N.S.)* 30: 189-194.

APPENDIX I:
Keha nī Paramparā Chai – Text in Old Gujarātī[304]

paramparā likhīiṃ chaiṃ, ketalā eka ima kahai chai śrī vīra nī paramparā ima kahai chai, te kihāṃ chai.[305]

1. *gharim pratimā ghaḍāvī maṇḍāvai chai, te keha nī paramparā chai?*[306] – *celā celī vecānā leī teha keha nī paramparā chai?*[307]
2. *nānhā chokarā nai*[308] *dīkṣā dii chai, te keha nī paramparā chai?*
3. *nāma*[309] *pheravai chai, te keha nī paramparā chai?*
4. *kāṃna vadhārai chai, te keha nī paramparā chai?*
5. *khamāsamāsaṇa*[310] *viharai chai, te keha nī paramparā chai?*
6. *gṛhastha (nī) gharaiṃ baisī*[311] *viharai, te keha nī paramparā chai?*
7. *dīhāḍī dīhāḍī*[312] *2 teṇai*[313] *ghariṃ viharai, te keha nī paramparā chai?*

---

[304] Text based on L.D. Institute Ms. 2989, pp. 14b-15a.

[305] The meaning (*vivaraṇa*) of this sentence has been given by Vāriā (1976: 127) as follows: *have paramparā lakhīie chīe. keṭalāk ema kahe che ke vīra prabhue ā rīte paramparā kahī che.śrī loṅkāśāha praśna kare che ke ā paramparā kayāṃ śāstro māṃ kahīi che te batāvo.* The text was reproduced *verbatim* by Hastīmal (1995) (and Jain & Kumār 2003), which shows that the subsequently published versions are all based on Vāriā's transcription.

[306] Vāriā's (1976: 127) reproduction of the text uses the past tense here and in the following question: "*te keha nī paramparā thai*". Since the L.D. Institute Ms. No. 2989 uses the present tense, I have amended the printing mistakes in the published version in these two cases.

[307] This sentence has been left out in all published versions of L.D. Institute Ms. No. 2989, probably because it is regarded as too controversial.

[308] Hastīmal 1995: 691: *chokaranaiṃ*.

[309] Hastīmal 1995: 691 added in brackets: (*dīkṣa kāle*).

[310] Hastīmal 1995: 691: *khamāsamāsaṇu*.

[311] Hastīmal 1995: 692: *baisi*.

[312] Hastīmal 1995: 692: *dīhāṛī* and added in brackets: (*pratidin*).

[313] Hastīmal 1995: 692 added in brackets: (*usī ek*).

8. *aṅghola*[314] *kahai*[315] *kare,*[316] *te keha nī paramparā chai?*
9. *jyotiṣa nai marma prajuṃjai chai, te keha nī paramparā chai?*
10. *kalavāṇī karī āpai chai, te keha nī paramparā chai?*
11. *nagara māhiṃ paisatā paiṃ sāru sāḥamuṃ karāvai chai, te keha nī paramparā chai?*
12. *lāḍūā pratiṣṭai*[317] *chai, te keha nī paramparā chai?*
13. *pothī pūjāvai chai, te keha nī paramparā chai?*
14. *saṅghapūjā karavai chai, te keha nī paramparā chai?*
15. *pratiṣṭā karai chai, te keha nī paramparā chai?*
16. *pajūsaṇaiṃ pothī āpai chai, te keha nī paramparā chai?*
17. *tathā yātrā vecai chai, te keha nī paramparā chai?*
18. *tathā mātra āpai chai, te keha nī paramparā chai?*
19. *tathā ghāṭaḍī donuṃ toraṇa*[318] *bāṃghai chai, te keha nī paramparā chai?*
20. *ādhākarma posāliṃ rahai chai, te keha nī paramparā chai?*
21. *siddhānta prabhāvanā pākhai na vāṃcai, te keha nī paramparā chai?*
22. *māṇḍavī karāvai chai, te keha nī paramparā chai?*
23. *gautama paḍagho*[319] *karāvai chai, te keha nī paramparā chai?*
24. *saṃsāra-tāraṇa karāvai chai, te keha nī paramparā chai?*
25. *candanabālā nu tapa karāvai chai, te keha nī paramparā chai?*
26. *sonā rūpā nī nīsaraṇī karāvai chai, te keha nī paramparā chai?*
27. *lākhāpaḍavi karāvai chai, te keha nī paramparā chai?*

---

[314] Hastīmal 1995: 692 added in brackets: (*snān*).
[315] Hastīmal 1995: 692 added in brackets: (*koī*).
[316] Hastīmal 1995: 692: *karai*.
[317] Hastīmal 1995: 692: *pratiṣṭhaī*.
[318] Hastīmal 1995: 692: *ghāṭaṛī* and added in brackets: *(vanaspati ke toraṇ)*.
[319] Hastīmal 1995: 692: *paṛagho*.

28. *ūjamaṇā*[320] *ḍhovarāvai chai, te keha nī paramparā chai?*
29. *pūja pūḍhāiṃ chai, te keha nī paramparā chai?*
30. *āsovṛkṣa bharāvi*[321] *chai, te keha nī paramparā chai?*
31. *aṭṭhottarī sanātra karāvi chai, te keha nī paramparā chai?*
32. *navā ghāna navā phala pratimā āgali ḍhoi chai, te keha nī paramparā chai?*
33. *śrāvaka-śrāvikā nai māthai vāsa ghālai chai, te keha nī paramparā chai?*
34. *parigraha ḍhūṇḍha māṃ bāṃdhai chai, te keha nī paramparā chai?*
35. *śrāvaka pāīṃ mūṇḍakuṃ apāvī ḍuṅgara caḍhāvī*[322] *chai, te keha nī paramparā chai?*
36. *mālāropaṇa karai chai, te keha nī paramparā chai?*
37. *padīka śrāvaka śrāvikā suṃ bhelī jāiṃ chai, te keha nī paramparā chai?*
38. *nāndi maṇḍāvai chai, te keha nī paramparā chai?*
39. *padīka cāṅka bāṃdhai chai, te keha nī paramparā chai?*
40. *pāṇi māhiṃ bhūko*[323] *muṃkai chai, te keha nī paramparā chai?*
41. *vāndaṇā divarāvai*[324] *chai, te keha nī paramparā chai?*
42. *oghā pheravai chai, te keha nī paramparā chai?*
43. *devadravya rākhai chai, te keha nī paramparā chai?*
44. *pagai lāgai nīcī pacheḍī oḍhai chai, te keha nī paramparā chai?*
45. *sūrimantra leiīṃ iṃ chai,*[325] *te keha nī paramparā chai?*
46. *dīhāḍī sūrimantra gaṇai chai, te keha nī paramparā chai?*

---

[320] Hastīmal 1995: 692: *ūṃjamaṇā̃*.

[321] Vāriā 1976: 129: *bharāvaī*.

[322] Hastīmal 1995: 693: *dūṅgara caḍhāvaī*.

[323] Vāriā 1976: 129: *bhūṃko muṃkai*; Hastīmal 1995: 693: *bhūṃko mukai*.

[324] Hastīmal 1995: 693: *dirāvai*.

[325] Vāriā 1976: 130: *sūrimantra leīṃ chaī*.

47. *kalapaḍā ṭhaṭai*[326] *chaiṃ, te keha nī paramparā chai ūjalā?*
48. *pajūsaṇa māhiṃ bairakanhai tap karāvai chai, te keha nī paramparā chai?*
49. *ghaḍūlā karāvai chai, te keha nī paramparā chai?*
50. *āṃbila nī olī siddhacakra nī karāvai chai, te keha nī paramparā chai?*
51. *mahātamā nāla*[327] *karā pachī te ūṭhamaṇuṃ karai chai, te keha nī paramparā chai?*
52. *pratimā jhūlaṇuṃ*[328] *karāvai chai, te keha nī paramparā chai?*
53. *padīka āgali ṭhavaṇī*[329] *māṇḍai chai, te keha nī paramparā chai?*
54. *pajūsaṇa parva nai cauthaiṃ*[330] *paḍikamai chai, te keha nī paramparā chai?*

---

[326] Vāriā 1995: 693 *thaṭai.*

[327] Vāriā 1976: 130: *kāla.*

[328] Vāriā 1976: 130: *jhūlaṇaṃ.*

[329] Vāriā 1976: 130: *Uaṃbaṇī.*

[330] Hastīmal 1995: 693: *cauthanaiṃ paḍikamai chaiṃ.*

APPENDIX II:

Loṅkā's assertions according to Candanākumārī 1964 in Hindī

1. *āgam-sammat ṭīkāoṃ ko hī prāmāṇik mānā jāy.*
2. *āgam ke anusār dṛṛhatāpūrvak samyamoṃ jīvan vyatīt kiyā jāy.*
3. *dharmdṛṣṭi se 'pratimā-pūjan' śāstra-sammat nahīṃ hai.*
4. *śuddha sāttvik śākāhārī pratyek kul kā āhār liyā jā saktā hai.*
5. *sthāpanācārya kī sthāpanā kī koī āvaśyaktā nahīṃ hai.*
6. *upavās ādi vratoṃ meṃ sabhī prakār kā prāsuk jal liyā jā saktā hai.*
7. *parv-tithi ke binā bhī upavās kiyā jā saktā hai.*
8. *sādhuoṃ ko mantra-tantra tathā yantra ādi vidyāoṃ kā prayog nahīṃ karnā cāhie.*
9. *śrāvak bhikṣā kar saktā hai, par dān nahīṃ le saktā.*
10. *dayā bhāv se garīboṃ ko dān denā pāp nahīṃ hai, apitu puṇya kā kāraṇ hai.*
11. *daṇḍ nahīṃ rakhā jānā cāhie.*

APPENDIX III:

Loṅkā's Sāmācārī according to Seṭh 1970 in Hindī

1. *upadhān tap kiye binā bhī śāstra-abhyās karāyā jā saktā hai.*
2. *jin pratimā kī dharma-dṛṣṭi se pūjā karnā 45 āgamoṃ meṃ nahīṃ hai.*
3. *mūl sūtra, āgam aur mūl śāstra, samasta ṭīkāoṃ ke sivāy anya āgam evaṃ ṭīkā sarvathā amānya hai.*
4. *vidyā kā prayog niṣiddha hai.*
5. *pauṣadh pratikramaṇ svatantra rīti se karnā.*
6. *cāturmās ke sivāy bhī pāṭ kā vyavahār jā saktā hai.*
7. *daṇḍ nahīṃ rakhā jānā cāhiye.*
8. *pustakeṃ rakhī jā saktī haiṃ.*
9. *sātviktā aur śuddhi kā dhyān rakhte hue pratyek kul meṃ gocarī kī jā saktī hai.*
10. *śrāvak bhī gocarī kar saktā hai.*
11. *śrāvak dān nahīṃ le saktā.*
12. *upavās pratyākhyān meṃ chāch-pānī kī āch prāsuk le sakte haiṃ.*
13. *binā upavās ke bhī pauṣadh kiyā jā saktā hai.*
14. *tithi-parv ke binā bhī upavās kiyā jā saktā hai.*
15. *ek sāth upavās paccakkhe jā sakte haiṃ.*
16. *kalyāṇakoṃ ko tithi meṃ nahīṃ ginnā cāhiye.*
17. *jis din goras liyā jāy us din kaṭhor (dvidal dhānya) kā prayog nahīṃ honā cāhiye.*
18. *sthāpanācārya kī sthāpanā anāvaśyak hai.*
19. *dhovan pānī meṃ do gharī ke anantar jīvotpatti sambhav hai.*
20. *apātra ko dharma buddhi se dān dene se hiṃsā hotī hai (anukampā se garīb ko denā ekānta pāp kā kāraṇ nahīṃ hai).*

PICTURE:

Loṅkā nā Aṭhāvana Bolo, Ms. No. 2989,
L.D. Institute, Ahmedabad, p. 14b

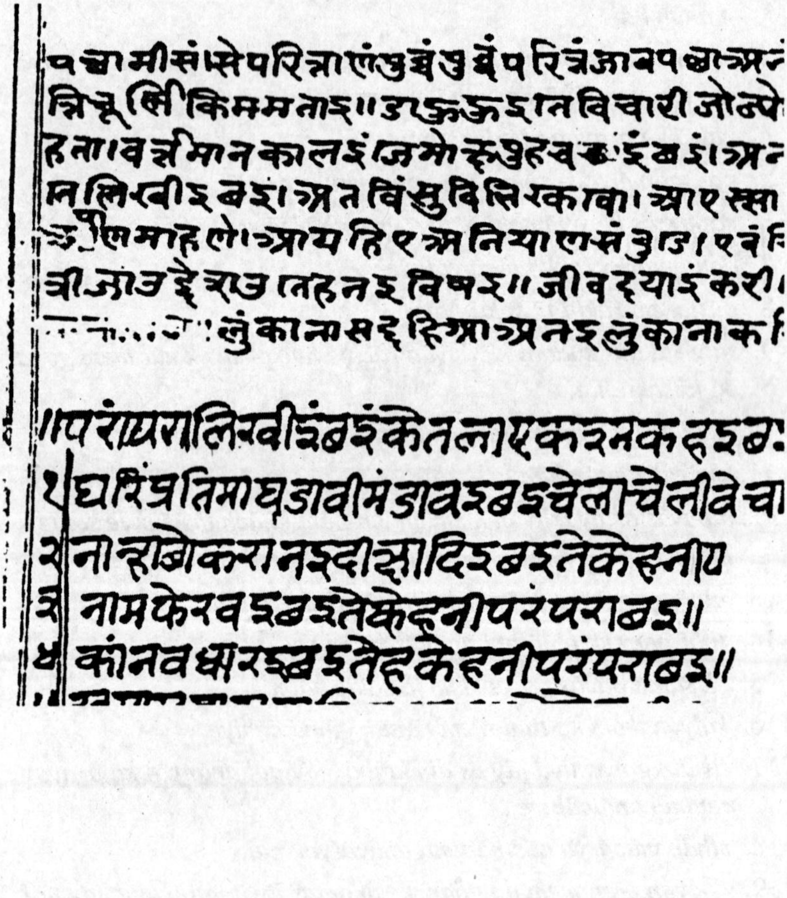

INDEX

(Italicized page numbers refer to the footnote section)